wide necked Bottles a layer of
sugar and a layer

Tye the jars down
bladders – let them
cold water on the
full half an hour – or untile you
think the fruit is enough done –
Take it off the fire and let the jars
stand in it until it is stone cold
then cover the bladders with double
paper – Apples, Pears, Siberian Crabs
may be done in this way

Custard Pudding

A pint of good milk (better with
some cream) 4 Eggs – a small
Spoonful of Flour – boil it 40 minutes
then take it out of the water, and
hang it up ½ an hour at least –
Put it in the boiling water again
for from 5 to 10 minutes

Yeast

Boil 1 oz of hops about 10 minutes
in 6 quarts of water – Strain it and
mix it immediately with 2 lb of
flour and a tablespoonful of sugar

Cooking and Dining
with the Wordsworths

FRONTISPIECE - The ladies who cooked for William Wordsworth; his wife Mary, sister Dorothy, and (below) sister-in-law Sara Hutchinson.

Cooking and Dining
with
The Wordsworths

From Dove Cottage to Rydal Mount

Peter Brears

Excellent Press
Ludlow

First published in 2011 by Excellent Press
9 Lower Raven Lane
Ludlow SY8 1 BL

ISBN 1 900318 43 1
ISBN 978 1 900 318 43 3 (*paperback*)

ISBN 1 900318 47 4
ISBN 978 1 900 318 47 1 (*cased*)

*The author has donated his royalties from sales of this book
to the Wordsworth Trust and Dove Cottage*

Printed in Malta

CONTENTS

Preface   7

Acknowledgements   9

Introduction   11

1. The Wordsworths & their Recipes   17

2. At Home in Grasmere   31

3. Of Main Courses   55

4. Of Cold Puddings   79

5. Of Hot Puddings & Sweet Pies   93

6. Of Bread & Cakes   105

7. Of Sweets   131

8. Of Preserves & Pickles   137

9. Of Cheese & Curds   149

10. Of Drinks   157

11. Of Pace Eggs   175

12. Of Home Remedies   181

Appendix   195

Bibliography   197

Notes   199

General Index   205

Recipe Index

PREFACE
by
Jeff Cowton MBE
Curator, The Wordsworth Trust

As curator of the Wordsworth Trust's collections, I have been privileged to work with Peter in the preparation of this book. His enthusiasm and knowledge have brought alive a subject hitherto unexplored in such depth; his research adds greatly to our understanding of life in Dove Cottage during the Wordsworths' residence from 1799-1808.

Dove Cottage, at the heart of the English Lake District, is the house most closely associated with Wordsworth's major writing. He chose it as his home when he was 29 years old, looking to dedicate his life to poetry amongst his 'native mountains'. His devoted sister, Dorothy, shared his home and was to live with him for the remainder of her life. Between 1800 and 1803 she kept a journal, she wrote, 'for the pleasure it will give William', and this records beautifully their life together, the places they visited and the people they met. Wordsworth married Mary Hutchinson in 1802, and three of their five children were born in Dove Cottage. It became a family home, often noisy and crowded, and led Dorothy to write at the age of 34: 'I think these years have been the very happiest of my life.' It was where Wordsworth wrote his most popular lines, 'I wandered lonely as a cloud', as well as the first full-length version of the great poem of his life, *The Prelude*.

The Wordsworths shared this hamlet of Town End with only three neighbouring dwellings; the road passing through its centre was a main thoroughfare, described by Dorothy in 1805 as 'the highway of the Tourists', busy enough even then for her to complain to a friend about its noise! In her journal she describes passers-by knocking and begging at her door. Life in Grasmere could be idyllic: daily walks, rowing and fishing on the lake, creating and enjoying their orchard and garden (their 'little domestic slip of mountain'), reading books and having friends call in or to stay (including key figures of the day, such as Samuel Taylor Coleridge and Sir Walter Scott). But as Wordsworth himself wrote: 'Yet 'tis not to enjoy that we exist...something must be done.' That something was the writing of poetry 'On Man, on Nature and on Human Life', subjects with which we are equally concerned today. The research that Peter has done, and the books that he has published help us better understand life in the modest white cottage that was the background to the writing of some of the greatest poetry in the English language.

The cottage, and most of the hamlet, is now owned and cared for by the Wordsworth Trust, established in 1891. Its purpose is to preserve Dove Cottage and its environs, and its growing collection of manuscripts, books and art, and to use them to promote a greater appreciation of the life and work of Wordsworth and the writers and artists of what we now call the 'Romantic period'. We are fortunate that their lives are extremely well documented through their poetry and prose, and that the Jerwood Centre at the Wordsworth Trust has such a rich reserve of archive material. Amongst the many thousands of manuscripts are the recipe books described in such detail in this book. Peter has used these materials to provide the context for the food that they ate, and at the same time given colour (and taste!) to what we already know.

Peter has drawn upon two principal manuscripts for his work: the first is a notebook shared by Dorothy and Mary, which came to the Trust in the late 1970s, as part of a collection that was discovered in Carlisle and which included the now famous 'love letters' written between William and Mary in 1810 and 1812. The second notebook was compiled by Joanna Hutchinson, Mary Wordsworth's sister, and came to the Trust in 1981, having descended through the family. A third source is still in private hands, and has been kindly loaned to the Trust by a great-great-great-grand-daughter of Samuel Taylor Coleridge: it contains recipes recorded by the Fricker family, two of whom (Sara and Edith) married the poets Coleridge and Robert Southey. These two poets and their families joined Wordsworth in the Lake District, settling in Keswick, 13 miles north of Dove Cottage. We are very grateful to Rosemary E. Coleridge Middleton for her generosity in lending these beautiful manuscripts.

It has been such a great pleasure to get to know Peter during his time in Grasmere. Memorably, he gave a talk on this subject and provided tablefuls of delicious food prepared using the recipes and methods described in the book. The lecture was fascinating, and the samples a treat. I recommend you not only devour his words and knowledge, but put the recipes to the test as well. You won't be disappointed.

ACKNOWLEDGEMENTS

I would like to thank Esther C.B.Rutter for first asking me to lecture at Dove Cottage. Following this, Jeff Cowton, Curator at the Wordsworth Trust, informed me of the Wordsworth, Hutchinson and Fricker manuscript cookery books in the Trust's extensive archives. Since I had already undertaken studies of the traditional foods of the Lake District, and re-created the kitchen of the poet's childhood home at Wordsworth House, Cockermouth, I fully appreciated their unique interest. I cannot thank Mr Cowton and all his staff at Dove Cottage enough for all their help while I was working there. Both he and Mrs P. Woof, President of the Wordsworth Trust, also read through my initial text, making valuable suggestions.

I would also like to express my warmest thanks to Susan Houghton for all her considerable assistance, my publisher, David Burnett, for his care in putting the book through the press, and Miriam Macgregor for her artwork, seen on the front cover. A special word of thanks to Valerie Thomas for her scrupulous care in preparing the manuscript for press, and for many valuable suggestions. Finally, I would like to record my appreciation of the Red Lion and Lamb Inn, Grasmere, a warm and welcoming retreat from the torrential rains, deep snows and biting frosts during the harsh winter of 2009-10.

Peter Brears
Leeds, 2010

INTRODUCTION

Throughout the English-speaking world, the works of the Romantic poets of rural late Georgian Britain are recognised as some of the greatest of all literary achievements. William Wordsworth and his vision of the Lake Counties are inseparable from this movement, continuing to give the greatest pleasure to his readers, in addition to providing a seemingly endless source of study for scholars. For over a hundred and fifty years there has been a continuous stream of books on Wordsworth, his family and friends, some being labours of love developing the very highest standards of research, writing, and editorship. There is, however, one fascinating aspect of his life that has received very little attention and on which there is a considerable body of valuable information.

In the extensive collections of the Wordsworth Trust at Dove Cottage, William's first home in Grasmere, are four early nineteenth century recipe books, the first written by his wife Mary, the second by her sister Joanna, the third by Martha Fricker, sister-in-law to both Samuel Taylor Coleridge and Robert Southey, and a fourth from the Fricker family. In all, they provide over 125 recipes used in their households. They have never been subject to any previous detailed study, and so are presented here for the first time. One of the primary purposes of this book is therefore to enable readers to cook and taste the same dishes as William Wordsworth and his circle, the necessary instructions being drawn from the original manuscript sources. A second, but more interesting and enlightening aim, is to combine the information in the recipe books with the vast wealth of other material and manuscript sources, including Dove Cottage itself, Dorothy Wordsworth's great Grasmere Journals of 1800-1803, and the correspondence of William, Dorothy and Mary Wordsworth, and of Sara Hutchinson, together with other contemporary documentation. It purposely avoids most of the creative and biographical aspects of their lives, since these have already been subject to considerable study, but instead concentrates on all matters culinary. In taking this approach I hope to review and reveal much additional information on the homelife of the Wordsworths, not so much as poets and writers, but as members of a somewhat irregularly organised household, growing ever more conventional with the acquisition of larger houses and higher social status.

The ladies responsible for preparing the poet's food and organising his domestic life came from the professional and minor gentry classes. In their earlier years they had experienced similar circumstances, but with significant differences, all of which influenced their approach to food and the levels of skill they developed in their kitchens. We must therefore start by introducing each of them in turn, following their lives up to the point of William and Mary Wordsworth's marriage towards the end of 1802, and describing their recipe books. Only then can we move on to explore the practical aspects of life at Dove Cottage and the increasing reliance on servants to undertake the cookery in the family's later houses.

In each succeeding chapter, the type of food eaten by the Wordsworths is considered in turn. Having drawn together all the relevant references from the family's extensive writings, they go on to provide transcripts of the original recipes, followed by instructions for making them today, if still practicable, which most are. For the convenience of today's cooks the modernised instructions are for reduced quantities, since today's households are far smaller than those for whom most of the originals were prepared. Where the Wordsworth recipe books do not contain details of a particular dish, its recipe has been drawn from an associated source such as one of the contemporary local cookery manuscripts, Coleridge's notebooks, or regionally significant publications like Mrs. Raffald's *The Experienced English Housekeeper*. Working directly from the original recipes can prove highly problematic, for their methods may be unclear, the quantities unsuitable for modern use, or the oven temperatures and cooking times missing. In addition, they frequently assume a level of knowledge that we may lack today, being written more as aides-mémoires for personal use, rather than as comprehensive instructions for strangers. For this reason each recipe is accompanied by an authentic yet modernised version, with measurements in pounds, ounces, pints and tablespoons, as well as in grams and litres. All measurements of volume are for level, rather than heaped quantities, while all eggs are of 'medium' size. As for temperatures, these are given in degrees Centigrade, Fahrenheit and Gas mark for a conventional oven. If using a fan-assisted oven these should be reduced accordingly. No attempt has been made to provide healthy alternatives for the authentic ingredients. Traditional recipes abound in saturated fats etc., which can lead to health problems, since our life-styles no longer burn them off. Similarly more people today require vegetarian or vegan options. It is therefore left to personal preference to use low-fat or vegetarian alternatives for the cream, butter, suet etc. quoted in the recipes. For every other ingredient, however, it is best to use local organic produce, such as Herdwick lamb or mutton, beef, pork, poultry, fish and game. As for flour, any good plain wheat variety may be used, but certainly not wholemeal, which the Wordsworths would never have bought, it then being considered decidedly third-rate.

In today's England, there is an enormous demand for ethnic or 'fusion' foods from everywhere but England. This is largely due to the economic problems and periods of rationing which marked the first seventy years of the twentieth century here. In ordinary homes, in country houses, inns, hotels and restaurants, the great national tradition of excellent cooking and baking suffered enormously, many of our finest dishes and highest culinary skills being largely forgotten. Instead of being revived when circumstances allowed, they were replaced by a hotch-potch of foreign dishes from France, Spain, Italy, Greece, India, China and even America. In contrast, the recipes reproduced in the following pages illustrate few international influences, being essentially those of the Georgian north-country middle-class. Their tea, coffee, rum, sugar, spices and other exotic ingredients were certainly shipped in from around the expanding Empire, but perhaps the only imported recipe in this collection is that for an excellent lemon pickle, based on those from India. As for the rest, they are purely English, using basic methods to convert local produce into a range of satisfying dishes, all of which are well worth reviving for everyday modern use. Some may prove rather surprising: those hostesses who boast of their pannacotta, for instance, will discover that it is just an inferior-flavoured English blancmange which in its delicious native version still makes by far the best accompaniment for Lythe Valley damsons, preserved to Mary Wordsworth's own recipe. Certainly all the recipes carefully noted down by Mary, her sister Joanna, and their Fricker contemporaries should not only be read, but also tried, in order to gain a fuller knowledge of the lives and lifestyles of all those who made up their illustrious households.

Chapter One

THE WORDSWORTHS
& THEIR RECIPES

Throughout his working life, from 1794 to 1850, William Wordsworth was fortunate in having a succession of practical ladies who provided him with every domestic service he could ever require, leaving him free to concentrate on his work.

His sister Dorothy acted as his secretary and copyist. She was also responsible for running his household – a responsibility she largely relinquished to William's wife, Mary, after his marriage in 1802. Dorothy and Mary had been close friends since childhood, and the household duties were often shared out even more widely during frequent long visits and residences from Mary's sisters, Joanna and Sara Hutchinson. This chapter explores the backgrounds of these key figures in William's life and their effect on the domestic arrangements at the houses where they lived in and around Grasmere: Town End (later renamed Dove Cottage), Allan Bank, Grasmere Rectory and finally Rydal Mount, a large house overlooking the vale of Rydal.

William himself had enjoyed an idyllic childhood at Cockermouth, where his elder brother Richard and younger siblings Dorothy, John and Christopher were under the tender care of their mother Ann. Unfortunately this period of great happiness and security came to an end on the death of his mother in March 1778, when William was just seven years old. This close family was now scattered, the last links with Cockermouth being cut when their father died in 1783.

From 1779 to 1787 William attended the grammar school at Hawkshead, lodging in the home of Ann Tyson, who acted almost as a foster-mother to several schoolboys. 'She gave all she could of that sort of simple, unpretentious rustic affection and discipline that seems like the very quality of the countryside distilled into human terms.'[1] Working on a fixed budget, she provided basic and nourishing food though William recalled that it was not over-plentiful:

> No delicate viands sapp'd our bodily strength;
> More than we wish'd we knew the blessing then
> Of vigorous hunger, for our daily meals
> Were frugal, Sabine fare! And then, exclude

> A little weekly stipend, and we lived,
> Through three divisions of the quarter'd year
> In pennyless poverty.[2]

When he moved on to St. John's College, Cambridge, in 1787, William found himself in rooms in the first court, where

> Right underneath the College kitchens made
> A humming sound, less tuneable than bees,
> But hardly less industrious; with shrill notes
> Of sharp command and scolding intermix'd.[3]

Meals were constantly available in hall, but, especially as a 'fresher',

> ... The weeks went roundly on,
> With invitations, suppers, wine, and fruit.
> Smooth housekeeping within, and all without
> Liberal and suiting Gentleman's array! [4]

The years following his departure from Cambridge in 1790 were spent in travelling through France and Switzerland, touring Wales and Wiltshire, and spending long periods in London. In January 1794 he was able to achieve a long-planned reunion with his sister Dorothy, spending six weeks with her with friends, Elizabeth and William Rawson, in Halifax, before travelling on to Keswick, walking the last thirty three miles from Kendal via Ambleside and Grasmere. It was in Keswick, at Windy Brow, that Dorothy first exercised her skills as housekeeper for William. 'We please ourselves in calculating from our present expences for how very small a sum we could live. We find our own food, our breakfast and supper are of milk and our dinner chiefly of potatoes and we drink no tea.'[5]

Dorothy's training for this lifelong role had probably started in the family home at Cockermouth, where she had been born in 1771. Here her father, John Wordsworth, was the attorney and 'law-agent' to Sir James Lowther, the chief landowner and political magnate of the district. To enable him to fulfil his professional and social duties, Sir James housed John Wordsworth in one of the finest properties in town. Standing at the west end of the main street, with a large walled garden extending down to the River Derwent, it had been built by Richard Bird around 1690, and then extensively remodelled to the highest standards around 1745 for John Lucock, Sheriff of

Fig 1. The kitchen at Wordsworth House, Cockermouth, was fully equipped with stewing stove, roasting range, oven and boiler. Here the Wordsworth children would have seen their mother Ann prepare fine dinners for her husband's guests, until her early death in 1778, when they were dispersed to school and distant relatives.

Cumberland. Its elegantly panelled entrance hall, office, dining room and first-floor drawing room were ideal for conducting the business and entertainment required to promote Sir James's extensive interests. Most of the other rooms were severely utilitarian, being used to house the family and a few servants. However, the house was provided with all the necessary offices. The semi-basement contained a dairy, a wine and ale cellar and a larder, while the kitchen had a large charcoal stewing stove, a roasting range, oven, and built-in dresser. Dorothy would have seen all of these in full operation in her early childhood, but had little chance to absorb any of the skills practised there before her mother died when she was six years old.

Unable to look after all his young family, John sent Dorothy to live with his mother's cousins, Elizabeth and William Threlkeld of Halifax. This extended household, already occupied by Elizabeth's orphaned nieces and nephews, provided both happy memories and lifelong friends. But all was to change in May, 1787, when Dorothy, who had been orphaned at John's death in December 1783, joined her maternal grandparents and her brothers, for the summer in Penrith. The young Wordsworths had had a miserable time here, being subject to constant indignities and insults, particularly from the servants. This time, however, it did bring a renewal of friendships made years earlier at the local dame school with the Hutchinson children, who were also orphaned and now in the care of their Penrith grandfather. Following their brief reunion, Dorothy went to live at the rectory of her uncle, William Cookson, at Forncett in Norfolk, staying with him until reunited with her brother William, first at Halifax and then at Windy Brow in 1794. A year later William and Dorothy moved on together to Racedown Lodge in Dorset and to Alfoxden House in Somerset in 1797. They visited the Wye Valley, and then embarked on a study-expedition to Germany, finally returning to England in May 1799. After a few months with the Hutchinsons, now at Sockburn-on-Tees in the south of County Durham, Dorothy joined William at Town End, Grasmere, setting up home in the former Dove and Olive Bough Inn on 20th December 1799, now Dove Cottage.

In her Grasmere journals, which run from May to December 1800 and October 1801 to January 1803, Dorothy recorded many of the cooking operations she carried out there. This considerable body of archival evidence has led a number of writers to assume that she was a great cook, running the Wordsworth's domestic affairs for the rest of her life. However, a closer reading of the journals and letters shows that this was not the case. Throughout much of her early life she had lived in relatively small households which employed only the basic standards of everyday cookery. There is no evidence to suggest that she ever had any opportunity of being trained to the levels of culinary skill usual amongst most contemporary middle and upper-class families, in which ability in domestic management was seen as an essential requisite for making a good marriage. Record offices and private family archives contain probably thousands of manuscript books of recipes collected by well-to-do young women, some being continued throughout their adult lives. They all demonstrate a high degree of practical competence, including a knowledge of both materials and techniques which it would be difficult to achieve even today.

As the journal entries show, Dorothy was perfectly capable of baking, brewing, and of producing basic nourishing meals composed of potatoes, vegetables, plainly-cooked meats and fish, and pies. When she had no other help but Old Molly Fisher, this is what she produced. However, when anything more was required, she found herself in difficulties. She was unable to raise the oven to its correct temperatures in July 1800, so that the pies could not be baked, while in May 1802, still susceptible to bad advice, she managed to produce a cake 'as black as a genuine child of the coal-hole' and completely inedible.[6] In August 1800 she was so uncertain of the proportion of sugar to fruit necessary when preserving, elementary knowledge to anyone with basic cookery skills, that she had to try three different batches and record the results.[7] It is interesting to note that the journals of 1800 – 1802 only mention cake-making when one of the Hutchinson sisters was a guest at Dove Cottage, except for one seed cake for her friend Mr Simpson.[8] Another telling comment on Dorothy's cookery at this period comes from a letter which William wrote to Mary in May 1812, after meeting Mr Carr, Solicitor to the Excise, in London. In it, he recalled 'the very bad dinner which he had the misfortune of receiving, or rather dearest Dorothy and I had the vexation of giving him in our Little Cottage at Grasmere, before you and I, my Love, were married.'[9] After Mary's permanent entry into the household as William's wife in October 1802, there were no more culinary disasters. Then, as Dorothy recorded in her journal: 'We made cakes' on 16th October, Mary was baking on 23rd October and 8th December, while on 24th December we find 'Mary... in the parlour below attending to the baking of cakes', and on 16th January 1803 'we [are] going to... make Gingerbread ourselves.'[10]

Mary seems to have been rather too busy cooking, child-rearing and managing the family's finances to have had time to record her own daily activities. For this reason, it has frequently been presumed that she did very little beyond the incidental activities that Dorothy noted in her journal, but there is substantial evidence that this was not the case. In reality she and Dorothy carried out their domestic responsibilities in tandem, assisted for long periods by Sara and Joanna Hutchinson, and demonstrated a remarkably good-humoured and mutually rewarding relationship - united in providing their beloved William with every opportunity to pursue his amazing creativity.

The Hutchinson family had been brought up in Penrith, where their father John was a tobacconist. There were four brothers, John, Henry, Thomas (Tom) and George, as well as three sisters, Mary, Sara, and Joanna, who had attended the same local dame school as the young Wordsworths. Their father died in 1785, being buried in Penrith on 2nd April. Sara then went to live with her cousin Margaret Robinson who had married James Patrick, a Scottish pedlar now settled in Kendal. All the other children moved in with their maternal aunt Elizabeth Monkhouse, under the watchful eye of their grandfather John Monkhouse, post-master of Penrith. William Wordsworth later described him as 'the most gentlemanly man, both in looks and manner, that I ever knew in Penrith.'[11] In addition to his town property, he owned a small estate at Sebergham, a few miles south of Carlisle, where the children spent very enjoyable holidays. His wife was Margaret Richardson of Nunwick Hall on the Eden, a member of one of the most considerable county families in the district. The Hutchinson children were therefore being brought up in much happier, more prosperous and more gentlemanly circumstances than their Wordsworth contemporaries. In addition, since they all could expect either to inherit estates or marry into good families, their guardians appear to have provided them with the necessary practical and social skills. In contrast the Wordsworth boys needed a grammar school education and professional training to counteract the uncertainty of their futures caused by Sir James's arbitrary decision to withhold massive sums owed to their deceased father. It is probable that there was a strong tradition of good housekeeping in Mary's family, for in the year of her birth Arthur Young, the great agriculturalist, published a description of hospitality he had received at Penrith, at Mr Monkhouse's New George inn. This, he found, was 'Exceedingly good, reasonable, and very civil. The dinner was roast beef, apple pudding, potatoes, cellery, potted trout and sturgeon. 1s a head.'[12]

When Dorothy came to live with her Cookson grandparents in Penrith in 1787, and William started to spend his vacations from Cambridge there in 1788 and 1789, their friendship with the Hutchinsons began to centre around the eldest sister, Mary, who would eventually would become established as Dorothy's lifelong friend and as William's wife. In the meantime, however, Tom Hutchinson had inherited his great-uncle's farm of Sockburn Hall, a peninsular of County Durham, where the Tees looped into Yorkshire just east of Darlington. The elder Thomas Hutchinson had been one of the great livestock breeders of the eighteenth century, his Sockburn sheep and shorthorn cattle enjoying a very high reputation in agricultural circles. As Dorothy recorded in 1795, the house was:

> ...built by their uncle, who left them the furniture and eighteen hundred pounds, which with what they had makes them very comfortable. It is an excellent house, not at all like a farm-house, and they seem to have none of the trouble which I used to think must make farmers always in

a bustle, for they have very little corn and only two cows. It is a grazing estate, and most delightfully pleasant, washed nearly round with the Tees (a noble river) and stocked with sheep and lambs which look very pretty, and to me give it a very interesting appearance.[13]

This now became the family home, with brother Tom at its head, and Mary as his housekeeper, assisted by her younger sisters. George, the youngest brother, also lived here, the eldest brother John being in business in Stockton-on-Tees, and the second brother Henry then at sea. Having no permanent home of their own, William and Dorothy Wordsworth spent considerable periods here as friends and house-guests, including a continuous seven months from May to December, 1799. Even after the Wordsworths moved into Dove Cottage, they continued to keep in close touch with the Hutchinsons through letters and visits.

In 1802 Tom, Mary and Joanna moved from Sockburn to Gallow Hill near Scarborough, while George took a farm at Bishop Middleton near Bishop Auckland in County Durham. Thus it was to Gallow Hill that William and Dorothy returned after their tour of Germany, arriving in the middle of the corn harvest at the end of September 1802. A few days later, on 4th October, William and Mary were married at Brompton Parish Church, returning only briefly to the house to have breakfast and board the chaise hired to take the three back to the marital home in Grasmere. As Dorothy recorded in her journal, 'Mary was much agitated when she parted from her Brothers and her Sisters and her home.'[14] This was to be expected, for even though she had already stayed at Dove Cottage for several months, and knew it well, she would now have to establish herself as wife and principal housekeeper of an already established household, and one not as extensive or so well provided for as the one she was leaving. In effect, she had been the chatelaine of a relatively well-to-do establishment for eleven years, fully responsible for its domestic management, except while making visits elsewhere, when her sister Joanna had taken over.

Compared to Dorothy, Mary was very competent and experienced in all things domestic. This is illustrated by her surviving recipe book. It takes the form of a vellum-bound pocket-book with marbled end-papers, measuring some six and a half by four and a half inches (16·5 x 11·5cm).[15] There are only eighteen recipes, but these include instructions for making blancmange, jaunemange, artificial ginger, and Portuguese vegetable soup, all of which might be expected in a rather more prosperous and pretentious house than Dove Cottage. It also contains remedies such as tonics, footbaths, eye waters and horse plasters. There is little internal evidence for its date. At the end of the recipes, and therefore most probably written some time after they were in use, are several pages of miscellaneous accounts, most being in Mary's hand and dated between 1815 and 1820, when the family had settled at Rydal Mount. Among them are entries such as:

'Rydal Mount up to Jan 7 1817	9 3 9'
'4 Days house work	4 -'
'Tom's Clothes [the Wordsworth's second son]	
2yd and half of calico at 1/8 per yard	[3 4]
2 and a half of checks	1 4
pair of shoes	7 -
2 yards of check for shirt	- -'
'1820 2 Baskets	3 -
Received of Mrs [?] for candlestick	1 3
2 flower pots (self)	6
2 Candlesticks	6
Match Boxes	8'
'butter sold	
Mary young 2pd paid	2
Nanny Patty 3pd	3
Mary Young 1pd	
Nanny Patty 1pd'	

There is also a list in Dorothy's hand of what she had paid for 'J. Hutchinson', presumably Joanna, including accounts with various ladies, £2. 4s for tartan, 11s for rugs, and £6. 6s 'For Taffy to Boy', along with £3.13s 2d for corn and 2s 8d for a blacksmith. However, the most moving of all is a separate entry for August 1816 'Tombstone £3. 4s -.' This would be to mark the grave of William and Mary's six-year-old son Thomas, who died in 1812. Later Mary was to complain that it took William 'years to produce those 6 single lines upon the stone at the head of the earthly remains of our own dear Boy'.[16] With the exception of these accounts, the recipes in this book are far too few in number to represent the working collection of a full-time housewife and cook. They are essentially Mary's working copies, made for occasional use - but copies of what? Three of them, those for rice, a pickle for hams, and the Portuguese vegetable soup, are actually in the handwriting of her sister Joanna. As for the remainder, the best clue comes from her recipe for

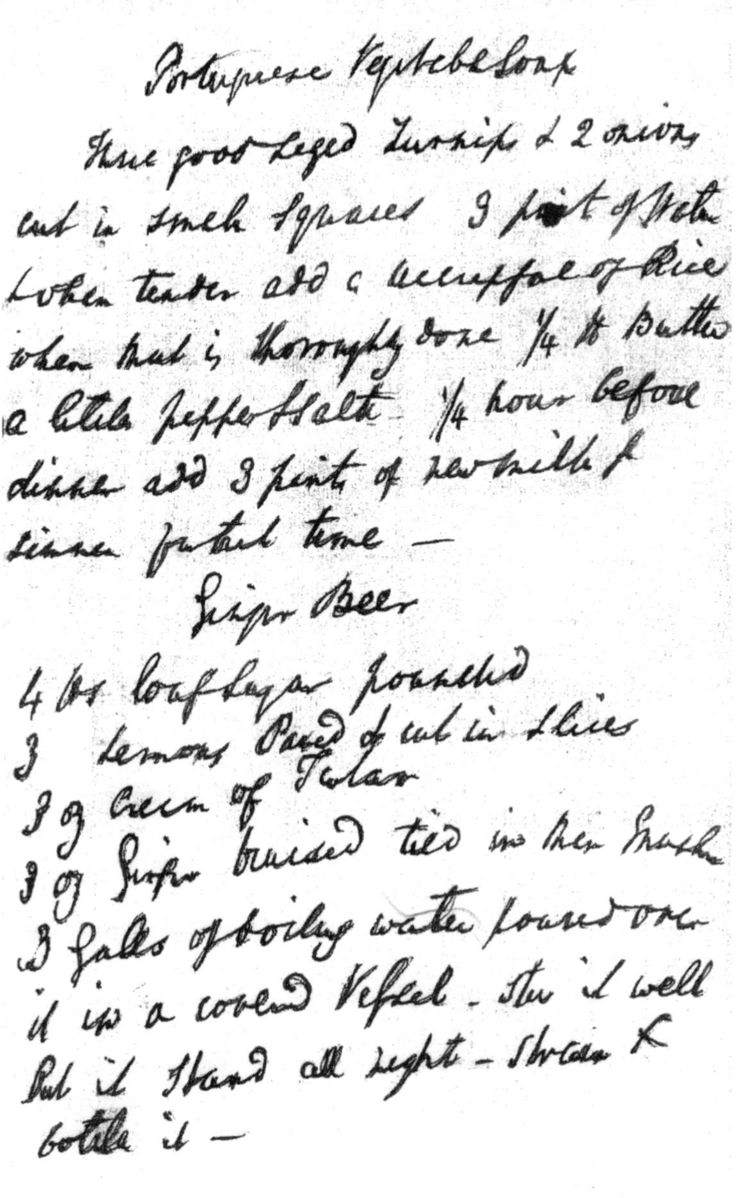

Portuguese Vegteble Soup

Three good Leged Turnips & 2 onions
cut in small Squares 3 pint of Water
when tender add a teacupfull of Rice
when that is thoroughly done 1/4 lb Butter
a little pepper & Salt. 1/4 hour before
dinner add 3 pints of new milk &
dinner put at time —

      Ginger Beer

4 lbs loaf Sugar pounded
3 Lemons Pared & cut in Slices
3 oz Cream of Tarar
3 oz Ginger bruised tied in thin Muslin
3 Galls of boiling water poured over
it in a covered Vessel — Stir it well
Put it Stand all night — Strain &
bottle it —

Fig 2. A page from Mary Wordsworth's recipe book, showing an example of her handwriting below, and that of her sister Joanna Hutchinson above.

gooseberry wine. This was either copied from one in the second recipe book in the Wordsworth Trust's collection, that of her sister Joanna, or from a common source, such as that of the unidentified original 'Mrs Kes...', or from an earlier Hutchinson family recipe book. Whatever the case, we may be sure that, as in most polite Georgian families, all the sisters would have developed similar repertoires of recipes during the long years they had spent together at Penrith and Sockburn. In essence, it is reasonable to assume that Mary would be familiar with the practical use of all the recipes in Joanna's book. Joanna herself never visited Grasmere before Mary's marriage, but already shared a close friendship with the Wordsworths, having given Dorothy a fine shawl in April 1802.[17] She first stayed at Dove Cottage in the autumn of 1803, providing company for Mary and baby John while William and Dorothy went off on a tour of Scotland with William's friend and fellow poet Samuel Taylor Coleridge. She was later to spend considerable periods in the Wordsworth household.

Joanna's recipe book, commenced in 1816 or earlier, and later inscribed 'Miss Joanna Hutchinson, Hindwell Hall, July 14, 1821', is fully worthy of that title. It is a card-covered book measuring some seven and three-quarters by four and a half inches (19·5 x 11·5cm), its thirty-six pages being packed with seventy-four closely-written recipes.[18] It has main courses of chicken, calf's head, pig, chicken, and game, eight hot and cold puddings, ten cakes, eight pickles and preserves, and thirteen wines and drinks, as well as a good selection of household and medicinal recipes. It is interesting to speculate whether William really did carry the odour of mothballs with him, having shaved with its home-made wash-balls containing camphor, or if his wife and sisters were scented with the rosewater and almond oil used in its cold-cream.

The third recipe book, loaned to the Trust, belonged to Martha Fricker. She had very little contact with the Wordsworths, spending most of her life in the south of England. The fourth daughter of the Fricker family of Bristol, she had been born in the family home on Redcliffe Hill in 1777. Her three elder sisters had been caught up in the idealistic plans for Pantisocracy, a scheme for setting up Utopian communities in which all were equal and all ruled. In the mid 1790s, when three of the girls were in their early twenties, they had each married one of its charismatic leaders, Sara, the eldest, marrying Samuel Taylor Coleridge, Mary, the second, marrying Robert Lovell, and Edith, the third, marrying Robert Southey. The Pantisocratic life they envisaged marked a giant leap from the conventions of the day. As

Coleridge described, they would:

> "let the married Women do only what is absolutely
> convenient and customary for pregnant Women or nurses
> - Let the Husbands do all the Rest & Washing with a
> Machine and cleaning the House. One Hour's addition to
> our daily Labor" [19]

He even noted down recipes for stew, ginger wine etc. ready for use
as part of his husbandly duties.[20] Even when married and responsible
for his first son Hartley, Coleridge still believed that he could live by
working:

> "very hard as Cook, Butler, Scullion, Shoe-cleaner,
> occasional Nurse, Gardener, Hind, Pig-protector, Chaplain,
> Secretary, Poet, Reviewer, and omnibotherum shilling-
> scavenger in other words, I shall keep no Servant, and will
> cultivate my Land-acre, and my wise-acres, as well as I
> can." [21]

Needless to say, when these high intentions came up against the harsh
realities of life, they rapidly crumbled. If the married Fricker girls
really believed that their husbands would undertake every domestic
chore and maintain them in the manner to which they aspired, they
were to be sadly disappointed.

William and Dorothy Wordsworth had first met Coleridge during
a five-week visit to Bristol in August-September 1795, immediately
preceding Coleridge's marriage to Sara Fricker, which took place at
the magnificent church of St.Mary, Redcliffe, on 4th October. Their
friendship and working relationship then flourished through their
time at Racedown and Alfoxden, at Sockburn, in Germany and into
the years at Dove Cottage. After returning to the West Country in May,
1800, Coleridge came back to the Wordsworths at the end of June, now
accompanied by Sara, baby Hartley, and all his books, in preparation
for moving into Greta Hall, Keswick, on 24th July. Eventually his
brother-in-law Robert Southey brought his family up to share the
Hall, along with Robert Lovell's widow and young son. This, in effect,
meant that its domestic affairs were entirely in the hands of the three
re-united Fricker sisters, Sara, Mary and Edith. As for Martha, she
had been courted by George Burnett, another Pantisocrat, but had
rejected him and remained single in the south of England. She hardly

ever travelled to Keswick to see her sisters, but did spend some time at Greta Hall in the summer of 1812.[22]

Martha Fricker's recipe book measures some six by four inches (15 x 10cm), is vellum-bound, and inscribed 'Martha Fricker January 1st 1814' inside its cover.[23] Its contents are chiefly medical remedies and instructions for whitening marble, removing ink stains, or making Indian glue, etc. There are culinary recipes too, for typical middle-class dishes of the period, from curing hams and making broth, to making cakes and puddings.

The fourth recipe book, on loan to the Wordsworth Trust, is also associated with the Fricker family, but it does not bear the name of any individual.[24] It measures eight and a quarter by five inches (21 x 12·5cm), with twenty-six pages containing twenty-seven recipes. Its main significance is that, unlike the previous books, it concentrates on cookery for a family used to giving high-class dinners. There are no egg and bacon pies, no boiled puddings. Its recipes are largely for fashionable confectionery, the kind of dishes intended to grace dining rooms and drawing rooms in the fine Bath-stone merchant houses of prosperous Bristol. Here are the lightest of sponge cakes, rich iced plum cakes, delicate creams and jellies, and even crème brulée. Given these aspirations and this standard of domestic training, the Fricker sisters were brought up to a more leisured way of life than the Wordsworths and the Hutchinsons. It is not surprising that Dorothy, while respecting Sara Coleridge's 'several great merits', found her to be 'a sad fiddle fuddler', taking three and a half hours just to dress herself and her two young children, only then coming down to her family's Sunday dinner, obviously prepared by others.[25]

It is particularly fortunate that the recipe books of Mary Wordsworth and Joanna Hutchinson have survived, since they provide instructions for making over ninety of the dishes probably served in the Wordsworth household. However, as with most records of this kind, they present an essentially incomplete account of most of the food actually cooked and eaten on a daily basis. No-one needed an aide-mémoire for making porridge, boiling or roasting meat, or cooking vegetables. Again, it is truly remarkable that so much of the Wordsworths' correspondence has not only survived, but has also been published in full, to provide a wealth of information regarding even these seemingly most insignificant of details. By combining such essential sources with close observation of their first marital home, Dove Cottage, it is now possible to reconstruct their domestic life with a high degree of accuracy.

Chapter Two

AT HOME IN GRASMERE

What kind of household did Mary Wordsworth enter as a new bride in October 1802? As her husband recorded, their house was a former inn called The Dove and Olive Bough which had:

> Offered a greeting of good ale
> To all who entered Grasmere Vale ...
> There, where the Dove and Olive-Bough
> Once hung, a Poet harbours now,
> A simple water-drinking bard.[1]

In a later letter to the Rev. Francis Wrangham, Wordsworth described it as 'our tiny cottage', where there was only 'very homely fare, no wine and even little beer'.[2] Over the following years, this concept of 'plain living and high thinking' was maintained and perhaps even developed with Eleanor Rawnsley describing how they had lived on nothing but bread, porridge, potatoes and milk, tea being far too expensive, and how they considered themselves fortunate to have a well of water in the garden, so that they could at least quench their thirsts.[3] Similar passages have effectively created a myth of William and Dorothy's 'noble poverty' at Dove Cottage. The only poverty they encountered was that which they observed in others, the homeless beggars wandering by their door, or the local families working every hour of the day to place even the most basic level of subsistence food on their tables. Being provided with a totally unearned income to support private grammar school education, years at Cambridge University and continental tours, and also to maintain a sequence of houses and a decidedly middle-class lifestyle, is to be considered prosperous, even wealthy, by both Georgian and modern standards. Plain living should never be confused with real poverty.

Similarly Dove Cottage could only be described as 'tiny' by someone like William who was used to life in mansions which today would be valued at around a million pounds or more. The real tiny cottages of the Lake counties were very basic one or two-roomed structures with walls of either beaten clay or local stone, roofed with thatch or slate, their only fire being lit in open smoke-hoods at one end.[4] Despite its relatively modern title of 'cottage', in 1800 'Town End' as it was then known was one of the best houses in Grasmere. It was two-storeyed, well-built with six main rooms, all but one having their own fireplace fitted with an iron grate. The culinary activities were centred on three ground-floor rooms.

In common with most middle-class families, the Wordsworths used two kitchens. The back kitchen, half-buried in the rising ground to the rear of the house, served as a combined pantry/ scullery/ washhouse/ and general kitchen for food preparation. To one side, it had a larder, with a channel of fresh water running beneath its slate floor to ensure that it always remained ideally cool. Here, on its shelves and its slate-slab-topped 'stone' or bench, all raw and cooked foods should have been stored, as in a modern domestic refrigerator. However, the unconventional Wordsworths apparently chose to use this room as their peatroom, giving them an indoor supply of domestic fuel. It is probable that they stored their ale barrels here too, since all the other rooms would have been far too warm for keeping ale in good condition. This meant that the back kitchen had also to serve as a pantry for the storage of food, its left-hand wall having a large cupboard furnished with shelves to hold all the family's dry stores - everything from rice, tapioca and dried fruits, to jams and preserves. The back kitchen/pantry had a slate-flagged floor and a low, beamed ceiling with wrought iron hooks at its centre. These were carefully positioned for hanging hams and pieces of bacon up in the slightly warm draughts drawn towards the fire, keeping them in ideal conditions and well away from people's heads, since the main worktable would be directly below. It would be from here that Coleridge probably cut himself a rasher of bacon to accompany the peas he had gathered from the garden in early August 1802, making a meal for himself while the Wordsworths were away in Calais.[5] The present fireplace is fitted with a mid-nineteenth-century cast iron oven to the right, a soot-door just below it, and the brass knobs above to operate a scraper, which prevented soot accumulating on its top, behind the faceplate. The wrought iron firebox of the grate extends to the left, terminating in a rectangular cast iron boiler with a brass tap from which to draw off supplies of hot water. All of these features date from long after the Wordsworth's departure, however, and in their place we should imagine a typical Georgian open fireplace, a single, large rectangular opening extending from the floor up to a long horizontal mantle-beam. Since coal would be burnt here, a wrought iron grate would have been set in the middle of the back wall, ready to roast or toast anything placed before it. Above, bridging across the chimney opening, there would be a high-level randle-balk or beam, from which cooking pots could be hung over the fire, by means of adjustable iron reckon-hooks. The oven would have taken the form of a large masonry-domed chamber, its rectangular door opening at about waist height into the side of the fireplace, so that its smoke would be readily carried away up the chimney. If there was a sink, it would have closely resembled the lead-lined example still to be found here, but it is equally likely that the function of a sink was then performed by a freestanding coopered tub mounted on a low stool-like stand.

The front kitchen, or kitchen parlour, the room that Dorothy referred to as 'the Kitchen' or 'the Parlour', was the main room at the front of the ground floor.[6] As the 'bar parlour' of the Dove and Olive Bough, it had a hard-wearing slate-flagged floor and walls clad in panelling most atypical of traditional cottages. The present whitewashed plaster ceiling is a later addition, for in the Wordsworth's day it was still open to the floorboards, so that all conversations held here could be easily overheard by all in the room above.[7] This was the main living room, a combination of entrance hall, dining room, parlour and kitchen. The panelling around the present inserted fireplace shows how it was originally much larger, housing a cooking grate to complement that in the back kitchen. In 1800 Dorothy described how 'after the dishes are washed up we let [this] kitchen fire go out, and we never light it till it is time to dress the dinner.'[8] By its side casual visitors were entertained as they told their stories. Here too Dorothy continued her writing while keeping a watchful eye on the roasting mutton, the family also reading around it, and sometimes taking their teas and dinners.[9] This was the bustling, cramped room in which William would:

> ... sit without emotion, hope or aim,
> By my half-kitchen, my half-parlour fire,
> And listen to the flapping of the flame,
> Or kettle whispering its faint undersong.[10]

The adjacent parlour was used as a bedroom, initially by Dorothy, then by William from the summer of 1802, and by both William and Mary after their marriage. Having a door into the front kitchen, it was ideally placed for serving breakfasts or suppers to William, on those occasions when he took these meals in bed.

Two short flights of stairs and a half-landing led up to the first floor, where the room over the kitchen/parlour was used as the family's more private sitting room. Breakfasts and teas were taken here, as well as dinners. On Christmas Day, 1805, for example, Old Molly and John Fisher were to leave the kitchen 'when dinner is ready ... to come upstairs and partake' in this family sitting room.[11] Before the houses were built across the road, it enjoyed splendid open views across Grasmere to Silver How and the encircling fells. This was William's refuge when foul weather kept him indoors, Dorothy describing how it:

> ...often compelled my brother to [remain in] the sitting room when in a milder season he would have composed in the open air, indeed I cannot but admire the fortitude and wonder at the success with which he has laboured in that one room, common to all the family, to all visitors, and where the children frequently played beside him.[12]

The room over William's bedroom was used as a lodging room for their numerous visiting friends and relations, while that over the larder/peat room was improved to provide a separate bedroom for Dorothy.[13] The last room upstairs, that over the back kitchen/pantry, served as a lumber room.

As for the Wordsworths, it can be confirmed that, as Eleanor Rawnsley stated, they ate bread, porridge, potatoes and milk. However, she was totally incorrect in claiming that they consumed nothing else. Meat, including beef steaks, veal and mutton as well as bacon was probably delivered by the butcher's man from Ambleside.[14] There were also geese and turkeys in the winter months, as well as occasional gifts of game, such as partridges from their friend Lady Beaumont.[15] Freshwater fish for the table were the product of local fishing expeditions. Between May and August 1800, for example, William and his brother John caught three pike and three bass in Grasmere, and three pike in Wythburnwater (now under Thirlmere).[16] The pike weighed up to 4¾ and 7½lb. For these their methods included both rod and line, and setting hooks baited with small dead fish on floated lines.[17] They also fished in Rydalwater and in Langdale, but their catches there were not recorded.

Most of their fruit and vegetables were either home-grown, or received as presents from friends. Peas, for example, were sown around early April, tended both by John and Molly Fisher, by Dorothy, provided with sticks, some made by William, in June, and harvested in baskets from late June through to the end of August, some being kept as seeds for the following year.[18] Considered a delicacy, some fresh green peas were given to their neighbour Mrs Simpson, and by a chaise returning to Keswick, to the Coleridges.[19] Scarlet or French beans came a little later, being sown in early June, tied and nailed up by Dorothy in early August, and harvested from July to the end of September.[20] In 1800 she described Dove Cottage being 'covered all over with green leaves and scarlet flowers, for we have trained scarlet beans upon threads, which are not only exceedingly beautiful but very useful, as their produce is immense.'[21] Given the basic details given in her journal, it is possible to reconstruct the seasonable availability of vegetables from the garden:

Beans, French[22]	late July – September
Beans, Kidney[23]	July – August
Broccoli[24]	October – March
Carrots[25]	October – March
Onions[26]	October – March
Peas[27]	June – September
Potatoes[28]	Most of year
Radishes[29]	May – September
Spinach[30]	October – June
Turnips[31]	October – March

The garden was also used to grow both culinary and medicinal herbs such as the 'lemon thyme and several other plants' that Dorothy planted by moonlight after a visit to the Simpsons, or the wild thyme gathered on a ramble on the hillside above the house.[32] Apple and pear trees in the orchard provided both fresh fruit and ingredients for pies and tarts, and there were rhubarb, gooseberries and strawberries to be had too.

William probably acquired both a taste for honey and the knowledge of how to collect it while at school in Hawkshead, where, returning for his vacation from Cambridge, he laid himself 'down to any casual feast of wild wood-honey' in the surrounding countryside. Ann Tyson had previously purchased honey for William, to satisfy his schoolboy yearnings for this sweet treat.[33] Peggy Ashburner gave Dorothy 'some honey – with a thousand thanks', in November 1801, in return for a gift of hot roast goose. Dorothy then decided to 'set her right', explaining that there was neither expectation nor need to repay such presents from a friend.[34] There might have been a hive in use in the garden by 1802, however, the bees buzzing around it

Fig 3. John Fisher's bee-stand at Sykeside, just opposite Dove Cottage.

in late January, and John Fisher sodding 'about the Bee-stand' at the end of April.[35] Bee-stands are shown in W.J. Blacklock's painting of a farmstead in Little Langdale of 1850, small four-legged tables, each of them supporting its traditional domed lipwork straw skep protected by what appears to be a white linen cover.[36] The garden at Sykeside, the Fishers' cottage just opposite Dove Cottage, still retains a bee-stand much more substantially constructed in stone. It has an open-fronted cupboard-like recess for the hives, and is protected by a sloping roof above. The hives at Town End would have provided the Wordsworths with sufficient honey to spread on their tea-time toast, as well as wax for polishing the furniture, making cold-cream, and similar domestic preparations.

As for the drinks taken by this 'simple water-drinking bard' and his sister, they included home-brewed beer, wine, coffee, and quantities of very expensive tea. There was milk, too, but not in large quantities, as the family did not acquire its own cow until after leaving Dove Cottage.

Fuel to cook the food, as well as to keep warm, came in three different forms. Dry fallen branches and sticks were collected during the course of frequent local walks, some being formed into faggots to heat the oven, and others being chopped into logs by William to burn as fuel.[37] Peat was also burned here, Dorothy recording the raising of the former peat-room roof to create her new bedroom in June 1805.[38]

It was cut from local peat-beds in late spring: 'The people were graving [digging] peats under Nadel Fell' in mid May 1802, which were laid out in strips to dry, and then carted back to the homesteads at midsummer, when the Wordsworths saw Colwith 'wild and interesting, from the Peat carts and peat gatherers.'[39] Some of the small farmers in Grasmere then sold part of their stock of dried peats to those unable to obtain their supplies in any other way, George and Sarah Green of Easedale earning much-needed money in this way.[40] This is how Dove Cottage peats would have been obtained. When looking for a new house in 1810, the Wordsworths had considered Bouth, six miles south of Kendal, one of its positive factors being that it enjoyed peat-digging rights, the expense of collecting them being only £8, a much cheaper way of heating a house than using coal.[41]

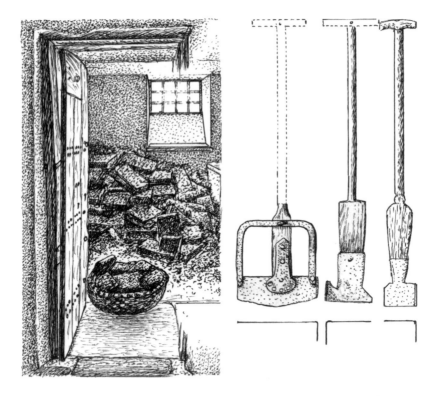

Fig 4. The Dove Cottage peat-house was in this small room off the back kitchen/pantry. In the Lake District peats were cut out of the moors and fells either in broad slabs, as with the spade from Wasdale Head near Shap (left) or in narrow strips, as with the spades from Hawkshead (middle) and Lowick, High Furness (right).

There were no coalfields near Grasmere, but coal was extensively burned in the more urban areas, Keswick being supplied from the great West Cumberland mines around Whitehaven, and Kendal from Ingleton etc., full access to the Wigan pits not being possible until the completion of the Lancaster Canal in 1819. Between 16th May and 1st November 1800, Thomas Ashburner, the local carrier and their close neighbour, delivered ten loads of coal to Dove Cottage, that is about one load per month.[42] They usually came from Kendal, only being carted more expensively from Keswick in times of scarcity.[43]

Having supplied Dove Cottage, the nature of the daily routine of its inhabitants can now be considered. In most households the needs to take the maximum advantage of daylight working hours, of feeding staff, and foddering livestock, together with other practical considerations, made it imperative to maintain a regular domestic timetable. One of the distinguishing characteristics of Dorothy's housekeeping, however, was that there was hardly a trace of any routine of any kind. To provide William with the maximum freedom to work as he wished, spending as much time as possible composing or travelling in the open air, every trace of a timetable was abandoned. Most houses would devote a particular day of the week to a particular purpose, such as cleaning, laundry, baking, etc., but as Dorothy's journal shows, this was not the case at Dove Cottage. Baking might happen not only on any weekday, but also on a Sunday, the established day of rest throughout the rest of the community, when best clothes were worn, the Bible read, and as little domestic work as possible carried out.[44]

It was generally accepted that the efficiency of a household could be judged by the regularity of its mealtimes. Coleridge's notebooks contain the following routine:

> Six o'clock, light the fires, Clean out the Kitchen, Put on the Tea Kettle. Clean the Insides of the Boiling Pot, Shoes &c. ...
> Eight o'clock. Tea things &c, put out [for breakfast] & after cleared up ...
> One o'clock – spit the meat
> Two o'clock – Vegetables &c ...
> Three o'clock – Dinner
> Half past three – 10 minutes for cleaning Dishes [45]

In contrast, under Dorothy's management, breakfast might be served at any time from around 8am to 1pm, dinner from around noon to 5pm, tea up to around 7.30pm, and supper some time later.[46] Such flexibility might suit the poetic mind, but is hardly ideal for promoting good digestion. It is therefore no surprise to find that the journal makes frequent references to stomach upsets. Dorothy must have been well aware of the situation, explaining to her close friend from her Halifax days, Jane Marshall, that 'I [can] [?not] tell you how we pass [the time] because our employ[ments are] not very various yet they are irregular.'[47]

Having spent some eleven years as mistress of a working farm, Mary Wordsworth must have found such a deliberately disorganised house extremely difficult to comprehend when she took up her role as William's wife. It is interesting to speculate why Dorothy's journal and letters makes little or no reference to her personal involvement in the subsequent changes. It is quite certain, however, that Mary's need to maintain a well-organised household was effectively adopted by Dorothy, who by early 1804 was explaining to Lady Beaumont that 'it is an affair of great consequence to us that we should be well served and that all things in our little establishment should be regularly organised.'[48] How different from 1800 – 1802! Mary's efficiency as a domestic manager greatly impressed all who saw her carrying out this role. When Canon Rawnsley interviewed those who remembered her, they recalled how she was:

> ...terb'le particular in her accounts, never allowed you an inch in the butching book.
> A close-fisted woman, that's what she was.
> ...and she was a manasher an 'aw', an kepp t'accounts. For ye kna he nivver knew aboot sec things, nayder what he had or what he spent.
> Mrs Wudsworth, she was a downright clever woman, as kep' accounts and was a reg'lar manasher. He never know'd, bless ye, what he hed, not what he was wuth, not whether there was owt to eat in t'house, nivver.
> Why, she was a manasher, niver a studier, but for a' that there's nea doot he and she was truly companionable, and they wer terr'ble fond o' yan anudder. But Dorothy hed t'wits on 'em boath.[49]

Since Mary's death in January 1859, successive writers have seen Dorothy as the chatelaine of Dove Cottage and the Wordsworths' later homes in Grasmere and Rydal, relegating Mary's contribution to the shadows. Nothing could be more unjust and untrue. Providing all essential domestic services for her family, and its numerous long and short-term guests, and fulfilling William's particular needs, were full-time and challenging tasks. Mary appears to have executed them with commendable efficiency and skill. Unlike her husband and sister-in-law, she apparently lacked both the free time and probably the inclination to record her experiences for posterity, but her contribution to their comfort, security and well-being should never be under-estimated.

To run their growing household, both Dorothy and Mary relied on practical help from servants and female relations. On moving into Dove Cottage, Dorothy found that the sister of their neighbour John Fisher had aired it by lighting small coal fires over the previous days. This was Mary, better known to the Wordsworths as 'Old Molly'. As William told Coleridge in a letter written on Christmas Eve, 1799:

> We do not think it will be necessary for us to keep a servant. We have agreed to give a woman [Old Molly], who lives in one of the adjoining cottages two shillings a week for attending two or three hours a day to light the fire wash dishes etc., etc. In addition to this she is to have her victuals every Saturday when she will be employed in scouring, and to have her victuals likewise on other days if we should have visitors and she is wanted more than usual. We could have had this attendance for eighteen pence a week but we added the sixpence for the sake of the poor woman, who is made happy by it. [50]

By September 1800 Molly's duties had been expanded to include gardening and laundry, Dorothy describing her as:

> ...an old woman 60 years of age whom we took partly out of charity and partly for convenience. She was very ignorant, very foolish, and very difficult to teach, so that I almost despaired of her, but the goodness of her disposition and the great convenience we should find if my perseverance was at last successful induced me to go on. She has now learned to do every thing for us mechanically, except those parts of cooking in which the hands are much employed, for instance she prepares and boils the vege[tab]les and watch the meat when it is made ready for roasting, looks to

the oven etc ... she has washed the linen of all our visitors except the family of the Coleridges during that month. [We have] great washes about once in 5 weeks, and she washes towels, stockings, waistcoats, petticoats etc. once a week, such as do not require much ironing. This she does so quietly, in a place apart from the house, and we know so little about it as makes it very comfortable. She sleeps at home ... and in winter it is a considerable saving of fire that her home is so near, for after the dishes are washed up we let the kitchen fire go out, and we never light it till it is time to dress the dinner, and she employs herself at home. She is much attached to us, and good as ever was a human being.[51]

Mary got on well with old Molly from her visit in the autumn of 1801, being provided with such information, irrelevant to her marriage, as 'Ye may say what ye will but there's nothing like a gay auld man for behaving weel to a young wife. Ye may laugh but the wind blows no favour – and where there's no love there's no favour.'[52] Her help in most aspects of domestic work was considerable, Dorothy finding herself extremely 'tired with making beds, cooking etc' when Molly fell ill in June 1802.[53] She was soon back to her duties, however, including helping Dorothy and sitting with Mrs Simpson during her convalescence.[54] In early May, 1804, following her sister-in-law's death, Molly had to take on the full responsibility for John Fisher's housekeeping.[55] The friendship with the Wordsworths continued as close as ever, however, young John Wordsworth cramming himself with her cream porridge and cakes, and Dorothy accepting her presents of home-made butter, for example. It only ended with Molly's death at Grasmere on 3rd June, 1808.[56]

From May 1804 her place was taken by a fifteen-year-old servant from the Vale of St. John.[57] In the Lakes it was customary for all male and female servants to attend the hiring fairs held in the market squares each Whitsuntide and Michaelmas, there to be inspected and interviewed by potential employers, who would hire them for the following six months. It would have been at such a fair that someone to whom Dorothy referred as their 'Old servant' (probably Mary Dawson), found fresh employment in May 1806, leaving only a twelve-year-old girl to serve them. Dorothy hoped to hire someone else by the end of June, but female labour was fast disappearing into the cotton mills, where the wages were far higher.[58] By March 1808 the family was being served by two servants and little Sally Green, the daughter of the Easedale couple who had recently been found dead in the snows towards Langdale. The pressure of housing William, Mary, Dorothy, Sara Hutchinson, the four Wordsworth children and three servants in the confined space of Dove Cottage was now causing severe problems, but these were largely alleviated by the removal to the much larger Allan Bank, Grasmere, towards the end of May.[59]

In addition to servants, the unmarried Hutchinson sisters also provided domestic help during their visits. Sara, the youngest, first stayed here in November and December 1800, sharing 'a great baking' with Dorothy, and returning again in December-January 1802-3.[60] From the following year she acted as Tom Hutchinson's housekeeper at Park House near the foot of Ullswater, then joined the Wordsworths from October 1806 on their winter visit to Coleorton in Leicestershire, after which she became their virtually permanent companion.[61] In June 1803, Mary had given birth to the Wordsworth's first child, John. When he was just two months old, William, Dorothy and Coleridge deserted her for a six-week tour of Scotland. Fortunately Joanna Hutchinson, author of the recipe book, was able to move to Dove Cottage in order to provide the necessary support. She stayed on for a whole year before moving in with Tom at Park House, but retained strong links with her Grasmere relations.[62] In June 1806, for example, Dorothy recorded how;

> 'Johnny likes being with his Aunt Joanna very much and she says he is a good Boy; he is quite at home among horses and cows.'[63]

Descriptions of some of the meals cooked at Dove Cottage were given by Dorothy in her journal, and it is probable that details of those taken in the family's later houses were very similar. As one indoor servant remembered:

> Nay, nay, Wudsworth was a man as was fond of a good dinner at times, if you could get him to it, that was't job; not but what he was a very temperate man i' all things, vara, but they was all on 'em mean livers, and in a plain way. It was poddish for t' breakfast, and a bit o' mutton to t' dinner, and poddish at night, with a bit of cheese happen to end up wi'...Mrs. Wudsworth would say "Ring

the bell" but he wouldn't stir, bless ye, "Goa and see what he's doing," she'd say, an we wad goa up to study door and hear him a mumbling and bumming through it. "Dinner's ready, sir," I'd ca' out, but he'd goa mumbling on like a deaf man, ya see. And sometimes Mrs. Wudsworth 'ud say, "Goa and brek a bottle, or let a dish fall just outside in passage." Eh dear, that maistly wad bring him out, wad that. It was nobbut that as wad, howivver. For ye kna' he was a vera careful man, and he couldn't do with brecking t' china.[64]

In taking porridge for breakfast, the Wordsworths were following the north-country practice of most poor and many middle-class families.[65] Made by sprinkling coarse oatmeal into a pan of boiling water while stirring vigorously, and continuing to stir as it slowly thickened, it was hot, satisfying and nutritious. The usual way of eating it was to hold a mug of milk in the left hand, dipping in each spoonful of porridge before raising it to the lips, but there is no evidence to confirm that this method was followed at Dove Cottage. Broth might also be taken at breakfast, as a lighter and more savoury alternative. In March 1802, for example, Dorothy made William 'his Basin of Broth ... and little plate of Bread and butter [as] he wrote a Poem to a Butterfly!'[66] Bacon and eggs were certainly available, but probably appeared at breakfast only when requested by visitors such as Coleridge.

Dinner, the main meal of the day, was again plain but nutritious in the 'meat and two veg' tradition which continued in England to the late twentieth century. Potatoes and seasonal vegetables provided the usual accompaniment to joints of legs of mutton, William's favourite meat, these being roasted, and probably boiled too.[67] Other meats included mutton chops, beefsteaks, pork and, rarely, hare and partridge, some of which would be roasted before the fire, broiled on an iron grill, or put into a dish, covered with pastry, and baked as pies.[68] Poultry appeared only rarely: goose when at its best in late autumn, turkey on Christmas Day, and fish only when caught locally by the family or its friends.[69] For dessert, there might be pies made from home-grown apples, pears, gooseberries, etc., or local damsons, either fresh or preserved.[70] The family also enjoyed richer dinners from time to time: for example, one served in September 1820 included hare soup, Stickle Tarn trout and venison.[71] They enjoyed similar fare when dining out, Mary describing to Dora the 'turbot, then a leg of most tempting looking mutton, Pidgeon Pye, Lemon Pudding and open sweetmeat tart, Dessert etc.' taken with young William in Carlisle. [72] Such dinners were sometimes replaced by much lighter snacks if appetites were low, Dorothy recording a dinner composed solely of 'a bason of Broth ... which seems to settle well with me', or another of two boiled eggs and two apple tarts. [73]

The best description of teatime at Dove Cottage comes from Thomas De Quincey:

> This, with the Wordsworths, under the simple rustic system of habits which they cherished then, and for twenty years after, was the most delightful meal of the day ... because it was prolonged into a meal of leisure and conversation ... [74]

In addition to the all-essential pot of tea, their favourite tea-time treat was fresh, hot buttered toast, William later recalling one afternoon when:

> My sister and I were in the habit of having the tea-kettle in our little sitting room and we toasted the bread ourselves ... one morning when we had a young prig of a Scotch lawyer to breakfast with us, my dear sister, with her usual simplicity, put the toasting fork, with a slice of bread, into the hands of this Edinborough genius. Our little bookcase stood on one side of the fire. To prevent loss of time he took down a book and fell to reading, to the neglect of the toast, which was burned to a cinder. Many a time we have laughed at this circumstance, and other cottage simplicities of that day. [75]

De Quincey recalled how William conducted himself when both reading and toast were being enjoyed simultaneously:

> Wordsworth took down the volume [as] tea was proceeding ... Dry toast required butter; butter required knives; and knives lay on the table; but sad it was for the purity of [the book's uncut] pages, that every knife bore upon its blade testimonies of the service it had rendered. Did that stop Wordsworth? Did that cause him to call for another knife? No at all: he
>> Look'd at the knife that caused his pain,
>> And look'd and sigh'd and sigh'd again

and then, after this momentary tribute of regret, he tore
his way into the heart of the volume with this knife, that
left its greasy honours upon every page, and are they not
there to this day?[76]

William appears to have been something of a connoisseur in the
matter of buttered toast, observing at an inn breakfast at Baldock that
it was 'for all the world as if it had been soaked in hot water'.[77] John
Pippingill's depiction of William seated at just such a coaching inn
table shows rolls, rather than toast, being kept hot on a plate placed
over a deep basin of hot water.[78] Other teatime specialities would
include home-made preserves and honey to accompany the toast, cakes
and gingerbread.[79]

As in most households supper was a relatively light meal, probably
based on the cold meat left over from dinner, cheese and bread and
butter and pickles. Its informality is illustrated by the supper-dishes
mentioned in Dorothy's journal, these including cold mutton, eggs,
broth, or pasty-pudding, while a later servant's account of the family
describes them supping on basins of new milk and a loaf of bread.[80]

More elaborate meals would certainly have been cooked and
served when entertaining guests, or when celebrating the major
annual festivals. On Christmas Day 1805, for example, young John
Wordsworth was 'all alive at the thought of two plum-puddings which
are now rumbling in the Pot, and a Sirloin of Beef that is smoking at
the Fire', their alternative Christmas roast being the turkey.[81]

Within a few months of arriving at Grasmere, the Wordsworths had
discovered the delights of rowing out to the island in its lake, there to
light a fire and enjoy a picnic. It was here that they entertained the
Coleridges just before they moved into Greta Hall, Dorothy's journal
recording how they all 'drank tea at the island. The weather was very
delightful ...'[82] Coleridge's account conveys a much fuller and more
enthusiastic image of the event:

> We drank tea the night I left Grasmere, on the island in
> that lovely lake; our kettle swung over the fire hanging
> from the branch of a fir-tree, and I lay and saw the woods
> and mountains, and lake all trembling, and as it were
> idealised through the subtle smoke which rose up from the
> clear red embers of the fir-apples, which we had collected:
> afterwards, we made a glorious bonfire on the margin,
> by some elder bushes, where twigs heaved and sobbed at

the uprushing column of smoke – and the image of that bonfire, and of us that danced round it – ruddy laughing faces in the twilight – the image of this in a lake as smooth as that sea, to whose waves the Son of God had said Peace! May God and all his Sons love you as I do.[83]

Such delightful picnics were repeated over the years, Dorothy noting 'the Ashes of the fire and the smoky stones we had left after boiling our kettle upon the Island' in 1803.[84] As with all the best- planned of Lakeland's outdoor events, the region's unpredictable weather could cause real problems. In August 1808 'Nineteen [of] us were to have [had] a Picnic upon Grasmere Island ...and all were caught in a thunder shower, and all wet to the skin on the way to the lake side. The feast was Mr Crump's, our [Allan Bank] Landlord ...We dined at the Inn.'[85] After removing to Rydal Mount, picnics were taken by Rydalwater, using two nice new boats; 'we take our Tea bathing & load with fuel at [the island] I stand and dr[ink] Tea on the opposite shore for the Islands

Fig 5. Dinners taken at Robert Newton's inn next to Grasmere churchyard cost just 10d (4p) each.

are so full of wood that there is no safety in making a fire upon them ... It is beautiful beyond all description,' wrote Sara Hutchinson.[86] Picnics continued to play an important part in every summer's social entertainment over the following years, as in September 1826 when 'we had a huge picnic party into Easedale', or in late August 1827, when 'we also had a picnic meeting under Raven Crag lying by the margins of Wytheburn – the families of Greta Hall and Rydal Mount, with other vagrants, making a party of about 30 – merry group we formed round a gypsey fire upon the rocky point that juts from the shore, on the opposite side of the lake from the high road.'[87]

Outdoor meals were as much a necessity as a pleasure when taken on the Wordsworth's long walks and rides across the region. The most convenient food for such journeys appears to have been sandwiches: William's sandwich tin, with its hinged lid, still survives in the Wordsworth Museum at Grasmere. Their contents were either cold meat or potted meat, sometimes supplemented with a piece of sweet cake or apple.[88] Inns and ale houses provided further refreshment. At its best, this could represent excellent quality and value, as at Seathwaite in the Duddon Valley, where they enjoyed 'Tea, Supper and Breakfast – Excellent cream and delicious bread and butter – broiled Char fresh out of the Tarn to supper. – Tea 1s – Supper 1s – Breakfast 1s – Horse 1s – ale 6d – Total 4s 6d!'[89] At another inn near Ullswater, 'We had a good supper; ham, veal, cutlets, preserved plums, ale, rum and water, dry beds and a decent breakfast. We paid 7/– one shilling too much.' At another at Kirk Ulpha they enjoyed tea, boiled ham and eggs.[90] Usually their chosen travellers' fare was rather simpler, however, such as the tea and ale, bread and cheese, etc. eaten heartily at the King's Head, Thirlspot, beneath his sign:

> J STANDLEY lives here & sells good Ale
> Come in & drink before it grows Stale -
> John Succeeded his Father PETER
> But ith' old mans time 'twas never better [91]

Alternatively there might be a first course of porridge followed by Christmas pies, as eaten in a public house in December 1801.[92]

It is interesting to follow the quite separate diet prepared for the Wordsworth children while in their infancy at Dove Cottage. John, or 'Johnny', the eldest, was born on 18th June 1803, the christening at Grasmere Church on 15th July being followed by 'christening cake, tea and coffee' at the cottage.[93] Mary appears to have suckled him from the start, but by the time he was five months old he was only taking milk and 'what he sucks out of a piece of meat or a crust of Bread while we are at our meals. He is generally so quiet at these times that it is quite a trial [i.e. problem] to have him at table with us ...We are going to get him a tall chair that he may sit up at Table by himself, for in a little while it will not be very convenient to eat with him upon our knees, he stretches out for everything.'[94] In February 1804 he was inoculated with cow-pox, to prevent him catching the deadly and disfiguring smallpox, but it failed to take, and had to be repeated a little later.[95] On 8th April Dorothy noted that he was taken from his mother's breast: 'At first he was silent & low spirited not very fretful. In two or three Days he began to ask for food very impatiently ... NB on Thursday 14th April he first got upon his feet by himself, with the aid of a stool ... William wagered a guinea with me that he would walk in a fortnight.'[96] By the time he was eighteen months old he had already been fed on broth too, but since it was thought to inflame a skin problem on his forehead, it was decided that he should be fed solely on bread and milk, quite a common regime for babies at this period.[97] One of his favourite dishes now became the rich 'Cream porridge which he sucked in most greedily at Molly's', but he was soon taking his share of his parents' meals.[98]

After the Wordsworths' move to Allan Bank in May 1808, their domestic circumstances changed considerably. This was a gentleman's villa, offering more and better rooms for both family accommodation and domestic services. It also offered sufficient land for Mary and Sara to utilise their farmhouse experience in keeping a cow to provide milk, cream and butter, as well as pigs for bacon.[99] The house incorporated numerous severe practical faults, however, including wet cellars and chimneys that perpetually smoked. It was so bad that they had to cook in the study 'and even heated water there to wash dishes, for the Boiler in the Back kitchen could not be heated, much less the kitchen fire endured ... we have been more than a week together at different times without a kitchen fire ... Dishes are washed, and no sooner set in the pantry than they are covered with smoke ... the smarting of the eyes etc., etc. you may guess at.'[100] Sara confirmed this appalling situation:

'Not a chimney will draw the smoke, and one day we could not have a fire except in the Study; and then you could not see each other. In the rest of the rooms the fire was actually blown out of the Grates.'[101]

Martha Fricker's recipe book offered this solution:

Cure for Smoky Chimneys

A wire-gauze front to be fitted over the [fire] place, of about twenty two wires to the inch. The effect of which is said to be instantaneous. [102]

The Wordsworths had no knowledge of this method, and it would probably have been ineffective against their hurricane-like down-draughts. These and other difficulties continued throughout their occupancy, despite the efforts of workmen to rebuild chimneys, improve the dining room etc.[103] In terms of domestic management, one of the major changes was the employment of a full-time cook/cow-keeper, 'a very good servant', to prepare the meals including dinner at 3pm.[104]

In early June 1811, they removed from Allan Bank to Grasmere Rectory, a house which had two parlours, four bedrooms for the family and one for the servant, a store-room, cellar, dairy, pantry, and 'a decent small kitchen'. The Rector, Mr. Jackson, agreed to add a library and a new back kitchen.[105] There were also a kitchen garden, space enough for breeding cows and pigs, and fields in which to grow hay for the cattle and potatoes for the house.106 Dorothy described the

> 'hay-making which was a throng [busy] time, for both our Servants were obliged to go out constantly, therefore Mary and I had to make beds, cook and attend the children. I made a large seed-cake ... and was employed in making preserves and picking gooseberries.' [107]

On May Day, 1813, the Wordsworths moved again, this time to Rydal Mount, which was to become their home for the rest of their lives. It was originally a farmhouse called Keens, but a fashionable front suite had been added in about 1760, with elegant rooms offering open views across the vale of Rydal on to the fells opposite. It was a gentleman's house, and was furnished accordingly, the dining room being provided with an expensive Turkey carpet, Wedgwood tableware and fine glass decanters.[108] 'You stare, and the simplicity of the dear Town End Cottage comes before your eyes,' wrote Dorothy, 'and you are tempted to say "are they changed, are they setting up for fine folk? for making parties – giving Dinners etc? No, no." ' [109] In fact, despite

Fig 6. Rydal Mount, drawn by Dora Wordsworth around 1830. The family moved in on Mayday, 1813, and remained here for the rest of their lives.

their wish to retain their simplicity of lifestyle, they were in reality setting up a conventional well-to-do household, complete with a butler; one that had nobility to dinner, and held balls. 'Were I to give you a list of the folks we have had & our consequent engagements,' wrote Sara, 'it would make a list as long as that of Crosthwaite Museum [in Keswick].' 'The dining room looks so comfortable, warm & genteel you would be delighted with it.' [110] Mary also described a ball for which 'the dining room was ridded of all superflous furniture and dressed out in Christmas's gayest garb – the festoons of glittering Holly with its red berries etc. etc., was carried round the walls – the floor chalked in great taste.' [111] Chalking the floors of ballrooms was a highly skilled task, usually undertaken by a professional, who used coloured chalks to give the boards the appearance of an elegant parterre, or a richly inlaid marble floor. They were a transient luxury however, as William had described in *Personal Talk* written back at Dove Cottage:

> These all wear out of me, like Forms with chalk
> Painted on rich men's floors, for one feast-night.

To carry out such entertainments effectively, it was essential to have the services of a good cook, but at the end of April 1814, Dorothy found that:

> Unfortunately we happen for the last year to have had the worst cook in England - but Mary Dawson is coming to live with us at Whitsuntide (whom you remember was our servant at Town End) and Sara and I intend to give her unlimited commission to cook all sorts of nice things for Mary [who] in these little things would be far more easily ruled by a servant than by us.[112]

Mary Dawson was later replaced by a cook called Jane, who apparently proved unsatisfactory, for in September 1819, following 'our unhappy cook's misery, we have got a delightful young woman in her place, who is always cheerful, tidy and good humoured, and in the management of her fires, that never-ending plague when Jane was here, she is exactly the opposite of Jane, and cooks well with less fuel than any servant we ever had.'[113] Within a year, however, there were renewed problems, Sara describing how she was awaiting the return of Mary Bill at Martinmas, since the current cook at Rydal Mount, one Mary Anne, was 'as smooth & polite as possible, but I do not like such smoothness if I were to say black was white to my face she would agree to it. Cross-tempered maids shall always have my favor in preference & I should be sorry if this smooth-faced, & insincere creature were here to greet you. I have hired a cook from Keswick, who I hope will do well, 'tho I have not seen her.'[114] Throughout their years at Rydal Mount the family always employed a full-time cook, only coming into the kitchen either to give orders or to undertake the preparation of a particular dish.[115] Their last cook was a typically practical and down-to-earth lady, who took no pleasure from the beauties of nature. When asked if she had seen a particularly wonderful sunset, she replied, 'No & I'm a tidy cook, I know, and, they say, a decentish body for a landlady, and sic-like, but I nivver bodder nowt aboot sunsets or them sort of things, they r'e nowt ataw i' my line.'[116]

Back at Dove Cottage, between Mary Wordsworth's arrival as a new bride in 1802 and the family's departure to Allan Bank in 1808, she and Dorothy had undertaken all the cookery required for their family and its numerous guests. Along with her sisters Joanna and Sara, she had previously been provided with an excellent training in culinary skills, and had had many years experience as housekeeper to a gentleman-farmer's establishment. The survival of Mary's recipe book, and that of her sister Joanna, is extremely fortunate, since it provides an invaluable insight into the dishes that would have been cooked at their Grasmere and Rydal homes. In the following Chapters all the recipes are reproduced and explained, along with those of Martha Fricker, and others from contemporary sources, for dishes mentioned by the Wordsworths, but for which no manuscript recipes survive. Together they provide a unique insight into the domestic life of one of the English language's greatest poets.

Pickle for Hams
To each ham 1 lb of bay Salt 1
of common Salt 2 oz Salt Pete
1 oz of black pepper – beat all
these very fine & rub upon th
let it lay 4 days. then powr o
...t 1¼ lb of Treacle ...led it st...
...nth turning it every ...
...nt... cold w...t...

Chapter Three

OF MAIN COURSES

The foods served at dinners and suppers in late Georgian Grasmere varied enormously in their quality and quantity, according to the wealth and resources of each individual or family. Those who took their meals at Robert Newton's, the inn just to the north of the churchyard, might pay only tenpence for:

> Roast pike, stuffed; a boiled fowl; Veal cutlets and Ham; Beans and bacon; Cabbage; Peas and Potatoes; Anchovy sauce; Parsley and butter [sauce]; Plain butter [white sauce]; Wheat bread and oat cake; Three cups of preserved gooseberries, with a bowl of cream in the centre.[1]

This was by no means exceptional travellers' fare, for at the King's Arms in Kendal Christopher Fenton would provide:

> A boiled fowl and sauce, roast partridge, potted charr, cold ham, tarts, and three or four foreign sweetmeats 8d a head. [or] cold ham, tarts, potted charr, anchovies, butter and cheese 6d a head.[2]

In contrast, families such as the Greens of Easedale were so poor that they had to barter their bridles etc. for a few potatoes. These, with a little oatmeal, a few pieces of lean dried mutton, and a daily quart of milk from their cow, were all that they could afford even in the coldest months of winter.[3] The Wordsworths' close neighbours, the Ashburners, may have been better off, but even they had to subsist on a mean diet of 'oatbread, milk and porridge by a fireside'.[4] In a letter to her lifelong friend Catherine Clarkson, Dorothy confirmed that she would rather survive on such poor fare than go into the banishment of emigration forced upon some of her contemporaries. However, the food they enjoyed at Dove Cottage was certainly superior to this, even if not of the quantity served in the local inns.

Various references show that their kitchen fire was equipped with pots and pans for stewing and boiling, a gridiron for broiling or grilling, some means of roasting meat before the fire, and most probably a frying pan too. These, in addition to an oven in the back kitchen/pantry, enabled them to prepare their food in every usual way. To make the broths sometimes served for breakfasts or suppers, and as a first course at dinner, for example, they would have used a covered boiling pot to simmer a joint of meat. Its stock could then be thickened with barley in the local tradition or with dumplings, such as Dorothy once made for John Marshall, proprietor of the world's largest flax mill, and husband to Dorothy's friend Jane Pollard.[5] Mutton broth appears to have been a favourite, even being served to Sir Francis and Lady Vane, the Wordsworths' friends and patrons, when they dined at Rydal Mount.[6] For such occasions it may have been made either from

Fig 7. The Wordsworth's favourite mutton would come from the local flocks of Herd wicks. This woodcut from the Shepherds' Guide of 1810 shows how they were identified by different 'lugmarks', such as 1. fold bitted, 2. slit, 3. cropped or stoved, 4. forked, 5. shearhalved, 6. halved, 7. key bitted and 8. punched.

stock from a joint, or from meat specifically intended for producing a good broth, as in the following recipe:

To make Mutton Broth

Take the scrag end of a neck of mutton, chop it into small pieces put it into a saucepan and fill it with water. Set it over the fire, and when the scum begins to rise take it off and put in a blade or two of mace, a little French barley, or a crust of white bread to thicken it. When you have boiled your mutton that it will shake to pieces, strain your broth through a hair sieve, scum off the fat, and send it up with dry toast.[7]

> 1-1½ lb/450-675g neck of mutton, chopped in pieces
> 1½ oz/40g pearl barley   1½ tsp salt
> 2 blades mace   pepper to taste

Put the meat into a pan with 3pt/1·8l cold water, bring to the boil, remove all the scum, add the barley, mace, salt and pepper, cover and leave to simmer for about 2 hours, then skim off the fat and strain through a fine sieve into a clean pan or tureen, and serve immediately, accompanied by fresh dry toast.

[For a thicker broth, strip the meat from the bones, return it to the barley, rinse in cold water, return the meat and barley to the broth, and re-heat before serving.]

Martha Fricker provided another good recipe which used sheep shanks, these probably being the shinbones with the knuckles of the forelegs, cut from the shoulders, along with the shins cut from the back legs. The left-over bones were often recycled as pegs for holding slates on roofs, or carved into the apple-scoops used to scoop out the pulp and carry it up to the lips.

Shank broth or Jelly, cheap & nourishing

Soak twelve mutton shanks four hours then brush & scaur them very clean, put them into a saucepan with one pd of lean beef, a crust of Bread made brown [by toasting], an Onion & herbs, add four quarts of water, simmer gently five hours, then strain it off.[8]

The only soup recipe in Mary Wordsworth's book was added to it by her sister Joanna. It is very plain, despite its continental attribution.

Portuguese Vegetable Soup

Two good ... Turnips & 2 onions cut in small squares 3 pint of Water, when tender add a cupful of Rice, when that is thoroughly done ¼lb Butter a little pepper & salt. ½ hour before dinner add 3 pints of new milk & simmer until time[9]

1 onion	1tsp salt
1 turnip	pinch of pepper
3oz/75g pudding rice	1½pt/900ml milk
2oz/50g butter	

Cut the vegetables into small dice, stew in 1½pt/900ml water for 20 min., add the rice and simmer for a further 20 min. Add the butter, salt, pepper and milk, and simmer gently for 30 min., then serve hot.

Such broths, thickened with cheap imported rice, were popular about this period, as were very similar stews. The following example is from Coleridge's notebook of 1796, when he was still gathering useful information for his Pantisocratic life in which men would do all the cooking. It is a simple, economical and yet healthy and substantial dish, resembling the style of catering normally used in institutions such as workhouses rather than in family homes. Just like William and Dorothy's experiment of living largely on milk and potatoes two years earlier at Windy Brow, this represented a concept of plain, economical fare, rather than the food they usually ate.

[Coleridge's Stew]

Take a pound of Beef, Mutton, or Pork; cut it into small pieces; a pint of Peas; four Turnips sliced; six or seven Potatoes cut very small; four or five Onions; put to them three Quarts of Water, and let it boil about two hours and a half ... then thicken it with a pound of Rice – and boil it a quarter of an ... hour more - after which season it with salt & pepper –
N.B. better season it at first-peppering & salt the Meat &c.[10]

Artist's impression of the Wordsworth family at home. (Illustration by Peter Brears)

A cutaway view of Dove Cottage as it appeared when the Wordsworths lived there, showing the kitchen and living spaces. (Illustration by Peter Brears)

P. BREARS

Dove Cottage as it is today. The original line of upright boundary stones has been replaced with a drystone wall and the small vegetable and herb garden is situated to the left of the gate.

Rydal Mount as it appears today.

8oz/225g cubed beef, mutton or pork
8oz/225g short-grain rice   *1tsp salt*
8oz/225g turnips, sliced   *6oz/150g peas*
12oz/350g potatoes, in small cubes
8oz/225g onions, chopped   *pinch ground pepper*

Mix the meat, vegetables, salt and pepper in a large pan with 3pt/1·8l cold water, cover, bring to the boil, and simmer as gently as possible for 2½ hours. Stir in the rice, and continue simmering for 30 min., stirring the rice up from the bottom of the pan from time to time to prevent it sticking to the base of the pan.

The result is a very thick and plain meat, vegetable and rice stew, one that takes the bare minimum of time to prepare, occupies just one pot over a very low fire, demands little attention while cooking, and yet produces, in its original quantities, twelve pounds of economical and nourishing food from just one pound of meat.

It is probable that Herdwick mutton and Westmorland beef were slowly stewed over the fire for the Wordsworths' table, but there is no evidence to actually confirm this practice. There are a number of Joanna's recipes, however, that demonstrate the Hutchinsons' ability to produce extremely good stews, including:

Jugged Pigeons

Dress 6 pigeons, season them with beaten mace pepper & salt put them into a Jug with ½lb Butter. Stop up the Jug close, set it in a kettle of boiling water, let it boil an hour & half – put the gravy that comes from them into a pan with 1 spoonful of Wine, 1 of [mushroom?] Catchup a slice of Lemon, ½ anchovy, chopt, a bundle of sweet Herbs – boil it a little, thicken it with a little Flour, lay the Pigeons on a Dish & strain the gravy over them. [Garnish with] Mushrooms or Forcemeat[11]

6 wood pigeons, prepared   *1tbs mushroom ketchup*
8oz/225g butter   *1tbs red or white wine*
2 tsp salt   *1 slice of lemon*
½tsp mace   *1tsp dried mixed herbs*
½tsp ground black pepperflour

Mix together the salt, mace and pepper, and rub them over the breasts of the pigeons. Arrange them in a deep basin, add the butter, broken in pieces, and cover with a piece of aluminium cooking foil, pressed down over the sides all round. Set the basin on a trivet in a large pan, half-fill with boiling water, cover, return to the boil, and simmer for 1½ hours.

When cooked, pour all the liquid off into a clean glass or plastic jug, allow to settle, pour off the butter into a basin (it may be used for making any kind of savoury pastry), and the gravy into a saucepan. Add the ketchup, wine, lemon and herbs, simmer for 5 min., then add the flour beaten into the cold water. Return to the heat, stirring until it has thickened, then pass through a sieve on to the pigeons in a hot dish, and serve immediately.

Joanna also had a recipe for calf's heads, like the one Mr. Clarkson was carrying in his basket when met by William, Dorothy and Mary on New Year's Eve, 1801.[12] Unlike many Georgian versions, which serve the whole head in a dish, hers par-cooks it before stripping and cubing the meat, then converting it into a very tender and flavoursome high-quality stew. Today it may be tried using either veal or lamb:

Calf's Head

Boil the Head ½ an Hour, bone it, when cold cut it into square pieces, season it with Cayenne, white Pepper, salt & nutmeg – then cover it with Gravy, let it stew till quite enough, then put in some strong Gravy with Morrells, Mushrooms, Oysters Cockles and Mussels, (or as many of these things as you have) mix a little Butter & Flour to thicken the Soup, [i.e. the sauce] add [Mushroom?] Catchup, hard boiled Yolks of Eggs, & Force Meat Balls.[13]

By far her most interesting recipe, however, is one which must have been used at least as far back as Sockburn in the 1790s, even though written into her book around 1816. It is extremely rare to find a manuscript recipe for which there is a precise, datable description of who made it, who ate it, and what the diners thought of it, but all this information is available regarding the chicken sauce recipe from Joanna Hutchinson's book. In the summer of 1801 Coleridge used the excuse of a study-visit to Durham Cathedral library to escape from his failing marriage to the former Sarah Fricker. His real purpose, however, was to spend quality time with 'Asra', Sara Hutchinson, with whom he had fallen deeply in love. On 31st July he and Sara arrived at her brother Tom's farm at Gallow Hill, after a sixty-mile ride from Bishop Middleham. Since Coleridge's left knee was swollen and painful he was installed in the kitchen, with his leg up on a sofa, and there nursed and fed on fine meals prepared by Mary. In a letter to Sara written nine years later he could still recall how the three of them curled up on the sofa, Mary stroking his brow and Sara tickling his cheek with her eyelashes:

> The fire, Mary, you, and I at Gallow-Hill, or if, flamy, reflected in children's round faces – ah whose children? - a dog, that dog whose restless eyes oft catching the light of the fire used to watch your face, as you leaned with your head upon your hand and arm, & your feet on the fender ... Fowls at Table – the last dinner at Gallow Hill [9th August 1801], when you drest the two fowls in that delicious white Sauce ... [14]

This is the recipe that Coleridge found so delicious. It really is excellent – and eats well with either fresh-cooked vegetables or plain-boiled rice.

Chicken Sauce

The yolks of 8 Eggs hard boiled & bruised thro' a sieve, a little Lemon peel grated – a little Nutmeg Grated – or beaten mace. Mix all well with 3 or 4 spoonfuls of thick cream, then put it into melted butter made with strong white Gravy instead of Water. Squeeze some Lemon upon the Dish.[15]

1 3lb/1·4kg oven-ready chicken	*2oz/50g flour*
2 chicken stock cubes	*2oz/50g butter*
1 medium onion	*3 egg yolks, separated &*
4 cloves	*boiled, 3 min.*
¼pt/150ml double cream	*1 medium carrot, peeled*
juice and grated zest of a lemon	*6 black peppercorns*
pinch of ground nutmeg or mace	*pinch of salt*
bouquet garni	

Place the chicken, stock cubes, onion stuck with cloves, carrot, peppercorns, bouquet garni and salt in a pan, cover with water, cover with a lid, and simmer for 40-50 min. until tender. Remove from the heat, strain the stock into a jug, remove the vegetables, peppercorns and bouquet garni, place the chicken on a hot dish, cover with foil, and keep in a hot place until the sauce is ready.

Rub the egg yolks through a sieve. Melt the butter in a saucepan, stir in the flour, and cook gently while stirring for 1 min. Remove from the heat and gradually stir in 1pt/600ml of the stock, together with the yolks, cream, zest and nutmeg or mace. Return to the heat and stir continuously until it has boiled and thickened. Simmer for 2-3 min., add ½tsp salt and a little white pepper if required, and adjust the consistency with the remaining stock.

Remove the foil from the chicken, pour the lemon juice over it into the dish, and the sauce all over the chicken just before serving. Alternatively remove all the meat from the chicken, and arrange on a hot dish before pouring on the lemon juice and sauce, this being far more convenient to serve while still hot.

Instead of being stewed in a pan over the fire, meats could be placed in a ceramic baking dish, covered with a pastry crust, and baked in the oven, the gentler heat often producing more tender results, while still retaining all the essential juices. Dorothy's 1805 report of the twenty-month-old John Wordsworth's use of 'pie and 'taters' to signify food of every kind shows that the majority of meals served at Dove Cottage featured some form of savoury pie.[16] Most pies would probably be of their favourite mutton, but other varieties were made, such as those she made from goose giblets.

Goose-giblet pie is now a virtually forgotten dish, but up to the late nineteenth century it was relatively popular, served either alongside the roast goose, or as a separate meal in itself. Dorothy made giblet pies between late October and late November, rather than on the traditional feast of Michaelmas on September 29th, one that she baked on 11th November, 1801, apparently being eaten before the goose itself was roasted.[17] In the Lake District giblet pies included black puddings of goose or pig blood, but most better off families in the north added beef, mutton or veal steaks, which added the required bulk, and absorbed the rich flavour of the giblets, as in this version of 1812:[18]

Giblet Pie

After very nicely cleaning goose or duck giblets, stew them in a small quantity of water, onion, black pepper, and a bunch of sweet herbs, till nearly done. Let them grow cold, and if not enough to fill the dish, lay a beef, veal, or two or three mutton steaks at the bottom. Put the liquor of the stew to bake with the above, and when the pie is baked, pour into it a large tea-cupful of cream. Sliced potatoes added to it, eat extremely well.[19]

Goose giblets	*4oz/100g flour*
1 small onion, chopped	*2oz/50g lard*
pinch ground black pepper	*pinch of salt*
1 bouquet garni	*¼pt/150ml cream*
12-16oz/350-450g beef or mutton steaks, trimmed	
1 large peeled potato (optional)	

Prepare the giblets by removing the gall-bladder from the liver, squeezing and washing the heart, skinning and removing the pipe from the neck, opening and washing the gizzard, and tearing away its thick lining. Put the giblets into a small pan with the onion, pepper, salt and bouquet garni, barely cover with water, and simmer very gently for 30 min. before removing from the heat and leaving to cool.

Rub the lard into the flour and a pinch of salt, and mix in about 2tbs cold water to form the pastry. Place the steaks in the bottom of a 1½ pt/900ml baking dish, remove the neck bone and chop the giblets into pieces, laying these on top, and almost cover with the strained giblet stock. If required, the potato may now be sliced and laid on top.

Roll out the pastry, use it to cover the baking dish, having moistened the rim, cut a hole in the centre, and use the trimmings to make a raised border, pressed down with a fork. Bake at 200°C, 400°F, Gas mark 2 for a further hour, before serving hot.

Dorothy left no recipe for the veal pies she made in July 1802, but below is the Fricker version:[20]

Veal Patties

Make a short crust, and roll it out thick, take the kidney part of a very fat loin of veal – Chop the kidney, veal and fat very small all together – season it with mace, pepper and salt to your taste – fill your Patties and cover them with a Crust – colour them with the yolk of an egg & bake them.[21]

To make 6 patties take:

1lb/450g veal or lamb, including a kidney
1tsp salt   *½tsp mace*
¼tsp pepper   *1 egg, beaten*
Shortcrust pastry made from:
8oz/225g flour,   *4oz/100g lard,*
a pinch of salt, and about 4 tbs cold water.

Finely chop/coarsely mince the meat, and mix in the salt, pepper and mace. Use ⅔ of the pastry to line six 3ins/7·5cm straight-sided small pie or deep bun tins, fill almost to the brim with the meat, brush the edges with the beaten egg, and pinch on the lids, each having a hole cut through its centre. Brush the top with egg, place on a baking sheet and bake at 200° C, 400°F, Gas mark 6 for 10 min., then reduce to 150°C, 300°F, Gas mark 2 for a further 25-30 min. Allow to cool a little, and the juices to be absorbed into the meat, before removing from their tins. Either serve immediately, or when cold, accompanied by pickles.

Joanna appears to have made really good hare pies, which again work well with venison:

Hare Pie

Cut a hare in pieces, season it well, put it in a Jug with ½lb of Butter, cover it close, set it in a pan of boiling water, let it stew an hour & half – make force meat of bread crumbs, bacon scraped & a little of the liver & sweet Herbs &c. season it high – put the Hare into the dish with the gravy that comes out of it, & the force meat – when cov [ere]d an hour will bake it.[22]

1 hare, drawn & skinned	*grated zest of ½ lemon*
1½tsp each marjoram & thyme	*8oz/225g butter*
2 rashers streaky bacon	*2 anchovy fillets*
½tsp ground black pepper	*¼tsp salt*
⅓ of a nutmeg grated	*1 egg, beaten*
6oz/150g fresh white breadcrumbs	*2tbs red wine*
Shortcrust pastry made from	
12oz/320g flour,	*6oz/150g lard,*
a pinch of salt and about 5 tbs cold water.	

Remove all the meat from the carcase, carefully taking out all the sinews etc. and cut into cubes about an inch across. Put them into a ceramic basin, along with the butter cut into small pieces, and cover with a piece of cooking foil pressed down tightly over the rim and outside. Place the basin on a trivet in a large pan, pour in boiling water until half-way up the basin, cover, return to the boil, and simmer for 1½ hours, stirring the contents after 30 min. to separate the pieces of hare.

Meanwhile make the pastry and set aside to rest in a cool place. Finely chop the bacon and anchovies, and mix into the breadcrumbs along with the remaining dry ingredients, then work in the egg and wine to produce a smooth forcemeat. Roll this into balls about ¾ins/2cm diameter.

Pour the hare stock from the basin into a glass or plastic jug, leave to settle for a few minutes, then pour off the clear butter into a separate vessel. Arrange the drained hare in a large pie-dish, along with the forcemeat balls, and almost fill with the stock and a little of the butter. Roll out the pastry and use to cover the pie-dish, having moistened its rim. Use the trimmings to add a raised edge, a border to a hole cut in the centre, and any leaves etc. as decoration. Brush with milk and bake at 220°C, 425°F, Gas mark 7 for 20 min., then reducing the temperature to 180°C, 350°F, Gas mark 4 for a further 20 min., then serve immediately.

As well as these rich meat pies, Joanna made others of bacon and egg, the predecessors of the thin, double-crusted plate pies of the later nineteenth and twentieth centuries.

Egg & Bacon Pie

Steep a few thin slices of Bacon in water, beat 8 Eggs with some milk put the Bacon on the Bottom of the Dish Pour the eggs over it season it with pepper & salt cover & bake it, in a moderate oven.[23]

4oz/100g flour	*6 eggs, beaten*
2oz/50g lard	*½tsp salt*
4 rashers bacon, soaked in water for 15 min.	

Rub the lard into the flour, with a pinch of salt, and mix in about 2 tbs cold water, to make the pastry. Roll out to fit a 1½pt/900ml baking dish, cut a small round hole in the centre, surrounding it with a ring of pastry, moistened, and stuck in position.

Line the dish with the drained bacon, beat the salt into the eggs, and pour on top. Use a little of the egg to wet the rim of the dish, place the pastry lid on top, trim the edges, and use the trimmings to make a raised border, forking the top to press it into position. Bake in an oven pre-heated to 200°C, 400°F, Gas mark 6 for 20 min., then reduce to 150°C, 300°F, Gas mark 2 for a further 30 min., then serve hot.

Joints of meat such as mutton, sirloin of beef, goose or turkey were roasted before the radiant heat of the kitchen fire, rotating there and being basted until done to a turn.[24] There is neither documentary nor physical evidence for any particular kind of spit mechanism. The most probable method would have been to suspend the joint on a twisted skein of twine, and spin it by hand at frequent intervals, to maintain its motion. The resulting roast was well worth the effort of watching and turning, since it gave far more delicately-flavoured and moist results than are achieved today. The Hutchinsons must have been in the habit of having a roast suckling pig for dinner on special occasions, this being amongst the finest of all spit-roasts.

The Wordsworths' friend Charles Lamb wrote one of the most enthusiastic, enjoyable and saliva-producing passages in the whole of English culinary literature in its praise. His *'Dissertation upon Roast Pig'* celebrates the incomparable flavour;

'of the crisp, tawny, well-watched, not over-roasted crackling, as it is well called the very teeth are invited to their share of the pleasure at this banquet in overcoming the coy, brittle resistance with the adhesive oleaginous O call it not fat!, but an indefinable sweetness growing up to it the tender blossoming of fat & the lean, no lean, but a kind of animal mannu or rather fat and lean so blended and running into each other that both make but one ambrosial result, or common substance'

This would have been a far too luxurious dish for the Wordsworths' table but, when the Hutchinsons cooked it, Joanna made the following as soon as it came off the spit:

Pig Sauce

Chop the brains a little with the gravy from the Pig & a little bit of anchovy a little salt, a spoonful of white wine a slice of Lemon, put all into melted butter [white sauce] & heat it over the Fire. [25]

Broiling also used the radiant heat of the fire, but employed the narrow horizontal bars of the gridiron to hold steaks and other relatively thin pieces of meat a few inches above the glowing coals. Dorothy used this method to cook beefsteaks, mutton chops etc., and may have broiled rashers of ham and bacon in the same way.[26] This would certainly have produced ideally crisp results, but would have wasted all the lard or bacon-dripping. For this reason ham and bacon was usually fried to produce sufficient fat for frying the eggs etc. In 1800 Dorothy was buying her bacon, but from around 1812 the family was breeding pigs to home-cure as bacon and ham.[27] Mary's recipe book provides the following instructions: The word 'genel' is not in general use now, but meant an entry, or a passage, especially between houses.

Pickle for Hams

To each ham 1lb of bay salt, ½lb of common salt 2oz salt Peta, 1oz of black pepper beat all these very fine & rub upon the ham let it lay 4 days then pour over it 1½lb of Treacle & let it stay a month turning it every day then put the ham into cold water for 12 hours when it has hung 2 months cover it well up in a brown paper bag & keep it in a genel or dry cellar: if it moulds it will be good.
Mrs Hugessen[28]

The Frickers' meanwhile used a simpler basic method, but then brushed the ham with a crude vinegar made from wood, called pyroligneous acid, to replicate the effect of smoking in a smoke-loft. A good example of such a loft can still be seen above the kitchen fireplace at Town End, Troutbeck.

Smoking Hams &c

Salt your meat in the usual way taking care to put the salt well in, & to turn the meat in the brine once every day. At the end of three or four weeks hang the meat up to drain 24 hours, then with a brush, such as is used for oiling Harness's dipped in the concentrated rough Pyroligneous Acid, smear the meat well over, and hang it up in an airy place. One application of the Acid is generally sufficient, but a second or third will produce a more powerful Westphalia [ham] flavour.[29]

Many local households used salting and sometimes subsequent smoking to preserve legs of mutton or joints of beef, especially for boiling over the winter months. There is no evidence that the Wordsworths did this, since they bought in, rather than bred, their butcher-meat. It would almost certainly have been practised by the stock-breeding Hutchinsons such as their great-uncle Thomas, who could produce sheep weighing seventeen and a half stone, or brother John, who exhibited his fat heifer at the Smithfield Christmas show of 1822.[30] Coleridge was interested in the practice, recording the following method in 1799.

[Salt Beef]

Thin flank of Beef is taken out, sprinkled with salt petre n. b. not with common Salt. to lay a fortnight, turning it every day it must be & tied very close boil it three or 4 hours according to the size till quite tender then press it with a small weight[31]

For keeping over winter, the salted but uncooked joints were hung up in a secure, well-ventilated location. When staying at an inn at Ingleby in 1800 Coleridge particularly noted a large buttock of beef hanging up in the thatch of the living room, from which portions could be cut, soaked and boiled as required.[32]

Moving on from meat to fish, there is very little evidence for the

Fig 8. In Westmorland these long-homed cattle were still the main source of beef for the local market

ways in which it was cooked at Dove Cottage. Presumably those caught by William, his brother John etc. were simply cleaned and either fried or grilled, still one of the best of all methods. In August 1800, however, Dorothy recorded that she had stuffed two small pike, and baked a loaf.[33] Since the oven would be hot, this suggests that she baked them, a much more reliable method than either simmering or roasting. Most of the baked pike recipes of this period recommended very rich stuffings with flavours which permeated the delicate flesh as it slowly cooked:

To Stuff and Bake & Pike

Having scaled and cleaned the fish without cutting open much of the breast, stuff them with a maigre forcemeat made thus; Beat yolks of eggs, a few oysters bearded and chopped, and two boned anchovies & grated bread, minced parsley, and a bit of eschalot or an onion, mace pounded, black pepper, all-spice, and salt. Mix these in proper proportions; and having beat a good piece of butter in a stew-pan, stir them in it over the fire till the consistence of a thick batter, then adding more & flour if necessary. Fill the fish, and sew up the slit. Bake them in a moderate oven, basting with plenty of butter, and sticking butter all over them, serve pike with anchovy sauce [made from the juices from the baking dish, thickened with a roux][34]

> 1 pike, scaled, cleaned, opened at the breast, rinsed in cold
> water, and dried with a cloth or paper towel

4 egg yolks, beaten	*¼tsp mace*
8oz/225g fresh white breadcrumbs	*¼tsp allspice*
1 medium onion, finely chopped	*½tsp salt*
¼tsp ground black pepper	*4oz/100g butter*
4 oysters, bearded & chopped	*4 anchovy fillets*
2tsp chopped parsley	

Melt the butter in a saucepan, stir in all the ingredients, except the pike, and stir over a gentle heat until thickened. Adjust the thickness with either a little more butter, or flour, as necessary to produce a thick but moist stuffing.

Pack this into the pike, sew up the opening, place in a large baking dish, and cook at 180°C, 350°F, Gas mark 4 for 30-40 min., regularly basting with butter.

Joanna Hutchinson's only fish recipe is for eels, traditionally caught in the north country by using a special multi-pronged spear called a glave. Like pike, they are quite a challenge to prepare for the table, the skins being both slippery and tough. She merely directs the cook to 'Case the Eels', that is to skin them, but this is easier said than done. The best instructions for this process are given in Bill Fowler of Eskdale's *Countryman's Cooking* of 1965:

> If you have a big eel that you want to cook yourself, you go about it like this: Get a piece of strong string, about two feet long, and tie the ends together. Pass the knot through the loop at the other end, so as to form a noose. Put this noose around the eel's neck, just below the head, pull tight, and hang the eel up by a strong nail. With a sharp knife, cut round the skin just below the string; now take hold of the edge of this skin with a pair of pliers. A strong, long tug downwards will remove the skin entirely inside out. Cut off the head [and] clean out the guts.

Joanna then goes on to remove the bones, to produce long fillets which are then collared in a similar method to that used for soused herrings:

Eels to collar

> *Case the Eels, cut off the Heads, slit open the bellies, cut off the Fins, & take out the Guts & bones lay them flat on the Back, grate over them a Nutmeg, two or 3 blades of mace beaten fine a little Pepper & salt strew them over a little Sage & parsley shred fine roll them up tight in a cloth & bind it well.*
> *If a middle sized eel boil it ¾ of an Hour in salt & water Hang it up all Night to drain add to the Pickle a pint of vinegar, & a few Pepper Corns, a sprig of sweet Marjoram boil it 10 minutes next day take off the Cloth & put the Eels into it.*[35]

It would be surprising to find no mention of char in the Wordsworth papers, for this trout-like fish, found in Windermere, Coniston Water, and a number of other local lakes and tarns, had been caught and preserved locally for centuries. Originally they were baked in butter in large pies. The Fleming account books of 1665 describe how they were 'sent up to London only between Xmas and Easter by reason ye Fish is at ye best and ye weather ye coolest for carryage'. And in March 1663; 'Ye carryage of 2 Pies to London (to ye Lord Arlington and Joseph Williamson Esq) Weight 7 stone 6lbs ye sum of £1.'[36] By 1675 tinplate pie crusts were also in use, but the early eighteenth century saw the introduction of char-pots, many being made at the Liverpool delftware potteries. Broad and circular, they had short vertical walls around which a number of colourful char were painted. At the opening of the nineteenth century around 1,800 such pots were required every year to pot around 10,800 char, illustrating the importance of this seasonal local industry.

In 1804 the Wordsworths had enjoyed broiled char fresh out of the tarn at Seathwaite in the Duddon Valley, but in later years they appear to have purchased some potted char, arranging them to be dispatched to Thomas Monkhouse in London.[37] In March 1813 Sara informed him that he was being sent 'in the Box a Pot of Chars which I hope will be acceptable to you & The Pots were not as large as I supposed, therefore I send two I should be glad to hear of their safe arrival.'[38] Sara also potted the fish caught by her family's menfolk. One Saturday her brother Henry 'went off again this morning before [I] was up so eager is he after his fishing He brought a fine lot which I potted, or rather

Fig 9. The char caught in lakes such as Windermere and Coniston Water (top) were cleaned, salted, baked, and packed into char pots (bottom) ready for despatch all over England. In the early nineteenth century the local trade required about 1,800 of these pots every year.

intended to pot but Mary Anne, being in love, chose after they were baked to leave them in the way of the dog, who dispatched the greater part.'[39]

Recipes for potting char were given by a number of contemporary authors, such as Mrs Raffald of Manchester, Mrs Burton, wife of the Rector of Windermere, and others. They all use very similar methods, only varying in the variety and quantity of their spicing, the following giving excellent results.[40]

To Pot Char, or Trout

1½lb/625g char or trout, after having had their heads, tails,
fins and backbones removed.

1-2oz/25-50g salt	*1tsp ground mace*
1½tsp ground white pepper	*½ a nutmeg, grated*
¼tsp ground cloves	*8oz/225g butter*

Sprinkle the salt and pepper inside and outside the fish, place in a dish, and leave overnight in a cool place. Put the butter in a saucepan with ¼ pt/150ml water, bring to the boil, and when all the butter is melted, also leave in a cool place overnight.

Next morning, pour the butter into a sieve, discard the brine, and heat the butter in a saucepan to evaporate the remaining water. Remove from the heat when the bubbles have subsided, and then set aside.

Rapidly rinse each fish to remove the brine, wipe dry with a cloth, and sprinkle with the mixed spices inside and out. Keeping the skin sides outwards, pack each double fillet into a baking dish, cover first with the clarified butter, then with a piece of cooking foil, and bake at 110°C, 225°F, Gas mark ¼ for four hours. Remove from the oven, and pour all the butter off into a glass jug. Pack the fish into a clean baking or serving dish about 1½ ins/4cm deep, arranging them head-end to tail-end, backs upward, as closely as possible. Pour in the melted clarified butter from the jug, carefully excluding the dull liquid beneath, and leave in a cool place to set, gently pressing down the fillets with the back of a fork to keep as much as possible under the butter.

Keep in a cool place for 2-3 days if then required for use, or cover with a ¼ins/1cm layer of more clarified butter if intended to be kept for a longer period, always storing in the cool.

The butter-sealed char pots were then wrapped in paper and packed into casks ready for transport to London and elsewhere. The wooded hills of Furness had a long-established cask and hoop-making industry with which William was intimately familiar, since John Tyson, husband of his Hawkshead 'dame', was a manufacturer of char-pot casks.[41]

Perhaps the most unusual recipe for cooking fish is the following example from Joanna Hutchinson. It simmers trout in seasoned beer and then thickens the liquid with egg yolks and the grated brown crust of a loaf to form a sauce. The bitterness of the hops, browned crusts and an onion completely overwhelms rather than complements the delicate flavour of the fish, and is little improved by the sharp acidity of the vinegar or lemon juice added at the end. Joanna must have enjoyed it, otherwise she would not have taken the trouble to enter Mrs. Montague's recipe into her book, but even around 1816 it must have been something of an acquired taste.

Receipt to stew Fish

Take half a pint of Ale or Porter, mix with it an onion chopped small and as much Parsley as will cover a Table spoon chopped very fine, a little salt, Cayenne Pepper, common Pepper, Anchovy Liquor or Catchup, or a little good gravy; Take your Fish and clean and wash them very well, cutting off the Fins and Heads; roll them in Flour and put them in a stew pan with some Butter the size of a Walnut broke into two or three pieces and laid in the bottom of the pan, rasp the upper crust of a loaf and dust the fish over with the brown raspings, then cover the fish with the ingredients above mentioned, and let the whole stew twenty minutes very gently; before the fish is dished, beat up the yolks of three Eggs, and mix them with the gravy, but do not set the fish again upon the fire after the Eggs are added:

Take the fish carefully out, pour the gravy (which ought to be thick) over it, and rasp the whole over with brown raspings, little vinegar or Lemon juice is an improvement, – the ingredients are for three good sized Trouts, they must be increased in proportion.

Mrs Montague[42]

3 trout, cleaned, head, tail & fins removed

2tsp mushroom ketchup or anchovy sauce	½oz/12g butter
	flour for dusting
1tbs chopped parsley	½pt/300ml brown ale
2-3oz/50-75g grated bread crust	¼tsp salt
pinch cayenne pepper	3 egg yolks, beaten
1-2tbs vinegar or lemon juice	pinch black pepper
1 small onion, finely chopped	

Just melt the butter in the bottom of a wide pan or a small frying pan, dust the trout with flour, and lay on top. Sprinkle with the parsley, salt, peppers and onion, pour in the ketchup or sauce with the ale, and cover with half the breadcrumbs. Cover, and simmer very gently for 10-12 minutes. Remove the pan from the heat, beat some of the cooking liquid into the egg yolks, return this to the fish, and stir in to thicken. Using a slice, transfer the trout to a hot dish, pour the sauce on top, cover with the remaining crumbs, sprinkle with the vinegar or lemon juice, and serve immediately.

There are no details describing how the Wordsworths cooked their vegetables, but it would be safe to assume that they prepared and plain-boiled them in salted water in the usual manner. The only recipe that has survived is the following version of creamed mushrooms, which Joanna served with 'sippets', fingers of fried or toasted bread set around the dish, but for today's use they are best piled onto hot buttered toast.

Stewed Mushrooms

Peel the Mushrooms & put them into a pan with a little water let them stew ¼ an hour, then put in a little pepper & salt, flour & Butter to make the gravy thick as Cream, before it is dished up put in a large spoonful of cream & stir it over the fire. Sippets.[43]

1lb/450g mushrooms	*½oz/12g butter*
½tsp salt	*½oz/12g flour*
pinch of pepper	*1tbs double cream*

Pull the stalks from the mushrooms, and wipe clean. Peel the caps by pulling the skin off upwards from its inner rim. Put all the mushrooms into a pan with ¾pt/450ml cold water, bring to the boil, and simmer for 15 min. before stirring in the salt, pepper and flour rubbed into a soft paste with the butter. Stir gently for a further 5 min. until the sauce has thickened, adding the cream just before serving. The edge of the dish may be decorated with sippets in the form of small triangles cut out of fried bread or toast.

Chapter Four

OF COLD PUDDINGS

Cold puddings were amongst the most luxurious dishes in Georgian cookery, partly because of the nature of their ingredients, such as rich cream, sugar and fruits, and partly due to the level of skill and length of time required to bring some of them to successful completion. It is interesting to note that some two-thirds of such recipes in the Wordsworth Trust's collections are from the Frickers. They represent the type of cookery which they would be expected to prepare in their Bristol home, and probably continued to make when running their own establishments. The recipes of Mary Wordsworth, and Joanna Hutchinson, though fewer in number and being a little plainer, still demonstrate that they too could produce excellent cold puddings whenever required.

When all these recipes were carefully noted down, the food manufacturing industry was still in its infancy, all wives and housekeepers still expecting to have to start every dish from its basic ingredients. Since there were no pre-prepared gelatins on the market, making something as simple as a clear well-flavoured jelly usually started off by buying in a 'gang' of four calf's feet from the butcher. After being cleaned, boiled for hours, chilled, and separated from both sediment and scum, their gelatinous stock was flavoured, clarified with the whites and shells of eggs, and finally filtered through a conical flannel filter-bag. The whole process might take several days. In the modernised version below gelatin has been substituted for the calf's feet, but the jellies retain their original flavours. To obtain good results it is essential to know how to mould jellies. It is easiest to use moulds made of tin-lined copper or aluminium. When the jelly has been set by standing overnight in a cool place, quickly dip the mould into warm water, which will release its contents. Working rapidly, hold the jelly mould at 45° in one hand, wet the other hand, the flat surface of the jelly and the serving dish, and slowly rotate and invert the mould until the full weight of the jelly is resting on the front of the fingers of the free hand. Hold the mould just above the serving dish, and pull the fingers away, allowing the jelly to slip down onto it. As the dish is already wet, the jelly may be slid into position, where it will soon stick, as the wetness is absorbed. When using moulds made of plastic, pottery or glass, dipping the mould in warm water rarely releases all the jelly before substantial parts of it have melted. The solution is to smear the inside of the mould with an extremely thin coating of butter, and pour in the jelly solution when cold, but not at the point of setting. This stops the jelly adhering to the mould, so there is no need to dunk the mould in warm water before proceeding as just described above.

Calf Feet Jelly

Wash & clean the Feet to a gang [ie 4 of them] *put 4qts of water, boil it down half, when cold take off the Fat. To a qt. of stock put a pint of white wine, a little brandy, the whites & shells of 4 Eggs beaten, some Cinnamon, the juice & Rinds of 2 Lemons. Sweeten it with loaf Sugar, boil all together 'till it breaks then run it thro' a bag (return it 'till it is clear) into Glasses* [1]

Calf's Feet Jelly

Boil 4 feet greatly in 5 quarts of water & strain it & when cold take off the fat, & scum the jelly from the sediment, put it into a saucepan with 1 quart of Madeira. 1 gill of Brandy, the rind & juice of 2 lemons, the whites of 6 eggs beaten to a froth & their shells broken small, boil it ten minutes, put in a small piece of cinnamon & sweeten it to your taste. Dip a Flannel jelly-bag into hot water, & keep stirring the jelly gently through it until it runs quite clear. [2]

7tsp/gelatin or 7 leaves	*¼pt/150ml Madeira*
1ins/2·5cmstick cinnamon	*3tbs brandy*
pared zest and juice ½ lemon	*3tbs sugar*

Mix the lemon juice with ¼pt/150ml water and strain into a pan. Add the Madeira, sprinkle and then stir in the gelatin (or broken up leaves). Soak for 5 min. then add the remaining ingredients and heat gently while stirring until it steams, and all is dissolved. Remove the pan from the stove, cover, and wrap in towels to infuse for 1 hour. Pour through a sieve into a measuring jug, make up to 1pt/600ml with cold water, stir thoroughly, and pour into a prepared mould, leaving this in a cool place overnight to set.

The only other gelling agent was isinglass, the swimming bladder or 'sound' of certain fish, particularly the sturgeon. Once cleaned and dried, it was formed into various shapes called 'book', 'pipe' or 'ribbon' for sale through high quality grocer's shops. Though much more expensive than calf's feet, it could simply be soaked, simmered and strained to produce a firm clear jelly, ready for sweetening and flavouring. The recipe below demonstrates how Georgian cooks were able to extract and retain as much as possible of the flavour of their expensive ingredients, all to make something we would now find virtually indistinguishable from a modern packet jelly.

Orange Jelly

Grate the rind of two Seville and two China oranges and two lemons, squeeze the juice of three of each and strain then add a quarter of a pound of lump sugar and a quarter of a pint of water boiled till near candying. Have ready a quart of isinglass jelly made with two ounces, put the syrup to it, and boil it once up but do not stir it after it begins to warm – Strain it through a flannel jelly bag dipped in hot water and let it spend half an hour to settle, before it is put into the Mould.[3]

7tsp gelatin	*1½ lemons*
1 large Seville & 1 large sweet orange	*2oz/50g sugar*

Sprinkle, then stir the gelatin into ½pt/300ml cold water, leave to soak for 5 min. warm over the stove or microwave for 1 min. until it has dissolved, then make up to ¾pt/450ml with cold water, and set aside.

Grate the zest off the oranges and a lemon, place in a pan with the sugar and 3.5fl.oz/100ml water, then boil rapidly for 15 min. and pour into the gelatin mixture. Line a sieve with a freshly rinsed and wrung-out piece of cloth, pour in the mixture, and let it filter through once or twice until it is virtually clear, and set aside until cold, but not set. Then pour into a 1pt/600ml mould and leave in a cool place overnight to set.

Blancmange, literally 'white-food', originated as a sweet chicken paté in medieval kitchens, then slowly transformed itself through the centuries to emerge as the cornflour 'shape' or mould of former school dinners and communal teas. It achieved its most delicious form during the eighteenth and early nineteenth centuries when it was a cool and delicate almond milk and cream jelly, ideal for all summertime entertainments. Since the bitter almonds in the original recipes contained potentially dangerous levels of Prussic acid, they have been substituted by almond essence in the up-dated version below. It eats particularly well when accompanied by the Wordsworths' preserved damsons. (See page 141)

Blanc Mange with Isinglass

Put 1oz of picked Isinglass to a pint of water with a bit of Cinnamon & boil till the Isinglass is melted, put to it ¾ of a pint of Cream, two ounces of sweet almonds and six bitter almonds, blanched and beaten, and a bit of lemon peel, sweeten it – stir it over the fire, and let it boil, then strain it, & stir it till it is cool – squeeze in the juice of ½ a lemon & put it in moulds – always wet moulds before you put in the blancmange. [4]

Blanc Mange

Pour a pint of boiling water over 2oz of Isinglass, when dissolved strain it off put to it ¼lb sweet almonds and 12 bitter beaten and beaten fine in a mortar with 3 spoonful of orange flower water & a pint of cream – put in sugar to the taste, boil ¼ hour stirring all the time – strain it off, stirring till it becomes thick – put it into moulds. [5]

5tsp gelatin	*½tsp almond essence*
2oz/50g flaked almonds	*3tbs sugar*
4½tsp orange flower water	*½pt/300ml cream*

Sprinkle, then stir, the gelatin into ½pt /300ml cold water, leave to soak for 5 min., then heat on the stove, or microwave for 1 min., and stir until it has completely dissolved. Blend this liquid with the almonds until they form a smooth cream, then add the remaining ingredients. Stir over a gentle heat until it rises in the pan, then set aside to cool.
Rub the inside of a jelly or blancmange mould with a little butter, making sure to cover every part, pour in the blancmange when cold but not set, then leave in a cold

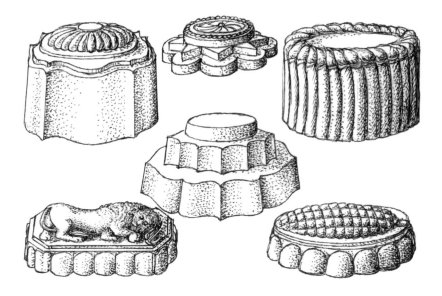

Fig 10. Blancmanges were very popular in the late Georgian period. These are some of the shapes produced by Wedgwood's moulds.

place for a few hours or overnight before serving.

In contrast to blancmange, jaunemange was 'yellow-food', its colour coming from the addition of egg yolks. Its alternative and perhaps less fashionable name was yellow flummery. Essentially a set custard, its initially bland and creamy flavours subside to leave a more mature lemon and wine after-taste, making it a good accompaniment to either stewed or preserved fruit.

Yellow Flummery

2oz of Isinglass beat & open it, put it into a bowl & pour a pint of boiling water upon it. Cover it up till almost cold, then add a pint of White Wine the juice of 2 & the rind of one Lemon, Yolks of 8 Eggs well beaten – sweeten to the taste, put it into a tossing Pan, stir it & when it boils strain it thro' a fine sieve– when almost cold put it into moulds.[6]

Jaune Mange

Two of Isinglass – pint of boiling water, when dissolved add ½ pint of wine – yolks of 8 eggs & the rinds of two [? Lemons] sweeten and let it boil, then pour into moulds [7]

4tsp gelatin	yolks of 4 eggs, beaten
¼pt/150ml white wine	pared zest of a lemon
3-5tbs sugar, according to the sweetness/sharpness of the wine.	

Put the wine, lemon zest, yolks and sugar into a pan with ½pt/300ml water, sprinkle on and then stir in the gelatin, and leave for 5 min. Stir all together over a gentle heat until hot and beginning to thicken, but do not allow to boil, then strain through a sieve into a jug, and set aside until cold but not set. Turn into prepared moulds and leave in a cool place overnight to set.

To avoid the troublesome use of gelatin, some later Georgian cooks began to replace it with a variety of starchy ingredients. This was the start of the slow transformation of the blancmange from a smooth, luscious delicacy into the solid, heavy-textured cornflour 'shape' of modern times. Martha Fricker's recipe clearly illustrates this change:

Receipt for imitation Blancmange

Take a quart of a pd of ground Rice a quarter of an ounce of Bitter Almonds beaten fine, mix them smooth in rather less than a pint of good milk, put pounded white sugar to your taste. When put into moulds it will turn out stiff [8]

4oz/100g ground rice	3tbs sugar
1pt/600ml full cream milk	
1tsp almond flavouring, to replace the dangerous use of bitter almonds	

Mix the ingredients in a pan, stir over a medium heat until boiling, simmer for 5 min., stirring continuously to prevent it from burning, then drop it into a freshly-rinsed mould, excluding any air-pockets, and level the top.

Leave to cool for a few hours, then turn out on to a dish,

and serve with either preserved (tinned) or fresh stewed fruit, or with fruit jams.

Smooth, rich and satisfying, cream provided an ideal basis for any number of cold puddings, in which its essential qualities were enhanced by the addition of contrasting bitter-sweet or sharp flavours. The blend of lemon, orange flower water and caramelised sugar make this a particularly good crème brûleé:

Burnt Cream

Take a Pint of Cream, boil it with sugar & a little lemon peel shred fine – then beat the yolks of six, and the whites of 4 eggs separately – when the cream is cooled, put in the eggs, with a spoonful of orange flower water & one of fine flour – mix it over the fire, keep stirring it till it is thick, then put it into a dish. When cold, sift ¼ of a pound of sugar all over; hold a hot Salamander over it, and when it is very brown, and looks as if a glass Plate were put over your Cream.[9]

1pt/600ml double cream	*1tbs flour*
4 yolks and 2 whites of egg	*2tbs sugar*
1tbs orange flower water	*½tsp grated lemon zest*
For the glaze: 4oz/100g caster sugar	

Simmer the cream, 2tbs sugar and zest very gently for 5 min. and leave to cool. Beat together the yolks, and whites, the orange flower water and the flour, stir into the cream, and stir over a gentle heat until it has just thickened, then pour into a heatproof dish, and set aside until perfectly cold. 2-3 hours before serving spread the sugar evenly across the surface and place under a hot pre-heated grill for 2-3 minutes until it has melted and taken on a colour, then remove, cool and chill.

Instead of setting the cream with eggs, it could also be transformed into a very smooth, thick curd by acidifying it with lemon juice and leaving it in a cool place overnight. Joanna's basic recipe is quite straightforward, but optimistic in its claim to achieve a sufficiently firm set to allow it to be turned out like a blancmange. In practice it is probably best to substitute the mould with a serving dish.

Lemon Solid

Grate the rind of a Lemon into a Dish and squeeze the juice upon it, boil a pint of thick [double] cream and sweeten it [2–3tbs sugar]. set the mould on the ground and strain the cream into it boiling hot, stir it well, let it stand all night, in the morning turn it out and stick it with Candied Orange &c.[10]

This could be converted into a Swiss or Stone Cream merely by adding cooked or preserved fruits in the dish with the lemon juice as in the following versions from Martha Fricker's recipe books:

Swiss Cream

Lay apricots or plums in the bottom of a dish, squeeze the juice of a lemon and the rind grated upon them, boil a pint of thick cream, and sweeten it to your taste; Set your dish in a cool place, and strain the cream very hot into it, let it remain all night, & ornament it with candied orange.[11]

Stone Cream

Put into the Dish you intend to send to Table Apricots, or other sweetmeats, cut small, & Three spoonfuls of lemon or orange juice, with a little of the peel grated –

Then take a pint of Cream, ¼ of an ounce of Isinglass, a little cinnamon and a few lumps of sugar, boil it till the Isinglass is quite dissolved – Then strain it into a jug that has a spout and when about the heat of new milk pour over the sweetmeats, round the Dish – it should be made some hours before it is wanted.[12]

> *1 standard tin of apricots, drained & chopped*
> *3tbs strained fresh orange or lemon juice*
> *grated zest of either an orange or a lemon*
> *1pt/600ml single cream*   *4tbs sugar*
> *2ins/5cm stick cinnamon*   *5tsp gelatin*

Arrange the apricots as an even layer across the base of a large dish, and sprinkle on the orange or lemon juice and zest. Put the cream, cinnamon and sugar into a pan, sprinkle and then stir in the gelatin, and leave for 5 min.

Heat gently while stirring until all is melted, but not to boiling point, then remove from the heat, leave until tepid, pour into a jug, and pour onto the apricots all over, from the height of a foot or two/30-60cm, to ensure it blends with the lemon juice. Leave in a cold place, preferably overnight, before serving.

Other creams were eaten in a semi-liquid state, and so were served either in dishes and bowls, or in individual custard glasses. For present day use they are most conveniently served in wine glasses and accompanied by sponge finger biscuits for dunking.

Custards

Take 1 Pint of Cream and 1 of new milk – set them over the fire with a little sugar, Cinnamon, Lemon Peel, 4 ounces of sweet almonds and 1 of bitter blanched and chopped small, when it has boiled, take it off the fire and add the yolks and whites of 4 eggs well beaten, then set it over the fire again till thick enough and take care to keep stirring it all one way & not to let it boil – pour it into a jug and when cold take out the Cinnamon and Lemon Peel and put a tablespoonful of Brandy & 2 of Madeira. [13]

½pt/300ml double cream	*½pt/300ml milk*
2oz/50g almonds, finely chopped	*½tsp almond essence*
2-3tbs sugar	*2 eggs beaten*
1 stick cinnamon	*½tbs brandy*
pared zest of ½ lemon	*1tbs Madeira*

Mix all the ingredients (except the eggs, brandy & Madeira) in a pan, simmer for 5 min., stirring to prevent it from burning. Remove from the heat, and pour a little onto the eggs, stirring vigorously to prevent curdling. Stir the egg mixture into the contents of the pan, return to a very gentle heat and stir continuously until just thickened, but not curdled. Remove from the heat and pour into a jug. Take out the lemon zest and cinnamon stick, stir in the brandy and Madeira, and pour into wine glasses to cool.

Lemon Cream

*Take a pint of thick cream and put to it the yolks of two eggs well
beaten, four ounces of fine sugar, and the thin rind of a lemon, boil
it up, then stir it till almost cold, put the juice of a lemon in a dish
or bowl, and pour the Cream upon it, stirring it until quite cold.[14]*

1pt/600ml double cream   *2oz/50g sugar*
pared zest and juice of 1 lemon   *yolks of 2 eggs, beaten*

Mix the cream, yolks, zest and sugar in a pan and stir
while heating almost to boiling point, then set aside to cool,
stirring frequently to prevent the formation of a tough skin
on top. When almost cold, pour onto the lemon juice either
in a dish or bowl. Alternatively stir in the lemon juice and
pour into individual wine glasses, and leave to go perfectly
cold before serving.

The following cold pudding is one of only four in the recipe book kept
by Mary Wordsworth. Essentially a moulded rice pudding, it is quite
different from anything we would recognise by that name today. It is
flavoured with salt rather than sugar to provide a relatively bland foil
for the sharper, richer flavours of marmalade, jam or stewed fruits. In
this it takes on a similar role to that of the bread in a jam sandwich.

Rice [Mould]

*Wash and put a little clear water to it, set it in the oven till all the
water is drained up, add good milk or cream, a little salt when
quite stiff beat it well with a spoon, let it be pretty stiff & put it in
a mould, to turn out – garnish it with Marmalade or sweetmeat
& pour over it coloured cream or custard.*
    *Rice prepared in this way may be laid over fruits and baked
instead of a Crust. It should be laid in separate spoonful & look
broken.* [15]

2oz/50g short-grain rice   *pinch of salt*
¼pt/150ml cream

Put the rice in a baking dish, cover with ¾pt/450ml cold
water, and bake at 150°C, 300°F, Gas Mark 2 for 30 min.,

stir, bake for a further 30 min., stir in the cream, and continue to bake for a further hour.

Remove from the oven, remove any skin, then sprinkle with the salt, and beat thoroughly. It may then be packed into a freshly-rinsed 1pt/600ml mould, and left in a cool place for a few hours to set. Turn out onto a dish and garnish with marmalade, jam, or preserved [tinned] fruit.

Pears were among the fruits which might be stewed from the raw to accompany the rice. This recipe states that they should be stewed for hours along with a new pewter spoon. This was a well-known method of turning the pears an attractive purple colour as they absorbed elements of the lead and tin components of the pewter released by the acids.[16] This practice should never be repeated today, the same effect being obtained from a few drops of modern food colouring.

Pears to stew

Pare the largest stewing pears & stick a clove into the blossom end then put them in a tin Pan with a new pewter spoon in the middle, fill it with hard water & set it over a slow fire for 3 or 4 Hours till soft & the water reduced to a small quantity. then put as much loaf sugar as will make it a thick syrup & let the pears boil in it, then cut lemon peel like straws & serve them up with the syrup in a glass dish [17]

6 cooking pears	1tsp purple food colour
6 cloves	pared zest of 1 lemon
6oz/150g sugar	

Peel the pears, stick a clove in the bottom of each one and stew with the sugar, food colour and sufficient water to just cover, for about 30 min. until tender. Strain the liquid into a clean pan and boil rapidly until reduced to half its volume, and leave to cool. Meanwhile slice the lemon zest into very fine straws and simmer in plain water for 5 min., drain, and rinse in cold water. Finally arrange the pears in a dish, pour the syrup over them, and sprinkle with the lemon straws.

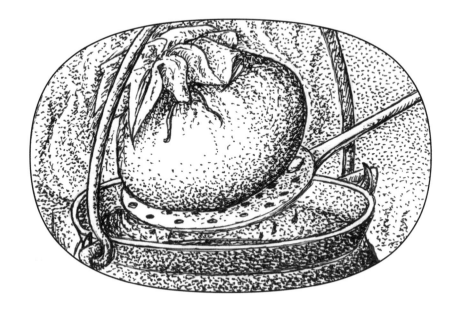

Chapter Five

OF HOT PUDDINGS
& SWEET PIES

Puddings are now thought of as being sweet dishes, but they originated as large savoury boiled sausages, including the black pudding, still an essential ingredient in any local breakfast or tatie-pot. By the Elizabethan period larger puddings became possible by enclosing ingredients in cloths, as well as prepared guts. Using combinations of flour, milk or cream and eggs, all mixed with various flavourings, very hot and satisfying puddings could now be made, ideal for providing substantial accompaniments to roast and stewed meats etc. It was only with the widespread use of potatoes to fulfil this role that the boiled pudding changed to an almost exclusively sweet dish. Around 1800 this change was actively taking place, and so recipe books still provided instructions for making unsweetened puddings either to accompany meats or to be served with a sweet white sauce. One of the most basic of these was the boiled batter pudding, Dorothy making a 'batter pudding for William' in May, 1802.[1] Since she did not record her own recipe, this example comes from a manuscript of around 1810 written in the North Yorkshire/County Durham area, which included the Hutchinsons' home at Sockburn.

Boiled Batter Pudding

Beat the Yolks of three Eggs with two large spoonfuls of Flour, a little Salt, a pint of good Milk or Cream, make it the thickness of a Pancake [batter], & beat all well together. An hour will boil it.
Mrs Bell Selaby.[2]

3 yolks of egg, beaten   8oz/225g flour, sifted
1pt/600ml milk or cream   pinch of salt

Beat the eggs into the milk or cream, then beat in the flour and salt until smooth and thick.

Take a double thickness of either very fine muslin or finely-woven cotton or linen, about 18ins/45cm square, soak it in boiling water, lightly wring it, shake out, lay on a flat surface, and smooth out any wrinkles. Sprinkle a thin layer of flour all over it, lift it up by the ends of one side, shake off any surplus flour, and lay inside a deep bowl, the edges overhanging the sides.

Half fill a large pan with water, and bring to a rapid boil. Pour the batter into the cloth, gather up the sides first, then the corners, until the batter is totally enclosed, and tie securely with string or twine. Immediately lift up the pudding and plunge it into the boiling water, using any long-handled utensil to turn it tied-side down, cover, return to the boil, and continue a strong simmer for 1½ hours, topping up with boiling water in order to keep the pudding floating.

When ready to serve, remove the pan from the heat, and scoop up the pudding in a strong wire sieve, or raise the corners of the cloth above the surface, and grasp either with strong tongs or with a double layer of thick towel, dip rapidly in and out of cold water in a basin just big enough to hold it, which will allow the cloth to be more easily untied, and the pudding turned out onto a hot dish.

Variations: add either 1-2 tsp ground ginger, or 1-2oz/25-50g currants, or 3-4tbs sugar to the batter.

Sauce: The usual sauce for puddings of this kind was made by melting together 4oz/100g each of butter, sugar and white wine.

On Christmas morning, 1805, young Johnny Wordsworth was 'alive at the thought of two plum-puddings which are now rumbling in the Pot.[3] Unfortunately their recipe has not survived, this one coming from Martha Fricker:

To Make a Plum Pudding

1lb of Currants, half lb of Raisins chopped, half lb of Suet, the rind of a Lemon grated half an ounce of Canddid Lemon two Tablespoonful of Sugar 4 Eggs & three table spoonful of Brandy [4]

1lb/450g currants	*grated zest of a lemon*
8oz/225g chopped raisins	*2tbs sugar*

8oz/225g suet	*3tbs brandy*
½oz/12g candied lemon peel	*4 eggs, beaten*
8oz/225g flour	

Mix the dry ingredients thoroughly, beat the eggs and brandy together, pour in and work together to form a uniformly stiff dough. Take a piece of fine cotton cloth or a doubled layer of muslin some 2ft/60cm square, scald, wring, spread out, and dust the top surface with flour. Shake off the surplus, lay across a bowl, and place the dough, formed into a ball, in the centre. Gather the cloth around it, centres of the sides first, and tie tightly with string.

Plunge into boiling water, cover, and continue at a strong simmer, topping up with more boiling water as necessary, for 4 hours. Scoop out of the pot with a strong wire sieve, place on a hot dish, remove the string, turn out of the cloth, and serve immediately.

Sometimes a plain pudding was required either at short notice, or when other demands left little time for the mixing, tying up and long period of boiling. Its place might then be taken by the appropriately-named Hasty Pudding, which Dorothy made for her supper after a busy day of gardening, walking and writing in May, 1800.[5] Since she used the word 'porridge' for its oatmeal equivalent, hers was most probably based on flour and milk.

Flour Hasty Pudding

Put four bay-leaves into a quart of milk, and set it on the fire to boil. Then beat up the yolks of two eggs, and stir in a little salt. Take two or three spoonfuls of milk, and beat up with your eggs, and stir in your milk. Then with a wooden spoon in one hand, and the flour in the other, stir it in till it be of a good thickness, but not too thick. Let it boil, and keep stirring; then pour it into a dish, and stick pieces of butter here and there.[6]

1 egg yolk	*2oz/50g flour*
pinch of salt	*2 bayleaves*
1pt/600ml milk	*1oz/25g butter*

Beat the yolk with a little of the milk, then add the remaining milk, salt and bayleaves, then sifting in the flour little by little while beating vigorously. Stir over a medium heat until it has boiled for 5 min., then pour it into a dish and dot with butter.

Some of the other boiled puddings were rather more delicate, Joanna Hutchinson's Custard Pudding, for example, being so lightly set with eggs that it tends to collapse into a mound when turned out onto its dish.

Custard Pudding

A pint of Good milk (better with some cream) 4 Eggs, a small spoonful of Flour, boil it 40 minutes; and hang it up ½ an hour at least. Put it in boiling water again for from 5 to 10 minutes [7]

| ½pt/300ml single cream | 4 eggs, beaten |
| ½pt/300ml milk | 3tbs flour |

Beat the cream, milk and eggs together, then sift in the flour while beating vigorously, then boil in a cloth, as described in the recipe for Boiled Batter Pudding above, removing it from the water after 40 min., hanging it up for 30 min. to cook through, and finally returning to boil for 10 min. just before serving.

Since this batter is quite thin, the initial plunge into hot water should be executed as quickly as possible. Alternatively pour it into a greased basin, cover with a piece of kitchen foil pressed over the rim, and steam instead of boiling.

One Sunday in early June, 1800, Dorothy 'walked up to Mr Simpson's to gather gooseberries it was a fine afternoon. Little Tommy [the son of a friend] came with me, ate gooseberry pudding and drank tea with me.' [8] We do not have her recipe, but it was probably similar to this one used by Rachel Whitwell of Kendal (1771-1833). It produces a very rich, moist and well-flavoured pudding, the gooseberries contributing their characteristic sharpness. It is useful in converting relatively few gooseberries into a very satisfying pudding. If a sauce is required, use double cream.

To make a boiled Gooseberry Pudding

6oz [150g] gooseberries
6oz [150g] grated bread
6oz [150g] Currants
6oz [150g] Sugar
1½ or 2 hours boiling [9]

3 Eggs (well beat)
Nutmeg [pinch]
Lemon peel [grated zest]
a [table] spoon of Brandy

Pick the gooseberries, trim off the projecting stalks etc. and chop each in half. Place in a bowl with the remaining dry ingredients, mix thoroughly, then stir in the eggs and brandy. Boil, as described in the recipe for Boiled Batter Pudding, above, for 2 hours.

Boiled puddings were relatively economical to make, since they could be cooked over any open fire. Baked puddings, meanwhile, even though less troublesome, required extra fuel to heat up the traditional stone-built ovens. Most of their recipes were very similar to their boiled equivalents:

Baked Batter Pudding

Two Spoonfuls of Flour, 4 Yolk of Eggs, & 2 Whites, one Gill of Cream, mix the Eggs & Cream together, then add the Flour, beat them all well for five Minutes, then bake them in Tea Cups for 20 Minutes.

Mrs Blakey, Minsteracres[10]

Use the butter or dripping to grease the insides of six heatproof basins or large metal bun-tins, and arrange on a baking tray. Beat the yolks into the cream, then sift in the flour while beating vigorously, to make a thick batter. [if possible leave to rest for 30 60 min.] Pour the batter into the basins/tins, and bake at 170°C, 325°F, Gas mark 3 for 20 min.

German Puffs were a rather more sophisticated version. Originally made by dropping spoonfuls of sweet batter into a deep pan of boiling fat to emerge as plum-shaped fritters, by around 1800 they had become puddings baked in cups.

To make German Puffs

Take the yolks of four eggs, two spoonfuls of flour, two ounces of sweet almonds beat fine, mix them well together and then add to it a pint of thick cream, two ounces of butter clarified; When cold, put that in, and sugar to your taste, add a little orange flower water. Bake them in little pans well buttered, and in a quick oven. Twenty minutes will bake them Your sauce must be melted butter with white wine and sugar. [11]

2 egg yolks, beaten	*1oz/25g butter*
4oz/100g flour	*2oz/50g sugar*
1oz/25g ground almonds	*2tbs orange flower water*
½pt/300ml cream	
The Sauce:	
4oz/100g butter 4oz/100g sugar	*¼pt/150ml white wine*

Beat the flour and almonds into the yolks, with a little of the cream, until smooth, then beat in the rest of the cream. Melt the butter in a small pan, allow to cool, and beat the clear into the mixture, along with the sugar and orange flower water. Butter six plain bun-tins, pour in the mixture, and bake at 170°C, 325°F, Gas mark 3 for 20 min, then turn out on to hot plates.

Melt the sauce ingredients together, and pour over the puddings.

3 Puddings [Gooseberry, Apple, Apricot]

Upon 2 handfuls of bread crumbs pour a pint of Cream boiling hot, when cold add 5 Eggs well beaten and 4 spoonfuls of the pulp of scalded Gooseberries, Apples, or Apricots the rind of a Lemon, sugar to the Taste, a glass of white Wine, or a little Brandy paste the dish & bake it [12]

4oz/100g fresh white breadcrumbs	*8oz/225g flour*
grated zest of 1 lemon	*3tbs sugar*
1pt/600ml single cream	
1tbs white wine or 1 tbs brandy	
6oz/150g cooked apricot, apple or gooseberry, pulped	
4oz/100g butter, or half butter	

Bring the cream to the boil, in a saucepan, stirring to prevent it burning, remove from the heat as soon as it has risen to the boil, and stir in the breadcrumbs. Cover, and set aside to cool. Meanwhile use the flour and butter to make a short pastry (alternatively use 1lb/450g puff pastry) and use to line a 2pt/1·2l baking dish.

When the cream mixture is cool, beat in the fruit, eggs, sugar, lemon and wine or brandy, until smooth. Pour this into the pastry-lined dish and bake at 150°C, 300°F, Gas mark 2 for 1½ hours until risen and just browning around the edges.

Earthenware baking dishes had been manufactured by most of the large pottery factories from the late eighteenth century. Relatively cheap to buy, they enabled 'pudding-pies' to be baked either without the necessity of raising a free-standing hot-water crust, or of providing any bottom crust at all. One of these 'bakers' was probably in use at the King's Head at Thirlspot a few days after Christmas, 1801. Here, after crossing Dunmail Raise on their way to visit Coleridge in Keswick, William, Mary and Dorothy 'roasted apples in the oven.[13]

Roasted Apples

1 medium cooking apple per person

Wipe and core each apple, and make a shallow cut through the skin all around its middle. Place on a baking dish, and bake at 200°C, 400°F, Gas mark 6 for about 40-60 min until soft. The Wordsworths' apples were probably baked in this way, but alternatively their centres may be stuffed with sugar and a knob of butter, with chopped dried and glacé fruits, or with mincemeat (*see p103*) before going into the oven.

Baking dishes were also useful for baking milk puddings, many of which were considered as much as invalid foods as puddings. This is certainly the impression given by Dorothy's decision 'to take Tapioca for my supper' in January 1803.[14] Mary's use of a stiff rice pudding to form the crust of a baked apple pie is both an interesting and a successful combination. The distinctive flavours and textures of the rice and apple complement each other ideally, and are an improvement on the usual shortcrust pastry. [15]

Rice [& Fruit Pie]

Rice prepared as in the recipe on p.126
1½lb/675g sliced apple or other raw fruit
2oz/50g sugar, pinch ground cinnamon

Arrange the fruit in the bottom of a baking dish about 6 x 8ins/15 x 20cm, sprinkling it with the sugar and cinnamon. Drop rough spoonfuls of the cooked rice on top to cover the fruit, and bake at 180°C, 350°F, Gas mark 4 for 30 min. until the top is lightly browned, and serve either hot or cold.

Dorothy's journal tells of the apple pies, gooseberry pies, apple tarts, and rhubarb tarts which she baked at Dove Cottage.[16] These were most probably simply made with shortcrust pastry, rather than the more elaborate puff-paste versions given in the published recipe books of the period. The prepared fruit would have been arranged in the baking dishes or in pastry-lined tart tins, sprinkled with sugar, perhaps with grated lemon zest, ground clove or cinnamon as appropriate, covered with an upper crust if intended for a pie, and baked in the oven.

When William, Mary and Dorothy Wordsworth called at the King's Head. Thirlspot, on 28th December, 1801, they found John Stanley's family making Christmas Pies.[17] The following day, as they approached Ullswater, they 'dined at the publick house on porridge, with a second course of Christmas pies'. At this time a Christmas Pie could take a number of forms, anything from a giant pie filled with all manner of poultry and gamebirds stuffed one within another, and weighing a stone or two, as in Yorkshire, to the equivalent of a modern meatless mince pie. The nature of the Lake District Christmas Pie in the eighteenth century was fortunately described in a letter sent by 'A Gentleman of Cumberland' to Richard Bradley, Professor of Botany at Cambridge University, who published it in 1732. Describing the local sweet haggis, called a hackin, he stated 'that it eats somewhat like a Christmas Pye, or is somewhat like that boil'd'.[18] Since its ingredients included minced lean beef, suet, shredded apples, currants, lemon peel and sugar, it was obviously a sweet minced pie, a forerunner of the traditional Cumbrian 'Sweet Pie'. This recipe, collected by Rachel Whitwell of Kendall (1771–1833) is much pleasanter, lighter and sharper than most modern mincemeats.

Fig 11. The late eighteenth century creamware potteries made wares ideal for baking pies, including bakers (top) which only required a top crust, patty pans (centre) and plates (bottom).

Mrs Mathew's Recipt for Minc'd pies

Two pounds [900g] of Beef Suet Shred fine, three pounds [1·8kg] of baking Apples, the Peel of a Lemon Shred Small, one pound & half [675g] of Sugar, two ditto currants, half a pound [225g] of Raisins, a quarter of a pound [100g] of Citron, a quarter [100g] of Lemon & orange peel, the juice of two or three Lemons, half a pint [300ml] of Brandy, an Ounce [25g] of Cinnamon, one Nutmeg, and a quarter of a pound [100g] of Almonds. [19]

Mix all the ingredients together (the quantity of suet has been halved to suit modern taste), press down into jars and seal, store in a cool place, and use within a month. Make up the plate or individual pies with either shortcrust or puff pastry, and bake at 220°C, 425°F, Gas mark 7 for about 20 min.

The final recipe in this chapter is for Raspberry Fritters, a useful addition to the dining table, especially for those dull, wet summer evenings so often experienced in the Lake District.

Raspberry Fritters

Pour ½ Gill of boiling cream upon some bread crumbs, beat the yolks of 4 Eggs to a froth, when the cream &c. is cold beat it a little then put all together very much & add 2oz of sugar & as much of the juice of Raspberries as will make it a pretty colour & give it an agreeable sharpness. drop them into a pan of boiling Lard the size of a Walnut. [20]

4oz/100g raspberries	*2oz/50g sugar*
5oz/125g fresh white breadcrumbs	*4 egg yolks*
⅛pt/75ml cream	*lard for frying*

Place the raspberries in a sieve over a jug, crush with a fork, and then use either the back of a spoon or the fingertips to press through all the juice.

Mix the bread and sugar in a bowl, pour on the cream heated to boiling, and stir in with a fork until completely incorporated, then leave to cool for 10 min. before stirring in the raspberry juice. Whisk the yolks until they are transformed into a pale yellow froth, and finally fold them into the mixture.

Heat a pan with sufficient lard [or oil] for deep-frying, using the lowest setting if using a deep-fryer. Using two dessert spoons, scoop up walnut-sized pieces of the mixture, and rapidly drop a number of these into the hot lard. They will sink at first, and may stick to the bottom unless eased off with a metal slice. When they have risen to the surface and their undersides are pale golden brown, checked by turning over, turn them all over to cook on the other side, then remove onto paper towels to drain, and keep hot while frying succeeding batches. Serve piping hot and sprinkled with sugar. N.B. If fried at too high a temperature, the outsides will be overcooked to dark brown while the insides are still virtually raw.

Chapter Six

OF BREAD & CAKES

Dorothy Wordsworth's Grasmere journal records her frequent baking sessions at Dove Cottage but, even though they might take place at roughly weekly intervals, no particular day of the week was selected for a baking day, as was customary in households with more regular domestic timetables. The oven at Dove Cottage was almost certainly of the traditional 'beehive' design, a domed masonry chamber a few feet in diameter built into the back kitchen chimney stack. Its only opening would have been a square doorway roughly at table height, into which were thrust bound bundles of small branches called faggots. William and Dorothy made one of these from trees blown down from 'John's Grove' after a storm in January 1802.[1] Having been ignited and pushed to the back of the oven, their flames roared against the domed roof, heating the masonry before emerging from the upper part of the doorway and escaping up the chimney. When sufficiently hot, the embers were raked out onto the hearth, the ashes swept out with a wet mop called a fruggan, the bakery inserted, and the door closed for the required cooking time. The efficient management of such ovens required considerable practical experience, but within a few months of arriving at Dove Cottage Dorothy had deputised much of this responsibility on to her neighbour and servant Molly Fisher. Writing to Jane Pollard in September 1800, she described how Molly 'looks to the oven', while in June 1802 she was able to tell Sara Hutchinson that 'Molly manages the oven entirely and as well as I can'.[2] Even so, Molly's opinions could still lead to absolute disaster. In May 1802 William explained to Coleridge the reasons why Dorothy would not be sending him his promised supper-cake: 'it died of a very common malady, bad advice. The oven must be hot, perfectly hot, said Molly the experienced, so in a piping red-hot oven it went, and came out (but I hate antithesis) in colours especially black as a genuine child of the coal-hole. In plain English, it is not a sendable article.'[3]

In the same letter he described Dorothy 'packing up a few small loaves of American flour'. These, being of hard or strong wheat, would have been lighter and spongier than those made from the traditional soft English wheats. Since dried forms of bread-yeasts had still to be developed, all bakers, whether working on a commercial or domestic scale, used ale-yeasts, sour-dough or home-made yeasts to raise their doughs. Dorothy appears to have changed to making home-made yeasts before 1802, when she told Sara Hutchinson that 'I am glad you found out how to bake bread in my way – we never want yeast now.'[4] Her method may have been either of the following, noted by Joanna Hutchinson:

To make Yeast

One Gallon of water, one ounce Hops 2 pounds flower, boil the hops 20 minutes then have your potatoes bruised small, then stir in the above quantity of flower, [min?] altogether with the liquor. when less than new Milk warm add 1 quart of old yeast to it & let it stand all night, it may be used in the morning, great nicety must be used to keep the stone bottles sweet it is kept in, the hops should be strained before they are mixed (boiling hot). you may omit the potatoes if you like [5]

Yeast

Boil 10z of hops about 10 minutes in 6 quarts of water, strain it and mix it immediately with 2lbs of flour and a tablespoonful of sugar, when the mixture is new milk warm add two spoonfuls of good yeast, put it in a stone bottle, cork it well and in two days it will be fit for use, half this quantity is sufficient for about 2 pecks of flour.

Reserve ½ a pint to make the yeast the next time. The night before you bake put a quart to a portion of the flour mixed then, in the morning knead it and bake in the afternoon.[6]

Joanna also obtained another recipe from a Mrs King:

Potatoe Yeast

Boil mealy Potatoes till quite soft, skin & mash them very smooth & put as much hot water as will make them the consistence of common Yeast. Add to every 1lb of Potatoes 2oz of coarse sugar, & when just warm stir into every lb of Potatoes 2 spoonful of common yeast & keep it till it has done fermenting & in 24 hours

*it may be used. 1lb of potatoes will make a quart of yeast & when
made it will keep 3 months. Make the Dough 8 hours before it is to
be baked.*

Mrs King [7]

Fig 12. This drawing after John Harden of Brathay shows a middle-class lady instructing
her servant in 1804. Their contrasting status is clearly defined by their respective poses
and dress, almost as if depicting Dorothy instructing Old Molly Fisher at Dove Cottage
in 1800.

As these recipes show, it was customary to start the bread-making process the previous night or at least eight hours before baking. The liquid yeast was mixed with sufficient flour to form a soft batter, which was then covered with more flour and allowed to ferment slowly. The rest of the flour was then kneaded into this 'sponge' and left to rise in the usual way. This method ensured that the bread was always well-risen and well-flavoured when it emerged from the oven. It was then ready for consumption either as bread and butter, toast, or as breadcrumbs in puddings, forcemeats and sauces.

This recipe from the Frícker recipe book shows how yeasted dough was used to make either rich caraway buns or hot cross buns:

To make light Barm [Buns & Hot Cross Buns]

Take 2 pounds & a half of Flour – rub into it ½ pound of sugar & some pounded Caraway seeds– mix 8 table spoonfuls of light barm with 6 eggs well beaten & rather more than ½ pint of warm milk. Make a hole in the Flour & pour in the liquid – cover it & set it by the fire for 2 hours to rise – make the buns up with as little Flour as possible – bake them in a quick oven
N.B. if you want them for Good Friday, add a few Cloves, a little Mace & Cinnamon beaten & sifted – and cross them.[8]

1lb/450g strong white flour	*3oz/75g sugar*
3oz/75g butter	*¼pt/150ml tepid milk*
1tbs caraway seeds	*2 eggs, beaten*
1tbs dried yeast	

Follow the manufacturer's instructions for the dried yeast, either activating it with 1tsp of sugar and a little of the tepid milk whisked together and left in a warm place for about 20 min. until frothy, before adding with the milk, or add the dried yeast with the caraway seeds etc.

Rub the butter into the flour, mix in the caraway seeds and sugar, make a well in the centre, pour in the tepid milk and eggs, and work together to form a dough. Knead on a floured board for 5 min. then place in a bowl, cover with a cloth and leave in a warm place to rise until doubled in size. Divide into 12 pieces, mould into round buns, place on a lightly greased baking sheet, a few inches apart, cover again, and return to the warm until doubled in size, then bake at 190°C, 375°F, Gas mark 5 for 15-20min., until golden brown.

For Hot Cross buns, add ½tsp each of ground clove, mace and cinnamon instead of the caraway seeds, slash their tops with a cross as soon as moulded into buns and brush over with 4tbs milk and water, and 3tbs sugar melted together just as they come out of the oven.

Martha Fricker also made this fruit loaf, which was made up and baked in the same way:

A Bun Loaf

½lb Raisins	½ [lb] Sugar
½lb Currants	two Eggs
½lb Butter	a little Nutmeg & Barm
2lb Flour	
To rise an hour [9]	

Some fruit cakes were also yeast-raised, just like modern plum-loaves, while others were raised either by a combination of yeast and eggs, or by eggs alone. A Fricker recipe advised that:

Whether black or white Plum cakes they require less butter and eggs for having yeast, and equally light and rich. If the leaven [yeast] be only of flour, milk and water and yeast, it becomes tough & is less easily divided than if the butter be first put with these ingredients & the dough afterwards set to rise before the fire.[10]

For these, as well as the lighter egg-raised cakes, the Frickers wrote down their:

Observations on making and baking Cakes

Currants should be very nicely washed, dried in a Cloth and then set before the fire. If damp they will make Cakes or puddings heavy. Before they are added a dust of dry flour should be thrown among them, and a shake given to them which causes the thing to which they are put to be lighter.

Eggs should be very long beaten, whites and yolks apart and always strained.

Sugar should be rubbed to a powder on a clean board and sifted through a very fine hair or lawn sieve.

Lemon-peel should be pared very thin, and with a little sugar beaten in a marble mortar to a paste, and then mixed with a little wine or cream, so as to divide easily among the other ingredients.

After all the ingredients are put into the pan they should be thoroughly and long beaten as the lightness of the Cake depends much on these being well incorporated ...

The heat of the oven is of great importance for Cakes, especially larger ones – if not quick their batter will not rise, but some paper should be put over the Cake to prevent it being burnt. If not long enough lighted to have a body of heat or it is become slack, the cake will be heavy.

To know when it is soaked take a broad-bladed knife that is very bright and plunge it into the very centre [of the cake], draw it instantly out, and if the least stickiness adheres put the cake immediately in and shut up the oven.

If the heat should be sufficient to raise but not to soak, fresh fuel might be quickly put in & the Cake kept hot until the oven was fit to finish the soaking – but great care should be taken that no mistakes occur from negligence in baking large cakes. [11]

Using this advice the Frickers were able to make rich fruit cakes such as this:

Plum Cake

lb of Raisins 2lb Currants ½lb Citron ½ of Lemon 1(?)lb of Flour 1lb½ Sugar 2 Nutmegs 1lb of Eggs (10) a Wine Glass of Brandy D° of Port wine 1lb & ¼ of butter without salt
beat the butter to a Cream then add the yolks of the eggs – then the whites well beaten – then all the other ingredients by degrees, except the Lemon, & Citron which are stuck upright between the layers of Cake in the dish – bake it in a moderate oven about 5 hours & ½ [12]

1lb/450g raisins	*8 eggs, separated*
2lb/900g currants	*3tbs brandy*
8oz/225g candied peel	*3tbs port*
8oz/225g citron, chopped	*2 nutmegs, grated*
1lb 4oz/550g butter	*1lb/450g flour*
1lb 8oz/675g sugar	

Line a 9ins/23cm square or 10ins/25·5cm round tin with buttered paper. Mix the currants and raisins, and the candied peel and citron.

The original recipe makes it difficult to prevent the butter from separating from the mixture, and so the following version adopts the usual modern method.

Cream the butter with the sugar, and work in, little by little, the beaten yolks, the whites whipped to a soft peak, and the brandy and port. Fold in the flour sifted with the nutmeg, and then the raisins and currants. Spread a third of the mixture into the tin, scatter on half of the candied peel and citron, then another third of the mixture, the rest of the peel and citron, and finally the remaining mixture. Bake at 150°C, 300°F, Gas mark 2 for 5½ hours, covering the top with paper after the first hour.

Icing for the Plumb Cake

ice it when nearly cold, rubbing it with flour first, the bottom is to be iced not the top.[13]

If intended for use as a bride-cake, as wedding cakes were then known, the cake was sometimes given a preliminary coat of almond paste (some 2lb 4oz/1kg for one of this size). Others had the icing laid directly on to their baked surfaces. This was made by whisking the whites of four small eggs to each pound/450g of icing sugar until they formed a thick cream which was applied using a flat spoon.

Most of the more delicate cakes of this period were variations of the fatless sponge, which relied on beating or whisking very fresh egg yolks and whites, then mixing in sugar, flour and some form of flavouring before baking in a cool or moderate oven. If skilfully made they were amazingly light and spongy, with a crisp crust and a sweet eggy flavour, absolutely ideal to enjoy fresh with either a cup of tea or a glass of wine. If hurriedly made, with insufficient beating, they failed to rise, and their sponge became decidedly chewy. Reputations were made or broken on the respective quality of a person's sponge cakes, so long as the tradition of home baking flourished in England.

White Cakes

1lb of Butter beaten to a cream, 9 Eggs leaving out the white of 3, 1lb of Flour well dried – 1lb of loaf sugar beat & sifted – the rind of a Lemon grated (also the juice when it is put into the the oven) ¼lb candied Lemon – 2oz of sweet & 2oz of bitter almonds. By adding ¼ of currants it will be an excellent 'fruit' cake. [14]

grated zest & juice of 1 lemon	*6oz/150g butter*
2oz/50g candied lemon peel	*6oz/150g sugar*
2oz/50g ground almonds	*3 eggs, beaten*
6oz/150g flour	*1tsp almond essence*
2oz/50g currants – optional	

Beat the butter to a cream, beat in the sugar until white and fluffy, then the eggs, little by little, and finally the lemon zest, lemon peel, almonds and, if chosen, the currants.

Line a 7ins/18cm cake tin with non-stick baking parchment, put in the mixture, levelling the top, and bake at 180°C, 350°F, Gas mark 4 for around 1 hour.

In the next recipe ground rice provides a pleasantly gritty texture, being an early version of the popular Victorian sand-cakes. It was considered to be an excellent cake for making trifles.

Rice Cake

15 Eggs leaving out 7 whites beat them well for an hour – add by degrees 1lb of loaf sugar beat & sifted with ½lb ground rice – beat in ¼ of an hour longer – butter the pan & bake it in a quick oven – don't fill the pan too full. [15]

6 eggs, less 3 whites	*4oz/150g ground rice*
6oz/150g caster sugar	

Line a 7ins/18cm cake tin with greaseproof paper, brush the inside with melted butter, and dust with a mixture of flour and caster sugar.

Beat the eggs until almost white, then beat in the sugar little by little, and finally the rice. Continue beating/whisking for 10 minutes, until the mixture is pale and foamy, then pour into the lined tin and place immediately into the oven pre-heated to 180°C, 350°F, Gas mark 4, baking it for 45 min. Allow to cool a little, and then remove the tin etc.

'Diet cakes' were very light cakes, suitable for delicate digestions, but their eggs and sugar were unlikely to encourage a loss of weight. Other contemporary versions suggest that either a little sugar should be sprinkled over them just before going into the oven, or that they should be iced when cold.[16]

Diet Bread Cake

Take a large Lemon & grate it into the yolks of seven Eggs ½lb of loaf sugar grated 4 whites of Eggs – beat the remainder for 20 minutes Stir in gently ½lb of flour bake it in a slow oven for ½ an hour – The yolks & whites must be beaten separate [17]

grated zest of a lemon	*4oz/100g caster sugar*
4 yolks & 2 whites of eggs	*4oz/100g flour*

Line a 7ins/18cm cake tin with buttered paper. Beat the yolks and sugar together for 10 min. until light and creamy. Beat the whites separately to a soft peak, and fold them into the yolks with the lemon zest. Sift the flour into the mixture, little by little, gently folding it in to form a smooth, light mixture. Pour this into the prepared cake tin, and bake at 150°C, 300°F, Gas mark 2 for some 40 min. until the top is a deep cream colour.

In March 1802 Dorothy Wordsworth baked a seedcake for her friend Mr.Simpson.[18] The distinctive flavour of caraway was greatly appreciated at this period, especially in sponge cakes enriched with butter, as in this recipe from Mrs Elizabeth Raffald of Manchester's *Experienced English Housekeeper* of 1769.

To make a rich Seed Cake

Take a pound of flour well dried, a pound of butter, a pound of loaf sugar beat and sifted, eight eggs, two ounces of carraway seeds, one nutmeg grated and its weight of cinnamon. First beat your butter to a cream, then put in your sugar. Beat the whites of your eggs half an hour, mix them with your sugar and butter. Then beat the yolks half an hour, put it to the whites, beat in your flour, spices and seeds a little before it goes to the oven. Put it in the hoop and bake for two hours in a quick oven and let it stand two hours. It will take two hours beating.[19]

8oz/225g plain flour	*8oz/225g butter*
1tsp grated nutmeg	*8oz/225g caster sugar*
1tsp ground cinnamon	*4 eggs, separated*
1oz/25g caraway seeds	

Line an 8ins/20cm cake tin with buttered paper. Beat the yolks until light and creamy, and the whites to a soft peak. Cream the butter with the sugar, fold in the whites, then the yolks, sprinkle in the caraway seeds and finally shake in the flour and spices little by little through a sieve, folding in to produce a soft mixture. Turn into the tin, and bake at 170°C, 325°F, Gas mark 3 for 1½ hours.

In the eighteenth century the word 'biscuit' was used not only for what we recognise as biscuits today, but also for what Americans now call cup-cakes or muffins. Some were baked in hand-pleated paper cases, while others went into 'pans', deep tart-tins made of either tinplate or salt-glazed stoneware.

Satin Biscuits [small cakes]

The yolks of 12 & the whites of 2 Eggs, beat them well with 2 spoonfuls of Rose water put them in a pound of loaf sugar beaten. stir it well – then add ¾lb flour well dried butter the pans & fill them ½ full.[20]

5 yolks and 1 white of fresh eggs	*8oz/225g caster sugar*
1tbs rosewater	*6oz/150g flour*

Butter a number of bun-tins, and dust with a mixture of caster sugar and flour. Beat the yolks, white and rosewater together, then gradually beat in the sugar, and continue beating until the mixture is very light, before folding in the flour very gently. Half-fill the bun-tins, and bake at 180°C, 350°F, Gas mark 4 for some 30 minutes.

Queen cakes were similar, but were baked in 'small saucers or fluted tins made for this purpose' or heart shaped tins.[21]

Queen Cakes

8 Eggs – 1lb loaf Sugar beat & sifted, whisk these together ½ an hour then add 1lb of flour dried 1lb of Butter beat smooth mix all together ½ an hour longer, Either put Currants, ½lb or Almonds & Candied Lemon, with a glass of brandy.[22]

2 eggs, beaten	2oz/50g currants or 2oz/50g
4oz/100g butter	ground almonds & candied peel
4oz/100g caster sugar	
4oz/100g flour 1tbs brandy	

Prepare a number of small bun-tins, about 2ins/5cm diameter, by brushing their interiors with melted butter and dusting them with a mixture of flour and caster sugar, knocking to remove the surplus.

Beat the eggs until they are in a pale, creamy state, fold in half the flour, then the butter beaten and warmed until semi-liquid, and finally the remaining flour and ingredients. Half-fill the pans and bake at 180°C, 350°F, Gas mark 4 for 20-25 minutes, allow to cool a little, then invert and tap, when they should fall free.

It is rather surprising to find instructions for jumbles in Joanna Hutchinson's recipe book, since these knotted biscuits originated as part of the sweetmeat banquet fare offered at well-to-do Elizabethan entertainments.

Jumballs

¼lb Butter beat to a cream ½lb flour dried ½lb loaf sugar beat & sifted, the rind of a lemon grated – a spoonful of Rose water-mix all together & make it into a paste with 2 Eggs – leave a little of the flour to make up the Cakes – let it stand 2 hours till stiff then make them up & bake them.[23]

2oz/50g butter	1½tsp rosewater
4oz/100g sugar	grated zest of ½ a lemon
1 egg, beaten	5oz/150g flour

Cream the butter with the sugar, then beat in the egg, rosewater and lemon zest, little by little, to form a smooth mixture, then fold in the sifted flour, little by little, and finally knead to make a soft dough. Set aside for 2 hours to firm up, then divide into pieces, roll out on a floured board to about ¾ins/2cm diameter and form into rings, knots (like pretzels), plaits etc. Place on a lightly greased baking sheet and bake at 180°C, 350°F, Gas mark 4 for 15-20 min.

In the late eighteenth and early nineteenth centuries macaroons had to be made from almonds still in their shells. Having been cracked open, their kernels were plunged into boiling water and allowed to cool, enabling their brown skins to be pinched off, and moistening their insides. After a preliminary chopping, they were ground in a mortar, great care having to be taken to ensure that their oil was not squeezed out, since this transformed them into an irrecoverable oily mass. Only when reduced to a smooth, stiff paste could they be used for marzipans or in bakery mixtures. Today it is far easier to use ground almonds instead.

Macaroons

To 1lb of blanched & beaten sweet Almonds put one lb. of sugar & a little rosewater then beat the white of 7 Eggs to a froth put them in & beat all well together drop it on wafer papers grate sugar over & bake them.[24]

5oz/150g ground almonds	*1tbs rosewater*
5oz/150g caster sugar	*2 whites of fresh eggs*

Mix the almonds, sugar and rosewater in a basin. Using another bowl, whisk the egg whites to stiffness then add the almonds etc. and fold all together to form a soft mixture. Using a teaspoon, scoop up portions and use the index finger to push them off onto a piece of rice paper (or baking parchment), leaving at least 1ins/2·5cm between each one.

Bake at 180°C, 350°F, Gas mark 4 for 20-25 min. until golden brown.

The final recipe for egg-raised cakes is for the lightest and most delicate of them all, meringues. It comes from the Frickers, being distinctly high-quality confectionery in comparison to the sound, though excellent, cakes and biscuits of the Hutchinsons.

Meranghes

Whisk the whites of nine Eggs to the rind of 6 lemons and a spoonful of Sugar to be put on a tin prepared for them, sift sugar over them and be very quick to put them in the oven, bake in a moderate oven, dry them on a dish before the fire, turning them first. Put sweetmeats between two.[25]

   3 medium sized fresh organic egg whites
   6oz/150g caster sugar   grated zest of 2 lemons

Grease 2 baking sheets or cover with non-stick parchment. Whisk the eggs until stiff, then whisk in half the sugar little by little, and then gently fold in the remaining sugar mixed with the lemon zest. Drop tablespoons of the mixture onto the baking trays, leaving a space of at least 1½ ins/4cm between each one, and lightly sprinkle with caster sugar.

Bake at 110°C, 225°F, Gas mark ¼ for about 2½ 3 hours, until firm and crisp, but not browned, then cool on a wire rack.

Just before serving stick the flat side of each pair together with a little sharply-flavoured fruit jam.

The word 'gingerbread' covers a number of quite different items of bakery, everything from a spongy ginger cake to a semi-hard semispherical 'nut', a crisp biscuit or 'snap', a 'brandy-snap', a moulded cake-cum-biscuit covered in gilt foil, or a small round cake baked in a tin and called a 'pigginbottom'. Barbara Grey's shop in Kendal stocked a number of these, her celebrated products including:

   'Her pigginbottoms, her brandysnaps,
   Her gingerbread cocks an' hens,
   An' men o' horseback decked i' gould
   They haa n't yan yet, by jems! &
   We nivver sall see sic a seet again
   As t' windo' at Barbr'y Gray's'.[26]

Fig 13. Barbara Grey's shop in Kendal stocked 'pigginbottoms' or spiced cakes baked in small tins, brandysnaps, and gingerbreads moulded as cocks and hens, and as men on horseback covered in gilt foil.

The Wordsworths bought their gingerbreads from Matthew Newton, 'the Blind Man', who earned his living by selling plants etc. In January 1803 Dorothy recorded how 'Wm had a fancy for some ginger bread. I put on Molly's Cloak and my Spenser and we walked towards Matthew Newton's. I went into the house. The blind Man and his Wife and Sister were sitting by the fire, all dressed very clean in their Sunday's Clothes, the sister reading. They took their little stock of gingerbread out of the cupboard and I bought 6 pennyworth. They were so grateful when I paid them for it that I could not find it in my heart to tell them we were going to make Gingerbread ourselves. I asked them if they had any thick 'No' answered Matthew 'there was none on Friday but we'll endeavour to get some.' The next Day the woman came just as we were baking and we brought 2 pennyworth.'[27] The thick gingerbread they were about to bake may have followed the usual form of 'block gingerbread' made throughout the northern counties, the following version being found in the recipe book of Rachel Whitwell of Kendal (1793-1833).

Gingerbread

*Flour & Treacle of each ¼St ½ Gill Brandy ½oz Carraway Seeds.
Do Clove Pepper, Do Ginger 2oz Butter 2oz Candied Lemon
½oz Pearl Ashes will be useful in making it rise [28]*

1lb/450g flour	3tbs brandy
½oz/12g candied peel	1lb/450g black treacle
1tsp bicarbonate of soda	½oz/12g butter
1½tsp each caraway seeds, ground ginger & allspice	

Line a loaf tin, or a 5ins/13cm square tin, with buttered
paper. Sift together the flour, spices and soda, rub in
the butter, add the peel, make a well in the centre, pour
the warmed treacle in the middle, with the brandy, mix
together, then knead until it is of an even colour. Pack into
the prepared tin, level the top, and bake at 140°C, 275°F,
Gas mark 1 for 2½ hours.

Both this and the next gingerbread emerge from the
oven with the hardness and density of a house-brick. They
should be wrapped in greaseproof paper and stored for
a month or two in a cold slightly damp larder or cellar to
mature and soften, and then sliced thinly and served with
a good white cheese, such as Wensleydale or creamy or
crumbly Lancashire.

Joanna Hutchinson's gingerbread has a lighter texture, provided by the
use of eggs, sugar and more butter:

Joanna Hutchinson's Ginger bread

*4lb Flour 2lb coarse sugar dried by the fire, 2lb of butter melted
in 2lb of Treacle, mix two eggs well beaten with 2 spoonfuls of
Brandy, put it into a dish & stir in the flour & sugar with some
beat Ginger beat it at least an hour or till it comes clear from the
bottom of the dish then set it by the fire till it is hot make it into
cakes & bake it upon untin'd papers, or tin sheets Dry a qr. of a
pound more flour to make the cakes up with.[29]*

8oz/225g black treacle
8oz/225g butter
2tbs beaten egg
1½tsp brandy

1lb/450g flour
8oz/225g Demarara sugar
3tbs ground ginger

Warm the treacle and butter in a large pan (or microwave in a ceramic bowl for 30 seconds) and stir together until blended, then mix in the egg and brandy. Work in the dry ingredients, until they form a mass of soft dough which does not stick to the sides. At modern room temperature this takes a few minutes, certainly not an hour.

Either weigh in 4oz/100g pieces, roll between the palms to form a ball, place three inches apart on a baking sheet, and bake at 150°C, 300°F, Gas mark 2 for 50 minutes, or pack 1ins/2·5cm deep in lined loaf or cake tins, and bake at the same temperature for 1½ hours.

Martha Fricker's recipe is also of the lighter variety, using 'Salts Tartar' as a raising agent, in addition to eggs, to give a rather more open and cake-like texture.

Receipt for Gingerbread

1¾lb Flour 1lb Treacle¼lb Butter1d pennyworth Ginger
1 Do Carraway Seeds half a pennyworth of Salts Tartar ¼lb
Brown Sugar 2 Eggs & if too stiff add 2 Tablespoonful of Milk.
Mix up well together & put into a tin
The Butter & Treacle put into a Jug and put into the oven until quite dissolved, stiring it occasionally [30]

12oz/350g flour
2tbs ground ginger
1tbs caraway seeds
2tsp cream of tartar
2oz/50g brown sugar

8oz/225g black treacle
2oz/50g butter
1 egg, beaten
2tbs milk

Line a loaf tin, or a 5ins/13cm square tin, with buttered paper. Mix all the dry ingredients in a bowl, and make a well in the centre. Place a small saucepan on the scales, weigh in the treacle, add the butter and stir over a gentle heat until combined. Allow to cool a little, then beat in the egg, pour the mixture into the bowl, and work in the flour etc. from the sides to form a dough, mixing in the milk to give a thick dropping consistency.

Pack into the prepared tin, level the top, and bake at 150°C, 300°F, Gas mark 2 for 1½ hours.

Gingerbread 'snaps' have to be kept perfectly dry in order to retain their essential crisp hardness. It is wise to try nibbling them before attempting a full bite, for they are far more solid than any modern ginger biscuit, but make up for this by having a richer flavour.

Gingerbread Snaps

Take 1 pound and half of Flour, and rub in ½ pound of Butter, one pound of coarse sugar & one ounce of Ginger beaten and sifted, mix the whole with 18 ounces of cold Treacle and a little Brandy – The Snaps will keep crisp any length of time in a Canister closely covered. [31]

12oz/350g flour	*2tbs ground ginger*
4oz/100g butter	*9oz/250g black treacle*
8oz/225g Demarara sugar	*1tbs brandy*

Rub the butter into the flour, mix in the sugar and ginger, make a well in the centre and pour in the treacle and brandy. Slip the hands into the flour beneath the treacle, and work the treacle into it, keeping the hands as free from the treacle as possible until all is combined into a firm even-coloured dough.

Roll out just over ⅛ins/·3cm thick, cut in 2-3ins/5-7·5cm rounds, and bake on greased baking sheets at 180°C, 350°F, Gas mark 4 for 20 minutes. Allow to cool before removing from the sheets.

Gingerbread [Snaps]

1½lb Treacle ½lb Sugar 9oz Butter Ginger to your taste A few cloves & a little lemon skin Rub the butter in as much flour as will make the paste stiff adding flour till it is so when you knead it. when the butter & treacle are stiff with cold put them within the air of the fire to soften. in warm weather this is not necessary. [32]

Gingerbread [Snaps] continued

12oz/350g flour	*12oz/350g black treacle*
4oz/100g butter	*2tbs ground ginger*
4oz/100g sugar	*¼tsp ground cloves*
grated rind of a lemon	

Make up and bake as for the previous recipe.

Gingerbread nuts, sometimes called hunting nuts since a number could be readily thrust into the pocket of a hunting jacket and eaten during the chase, were a rather more elegant form. The Frickers' recipe produces a much more open texture than any of the others reproduced here.

Gingerbread Nuts

Take 3 pounds of Flour, 1 pound of sugar, 1 pound &¼ of Butter, rubbed in very fine a large nutmeg grated 1oz &¾ of ginger, 2oz. of Carraway seeds, a few cloves, and a little mace and cinnamon beaten and sifted the rind of a large lemon grated mix all with the Flour melt a pint of Treacle with ¼ a pint of cream pour it into the Flour, & make it into a paste bake the nuts on Tin plates in a slack oven. [33]

12oz/350g flour	*¼tsp ground clove*
4oz/100g sugar	*¼tsp ground mace*
5oz/125g butter	*¼tsp ground cinnamon*
¼tsp grated nutmeg	*grated rind of a lemon*
4tsp ground ginger	*1lb/450g black treacle*
5tsp caraway seed	*tbs cream*

Rub the butter into the flour, and thoroughly mix in the dry ingredients. Just melt the treacle and cream together, without over-heating, and pour into a well in the flour etc. Mix in the flour from the sides until all is incorporated into a soft dough.

Lightly grease baking sheets, scoop up portions of the dough with a spoon, roll between the palms to form 1ins/2·5cm balls, and drop them on the sheets leaving about 1ins/2·5cm between each one. Bake at 180°C, 350°F, Gas

Above: Pace Eggs by James Dixon, general handyman, gardener and butler to the Wordsworths at Rydal Mount.

Below: Pages from Joanna Hutchinson's recipe book.

Top Left: A traditional char pot. Potted in such jars, the local fish were despatched in quantity to distant markets.

Top Right: The Wordsworths were used to fine tea-wares; Dorothy's cup and saucer survive in the collection at Dove Cottage.

Left: Wordsworth's "bait" tin contained the poet's sandwiches on fishing days.

Above: Jellies were always popular. Here, clockwise from the left, are a Madeira calf's foot jelly, a blancmange, a jaune mange, stone cream, orange jelly and strengthening jellies, all surrounding sponge creams.

Above: On Christmas Day 1805 plum puddings such as this were 'Rumbling in the pot' at Dove Cottage.

Below: Teatime cakes. Here are, from the back, thick and moulded gingerbreads, a rice cake, rice cake jumbles and cheesecakes.

mark 4 for 20 minutes, remove from the oven and allow to cool a little before transferring onto wire cooling racks.

On 6th November, 1800, Dorothy Wordsworth baked parkins.[34] The date is significant, for in the industrial West Riding, the centre of the north country parkin tradition, they had already become associated with Bonfire Night on November 5th ('Parkin Day' in Leeds), and was eaten over the next few days. [35] It would appear that Dorothy was following the practices of her mother's cousin, Miss Elizabeth Threlkeld of Halifax, with whom she spent her girlhood after her mother's death in 1778. Here, along with Miss Threlkeld's extended household of other orphaned nieces and nephews, parkins must have formed one of the most popular of all seasonal treats.

Parkins

7oz/200g medium oatmeal	*1tsp bicarbonate of soda*
7oz/200g flour	*8oz/225g black treacle*
1oz/25g brown sugar	*1oz/25g lard*
1½tsp ground ginger	*1oz/25g butter*

Thoroughly mix the oatmeal, flour, sugar, ginger and soda in a bowl, and make a well in the centre. Weigh the treacle into a saucepan, add the lard, butter, and 1tbs water, and stir over a gentle heat until just melted. Pour into the dry ingredients and stir until thoroughly mixed to form a soft dough.

Use a dessert spoon to form into balls about 2ins/5cm diameter, and place on a greased baking sheet leaving some 2ins/5cm between each one to allow them to spread. Bake at 150°C, 300°F, Gas mark 2 for 45 minutes, then remove onto a wire rack to cool. [36]

The American-style cheesecake, that heavy slab of creamy solidity mounted on a crushed-biscuit base found in every supermarket, has nothing in common with the English varieties, except for its name. In the north country cheesecakes came in the form of tartlets, their short pastry crusts being filled with the jam-like lemon curd or lemon cheese, with custardy rice mixtures, or, particularly in Yorkshire, with curds mixed with sugar, currants, nutmeg and eggs.

Lemon Cheesecakes

Lemon cheese, made to the recipe on page 142[37]

*Short pastry made with 8oz/225g flour, 2oz/50g butter and
2oz/50g lard, a pinch of salt, and about 3-4 tbs cold water.*

Use the pastry to line a dozen tart tins, fill with baking beans, and bake at 200°C, 400°F, Gas mark 6 for 10-15 min., remove the beans, return to the oven for 5 min. and allow to cool. Half fill the tarts with the lemon cheese, and return to the oven at 180°C, 350°F, Gas mark 4 for 5-10 minutes, before removing and leaving to cool.

Joanna's recipe for a rice cheesecake is amongst the most unusual in this collection, its combination of ingredients being unlike almost any of those found in the most popular cookery books of the period. The results, even if baked with skill, certainly fall into the category of 'interesting', rather than 'good'.

Rice Cheese Cakes

Boil 4oz of rice, put it in a sieve to drain 4 Eggs well beaten, ½lb Butter ½ pint of Cream, 6oz of Sugar nutmeg, a glass of Ratafia or Brandy, beat well together, & bake them in paste.[38]

1oz/25g pudding rice	*⅛pt/75ml double cream*
2oz/50g butter	*1tbs brandy*
1½oz/35g sugar	*⅛tsp grated nutmeg*
1 egg, beaten	
shortcrust pastry made from :	
8oz/225g flour, 4oz/100g butter (or lard, or ½ butter,	
½ lard), and 3-4 tbs cold water.	

Use the pastry to prepare a dozen blind-baked tarts as in the previous recipe. Simmer the rice in ½pt/300ml water for about 20 min. until tender, then drain. Cream the butter and sugar, beat in the eggs little by little, and beat in the cream, brandy and nutmeg. The butter in this recipe will separate out unless the mixture is very well beaten at every stage. Stir in the rice, ³/₄ fill the tarts and bake at

150°C, 300°F, Gas mark 2 for 20-25 min. until the tops are
a pale golden brown.

Throughout the Wordsworths' years at Grasmere and Rydal, most of
the working population of the Lake District still relied heavily on the
local, home-baked oatcake, as they had probably done for millennia.
Oats were still grown here, flourishing far better than wheat, and,
after being dried, were ground between gritstone stones in all the
smaller mills, the Wordsworths' supply almost certainly coming from
Tongue Gill Mill, on the Dunmail Raise side of Grasmere. At their
cottage, they appear to have used oats only to make their porridge, but
they certainly enjoyed the oatcakes offered to them by neighbours,
farmer's wives etc. When visiting the last farmhouse in Martindale,
for example, William was grateful for the 'welcome refreshment [to
which] the good woman treated us with oaten cake, new and crisp'.[39]
Dorothy was even more appreciative:

> 'And as for her, why Miss Wudsworth, she wad come into t'
> back kitchen an exe for a bit of oatcake and butter. She was
> fond of oatcake, and butter till it, fit to steal it a' most.'[40]

Compared to the Scottish oatcakes with which most people are now
familiar, that of the Lake District was of a distinctly superior quality. To
make it, the fresh-ground meal was first carefully sieved to extract the
finest oat-flour, the remainder being used for bannocks or porridge.
A small quantity was then mixed into a stiff dough with a little
warm water and clapped out on a wooden board until about twenty
inches/50cm in diameter and about one-sixteenth of an inch/2mm
in thickness. Since oats contain hardly any gluten, the ability to make
such cakes without them breaking up or cracking was a feat of real
skill, only acquired by being brought up to it from girlhood. Originally
they were baked by being slid onto a large flat slab of fireproof stone
supported a few inches above a peat fire on the hearth. The local source
of these was probably at the appropriately-named High Bakestones
between Scandale Fell and Dove Crag, three miles to the north-west of
Grasmere, as the crow flies. By the nineteenth century, however, many
had been replaced by large round plates of cast iron.[41] Although not of
the same size, oatcakes of the same thickness, crispness and flavour
can still be made today, using the following traditional recipe:-

Fig 14. The oatmeal for the oatcakes which Dorothy enjoyed at local farms, as well as for their breakfast porridge, was probably ground here at Tongue Ghyll Mill, just off the road from Grasmere towards Dunmail Raise. This drawing is by Sara Hutchinson, Wordsworth's niece.

Oatcake

4oz/100g fine oatmeal (Purchase 'fine oatmeal' from health food shops etc., pass it though a fine sieve to extract the fine 'flour', and retain the rest for making porridge etc.)

Place the sieved oat 'flour' into a small bowl and stir in a pinch of salt. Place a jug on the scales, weigh in 2oz/50g of tepid water, pour this into the oats, mix in and then knead rapidly to form a uniform dough. Scatter a thin layer of sieved oatmeal onto a board, place the ball of dough in the centre, and pat it out to form a 3ins/8cm disc, then press the centre down with the fingertips until about one sixteenth of an inch/2-3mm in thickness. Rotate it on its bed of dry oatmeal while extending the size to the thin central area, maintaining a thick even rim until it is about 8-9ins/20-22cm in diameter, then flatten the rim, and roll lightly to ensure an even thickness. By now it should be over 10ins/25cm in diameter. Place an upturned dinner plate on top, and cut off the uneven edges, to produce a perfect circle.

Place a circular iron girdle over a gentle heat until a sprinkling of flour browns very slowly, but does not smoke. Brush off the flour, very lightly grease the girdle, slide on the oatcake, using a piece of thick paper or thin card to transfer it from the board, and leave to cook until crisp, with slightly raised edges, but not browned. Finally remove from the girdle, and cool on a wire tray.

If no girdle is available, the oatcake may be slid onto a baking tray, and baked at 180°C, 350°F, Gas mark 4 for 15 min. Remove from the tray and leave to cool on a wire tray.

Chapter Seven

OF SWEETS

At the opening of the nineteenth century most large towns had a number of confectioners making fruit drops, comfits, tablets, candies, chocolates, lozenges, fruit pastes and mint cakes. Theirs was a highly-skilled profession, requiring specialist knowledge and equipment, but a number of the simpler sweets could be easily made in ordinary homes. Cumbrian youngsters used to enjoy 'Taffy-joinin's' for example, clubbing their pennies together to buy treacle etc. for a winter evening's toffee-making, at which the smearing of each other's faces provided great fun.[1]

Toffee

Take 4oz: of Butter, 4 of Sugar, and 4 of Treacle, half the rind of a large lemon grated and a quarter of a teaspoonful of pounded ginger mix them all together and boil them over a slow fire until the Toffee becomes crisp (which you must ascertain by dropping a little of it into cold water) then pour it into a Tin and cut it out when cold.[2]

4oz/100g butter	*grated zest of ½ lemon*
4oz/100g sugar	*¼tsp ground ginger*
4oz/100g black treacle	

Rub the base and sides of a shallow baking tin with a little butter, and set aside. Boil the remaining ingredients together, stirring constantly over a gentle heat, until a drop plunged into cold water rapidly forms a hard ball. Pour into the tin, allow to cool, then break up when completely set.

Alternatively the top may be marked out into squares when half-set using a buttered knife, so that it may be easily broken up into neat pieces when cold.

The Fricker family made two other sweets which may now be served at the end of a meal, or at parties. The first, called 'Strengthening Jelly' is an original form of wine-gum which slowly releases its rich flavour and alcohol as it dissolves in the mouth.

Strengthening Jelly

2oz of Isinglass, 2oz brown sugar, 1oz Gum arabic, 1 small nutmeg grated, the above to be boiled in a quart of Port or very good white wine, then strained when cold cut into small pieces the size of a nutmeg, & one occasionally put into the mouth.[3]

1tbs brown (Demarara) sugar	*4tsp gelatin*
½pt/300ml port or strong white wine	*¼ grated nutmeg*

Mix the ingredients in a pan, set aside for 5 minutes, then stir and heat until the gelatin and sugar have completely dissolved. Strain through a piece of muslin into jug, and leave until lukewarm, then pour into a metal or thin plastic box some 4-5ins/10-15cm square, and leave in a cool place until set firmly.

Dip the box briefly in warm water, and turn the jelly out on to a piece of wet muslin or greaseproof paper, and use a knife dipped in hot water to cut it into ½ins/1·5cm squares, arranging these separately on a serving dish or plate.

The second has a lemon or orange flavour, lightened by being whipped just before being left to set;

Sponge Cream

One ounce & ½ of Isinglass dissolved in a pint of water, the rind and juice of three large lemons, one orange, rather more than half a pound of loaf sugar, which rub upon the lemon and orange peel, mix all together and whisk it an hour when cold cut it in square pieces.[4]

9tsp gelatin	*8oz/225g lump sugar*
3 lemons	*1 orange*

Sprinkle then stir the gelatin into 1pt/600ml cold water, leave for 5 min., then stir in a pan over a gentle heat, or microwave for 1 min., until it has dissolved, then set aside. Rub the sugar lumps on the lemon and orange peels to extract their oils and colour, then squeeze their juice (which should produce ½pt/150ml), and strain it through a piece of muslin. Add both the sugar and the juice to the gelatin mixture, and stir (gently warming if necessary) until completely dissolved, then set aside until cold and just beginning to set.

Turn the jelly into a metal bowl set in a bowl of iced water and whisk until it has turned into a white foam. Pour into a deep metal tray or loaf tin in a ¾ins/2cm deep layer, leave in a cool place to set overnight, then turn out onto a sheet of wet muslin or greaseproof paper, and use a knife dipped into warm water to cut it into cubes. Arrange these on a dish, and serve.

Chapter Eight

OF PRESERVES & PICKLES

Today we can enjoy most foods throughout each year, but this has been achieved only through the development of freezing, canning and the rapid international transport of fresh foods. In the opening years of the nineteenth century there was still a great reliance on locally-grown seasonal foods, many of which were only available for a few weeks at a time. In order to enable them to be enjoyed beyond this period, the methods of home-preservation were quite limited, sugar being the main preservative for fruit, and salt and/or vinegar for vegetables. Some attempts were made to keep fruits etc. without any of these additives, in order to retain their original flavours intact as can be seen in this recipe. Boiling in bottles sterilised them very effectively, but the use of corks and rosin to provide an airtight seal was not particularly reliable, and if they failed, the contents would quickly decay.

Green gooseberries to Bottle

gather gooseberries before full grown, pick and put them into clean bottle with as much cold water as the Bottles (when nearly full of gooseberries) will hold. set them without corks into a pan of cold water over the fire, let them remain 'till scalded take them out when cold, cork & Rosin the Bottles
NB. if the Bottles are full they will burst.[1]

However, the success-rate of this method was greatly increased when sugar was added to the fruit. Not only did this form an excellent preserving syrup, but it also provided the housewife or housekeeper with a new convenience food.

Dorothy Wordsworth used sugar when preserving her gooseberries in August 1800, but, although in her late 20s, was still uncertain as to the best proportions of sugar to fruit. She therefore decided to experiment, noting in her journal 'Boiled gooseberries N.B. 2lbs of sugar in the first panful, 3 quarts all good measure 3lbs in the 2nd 4 quarts 2¹/₂lbs in the third.'[2] Assuming that all were bottled and sealed while still scalding hot, she should have had good results with each batch, only varying in their relative sweetness. Now she could open a bottle or jar whenever required to provide a dish of sweet, cooked fruit ready to be eaten with cream, to garnish a dessert, to fill pies, or to go into puddings. Other fruits could be preserved in the same way: These are Joanna's recipes.

Green Gage Plumbs

Put the plumbs (not quite ripe) into a Pan of Spring Water with the vine leaves, set them on a slow fire, when the skins begin to rise take them off & skin them carefully, put them on a sieve as you do them, then put them into the same water, cover them close & hang them at a great distance from the fire till they are green, which will be 5 or 6 hours at least. drain them. make a good syrup & give them a gentle boil in it twice a day for 4 days [before bottling][3]

Green Apricots to preserve

Gather the Apricots before the stones are hard, put them in a Pan of spring water with vine leaves, set them over a slow fire till yellow, take them out, rub them with a flannel & salt to take off the peal, put them into the same water & leaves cover them close, set them by the fire till they are yellow, then take them carefully out, and boil them two or three times in a thin syrup, when they look plump & clear make a thicker syrup of fine sugar. & give the apricots a quick boil in it.
N.B. for Tarts boil them in the first syrup.[4]

To preserve fruit of any kind

Gather the fruit when dry & to a pint of fruit take ¼lb Lump sugar (or fine soft will do), put the fruit & sugar into jars or wide necked Bottles a layer of sugar and a layer of fruit.
Tye the jars down with wet bladders, set them in a pan of cold water on the fire. let it boil full half an hour, or until you think the fruit is enough done. Take it off the fire and let the jars stand in it until it is stone cold, then cover the bladders with double paper. Apples, Pears, Siberian Crabs, may be done in this way.[5]

Mary Wordsworth used this method to preserve their damsons, this popular local fruit thus being converted from a sour plum into one of the most succulent luscious and richly flavoured of all preserves. It is well worth the effort of making today, either to serve cold with cream or ice-cream, hot with custard, or baked either in a pie or under a crumble.

[To Preserve Damsons]

To one pt of Damsons put 6oz of Sugar, tie the bottles over with bladders & bake after the bread is drawn [6]

Damsons Sugar

Fill a number of screw-topped jam jars with damsons, and shake in enough sugar to cover them (this gives the same proportions of fruit to sugar as the original recipe). Place, without lids, on baking trays, and bake at 150°C, 300°F, Gas mark 2 for some 30 min. by which time all the sugar should have dissolved to form a rich maroon syrup, and the damsons have split their skins. Remove from the oven, allow to cool a little, then screw on their sterilised lids.

The Wordsworths also made their own Seville Orange marmalade from fruit imported from Spain and Portugal. The earlier form of English marmalade had been a thick paste made from whole oranges, sometimes boiled with pippins, but the potted jam type, with strips of the peel added to give a more interesting texture and flavour, had already been adopted here by the 1670s. [7]

Marmalade

An equal weight of the cleanest Seville oranges & loaf Sugar Take off the rinds, boil them until Tender Scrape all the pulp from skin and seed. When the rinds are sufficiently boild 1½ hours cut them as thin as possible wiping the knife often else it will make them black. Put rind, pulp & juice in a preserving pan with the sugar boil over a slow fire about 40 or 50 minutes put it jars [cover?] when cold with brandy papers & tie them down close [8]

Seville oranges, and their weight of sugar.

Remove the peels from the oranges, and simmer these in plenty of water for about an hour until tender. Drain, allow to cool, and use a spoon to scrape off most of the pith, and cut the rind into narrow shreds. Slice the oranges thinly, removing the seeds and surplus pith, put into a pan with the shredded peel, sugar, and enough water to cover them, and stew gently for 40-50min. until they have come to a dark, jam-like consistency. If too thick, a little water may be added as they cook. Pour into sterilised jars and seal down.

Lemon curd, or lemon cheese, was probably the most popular lemon preserve. Both lemons and sugar were imported directly into the Fricker sisters' home town of Bristol:

Lemon Cheese

Grate the rind of 3 Lemons, then add the juice, & mix with it 8 ounces of Loaf sugar, 4?ounces of butter the yolks of 6 and the whites of 4 eggs well beaten set it over the fire in a saucepan, - keep stirring it until quite dissolved, and it begins to thicken take great care not to let it brown.

Then pour it into jars for use cover it like preserves with paper dipped in brandy, when you make Cheesecakes lay paste in your pattypans and half fill them with the mixture.
N.B. this mixture will keep a long time in jars well covered, in a cool place. [9]

3 small or 2 large lemons	*3oz/75g butter*
8oz/225g sugar	*4 yolks & 3 whites of egg*

Grate the zest from the lemons, put it into a saucepan with their strained juice, the sugar, butter and beaten and strained eggs. Stir continuously over a gentle heat until the mixture has thickened, then pour into sterilised jars, seal down, and keep for use, either for making lemon cheesecakes (*see p.126*), as a spread, or as a sauce on hot puddings, cold cheesecakes or ice-cream.

Jelly made from red or white currants was useful either as a preserve, or as an accompaniment to both hot and cold cooked meats. Joanna Hutchinson's recipe cooks the currants with sugar before passing them through a flannel filter bag,but this is a very slow process, particularly when it is cold. For this reason the modernised version below only adds the sugar after the juice has already been extracted and filtered.

Red or white Currant Jelly

Pick the currants very clean, to 1lb of fruit, 1lb of loaf sugar pounded, mix it in a pan, set them on a slow fire, stirring all the time, let it boil 5 minutes, then pass it thro' a flannel Bag into Glasses.[10]

1lb/450g red or white currants   1lb/450g sugar

Stew the currants with ⅓pt/200ml water for about 30 min. stirring from time to time to prevent them from sticking, then pour into a jelly bag or cloth hung over a clean pan and leave for about 12 hours. Add the sugar to the juice, heat gently while stirring, until it has dissolved, then boil rapidly for about 15 min., skimming it carefully. Test a little on a cold saucer, until it reaches setting point, then pour into sterilised jars and seal down.

Some imported preserves, such as ginger in syrup, were quite expensive. This led would-be fashionable housewives and housekeepers to make their own by flavouring lettuce stalks with ground ginger and sugar. The following version from Mary Wordsworth's recipe book is quite typical:

Artificial Ginger

When the Cos Lettuces are running to seed cut off the leaves & peel the stalks till quite clear cut them in pieces & throw them into water as you do them wash well – & have ready a syrup of sugar & water 5 pints to a lb & with some powdered Ginger tied up in a bag boil for 20 minutes set it aside for 2 days boil again for ½ an hour repeat the boiling 5 or 6 times leaving a day or two between then drain it & wipe the pieces quite dry make a syrup (a lb to a pint of water) of sugar & [mix] with a good deal of ginger well scraped & sliced boil it in them 2 or 3 times till quite clear & taste like Indian Ginger. at the last boiling put in the peel & juice of one Lemon.[11]

There were three distinct varieties of vinegar available from Georgian grocers and oilmen, the true vinegars made from either red or white wine, and the alegar made from malted liquors, which we know today as malt vinegar. All were useful preservatives and condiments, the wine vinegars giving more gentle and refined flavours than the much more robust alegars. However, since many households took pride in their self-sufficiency, and wished to avoid the probably dangerously adulterated purchased supplies, it was quite usual for families such as the Hutchinsons and Frickers to make their own:

Vinegar (Mrs Charlton's)

1¼lbs of coarse brown Sugar to every Gal. of Water, boil & skin it, pour it into a Tub to cool, when milk warm put it into the Cask with a little Yeast, set it in the Sun. Cover the Bung hole with a brown paper full of holes.[12]

Sugar Vinegar

one pound and a half of sugar, to one gallon of water boil it half an hour put it into a Tub to ferment with a little Barm upon a Toast for two days, put it into a Barrel, bung it up (not too close). Let it stand in a warm place until sour then bottle it.[13]

Pickles must have played a useful role in planning meals at Dove Cottage, enlivening the previously roasted and boiled joints when they reappeared cold over the next day or two, in addition to providing a fashionable accompaniment to the more formal dinners prepared for visiting friends. Compared to most of today's pickles, those of late Georgian England were very highly spiced, using the same ingredients and similar recipes to those that East India Company employees had first experienced during their sojourns on the sub-continent. The yellow pickle made by the Hutchinson sisters is typical in the use of salt to remove the surplus moisture from its vegetables and the use of a heavily-spiced alegar as a combined flavouring and preservative. The appearance of long pepper is a little unexpected, for it had gone out of general use in English cookery in the early seventeenth century, and never regained its former popularity. Sharper, hotter and sweeter than black pepper and in catkin-like spikes of tiny seeds about 2½ins/6cm long, it came from two separate species of shrub, one from the Himalayan foothills and southern India, and the other from

Java and Malaysia. In the late eighteenth century it became available again through the East India trade, but today can be very difficult to find. For this reason, it has been replaced by black pepper in the modernised recipe below.

Yellow Pickle

Take Cabbage, Carrots, Turnips, Cauliflowers, Apples, or any thing else you like, cut them into pieces, put them in a pan of boiling water for a minute, then drain them put them into a close pot with a good quantity of salt, press them down with a Weight let them remain for three days then dry them in the sun or by the fire 2 q.ts of Alegar, 2oz. Ginger, 2oz. White Mustard seed, 1oz. Long Pepper, 2oz garlic, 1oz White Pepper & plenty of Cayenne and a little Turmeric (steeped in vinegar & strained) to colour the vegetables The Pickle need not be boiled [14]

1lb/450g each of cabbage, carrot, turnip, cauliflower, and apple, cut in pieces around ½ ¾ins/1·5 2cm cubes	
2tsp white peppercorns	1pt/600ml malt vinegar
½oz/12g root ginger, sliced	6oz/150g salt
1tsp turmeric	2tsp black pepper
4tsp white mustard seed	½tsp cayenne pepper
4 cloves of garlic, sliced	

Bring a large pan of water to the boil, put in a batch of vegetables for a minute, then use a sieve or a pierced spoon to remove them into a bowl. Boil further batches in the same way, then leave the vegetables until quite cold. Layer the vegetables and the salt in a cylindrical saucepan, put a plate on top, then a weight, and leave in a cool place for the next 3 days.

Meanwhile divide the vinegar between two jars, stirring the turmeric into one, and the remaining spices in the other, cover, and leave to soak. Finally, drain the vegetables, pat them dry using a towel, and pack into jars. Pass the turmeric vinegar through a coffee filter paper, mix with the spiced vinegar, and use to fill up the jars before sealing them down. This crisp, hot and spicy pickle may be used after a couple of weeks.

In common with most recipes for pickled mushrooms, this version from Joanna Hutchinson's notebook imbues their usual mild flavour with one much more pungent and spicy. If a more subtle pickle is preferred, replace the 'alegar' with white wine vinegar.

Pickled Mushrooms (brown)

Rub the Mushrooms with a flannel & Alegar; 2qts. of good Strong Alegar, 4 spoonfuls of salt, ¼oz. Mace, ½oz Nutmegs, 2 drams Cayenne Pepper, ¼lb Anchovies, washed & picked, a large Lemon Peel, ½oz. Cloves put in the Mushrooms when the pickle boils, & let them simmer 20 minutes.[15]

Contents of a 50g tin of anchovies, drained	
1½lb/675g button mushrooms	1tsp salt
½ a nutmeg, finely chopped & rinsed	½tsp mace
1pt/600ml malt vinegar	10 cloves
pared zest of ½ lemon	⅛tsp cayenne pepper

Use a cloth or sponge dipped in vinegar to rub all smuts etc. from the mushrooms, rubbing from the top downwards to avoid tearing the skin and gills. Bring the remaining ingredients to the boil, add the mushrooms, and simmer for 20 min. Pack the mushrooms into jars, cover with the liquid, and seal down. They may be used either immediately, or over the following year.

The lemon pickle used to accompany curries in India was often replicated in English middle-class kitchens, using imported lemons and spices. Early eighteenth century recipes are for relatively simple methods, such as boiling in salted water and potting in white wine vinegar.[16] By 1800 the lemons were being salted, dried, spiced and pickled in processes taking around three months, after which some cooks discarded the lemons, retaining their liquor for flavouring white or brown sauces: 'It is a most useful pickle, and give a fine flavour to whatever it is to be used in. But remember always to put it in before you thicken the sauce, or put in any cream, lest the sharpness should make it curdle, which will spoil your sauce.'[17] In the modernised version below, the lemons are slowly dried in the oven rather than by sunlight, the latter commodity always being unpredictable in England, and even more so in the Lake District. Oven drying was also recommended by

John Farley, cook to the famous London Tavern, in his popular book *The London Art of Cookery*, first published in 1783.[18]

To pickle Lemons

Take 12 Lemons cut them across into 4 parts downwards but not quite thro', then put in as much salt as they will hold, rub them well & strew them over with it, let them lie in an Earthen Dish in the Sun & turn them every day, cut an oz. of Ginger very thin & 12 cloves of garlic salted for 3 days a small handful of Mustard Seed bruised one Pod of Red Indies Pepper to every Lemon, take the Lemons when dry, put them into a jar with juice & other ingredients, & cover with best white wine Vinegar They will be ready for use in 4 months, add Vinegar as the Pickle is used.[19]

½pt/300ml white wine vinegar	*6 lemons*
6oz/150g large crystal sea salt	*6 dried red chillies or*
½oz/12g root ginger, sliced thin	*1tsp cayenne pepper*
6 cloves of garlic, peeled	*2tbs mustard seed*

Take each lemon in turn, hold it upright with the stalk end uppermost, and make two diametric cuts almost down to the pointed top, to divide it into four equal segments. Ease the joints open, pack them with the salt, place in a baking dish, and leave to rest overnight.

Next day bake at 110°C, 225°F, Gas mark ¼ for 2 hours, and leave until perfectly cold. Very gently squeeze most of the juice (not the pulp) from each lemon, then strain all the liquid through a muslin-lined sieve to remove the surplus salt. Pack the lemons into one or two jars, pour in the strained juice, add the garlic, spices and bruised mustard seed, top up with the vinegar, seal down, and keep in a cool place for 4 months before using.

This lemon pickle has a remarkable saline/sour taste much more characteristic of oriental than English cuisine. In contrast, the practice of pickling unripe walnuts, as carried on here from the early eighteenth century, produces a rather fuller, spicier flavour. [20]

Walnuts to Pickle

Prick the Walnuts with a pin, put them in soft water, change it every day for a month, then put them in strong salt & water for a fortnight then take them out & wipe them clean Take vinegar Ginger, black pepper (Garlic) & any other warm seasoning boil them all with the vinegar & pour it upon the Walnuts, heat it 3 or 4 times & put it upon the Walnuts before they are closed up.[21]

Walnuts, salt, malt vinegar, root ginger, black pepper, garlic

The young green walnuts must be picked before the end of June, after which their shells become too hard for pickling. Wearing rubber gloves to prevent the hands being stained, prick each walnut all over with a long, strong needle. The preliminary 1 month soaking may be replaced by brining twice, soaking them in a brine of 3oz/75g salt to each pint/·5l of water for one week, then putting them in a fresh batch of the same strength of brine for a second week, then drain and wipe dry.

Make spiced vinegar by boiling ½oz/12g bruised root ginger, ½tsp black pepper and 3 cloves of garlic, chopped, to each pint of vinegar for 10 minutes, then leaving it to cool. Pack the walnuts into jars, cover with the strained vinegar, seal down and leave for 6 to 8 weeks before using.

Chapter Nine

OF CHEESE & CURDS

D airying in most Lakeland farms was carried out almost as much to serve the statesmen and their families as it was to produce a cash income. Much of the milking took place in the fields,some Cumbrian farms growing 'milkin' rings' of overhanging trees or bushes, usually holly, to provide a sheltered area for milking their cows in hot weather, one being noted at Causeway Foot near Keswick.[1] Having been carried back to the farm in wooden piggins or pails, the milk was strained through a muslin-based 'sile' into broad pans, and left overnight to allow the cream to rise to the surface. This was then removed by being blown off into a cream-kit.[2] Most of the cream was preserved by being converted into butter, cream-cheeses or cream curds, and much of the remaining blown- or blue-milk into either 'whangy cheese', or 'cum't milk', a dish made by curdling it with rennet.[3] The best farmhouse cheeses were made of whole milk curdled with rennets made from either the cured fourth stomach of a calf called a keslop skin, or the juice of Lady's Bedstraw, Galium verum, locally known as 'cheese-rennet'.[4] The curds were then placed in a muslin-lined cylindrical open-topped tub called a cheese-ring, and pressed to remove the remaining whey. Weighing some 10 to 12lbs each, these cheeses were then either stored for home use, or sold at the nearest markets.[5] It would have been cheese of this kind that the Wordsworths would have enjoyed with home-made bread when calling at John Stanley's at the King's Head, Thirlspot.[6]

Since there was neither space nor time to keep even a house-cow at Dove Cottage, all the milk and cream they required had to be bought in. In February 1802 Jenny Dockray brought a present of milk from her farmhouse at either Underhow or Butterlip How on the Easedale road. This appears to have been their main source of dairy produce, for in November 1801 Dorothy recorded how: 'We walked into Easedale to gather mosses and fetch cream. I went for the cream and sat under a wall. It was piercing cold and a hail storm came in the afternoon.'[7] On 30th April, 1802 a much more regular supply was obtained when Dorothy 'Began to get Milk from F. Baty's 1d in the Evening', Frank Baty, or Bateman, living nearby at Town End.[8] In the spring of 1804, when Molly Fisher took over the running of her brother's house on the opposite side of the road to Dove Cottage, she also looked after his single cow. This probably provided a more convenient source, including cream for Johnny Wordsworth's porridge and presents of pounds of butter.[9] A couple of years later William's one surviving daughter Dora would see the theme of her nursery rhyme 'Cushy cow bonny, let down thy milk' enacted here by Old Molly.[10] Shortly after the Wordsworths moved into Allan Bank in 1808 the newly-available land and staff made it possible for them to acquire a house-cow, Dorothy telling Clarkson in December that 'We keep a cow the stable is two short field lengths from the house, and the cook has both to fodder and clean after the cow.'[11] This provided all the household's milk and cream, the latter being churned to supply butter too.[12]

The introduction of dairying into the Wordsworth household was undoubtedly due to the previous experience of the Hutchinson sisters, who had kept house-cows for many years at Sockburn, and Gallow Hill. Their depth of knowledge is admirably demonstrated by the following advice which Sara sent to Mary Monkhouse who was apparently setting up a dairy at Tom Hutchinson's farm at Hindwell, Radnorshire:

> & as the for Churn I can do nothing for you the one Mr. Taylor recommended was Beetham's (patent Churn I believe) he lives in London But I dare say there are by this time improvements upon it Mr Taylor's only churn 12lb and a churn of that shape to churn only a firkin [56lb] would be very awkward I saw one advertised in the Courier yesterday; but it was a patent one also - & only made in Lancashire J. Woods, Ormskirk - It is worked by a lever with a weight & grit & performs more work with it than 2 women in the same time without it & price £2.12.6. What kind of Churns are used in the County? I would on no account advise you to get one that does not work with a Churn staff next to this a barrel churn is best that turns round altogether but then it requires most art in churning - & some people always churn ill with them (our Betty for instance).[13]

Getting a good dairymaid, ideally one with cold hands that did not spoil the butter, was to remain a problem. As Mary explained to Sara, then at Grassy Nook near Stockton on Tees,

'I dropped the thought of a servant from you as soon as I had sent my [last] letter off, for it occurred to me that a Durham or Yorkshire lass would not do in our cowhouse we have not got one nor heard of any.'[14]

By 1811, now transferred to Grasmere Rectory, the dairying activities were expanded by buying more cows to serve the needs of the family, as well as producing a surplus for sale. In early May, 1812, after a winter on hay, and before the benefits of new grass began to show, Dorothy noted that 'The cows do not give so much milk as they did, but very well considering we expect to sell butter this week. It is 14d pr. lb. As we have plenty of hay it is very well we kept the great cow & We have already got a guinea's worth of butter from her besides the calf a guinea and about 4/- new milk at Mr. Crump's, besides all the blue milk which we have sold, and we have not yet got a pig.'[15] The butter was made up for sale using carved wooden moulds called prints. While staying at Hindwell in October 1814, Dorothy received a note from young Dora, reminding her that 'Mary Dawson said I was to tell you not to forget the butter prints' which were to be used for this purpose.[16]

If butter was to be preserved either for sale or for use over winter, it had a little more salt than usual beaten into it and was packed down into airtight containers, barrels for large quantities, and ceramic jars for small, especially on a domestic scale. Martha Fricker used the following brining technique:

To Pot Butter

1 Teaspoonful of Salt Petre, to two Teaspoonfuls of white & finely beaten sugar & three spoonfuls of salt. To be pounded & boiled up with a little water, & when cold, poured on the Jar of butter, & covering close to the top of the Jar.[17]

The making of large hard cheeses was impractical in such a small household, but more delicate soft cheeses provided a pleasant addition to the Wordsworths' regular diet. The following recipe comes from Mary's recipe book:

[A Soft Cheese]

The Vat must be a plated Seive The Cheese Cloth thin muslin. To 3 qts of new milk & one of thick cream a little warm put as much Rennet as will make it come pretty stiff then put it into the Cheese vat lined with the muslin. lay on it a light sinker & weight till it comes to 4 pd. the next day turn it out on boards & salt & ....Cover it with nettles and if the weather is hot it will ripe in a week.[18]

Very similar home-made soft cheeses were made by her sister Joanna:

[Cheese]

Take 2 qts of Cream & 2 qts of New Milk warm from the Cow, if not warm enough to cum pour in a little boiling Water, a Table spoonful of [rennet] is sufficient, when it is turned take it into a fine Cloth & squeeze it, but not break the Curd if wanted to eat soon you must mould it in oval or round dish about 1½inches deep, turn it every day with a fresh Cloth wet & well wrung, let it be upon the Table so that the Whey may drain from it, and press it with a weight, then put it between 2 Pewter plates to ripen & it will be fit to eat in 4 days, if wanted sooner put Nettles round it & send it to Table upon Currant Leaves.[19]

Today virtually all available milk and cream has already been pasteurised. Cheese rennet, meanwhile, is almost unobtainable, while alternative curdling agents such as lemon juice or vinegar impart unwelcome flavours. For these reasons the above recipes are not really practical in a modern kitchen, but this Hutchinson version still gives good results, a delicious home-made cream cheese:

Cream Cheese

Take a qt of thick Cream out of the cream Pot, stir a little salt in it, & lay it upon a fine Cloth, & put it into a Hair Sieve (the Cloth must be wet) turn it once or twice a day till stiff & send it to Table.[20]

1pt/600ml double cream   *2tsp salt*

Rinse a 12ins/30cm square of fine muslin, wring it out, and use to line a sieve with as few creases as possible, then place the sieve over a bowl. Double cream can vary considerably in its consistency, so add the salt and whisk until a small cone remains on the surface on removing the whisk, otherwise the cream will probably run straight through the muslin. Leave overnight, in a cool place, then invert onto another square of freshly-rinsed muslin, and replace in the sieve for a further 12 hours. By this time it will be reasonably stiff and have a delicate flavour, which improves if kept for 3 or 4 days, turning it once or twice each day.

Cream curds were a popular dessert in many households where there was access to cream, milk, eggs and buttermilk. To make them, a very lightly egged mix of milk and eggs was poured into a very large pan of salted water with just sufficient buttermilk to form a soft curd, which was then drained on a muslin-lined sieve. When cold and completely drained, the curds were turned out onto a dish and served with redcurrant jelly and a sprinkling of sugar. However, in common with other apparently straightforward recipes, the production of good curds depended more on long experience of dairy practice than on the ability to follow a written recipe.

Cream Curds

Set on the Fire a brass Pan full of water with a little Salt, then take yolks of 4 Eggs well beaten & mix them with a pint of Cream & a pint of Milk; which when the water boils pour into the Pan with a small Tea Cup full of Butter-milk, When the Curd rises take it carefully out with a slice into a Muslin Bag spread upon a Seive.[21]

In the more prosperous later years at Rydal Mount the Wordsworths enjoyed Stilton cheese, which was supplied to them from London via Mr Powell, the poet and dramatist. As soon as the last one was about to be finished, Mary would ask him to arrange for others to be despatched northwards, where their arrival was eagerly anticipated. Those that their servant Ann unpacked in August 1837 were a great disappointment: 'one having been nibbled by Rats [was] brought in at dinner. To my dismay it is no Stilton what they may call the kind I know not, but it is not nearly so good or so rich as our Lancashire; of a hard stiff texture, and two weighing 13½ [lb] each. As Mr P. had no doubt ordered Stiltons it would be proper that he should know his orders were disobeyed. He is not the cheesemonger whose card was enclosed in the Packet.'[22] With her personal knowledge of dairy produce, Mary was not to be fobbed off with substandard cheeses, and no doubt eventually obtained full satisfaction from the suppliers.

Chapter Ten

OF DRINKS

'To drink wild water, and to pluck green herbs,' as William explained in *The Prelude*, engendered 'Pure passions, virtue, knowledge, and delight/The holy life of music and of verse'.[1] Pure, moving water was both symbolic of the plain living and high principles of the Romantic poets, and also a readily-available amenity at Dove Cottage. Described by Dorothy as 'the Syke as we call it, that diminutive Beck where we get our water', provided an unfailing supply.[2] In addition, there was a small round well which had to be cleaned out either by William or by John Fisher to keep it free from mud.[3] Eleanor Rawnsley considered that the Wordsworths were fortunate to have such a well in the garden, since tea was too expensive for them. In this she perpetuates a common myth of creative poverty, for they could always afford this most expensive beverage. It was certainly considered a real extravagance by many in Grasmere in 1802, as Betty Towers told Dorothy that the family of old Jim Jackson 'might have looked up with the best [here] if they had been careful ... The wife would make tea 4 or 5 times a day and sec folks for sugar! Then she would have nae Teapot but she would take the water out of a Brass pan on the fire and pour it on to the Tea in a quart pot. This all for herself, for she boiled the tea leaves always for her husband and their son.'[4]

In 1803 Dorothy was expecting the arrival of a box of tea from her brother-in-law, Captain John Wordsworth, commander of the East Indiaman The Earl of Abergavenny.[5] She later explained to Thomas de Quincey that 'the tea sold here being very bad and very dear, we always get ours from London.' They obtained their supplies from Mr. Twining, who had called at the cottage on 23rd August, 1800. It was Richard Twining, as Chairman of the Tea Dealers' Association, who had persuaded Prime Minister William Pitt in 1784 to remove the 100% import duty on tea, and replace it with a 12½% lump sum paid by the merchants. This virtually eliminated smuggling, and greatly encouraged the trade, reducing retail prices. The Wordsworths' practice was to order their tea, take delivery of it, and then ask their London brother Richard to settle their account for them perhaps ten months later, just before placing their next order.[6] In 1808-9 they owed £13. 4s,

Fig 16. The Wordsworths always bought their tea from Twinings, the leading tea merchants of the day.

but by January 1810 they had spent a further £31.16s for Twining's tea, although some of this represented a joint purchase with Mr Cookson of Kendal.[7] No wonder that they considered giving up tea-drinking at this point, but they still carried on, even after receiving a bill for a massive £45.10s in May 1810, this being for all the tea supplied by Twinings since 1808, Richard never having settled the earlier accounts.[8] Soon another order was put in, a whole chest of black tea being expected in November.[9] Similar orders were placed in later years, the varieties in 1813 being Souchong, Pekoe and another fine black tea.[10]

At Dove Cottage tea appears to have been taken in the parlour on most afternoons, but this location was often changed to suit particular circumstances. Sometimes it could be around the kitchen fire, at others in the orchard, while in June 1800 John and Dorothy carried a jug of tea to William who was fishing for pike at Rydal. He drank it on the roadside turf before returning home.[11] Tea was also found to be one of the best drinks for long walks on cold days, John Stanley, landlord of the King's Head at Thirlspot, providing it for the Wordsworths on one of their descents from Helvellyn as well as on their pedestrian journeys between Keswick and Grasmere.[12] Frequent invitations to take tea were also exchanged with many of their neighbours, including the Simpsons of High Broadrain and the Oliffs at the Hollins on the Keswick road, the Batys, Lloyds and Fishers in Grasmere, the Cockyns in Keswick, and the Ibbotsons of Ambleside.[13] It is not known how the tea was served by these families, but they probably followed the local tradition of providing a choice of either sugar and cream or a glass of rum to stir into each cupful.[14]

Coffee was also drunk at Dove Cottage, but probably not to the same extent as tea. It was about double the price of tea, and taken either at breakfast or after dinner, rather than being a general social drink. In November 1802 Dorothy appears to have used coffee as a mild stimulant after spending an afternoon in bed. Unfortunately she spilled some on her foot, causing a severe scald, which Mary treated with an application of vinegar. Even so, she was unable to get to sleep until 4am and had to spend the next day in bed.[15]

The usual way to make coffee was to use a finely perforated filter called a percolator, placing the ground beans in the bottom, pouring on hot water, and leaving it to drip through into the coffee pot below. The success of this method depended on having a percolator, and on the fineness of its filter. Coleridge's recipe relied on neither of these, using egg white to remove even the smallest particles to produce a good, strong clear beverage:

[To make Coffee, 1802]

*One half of the white of an egg – a cup of tepid water after the
egg has been beaten up – Water enough to make the Coffee moist
whatever it be /– Then put in the ground Coffee (1 heaped Coffee
cup to six cups of boiling water to be [added] after put in) mix up
the Coffee with the beat up egg & tepid water/ then put it into
the Coffee Boiler, & add boiling water in the proportion of 6 to
1 – put it on a quick fire - & let it boil up two or three times. Then
throw it into the China or Silver Coffee pot thro' a strainer / After
boil & decant the Coffee grains & use the Decantia instead of hot
water next time* [16]

½ raw egg white	*6 level tbs ground coffee*

Put ¼pt/150ml tepid water into a saucepan, beat in the
egg white, and then the coffee. Pour in 1pt/600ml boiling
water (he used water boiled with the dregs of his last batch
of coffee), boil until it has risen twice, then pour through a
fine strainer into the coffee pot.

On hot days something much cooler and refreshing was required.
Cold water was always available, but this could be rendered more
flavoursome by being used to make Imperial water, a mild lemonade.
This is Joanna Hutchinson's recipe:

Imperial Water

*¼lb cream of Tartar, 10oz of Sugar, 9 qts of water boiled 10
minutes, strain it into an earthen Pot upon the Rind of 3 Lemons* [17]

6pts/3·6l water	*3½oz/90g sugar*
1oz/25g cream of tartar	*pared zest of a lemon*

Boil the water, cream of tartar and sugar for 10 minutes,
pour onto the lemon zest in a large heatproof container,
cover, allow to go cold, then seal in sterilised bottles and
keep in a cool place ready for use.

Mary Wordsworth's recipe for ginger beer makes an excellent
summertime drink, easily and quickly made, lasting for a few weeks, and

containing no alcohol to blur the senses. It is quite sweet, with a flavour mid-way between the sharpness of lemons and the dry heat of ginger.

Ginger Beer

4 lb loaf Sugar pounded
3 Lemons Pared & cut in slices
3 oz Cream of Tartar
3 oz Ginger bruised tied in thin muslin
3 Galls of boiling water poured over it in a covered Vessel. stir it
well, let it stand all night, strain & bottle it.[18]

For 8 pints/4·8l take;   *1 lemon*
1lb 4oz/550g sugar   *1oz/25g cream of tartar*
1oz/25g ground ginger loosely tied in a 6ins/15cm square of
muslin

Pare the zest off the lemon, thinly slice the rest, and place in the bottom of a large heatproof container with the sugar, cream of tartar and ginger.

Bring 8pts/4·8l water to the boil separately, pour onto the lemon etc., cover with a lid and thick cloth and leave overnight, then carefully ladle out into clean bottles, without disturbing the sediment. The remaining liquid may then be poured into a jug, the sediment allowed to settle and the clear poured off into the last bottle. Cork or screw down, and store in a cool place for use.

The ginger beers made in some of the households visited by the Wordsworths were solutions of ginger, lemon and sugar fermented with yeast. In addition to being alcoholic, these versions were effervescent and could cause problems if high pressure built up within their containers. Years later, at Rydal Mount, a gift of 'a most capital Beverage' from John Monkhouse had just been bottled by their servants, Willy and James, and the corks tied down, when two bottles exploded. This was probably due to their yeast being re-activated by 'the warm hands, or the warm air of the household [which] did the mischief'. The strings were immediately cut and the corks raised to prevent any further accidents, only being replaced a day or two later in the safety and coolness of the cellar.[19] A bung blown out of a cask might lead to the loss of it contents, but a bottle sealed too tightly could explode like a grenade without any warning whatsoever, sending particles of glass flying in all directions. For this reason it is best either to cork the bottles lightly or to use plastic drinks bottles when trying the recipes today.

Ginger Beer

Boil 4 quarts of water 4lbs of loaf sugar 1oz of pounded ginger for 20 minutes – Pare the rind of 4 lemons & squeeze the juice into a Cask – when the liquor is cool put it into the Cask with 1 table spoonful of yeast. let it remain in this state 4 days, then bottle it for use.[20]

8pts/4·8l water	4 lemons
4lbs/1·8kg sugar	1 tbs dried yeast
3 tbs ground ginger	

Boil the water, sugar and ginger in a large pan for 5 min., add the pared zest and strained juice of the lemons, and leave to cool to 36°C, 95°F. Take out a cupful of the liquid, beat the yeast into it until completely dissolved, then return it to the pan, and stir thoroughly. Cover the pan and leave at room temperature for 4 days, wrapping in a cloth or towel to prevent it chilling, if necessary.

At the end of this period fermentation should have largely ceased, so transfer the clear liquid into bottles, lightly corking them if glass, or screwing down if plastic, leave in the warm for a further day, then keep cool ready for use.

The recipe used by Joanna was virtually identical, except that it used a quarter of the proportion of sugar, and added egg whites and shells to clarify the initial solution:

Mrs Hugessons Ginger Beer

Boil 6 galls of water, 6lb soft sugar, 6oz Ginger beat fine, let it boil on hour, clarifying it with the Whites & shells of 6 Eggs beat well together, scum it, run it through a bag into an open vessel, let it stand to cool, then add the Juice & Rinds of 6 Lemons with two spoonfuls of yeast, put it into a cask, let it stand a fortnight more & it will be ready for use.[21]

Ale and beer were the general drinks throughout most homes in the Lake District. Those who drank very little, or lacked the necessary equipment, would buy in what they needed from a local inn or ale-house. Here, of course, supplies were constantly available for all customers, such as the Wordsworths, who snacked on bread and ale at the King's Head, Thirlspot, on their journeys between Grasmere and Keswick.[22] As early as February 1801 William was able to offer visitors to Dove Cottage his own 'little beer'. This was probably home-brewed, Dorothy finding that her 'brother had indeed been in much better health since we began to drink the ordinary ale which we brew ... We are now drinking the last cask of our own ale' in May, 1804.[23] This interval in home brewing did not mark a return to drinking water, but the arrival of a cask of strong brown stout, a present from Sir George and Lady Beaumont. Thinking of them, wrote Dorothy in her letter of thanks, ' will add not a little to the good effects of this liquor; we shall all drink of it, though we were educated and lived by choice as water-drinkers for many years after we grew up we have, for different reasons, all been obliged to drink malt liquor ... We shall, as you were so good as to direct, put a tea cup full of sweet Oil into the Cask'.[24] The olive oil formed an airtight seal across the upper surface of the stout, ensuring that it did not turn sour as slowly drawn off over the following months. In a letter to Lady Beaumont at the end of July, Dorothy told her of the 'pleasure I have received from drinking of the Brown Stout, of which I take a certain quantity every day and it seems to make me stronger and do me good.'[25]

There is no evidence to suggest the strength of the Wordsworths' home-brewed ale, but it was probably similar to that of the Fricker family, which, using only 1·8 bushels of malt to each barrel, was a small beer, just over half the strength of common country ale. It was a good everyday drink, however:

Excellent Household Beer

1 Bushel of malt and ½ a lb of hops to every 20 gallons of water [26]

The Hutchinson method of ensuring that their home brews were crystal clear was:

To fine beer, wine or Cider and to recover either when sour
The whites and Shells of 12 Eggs 1oz Salt of tartar, ½oz Pearl
ashes, ½oz grains of paradise bruised fine, and mix with as much

powder of Chalk as will make it the consistency of paste, roll this into small balls, which put into the bung hole and stop down immediately. This preparation will render the liquor fine, mild and pleasant in a few days [27]

The only brewing recipe in Mary's notebook is not for anything we would recognise as ale today. It comprised a solution flavoured with elderflowers, raisins and gooseberries fermented to produce a sparkling wine:

Ale Mearnce

30lb of Sugar 10 Gals of Water boiled ¾ hour & when milk warm put in 5 qts of Elder flowers nicely picked from the stalks, then add one gill of yeast; stir it twice a day till the flowers turn brown then put it thro. a seive & let it stand a day or two. cask it and put in 6lb of chopped Raisins & a pint of the juice of green gooseberries, cover it up and let it stand six months try it & if not quite bright rack it off and dissolve an oz of Isinglass & 1lb of loaf sugar, stop it & let it stand 2 months longer. [28]

> *1pt/600ml elderflowers, picked from the stalks, or*
> *1pt/600ml elderflower pressé*
> *9oz/250g chopped raisins   1 sachet/7g dried wine yeast*
> *4tbs gooseberry [or lemon] juice]   3lb/1.3kg sugar*

Bring 10pt/6l of water to the boil in a large pan, stir in the sugar until dissolved, then allow to cool to 36°C, 95°F, before stirring in the elderflowers or pressé, and the yeast beaten into a little of the liquid until dissolved, and then mixed into the remainder. Cover, and keep at room temperature for about 4 days for the initial fermentation to take place. Transfer into demijohns, add the raisins and gooseberry juice, fit an air-lock, and leave in a cool place for 6 months before bottling.

Wine was not being drunk at Dove Cottage in 1801, but by Christmas 1802 Dorothy was able to tell her brothers that 'I continue to drink wine though not in so large a quantity as I did. I find myself stronger and better for it, but I hope in the summer I shall be able to leave it off again.' [29] She clearly considered it to be more of a tonic than a luxury, later becoming concerned that her sister-in-law Mary was not taking sufficient to maintain good health. 'We cannot persuade her to drink wine [and she] will never take a glass except when we have company, and we always find that she looks better and is stronger when she has been obliged to drink wine for a week or a fortnight together.'[30] Wine was certainly offered to house-guests and those who came to dine, as in every middle-class household, and bottles were opened whenever a suitable opportunity arose.

Some wines would be obtained through the usual dealers, but never by the following method described by Coleridge:

> Receipt for brewing Wine
> Get two strong faithful men by proper Instruments – Vide Thieve's Calendar – break into a Wine Merchants Cellar – carry off a hogshead of best Claret or other as arbitrium – given me by Mrs Danvers – expertae crede.[31]

Others were received as gifts, Mary apparently acting as her own butler to ensure that the contents were safely transferred from cask to bottle at the appropriate time. In July 1828, for example, she wrote to Edward Quillinan to confirm the arrival of his wine, now 'safe in the Cellar and I look forward to no pleasant job in the bottling of it.' Five months later, sufficiently settled and matured, it was found 'excellent, then being bottled and laid down for future use'.[32] Home-made country wines were also drunk. At Dorothy's birthday party on Christmas Day, 1817, for example, the assembled company toasted her with a bottle of cowslip.[33] Mary, being rather abstemious, was a little shocked, however, when her student son William asked for cowslip wine to drink with his Sunday dinner during his visit from Oxford University in September, 1820.[34]

It is probable that the Wordsworths adopted country-wine-making practices from the Hutchinson sisters, who appear to have had considerable expertise in this field. Evidence for this comes from Mary's recipe book which includes instructions for making her gooseberry wine. This would use up some of their annual home-grown crop:

[Gooseberry Wine]

3 Gallons of red & green Gooseberries 3 do. Water previously boiled & cooled 10½lb of Lump sugar; the Gooseberries must be broken small & remain 2 days in the water stirred frequently. The sugar to be added to the Liquor when separated from the fruit

& put into the barrel as soon as dissolved. The Barrel must be rinsed with Brandy: it must be stirred every day for a fortnight then stopped down. The colour is best when the greater part of the berries is red. To be tapped about Xmas If not bright rinse the cask and put it in again with a little Isinglass dissolved in the wine.[35]

This is clearly copied from the same original source as the following, which comes from Joanna Hutchinson's recipe book:

Gooseberry Wine (Mrs Kis ...)

Take three gallons of Red and Green Gooseberries, three Gallons of Water previously boiled and cooled, 10½lbs of lump sugar, the Gooseberries must be broken small and pour in two days in the water stirred frequently. The Sugar to be added to the Liquor when separated from the fruit and put into a Barrel as soon as dissolved. The Barrel must be rinsed with Brandy: it must be stirred every day for a fortnight then stopped up. To be tapped about Xmas. If not bright rinse the Cask and put it in again with a little Isinglass in some of yr. Wine[36]

As the following recipes show, Joanna was making wines from ginger, raisins and wild flowers, including cowslips.

Ginger Wine ... Mrs Powell

5 Gallons of water 12lbs Lisbon sugar, the rinds of 12 lemons ¼lb Ginger bruised, boil and skim it, when cool put to it a little yeast on toasted bread and the next day put it in the cask with 1lb of chopped raisins to each gallon, a little isinglass and the juice of 12 lemons[37]

Ginger Wine

Take 6 Galls of water & 12lb Sugar, ½lb of Ginger bruised, put it in a bag & boil it ½ an hour in the water with the Sugar & whites of 4 Eggs, pour it upon the juice & Rinds of 9 Lemons, when cold put to it a little Beer yeast, let it work a day or two, then put it into the cask with the Ginger, Rinds, and a little Isinglass.[38]

Ginger Wine (Mr. Joy's receipt)

To 9 Galls of Water 18lbs of Sugar, boil them together for half an hour, taking off the scum as it rises, pour it into a Tub, when cold put to it as much good yeast as you think will work it, let it stand 3 days, put into the barrel 1lb of Ginger Bruised, the rinds of 18 Seville Oranges & as many Lemons pared thin, the pulp of the Oranges & Lemons beat up with as much sugar as will make it very sweet & 2lbs of Raisins stoned, 1 qt. of Brandy, ½ oz of Isinglass cut small, pour the fermenting Liquor upon these Ingredients, when it has done working stop it up close & let it stand ½ year before it is drawn off.[39]

Raisin Wine

Put 7lbs of Malaga Raisins to every Gal of cold Spring Water, after standing for 3 days, draw as much off as will boil ¼lb Hops for a qr. of an hour, which must be put all together boiling hot into the Cask, leave the Bung open till done fermenting, close the Cask about 2 Months when it will be fit for drinking.[40]

Raisin Wine [Tho King]

To 7lb of Raisins, stalks & all, put one Gall. of cold spring Water, put them into a Hogshead, according to the Quantity you wish to make, allowing room for the swelling of the fruit & stirrings, which must be done every other Day for a Month, stop it close & let it stand on the fruit 10 or 12 Months. Draw the liquor from the fruit into a clean cask, take care that the Cask be full, to every 10 Galls. of Wine put one pint of Brandy. Let it remain in the Cask six Months or as long as you think proper. Fine it with blue Milk, to 10 Gallons one pint to be put in to the Cask at the time you draw it from the fruits. The sort of Raisins [& ?] are the Lexia, any other sort perhaps may do as well.[41]

Smyrna [Raisin] Wine (Mr Joy's receipt)

Boil the quantity of water wanted & when cold put in 8lbs of Fruit [Smyrna raisins] to the Gal. Let it stand a fortnight in a Tub & stir it 2 or 3 times a day. Then put all into the Barrel & stir it once a day till it has done working, which will be perhaps a fortnight or 3 weeks, it should not stand longer. Take it out of the Barrel & press the liquor from the fruit, then fill the Barrel full that it may again ferment out of the cask, & let it remain till that is over, take out as much wine as you put in Brandy (nearly 1 Gall to 18 of wine) add a Gill of skimmed Milk with a little Isinglass dissolved in wine & the whites of 2 or 3 Eggs. It may stand in the Cask [& ?] a year [42]

Cowslip Wine

To 20qts. of Water 15lbs of Sugar, & rather more than 1 qt. of picked Cowslips to each qt. Boil the water with the Sugar ½ an Hour, put in the whites & shells of 6 Eggs well beaten, skim it, and when nearly cold pour it upon the Cowslips & 6 Lemons skins & pared, let it stand all night, then put to it a Gill of Yeast & for 24 Hours stir it frequently, then put it in the cask with a little Isinglass dissolved in vinegar. [43]

Elderflower Wine [Mrs King]

Take 30lbs of Lump Sugar, 10 Gallons of Water (Ale measure) boiled ¾ of an Hour, and when Milk warm put 5 pts of Elderflowers nicely picked from the stalks, then add ¼ of a pint of yeast: stir it twice a day till the flowers turn brown, then put it through a sieve & let it stand a Day or two. Cask it & put in 6lb of chopped Raisins & a pint of the juice of Green Gooseberries. Close it up & let it stand for 6 Months, try it & if not very bright rack it off & dissolve an Ounce of Isinglass to a lb of lump Sugar, put that in, stop it & let it stand 2 Months longer. [44]

Clary is a herb found mainly in the south of England, which explains the use of its violet or white flowers in this recipe of the Fricker family:

Clary Wine

To 10 gallons of water, 1 peck of Clary flowers, 2lb & ½ or a little more (but not quite 3lbs) of Loaf Sugar to each gallon, boil the sugar and water, clear it with white of eggs, when cold put it into a barrel with a square hole at the top with a little yeast, when it begins to work put in the flowers and stir it twice a day for a

fortnight, then add a little Isinglass and bung it up. Bottle it in
3 or 4 months. The Barrel may be kept from year to year with the
flowers in it. measure the flowers lightly, 8 quarts to the peck.[45]

While staying overnight at Hawes at the head of Wensleydale in early October 1802, the Wordsworths enjoyed the evening with 'a shilling's worth of negus'.[46] This blend of port or sherry, sugar, flavouring and hot water had been invented by Colonel Francis Negus about a century earlier, but was still very popular throughout the country:

Negus

2-3 lumps of sugar
4 fl oz/ 100 ml port or sherry
1 lemon   *pinch of grated nutmeg*

Rub the sugar on the lemon rind to extract the oils, put this in a ½pt/300ml heatproof glass, add the port, and fill up with boiling water. Stir to dissolve the sugar and finish with a sprinkling of nutmeg.[47]

In the heat of a spring day in May 1802, William and Dorothy, accompanied by Coleridge, dined 'upon a moss-covered Rock, rising out of the bed of the River' at what is now Thirlmere. Here she 'drank a little Brandy and water and was in Heaven'.[48] Brandy, and particularly rum, were both popular in the Lakes, much being smuggled into the prosperous port of Whitehaven. On 1st September, 1800, the Wordsworths 'borrowed some bottles for bottling rum' from their friends the Simpsons.[49] These may have been of glass or perhaps 'grey hens', the imported salt-glazed bottles used for ale and spirits on the local farms. Dark rum can be a fiery liquor in the mouth and throat, but these properties could be remarkably transformed by adding sugar, lemon juice and lemon zest to produce 'shrub'. English travellers had first come across 'Scherab or Persian wine' in the mid seventeenth century, but its popularity here really started in the 1740s. It has a decidedly citrus flavour, its high alcohol content being detected more by a quickening pulse and a warm glow rather than by its deceptively mild taste.

Shrub

4qts of Lemon juice, 4lbs lump Sugar, 9 or 10 qts of Spirits. Pare the Lemons very thin & infuse the Peel in half of the spirit 24 Hours, then put all into a Cask, tumble it twice a day till the Sugar is dissolved, put into the Cask the white of 2 Eggs let it stand till fine, then Bottle it.[50]

1pt/600ml rum	*4oz/100g sugar*
6 lemons	*white of 1 egg*

Use a potato peeler to pare the zest from the lemons, then squeeze them into a measuring jug, to produce ½pt/300ml juice. Strain this through a fine sieve or a piece of muslin into a large jar, add the zest, rum and sugar, seal the jar, and shake it from time to time over two days, by which time the sugar should have dissolved, and the zest given up its oils.

Strain the liquid to remove the zest, beat the egg white thoroughly, with a little of the liquid, beat this into the remainder, leave for two hours, then pass through a coffee filter-paper which has been freshly rinsed in cold water. Pour the first few cloudy tablespoonfuls back into the filter paper, after which it will run through crystal clear over the next couple of days, when it can be bottled for use as a liqueur.

The final recipe in this section is for an extremely useful winter-time drink, blackcurrant vinegar. On 22nd April, 1802, Coleridge accompanied the Wordsworths on a walk up Easedale, where the whole party was drenched. After returning to dinner at Dove Cottage Dorothy and Coleridge 'drank black currants and water'.[51] Since fresh, ripe blackcurrants are only in season between July and August, they must have used this simple, sharp-flavoured cordial made up with hot water, to enjoy this most comfortable remedy for colds and chills:

Blackcurrant vinegar

Fill a jar with black currants, then pour in as much vinegar as the jars will hold; let it stand 4 days, stirring it well each day Then squeeze out the fruit & pass the liquor thro' a canvas bag to every pint of juice put a lb. of Loaf sugar, let it simmer ½ an hour, when cold bottle it for use

N.B. very good for colds. Raspberry vinegar may be made the same way.[52]

Chapter Eleven

OF PACE EGGS

Eggs have provided a potent symbol of the resurrection of Christ at Eastertime for many centuries. In Martindale they were collected by the priest as his Easter dues. During the sixty-seven years of his incumbency Richard Birkett used a piece of wood with a hole in it as a gauge, returning to each farmer all those which were so small as to pass through.[1]

In the opening decades of the nineteenth century it was customary for children in the Lake District to give 'pace eggs' to their friends, this name being derived from 'paschal', relating to Easter. Each egg was decorated to the utmost of the giver's skill, one method being to dip it in hot water for a few moments, then use the tip of a tallow candle to inscribe an appropriate name or date. This acted as a resist, the lines remaining white in contrast to the background, which readily absorbed colour when immersed in a pan of hot dye. Writing in 1825, 'Mr J.B.' of Maryport described how:

> Another method of ornamenting 'pace eggs' is, however, much neater, although more laborious, than that with the tallow-candle. The egg being dyed, it may be decorated in a very pretty manner, by means of a penknife, with which the dye may be scraped off, leaving the design white, on a coloured ground. The egg is frequently divided into compartments, which are filled up according to the taste and skill of the designer. Generally one compartment contains the name (being young and unsophisticated) also the age of the party for whom the egg is intended. In another is, perhaps, a landscape; and sometimes a cupid is found lurking in a third; so that these 'pace-eggs' become very useful auxiliaries to the missives of St Valentine. Nothing was more common in the childhood of the writer, than to see a number of these eggs preserved very carefully in the corner cupboard; each egg being the occupant of a deep, long-stemmed ale-glass, through which the inscription could be read without removing it. Probably

many of these eggs now remain in Cumberland, which
would afford as good evidence of dates in a court of justice,
as a tombstone or a family bible.[2]

One of the finest of all egg decorators was James Dixon who started
work as the Wordsworths' gardener sometime before 1829. He was
a much-loved servant, remaining at Rydal Mount as long as it was
inhabited by any member of the family, and regularly visiting their
graves to the end of his life. He was later remembered as 'yan they
called Dixon, smart lile chap as iver was seen in these parts, but ter'ble
given over to cold watter and temperance he woz. Coomed out of a
union [a workhouse], but verra neat, and always a word for onybody,
and a verra quiet man, particular quiet, nivver up to nea mischief, and
always sat at heam wi' t' lasses a mending and sewing o' evenings ye
kna.'[3] In 1830 Sarah Hutchinson described him as:

> our industrious and simple-hearted Serving-man James,
> who can do all sorts of little jobs, mend chair-bottoms,
> weave garden nets, make mats, list sheets etc., etc., has
> made cap stands for the Ladies of this house & By the Bye,
> his wedding present to Mrs. J.W. Was a paste-pin turned by
> himself, and a potato bruiser both made of wood grown in
> Rydal Mount Grounds.[4]

He was also a skilled gardener, even though:

> He knew nothing of gardening when he came to us but
> kindly took to the work; and is now even passionately
> attached to the gardens especially the ornamental part
> as my Sister [Mary] says he worships his flowers . Every
> morning from her bed-room window does she see him
> going his Rounds and standing over every particular Plant
> that pleases his family & His health is delicate and he could
> not stand hard exercise.[5]

From these accounts, it is obvious that he combined a real appreciation
of the beauties of nature with considerable ingenuity and dexterous
craftsmanship. Even so, the exceptionally high quality of the design
and execution demonstrated in his decorated pace eggs still comes as a
complete revelation. The Wordsworth Trust at Dove Cottage preserves
a number of those he made for William's grandchildren between 1868

and 1878. Compared to any other English examples, they are truly magnificent, standing at least equal to the very best in the whole of Europe.[6] He also decorated Easter eggs, conkers and snail shells, some being the treasured possessions of local families whose great-great-grandfathers received them as presents from him when he used to visit Langdale School in 1863.[7]

Unlike many other local egg-decorators, who used either natural materials or pieces of cloth with non-fast dyes to colour their eggs, James Dixon appears to have used the strongest of commercially-manufactured dyes or inks to achieve the richest of royal blues, purples, red-browns or blacks. Using a sharp-pointed blade, he then scratched through this layer to reveal the white shell beneath. Some of his eggs demonstrate an amazing degree of geometric accuracy, dividing their curving surfaces into tiny squares, or circular panels, while others are in much freer, but still well-balanced and highly detailed designs. These include swans, poultry and wild birds, as well as sprays of foliage and flowers informed by his occupation as a gardener. Without doubt, these are among the most important examples of English folk-art, always intended to be preserved and displayed, unlike most other locally-decorated examples.

It was during James Dixon's time that a remarkable distribution of pace eggs took place at Rydal Mount. The date was Tuesday 9th April, 1844, Wordsworth's 74th birthday, when a celebratory fête was provided by Miss Isabella Fenwick, a close family friend then living in Ambleside.

'The Grasmere boys and girls came first, and took their places on the benches placed around the gravelled part of the esplanade; their eyes fixed with wonder and admiration on the tables covered with oranges, gingerbread and painted eggs, ornamented with daffodils, laurels, and moss, gracefully intermixed & Neighbours, old and young, of all degrees, ascended to the Mount & and every face looked friendly and happy. Each child brought its own mug, and held it out to be filled with tea, in which ceremony all assisted. Large baskets of currant cakes were handed round and liberally dispensed; and as each detachment of children had satisfied themselves with tea and cake, they were moved off, to play hide and seek among the evergreens on the grassy part of the Mount & The children, who amounted altogether to above 300, gave three cheers to Mr. Wordsworth and Miss F[enwick]. After some singing and dancing, and after the division of eggs, gingerbread and oranges had taken place, we all began to disperse.[8]

The pace eggs intended to be given away to children calling at farmhouse and cottage doors on Good Friday were either simply dyed or dotted with tallow to present a piebald or bird's-eye appearance. Made by the younger boys who had still to aspire to motifs such as Cupid's bent bow and quiverful of arrows, a flaming torch or a heart and a true-lover's knot, their dyes were brown onion skins, green ivy leaves, yellow gorse flowers etc.[9] Often the children would arrive in a small group, perhaps dressed in character, those of the mid-nineteenth century appearing as Lord Nelson, Jolly Jack Tar, Old Tosspot and a female Old Muse with her bags. They started their performance with the traditional chant of:

> *Here's two or three jolly boys all of one mind,*
> *We've come a pace-egging, I hope you'll prove kind,*
> *I hope you'll prove kind, with your eggs and strong beer,*
> *And we'll come no more nigh you until the next year.*

Each character then stepped forward and exclaimed its particular line, after which the resident 'Ladies and gentlemen that sits by the fire' were requested to put their hands in their pockets and remember that it was pace-egging time.[10]

On Easter Monday the children disposed of their eggs in various ways, either tossing them in the air, rolling them down a particular local hill, or trundling them, as at Kendal.[11] Here pairs of children sat at each side of a piece of level turf and rolled their eggs so as to collide in the middle, until one was broken and forfeited to the winner, who probably gobbled it up immediately. Alternatively a child holding an egg in one hand would challenge another to give it a blow with his egg, the one that survived being given the title of a cock of one, two, three etc.[12] Unfortunately there are few early records of these customs in the Lake District, since they were probably so well-known that no one ever thought it worthwhile to mention them, but they formed an essential event in the annual cycle of celebrations. Egg-rolling was still practised in some villages into at least the 1950s, and egg decorating still continues as a hobby, but rarely, if ever, to James Dixon's remarkable standards.

Chapter Twelve

OF HOME REMEDIES

In common with most other personal recipe books, those of the Wordsworth, Hutchinson and Fricker families include practical remedies for alleviating minor medical conditions, as well as for coping with a variety of housekeeping problems. None of them should be used today, but they are reproduced here for their general interest, and to shed light on the ways in which the families dealt with ailments partly resulting from their particular lifestyles.

Dorothy's journal mentions that meals were occasionally missed due to unspecified illnesses, their appetites usually being quite good. However, the remedies recorded in Mary's recipe book suggest that they sometimes needed to modify their digestions:

Tonic for the Stomach

½oz red rose leaves
¼oz snepe root
¼oz bit. orange Peel
pour on the above 1qt. of boiling water. 2 in ye Day [1]

[The 'snepe root' may possibly be snake root, Polygale senega or Aristolchia serpentaria].

The Frickers, meanwhile, used a hop solution:

To create an Appetite

Put a handfull of Hops into a quart jug & pour boiling water on it with a little ginger [2]

Laxatives were apparently also in demand, the Wordsworths making up both Daffy's Elixir, a highly-regarded tonic invented by Anthony Daffy around 1680, and a mixture of heira picra (a compound of purgative aloes and wind-expelling cinnamon) and a starchy gelling agent called saloop:

Daffy's elixir

1½oz Rhubarb 1½ Senna
1lb Raisins shred 1oz figs sliced
1oz Liquorice sliced & scraped
1oz Cummin seeds
½ Dram Cochineal bruised
Do Saffron
infuse in 3 pints of brandy 8 days strain it off & put on 3 pints
more let this infuse 8 days longer pour it off & mix all together [3]

Mrs Hugessen

1oz Heira Picra
1 Do Salap to a bottle of White Wine – let it stand 6 weeks sheking
the bottle often – strain it - & add a glass of brandy – Dose ½ a
wine Glass with water. [4]

Joanna Hutchinson had a recipe for a similar purgative compound which included Castile soap:

Mrs Hugesson's Pills

Rhubarb and Ipicacuanha each ½ dram, Castle Soap 1 dram in 30 Pills [5]

while Martha Fricker recommended:

A Saline Draught

½ an oz of nitre to a pint of toast & water [6]

Even more troublesome complaints were treated with self-prescribed remedies. To dull the raging agony of her toothache, Dorothy sometimes dosed herself with laudanum, a strong opiate, for example.[7] Meanwhile the pile-wort (Ranunculus Ficaria or Ficaria verna) which 'spread out on the grass a thousand shining stars' of glossy yellow flowers in the garden at Dove Cottage, was probably used to heal William's piles.[8]

Even for people who were born and bred in the Lake District, the cold of the winter months presented a real challenge. Out of doors, especially with a hard frost and a biting wind, it could take the breath away, and it wasn't much better inside, except within the immediate radiance of the fireplace. After one February night in 1802 Dorothy described how: 'At first I went to bed I seemed to be warm, I suppose because the cold air, which I had just left, no longer touched my body, but I soon found that I was mistaken, I could not sleep for sheer cold.'[9] Only those who can remember sleeping in the usually sub-zero temperatures of pre-centrally heated winter bedrooms can fully appreciate her experience, and the symptoms it produced. Chilblains were a regular seasonal problem, tender and itchy inflammations on hands and feet exposed to the cold, which could easily degenerate into ulcers. To cure them Dorothy used this plaster:

For Chilblains

1oz Rosin 1 Do Bees wax 1 Do Lard, 2 Spoonful Sweet oil to be simmered in a new pimpkin. The feet to be washed, a plaister of this mixture to be spread thinly and applied fresh every third night.[10]

while Joanna Hutchinson recommended several others.

For Chilblains

one oz of White Copperas [zinc proto-sulphate] dissolved in a quart of water. This application must be used before they break [11]

Chilblains

Citrine ointment 1oz, oil of turpentine 2 Drachms, oil of olive 4 Drachms, mixed, to be well rubbed in night & morning.[12]

Do. Sir Astley Cooper

1oz of Camphorated Spirit of wine, ½oz of the liquor of subacetate of lead. Mix and apply 3 or 4 times a day [13]

[Chilblains]

1oz White Copperas in a qt. of Water will remove Chilblains [14]

Boils, infected wounds and gatherings were treated with salves which both helped to extract puss etc., and soothed and healed the inflammation. Of their effective ingredients, diachalum was a compound of lead oxide, boiled with olive oil and water to form a stiff paste. These recipes come from one of Dorothy's commonplace books, probably of the later 1820s:

Miss Barker's White Salve

Diachalum ½lb sweet oil 4oz (¼ pint) Chalk 4oz Vinegar 4oz
Cut the Diachalum into thin slices put into a new glazed pipkin
with the oil melt gently over a fire Add the Chalk finely powdered
& sifted, stirring till cold
Drawing Salve Do.
Millicot plaster 4oz Sweet oil 3oz
Melt by the fire
To be put on a bit of Lint, & to be applied to the & of a Boil or
Sore with a plaster of the White Salve above it. When sufficiently
drawn, the White Salve only is wanted.[15]

In addition to chilblains, the winter months also brought on coughs and colds, for which medicines were made up to recipes such as these:

Cough Mixture

1oz Elixir of Panegoric
1oz of Syrup of Poppies
½oz Sweet nitre
½oz Gum Arabic
These ingredients to be well mixed and a teaspoonful taken two or
three times a day [16]

For a Cough & cold

one drachm of Elixir of Vitriol & drachms of Laudanum, 3
teaspoonfulls full of honey, 30 drops of mixture to be taken three
times a day [17]

The Elixir of Panegoric was a camphorated tincture of opium with aniseed and benzoic acid, the laudanum also being an opiate, while the Elixir of Vitriol was aromatic sulphuric acid. Their sharp flavours were masked and soothed by the use of either the opiate syrup of poppies or the honey, but even so it would have been unwise to have taken these medicines for more than a short period.

The only remedy for a childhood illness to be recorded in the Wordsworth recipes is one for croup, which Dorothy noted down from the *Morning Chronicle* probably about the time of young John Wordsworth's birth in 1803. This disease caused inflammation of the larynx and windpipe, as well as a characteristic sharp, ringing cough, and frequently proved fatal. Since the mixture of camphor and sal ammoniac (ammonium chloride) could not be applied directly to the affected parts, they were both dissolved in volatile distilled spirits of wine. When applied to the external skin of the throat, either directly or on a piece of flannel, they were rapidly evaporated and inhaled, just like the medicinal vapour-rubs popular up to the mid twentieth century.

For the Croup   Ward's Essence

4oz of the best highly rectified Spirits of Wine 4oz Camphor to be thoroughly mixed & incorporated then add 4oz of the best soluble Sal Ammoniac.

If both the Spirits be not good the proper quantity of Camphor will not be taken up by them.

Tried by Dr Hawkins of Monmouthshire with good success. The throat to be bathed with the Essence & a piece of flannel to be dipped with it, & tied round.[18]

At a time when it was more usual to walk than to ride, it was essential to keep the feet in good condition, partly by using well-fitting footwear, and partly by treating corns etc. before they caused major problems. The Wordsworths used this remedy:

Bath for the feet

Muriacic Acid 2 of each
Warm water 3 gallons
The two acids to be added each separately to ½ a pint cold water & then mixed together, by the Druggist. Then put to 3 galls. warm water Feet to be kept in ¼ an hour at bed time every night. If a proper strength it lasts like & ?[19]

Unfortunately the recipe gives only one of the two acids. Muriacic acid is the now obsolete name for hydrochloric acid, which explains why the Wordsworths preferred to have their druggist carry out its initial mixing and dilution. Joanna Hutchinson's recipe used, as a safer alternative, a strong lye made by dissolving willow ashes in vinegar to soften both:

Warts & Corns

The bark of the Willow tree burnt to ashes and [mixed?] with strong Vinegar form a [& ?] which effectively eradicate by repeated application warts, corns, and all cutaneous excrescences [20]

For complaints which affected the limbs and joints rather than the feet, her remedies include:

Oliver's Oil for Sprains &

Hungary Water 2 ounces, Powers of Amber 2 do. Spirits of Lavendar 1 Dram, Spirit of Wine 4 ounces Spirit of Nitre, sweet, 1 Dram Tincture of Saffron 10 drops
Mix
For inward Bruises 8 to 10 drops taken twice a day [21]

The following remedy for rheumatism which was based on mustard, which the Wordsworths obtained from 'the Cockermouth traveller', a woman who called at Dove Cottage on her way to Ulverston, carrying her dry goods on her back, and planning to return in time for Ambleside Fair. [22]

For Rheumatism

Take of the best Durham Mustard seed 3 oz, boil it gently in three pints of water till reduced to one, then add one pint of skimmed Milk & strain it through a sieve, one Teacupful of warm [taken] every night & morning. [23]

Spending so much time in the open air in all weathers took its toll on the complexion. In 1810 Russell's poem To a Lady described the best available means of easing the combined effects of wind, rain and cold:

'A pot of cold cream to Eliza you send.
Who'er with this cream shall her countenance smear,
All redness and roughness will strait disappear.' [24]

Joanna Hutchinson used this recipe:

To make Cold Cream

Dissolve half a Cake of white wax in half a Pint of oil of sweet Almonds, then put the whole into a large basonful of cold spring water and beat it with a silver spoon for half an hour, change the water and beat it again for half an hour longer, this water must then be poured off and a quart of rosewater added in which it must be beaten an hour, put it in cups, leaving sufficient room to cover it with a little fresh rosewater, tie it close with paper.[25]

One Friday in March 1802, as dusk was falling, Coleridge arrived at Dove Cottage, having walked from Keswick via Dunmail Raise in torrential rain. As Dorothy recorded in her journal,

'His eyes were a little swollen with the wind, I was much affected by the sight of him he seemed half stupified & Poor C! I did not wish for, or expect him, it rained so.'[26]

The long hours which both he and the Wordsworths spent at their reading and writing, especially by candlelight or firelight during the long winter evenings, also produced eye strain. Coleridge sometimes had to work throughout the night to complete his essays for the newspapers, for example, while Dorothy described many evenings such as one in November 1801,

'all sitting by a nice fire. W. with his book and a candle and Mary writing to Sara'.[27]

Dorothy sometimes suffered problems with her eyes, as noted in her letters, but they were rarely, if ever, as bad as William's.[28] His problems were exacerbated with the smoke problems at Allan Bank, but continued to increase over the following years. In 1837, for example, he described how

'My eyes are not bad, but certainly weaker than I could wish, the eyelids reddening and the balls watering when exposed to strong light or sharp air, but very little bloodshot.[29]

This, it should be stressed, was when they were 'not bad'. This explains the presence of a number of home-made eye washes in Mary's recipe book:

Eye Water

2oz Rosemary Leaves
¼pt Port Wine
¼pt Water [30]
Eye Water
2 Dr. Borax
9qr vitriolated zinc
3oz rose or elder flower water [31]

Joanna Hutchinson's remedy was based on sassafras. This was a small elder-like tree, native to North America, whose bark was used as an alterative, restoring the organs to a healthy condition.

Sore Eyes

Take small sticks of salsafras split in 4 Pieces, put them in a Vessel with cold water, they impart a glutinous matter in the water, wash the Eyes with this Liquid & will cure without smarting or heals. [32]

Although not medicinal, the use of toilet soap was certainly necessary both for personal hygiene and for shaving. Camphor, whether prepared from the original Far Eastern shrub, or by the developing chemical industry, was a white, crystalline volatile substance, with a strong and very characteristic smell, which many people today still associate with mothballs.

Wash Balls

1lb of white Soap shaved fine 3d of Spermacete bruised & 3d Camphire dissolved in Spirit of Wine, 4d of the best sweet oil, put these ingredients into a jar & stir it till all is dissolved then take it off & continue stirring, till cold enough to make into Balls. [33]

The recipe books also contain instructions for keeping clothing and footwear in a good, presentable condition. Items of linen were relatively valuable, and so it was essential that each piece should be indelibly marked with the name of its owner, perhaps also with the date of its acquisition, and sometimes a number to relate it to a household inventory. Making the ink was a potentially dangerous operation:

To make ink for marking Linen

Pour a little nitric acid (aqua fortis) into a cup or glass and add to it a small piece of pure silver, when the effervescence ceases filter the solution through a piece of blotting paper, and put it into a small phial, then add to it a little gum arabic, and a little of the paint called Sap green, after the whole is perfectly combined and is fit for use [34]

Such an ink had to survive the repeated washings which usually improved the whiteness and texture of the linen. In contrast all wool, silk, velvets etc. had to be given some form of dry-cleaning, as washing could damage their surfaces. If dry-brushing or gentle sponging failed to remove stains, especially those of oily or waxy substances, the best treatment was to use a highly volatile ether:

Scouring Spirit

Pyreligneous Aether 1 ounce, essence of Lemons 3 drams, mix, the part should be well rubbed with Tow or woollen Cloth moistened with this Composition. [35]

For footwear, home-made liquid blackening was made by combining burnt ivory powder with an emulsion of vinegar, sulphuric acid (then known as oil of vitriol), olive oil and sugar. It was then stored in corked jars ready for use.

Blackening

4oz Ivory black, 2oz Coarse sugar mixed well with a quart of vinegar, add carefully ½oz Oil of vitriol stirring very well with a stick in a deep earthen vessel, last of all add two large spoonfuls of sweet oil. [36]

Much of the redecoration and maintenance of Dove Cottage was carried out by its occupants, rather than by local craftsmen. Repainting was best done in the summer months, when the longer days and warmer weather meant that the doors and windows could be left open to speed up the drying process. In June 1802 Dorothy made her start by actually grinding the paint, probably using a pestle and mortar to crush lumps of prepared chalk before mixing it to a thin creamy consistency with size, perhaps a bit of washing blue, and water. Next morning she used this to whitewash the ceiling, the effort leading her to spend the afternoon in bed. Her friend Miss Simpson then colourwashed the walls. [37]

The rubbing of the tables, or furniture polishing, appears to have been one of William's domestic chores, but the cleaning which most households carried out once a year involved washing off any accumulated dirt with vinegar before applying linseed oil. For mahogany, it was coloured red with the root of alkanet or Dyer's Bugloss (Anchusa or Alkenna tinctoria) and Rose Pink, a pigment made by dying whiting with red-purple Brazil-wood.

Clean Mahogany

First wash it clean with vinegar. Then take 4d. of Alkanet Root, 2d Rose Pink, 1 Pint of cold drawn nseed Oil. Put it into an Earthen pot & let it stand 24 Hours. Rub the Mahogany with this mixture, then after standing 24 hours rub it bright with a Linen Cloth. [38]

The next recipe comes from Mary Wordsworth's book. It is not domestic, however, but veterinary, describing how to make a plaster to cure warbles, the small hard tumours on a horse's back, caused by the pressure of the saddle, particularly if this area was not kept perfectly clean. She was an accomplished horsewoman, riding sidesaddle in a habit in her younger days, and probably learned simple vetinary cures of this kind while living at Sockburn and at Gallow Hill.

Warbles or sore back of a Horse

Com. Pitch [&] Pitch ea 3oz
Mastic[&] Francincence ea 1oz
Common Turpentine, Galbarum [&] Bole Armeriac ½oz
Powder the Bole armeriac & mix it with the other ingredients when melted over a gentle fire.
This plaster is to be spread on soft Leather & remain on the part till well. [39]

The final recipe is by far the most appropriate for the household of a major poet, and for one in which writing was such an important everyday occupation. It is Dorothy's instructions for making ink, written in the early years at Dove Cottage, and most probably used to make the ink with which William's finest poetry was first set down on paper.

To make Ink

an ounce of Gum arabick, 30 [oak] Galls, 1oz sulphate of iron. A wine quart of water of which put as much upon the Gum as will dissolve it & the rest on the Galls & iron. Let it stand 3 days without cork shake it after three days add the gum & it is fit for use.[40]

As this chapter clearly demonstrates, a considerable degree of training and expertise was required in order to manage even modest households. Compared to our current lifestyles, which enjoy ready access to every conceivable ready-made commodity, those of most country housewives and housekeepers of the early nineteenth century were amazingly self-sufficient. Medicines, cosmetics, cleaning materials, paints and polishes were all made up in the kitchen from a selection of raw materials, following traditions established by generations of trial and error experiences. Today they not only impress us with their comprehensive range of solutions to all manner of practical problems, but they also help us to comprehend otherwise intangible aspects of the everyday lives of the poets. These might include the almond and rosewater scents from their cold cream, the mothball smell from their wash-balls, or the heavy odour of linseed after furniture polishing. In the storecupboards we may also trace the aromas of rose petals, orange peel, liquorice, cummin, saffron, lavender, rosewater and elderflower water, along with those of the more dangerous acids and chemicals used to ease the symptoms of various illnesses and complaints.

It is extremely fortunate that Mary Wordsworth, her sister Joanna Hutchinson, and Coleridge and Southey's sister-in-law Martha Fricker all recorded so many of their recipes in their manuscript notebooks, and that these are now preserved by the Wordsworth Trust at Dove Cottage. Without them our knowledge of their lives, and also our ability to make and taste so many of their authentic dishes, would have been totally impossible.

APPENDIX

Table-Linen at Dove Cottage

One month after Mary's arrival at Grasmere as William's wife, a list was drawn up of all the linen which Mary's family had provided for her new home. It is interesting both for its content, and for the initials marking the origin of each piece. For centuries it had been the practice for families to grow their own flax, scotch and spin it into yarn, have it converted into cloth by a local weaver, and then make it up into sheets, tablecloths, towels, shirts, underwear etc. as required. Such pieces would then be handed down through successive generations, being extremely hard-wearing. This is shown by the initial marking each of Mary's linens:

G	Gamage
H	Hutchinson
JH	John Hutchinson (1736-1785) her father
MC	Margaret Cooper, her grandmother's niece
MM	Margaret Monkhouse (1717-1788) her grandmother
WM	Monkhouse (1746- 1809) her maternal uncle

The linen was made of distinctive weaves and yarns, the finest being damask, in which the loom was set to produce elaborate borders and patterns which absorbed or reflected the light on the otherwise uniformly white surface of the material. Next came diaper, a twill weave giving a small all-over diamond pattern, hence the American term 'dyper' for the English 'nappy'. Huckaback was usually thicker, with a chequerboard pattern, its absorbency making it suitable for hand-towels, as well as other uses. Mary's probably came from Darlington, the major national centre for its production. Finally, there was plain-woven linen, where the quality was largely dependent on the fineness of the yarn, anything from the almost transparent lawn to the roughest of coarse cloths. In addition to bedlinen and towels, this is the account of Mary's linen which came from Penrith to Grasmere in November 1802 (original spellings corrected):

1 small Damask Table Cloth
1 large Do
2 Diaper Table Cloths 1 marked WM the other unmarked
1 old Diaper, Do
2 Diaper Breakfast cloths one marked H the other unmarked
2 large Huckaback Table Cloths marked H
1 Do Do JH
2 coarse & strong, one marked G the other unmarked
3 breakfast Do

With a total of fifteen tablecloths to choose from, she could always provide a suitable cloth for any meal, fine damask for formal entertaining, diaper or huckaback for friends etc., and coarse and strong for everyday use.

BIBLIOGRAPHY

Anon., *15 Books of Old Recipes as used by the Pease and Gurney Households in the XVIIIth Century* (Newcastle upon Tyne c. 1910)

Bradley, R., *The Country Housewife and Lady's Director II* (1732)

Brears, P., 'Traditional Food in the Lake Counties', in Wilson, C.A., *Traditional Food East and West of the Pennines* (Edinburgh 1991)

Bowness, W., *Rustic Sketches* (1868)

Brown, P.B., *In Praise of Hot Liquors* (York 1995)

Coleridge, S.T., *The Notebooks of, I 1794-1804* ed. Coburn, K. (1957-62)

De Quincey, T., *Recollections of the Lake Poets* (Harmondsworth 1985)

Dickinson, W., *The Dialect of Cumberland* (1878)

Dods, M., *The Cook and Housekeeper's Manual* (Edinburgh 1829, reprinted 1988)

Farley, J., *The London Art of Cookery* (1793, reprinted Lewes 1988)

Fell, J., 'Some Illustrations of Home Life in Lonsdale North of the Sands in the 17th and 18th Centuries', *Trans. Cumb. & West. Arch. Soc. XI* (Kendal 1891)

Glasse, H., *The Art of Cookery Made Plain and Easy* (1747)

Griggs, E.L.,*Collected Letters of Samuel Taylor Coleridge* (Oxford 1956-71)

Hart, K., *Dove Cottage* (1966)

Holmes, R., *Coleridge, Early Visions* (Sevenoaks 1989)

Hone, W., *The Everyday Book* (1826-7)

Howe, H.W., *Greta Hall, Home of Coleridge and Southey* (Norfolk 1977)

Hutchinson, Sara, *Letters of,* ed. Coburn, K. (Toronto 1954)

Kipling, C., 'Charr, a Northern Fish', *Petit Propos Culinaires, 17* (Totnes 1984)

Lee, E., *Dorothy Wordsworth* (1894)

McCracken, D., *Wordsworth & the Lake District* (Oxford 1985)

Moorman, M., *William Wordsworth: I The Early Years, II The Later Years* (Oxford 1957)

Newall, V., *An Egg at Easter* (1971)

Nicholson, N., *The Lake District* (Harmondsworth 1982)

Nott, J., *The Cooks and Confectioners Dictionary* (1726)

Raffald, E., *The Experienced English Housekeeper* (1769, reprinted Lewes 1997)

Rawnsley, E.F., *Grasmere in Wordsworth's Time* (Kendal n.d.)

Rawnsley, H.D., *Reminiscences of Wordsworth among the Peasantry of Westmoreland*, intro. by Tillotson, G., (1968)

Rundell, M.E., *A New System of Domestic Cookery* (1813)

Rollinson, W., *Life and Traditions in the Lake District* (1974)

Stead, J., 'Prodigal Frugality: Yorkshire Pudding and Parkin', in Wilson, C.A., *Traditional Food East and West of the Pennines* (Edinburgh 1991)

Sullivan, J., *Cumberland and Westmorland Ancient and Modern*
(London & Kendal 1852)

Thompson, T.W., *Wordsworth's Hawkshead* (Oxford 1970)

White, F., *Good Things in England* (1974)

Wordsworth, C., *Memoirs of William Wordsworth* (1851)

Wordsworth, Dorothy, *Journal*, ed. Moorman, M., (Oxford 1971)

Wordsworth, Mary, *Letters of, 1800-1855*, ed. Burton, E., (Oxford 1958)

Wordsworth, William, *Guide to the Lakes*, ed. De Sélincourt, (2004)

Wordsworth, William & Dorothy, *Letters of*; ed. De Sélincourt
   The Early Years 1787-1805, (Oxford 1967)
   The Middle Years 1806-1811,(Oxford 1969)
   The Middle Years part 2, 1812-1820, (Oxford 1970)
   The Later Years part 1 1821-1828, (Oxford 1979)
   The Later Years part 2 1829-1834 (Oxford 1979)
   The Later Years part 3 1835-1839 (Oxford 1979)
   The Later Years part 4 1840-1853 (Oxford 1979)
   A Supplement of New Letters, ed. Hill, H.G.. (Oxford 1993)

Wondrausch, M., 'Char' in Walker, H., ed. *Disappearing Foods* (Totnes 1995)

Young, A., *A Six Monthly Tour through the North of England* (1770)

MANUSCRIPTS FROM THE WORDSWORTH TRUST COLLECTION

Dorothy Wordsworth's commonplace books	DC MS 26 & 120
Fricker Family recipe book	MS E 907
Joanna Hutchinson's recipe book	WLMS Hutchinson 1/8/52
Martha Fricker's recipe book	MS E 907
Mary Wordsworth's recipe book	MS G 2/14/1

NOTES

ABBREVIATIONS

Date only, e.g. 10/1/00, *Dorothy Wordsworth's Journal*
DCMS   manuscript commonplace books of Dorothy Wordsworth
F   manuscript recipe book, Fricker faniily
JH   "   "   "   Joanna Hutchinson
MF   "   "   "   Martha Fricker
MW   "   "   "   Mary Wordsworth
LMW   Letters of Mary Wordsworth
LSH Letters of Sara Hutchinson
LWDW   Letters of William & Dorothy Wordsworth

Chapter 1

THE WORDSWORTHS & THEIR RECIPES

1.   Moorman I 29
2.   Prelude II, 79-85
3.   *ibid.* III 49-52
4.   *ibid.* III 42-45
5.   Moorman I 245
6.   25/7/00, Hart 52, 81
7.   7/8/00
8.   28/8/00, 11/12/01, 18/12/01, 13/3/02
9.   LWDW VIII 96
10.   16/10/02, 23/10/02, 8/12/02, 24/12/02, 16/1/03
11.   Moorman I 16
12.   Young IV 59
13.   LWDW I 133
14.   4/10/02
15.   Wordsworth Trust MS 9/90/31
16.   LMW 88 19/9/22
17.   LWDW I 351
18.   Wordsworth Trust WLMS Hutchinson 1/6/52

19.   Holmes 78
20.   *ibid.* 374
21.   *ibid.* 133
22.   LWDW III 11, 42
23.   Wordsworth Trust E 907
24.   Wordsworth Trust E 907
25.   Hart 76

Chapter 2

AT HOME IN GRASMERE

1.   The Waggoner
2.   LWDW I 317
3.   Rawnsley, E.F., 2
4.   Brears (1988) 77
5.   Hudson I 60
6.   24/12/02, LWDW I 622
7.   LWDW I 188
8.   9/12/01, 7/5/02, LWDW II 38
9.   Dove Cottage Guidebook (1970) 10, 9/12/01
10.   Personal Talk
11.   LWDW I 661

12. *ibid*. 622
13. 8/11/00, 7,17 & 18/4/02, 3/7/02
14. 8/11/00, 7,17&18/3/02, 3/7/02, 14/2/02
15. 12&24/11/01, 24/1/02, LWDW I 636
16. 29/5/00, 9,11,13 & 19/6/00, 2/8/00
17. 12/6/00, 19/6/00
18. 10/6/00, 23 & 25/6/00
19. 15 & 22/5/00, 30-31/6/00, 21/8/00
20. 4-5/8/00
21. 9/6/00, 10/9/00
22. Hart 52
23. 9/6/00
24. 11/6/00
25. 9/6/00
26. 16/5/00
27. 16/5/00
28. 15/5/00 to 30/8/00
29. 22/10/00, 14/5/02, De Quincey 260
30. 16/5/00
31. 11/6/00
32. 19/5/00
33. 4-5/6/00
34. Prelude III 528-9, Thompson 106
35. 24/11/01
36. 27/1/02, 27.4.02
37. Christies, London Saleroom, 7/6/1996
38. 5/2/02, 23/2/02
39. LWDW II 205
40. 17/5/02, 16/6/00
41. LWDW II 394
42. 8/2/02, 16/6/00
43. 17/5/00, 30/8/00, 10/10/00, 1/11/02
44. 29/11/01, LWDW III 13
45. Coleridge 283
46. Hart 50, 6/3/02, 11/1/03, 30/4/00, 13/1/02, 20/10/00
47. Hart 56
48. LWDW I 476
49. Rawnsley, H.D., 15,23,28,35,36
50. Hart 18
51. 26/5/00. 2/6/00
52. Hurst 52
53. 11/6/02
54. 31/10/02, 21/11/02
55. LWDW I 471
56. *ibid*. I 480-81, II 19, I 275
57. *ibid*. I 480
58. *ibid*. II 31
59. *ibid*. II 207, Moorman II 133
60. 23/11/00, 5/12/00, 22/12/00, 7/12/02, 8/12/02
61. Moorman II 87
62. LWDW I 403, 415, 481
63. *ibid*. II 51
64. Rawnsley, H.D., 35
65. *ibid*. 28
66. 14/3/02
67. Rawnsley, H.D., 14
68. 1/9/00, 22/5/02, 7/3/02, 17-18/3/02, 11/2/02, 4/12/02, LWDW I 636
69. 12/11/01, 22/11/01, 24/11/01, 24/12/02
70. 4/3/02, 12/6/02
71. LSH 202
72. LMW 207, 4/4/38
73. LWDW I 362, 4/3/02
74. De Quincey 127
75. Lee 63
76. De Quincey 127
77. *ibid*. 218
78. National Trust, Cleveland Court, Somerset
79. 7/8/00, LWDW II 453, 13/3/02, 16/1/03
80. 11/1/03, 2/7/00, 7/4/02, 16/5/00, Moorman II 135
81. LWDW I 661, 22/12/02
82. 25/6/00
83. Coleridge to Humphry Davy 25/7/00
84. LWDW I 442
85. *ibid*. I 263
86. LSH 61, 1/8/13
87. *ibid*. I 324, 19/9/26, LWDW III 539
88. 30/12/02, 28/10/00, 28/12/01, Hart 145
89. LWDW I 419
90. Hart 144, LWDW VII 448
91. Coleridge 723
92. 10/12/00, 5/11/01, 29/12/01
93. Moorman I 578
94. LWDW I 419
95. *ibid*. I 440
96. DCMS 26. 143
97. LWDW I 461
98. *ibid*. II 480, 661
99. *ibid*. II 282
100. *ibid*. II 279-81

101. LSH 9, -/10/08
102. MF 26
103. LWDW II 376-8
104. ibid. II 282
105. ibid. II 407, 491-3
106. ibid. II 493, III 15, 38
107. ibid. II 114, 519, 554
108. ibid. III 86,11, 114
109. ibid. III 114, 519, 554
110. LSH 57, 60, 1/8/13
111. LMW 49, 12/1/19
112. LWDW III 140
113. ibid. III 554
114. LSH 203, 11/9/20, 206, 19/9/20
115. LWDW III 554
116. Rawnsley, H.D., 12-13

27. 15/8/00, LWDW III 38 26/7/12
28. MW 16
29. MF 23
30. Moorman I 436, LSH 247 9/11/22
31. Coleridge 584
32. ibid. 974
33. 3/8/00
34. Dods 188
35. JH 4
36. Wondrausch 229
37. LWDW 508
38. LSH 51 9/3/13, 163 28/10/19
39. ibid. 210 19/9/20
40. Raffald 24, Wondrausch 230
41. JH 22
42. Moorman I 24
43. JH 3

Chapter 3

Of Main Courses

1. Nicholson 309
2. Young IV 591
3. LWDW II 205
4. ibid. III 50
5. 14/3/02, 7/4/02, Thompson 102, Hart 52
6. LMW 190, 21/9/37
7. Raffald 161
8. MF 32
9. MW 18
10. Coleridge 173
11. JH 2
12. 31/12/01
13. JH 3
14. Coleridge 305-7
15. JH 3
16. LWDW I 357
17. 29/10/00, 11/11/0, 29/11/01
18. Dickinson 201 'Giblet Pie', Dods 387
19. Rundell 133
20. 3/7/02
21. F.12
22. JH 1
23. JH 2
24. 9/12/01, 12/11/01, 24/11/01, 24/1/02, LWDW I 661, 25/12/05
25. JH 2
26. 17/3/02, 22/5/02, 1/9/00

Chapter 4

Of Cold Puddings

1. JH 14
2. F 20
3. F 19
4. F 14
5. MW 20
6. JH 11
7. MW 20
8. MF 22
9. F 15
10. JH 10
11. F 25
12. F 3
13. F 23
14. F 19
15. MW 17
16. Glasse 84
17. JH 12

Chapter 5

Of Hot Puddings & Sweet Pies

1. 29/5/02
2. Private Collection
3. LWDW I 661
4. MF 37

5. 16/5/00
6. Farley 183
7. JH 35
8. 7/6/00
9. Anon. 80
10. Private Collection
11. Raffald 80
12. JH 1
13. 28/12/01
14. 11/1/03
15. MW 17
16. 8/12/01, 25/1/02, 12/6/02, 3/7/02,
    4/3/92, 29/3/02
17. 28/12/01
18. Bradley II 122-3
19. Anon. 57
20. JH 11

Chapter 6
OF BREAD & CAKES

1. 26/1/02
2. Hart 52, 175
3. Hart 81
4. Hart 175
5. JH 27
6. JH 35
7. JH 30
8. F 13
9. MF 37
10. F 16-18
11. F 16-18
12. F 26, Dods 443
13. F 25
14. JH 8
15. Dods 445
16. Dods 446
17. JH 31
18. 13/3/02
19. Raffald 135
20. JH 9
21. Dods 450, Nutt 19
22. JH 9
23. JH 10
24. JH 10
25. F 27
26. Bowness 40

27. 31/5/00, 16/1/03
28. Anon. 74
29. JH 8
30. MF 25
31. F 7
32. JH 34
33. F 6
34. 6/11/00
35. Stead 163
36. White 299
37. F 22
38. JH 1
39. Dove Cottage Guide 116
40. Rawnsley, H.D., 28-9
41. Brears (1991) 85

Chapter 7
OF SWEETS

1. Dickinson 202 Taffy-joinin
2. MF 5
3. MF 8
4. MF 2

Chapter 8
OF PRESERVES & PICKLES

1. JH 14
2. 7/8/00
3. JH 13
4. JH 12
5. JH 34-5
6. MW 20
7. Wilson 52
8. MW 19
9. MF 22
10. JH 13
11. MW 21-2
12. JH 17
13. MF 11
14. JH 5
15. JH 5
16. Nott 202 'To Pick Lemons'
17. Farley 237
18. Farley 236
19. JH 6

20. Nott 203 'To Pickle Walnuts'
21. JH 6

Chapter 9
OF CHEESE & CURDS

1. Dickinson 203 'Milkin ring'
2. *ibid.* 203 'Blown milk'
3. *ibid.* 203 'Cumt milk'
4. *ibid.* 203 'Cheese Rennet'
5. Rollinson 45
6. 10/10/01, 9/11/01
7. 13/2/02, 26/11/01
8. DCMS 143
9. LWDW I 470, 450-4
10. *ibid.* II 58
11. *ibid.* II 282
12. *ibid.* II 453
13. LSH 19, 19/4/09
14. LMW 4, 11/8/13
15. LWDW III 15
16. LMW 20, 11/10/14
17. MF 38
18. MW 9
19. JH 16
20. JH 16
21. JH 16
22. LMW 169, 19/8/37

Chapter 10
OF DRINKS

1. Prelude I 37, 44, 45
2. LWDW I 460
3. 27/4/02, 7/5/02
4. 21/6/02
5. LWDW I 385
6. *ibid.* II 361-2, 23/8/00
7. *ibid.* II 403
8. *ibid.* II 407
9. *ibid.* II 453
10. *ibid.* III 82,85,94
11. 7/5/02, 23/11/00, 1/8/00, 25/6/00
12. 25/10/01, 10/11/01
13. 26/10/01, 27-8/1/02, 28/10/00
14. Dickinson 75

15. 4-5/11/02
16. Coleridge 1300, ?/12/00
17. JH 15
18. MW 18
19. LMW 362, 28/4/28
20. F 9
21. JH 27
22. 2/1/03
23. LWDW I 317, 475-6
24. *ibid.* 466, 480
25. *ibid.* 494
26. F 10
27. JH 28
28. MW 10
29. LWDW I 317, Hart 207
30. *ibid.* III 140
31. Coleridge 164
32. LMW 127, 16/7/ 28
33. LWDW III 409
34. LMW 202, 11/9/20
35. MW 11
36. JH 23
37. JH 15
38. JH 20
39. JH 20
40. JH 19
41. JH 24
42. JH 37
43. JH 19
44. JH 23
45. F 1
46. 5/10/02
47. based on a number of contemporary recipes
48. 48 4/5/02
49. 49 1/9/00
50. 50 JH 15
51. 22/4/02
52. F 10

Chapter 11
OF PACE EGGS

1. Sullivan 164
2. Hone I 426-8, II 450
3. Moorman II 430, 602, 611,

Rawnsley, H.D., 31
4. LSH 350, 7/11/30
5. *ibid.* 175, 19/11/29, 177, 25/11/29
6. e.g. Newall 284-5 & colour plate XVIII
7. Information from R.Miller
8. Lady Richardson in Wordsworth, C., II 446-7
9. Hone, op. cit.
10. Sullivan 164
11. Newall op. cit. 336,339, Thompson 34
12. Hone, II 450

33. JH 25
34. MF 4
35. JH 29
36. JH 34
37. 24-5/6/02
38. JH 25
39. MW 12
40. DCMS 26 143

Chapter 12
OF HOME REMEDIES

1. MW 8
2. MF 8
3. MW 15
4. MW 15
5. JH 31
6. MF 9
7. 24/11/00
8. 21/4/02, 4-5/11/00
9. 8/2/02
10. DCMS 26 142
11. JH 33
12. JH 33
13. JH 33
14. JH 33
15. DCMS 120
16. JH 32
17. JH 32
18. DMS 26 142
19. MW 14
20. JH 7
21. JH 18
22. 10/10/00
23. JH 33
24. OED 204 'Cold Cream'
25. JH 29
26. 19/3/02
27. 4/10/00, 11/11/01
28. e.g. LWDW I 505, III 131
29. *ibid.* VIII 236
30. MW 8
31. MW 13
32. JH 7

GENERAL INDEX

A

Ale Mearnce 166
Allan Bank 19, 44, 48, 50–51, 53, 152, 189
Ambleside 20, 36, 161, 179, 188
Ashburner
    Peggy 37
    Thomas 40

B

Baldock 47
balls 51
Baty (Bateman), Frank 151
Beaumont
    Lady 36, 41, 165
    Sir George 165
    bees 20, 37. *see also* honey
    hives 38
Beetham's Churn 152
Bill, Mary. *See* Cooks
Bird, Richard 20
Birkett, Richard 177
Bishop Middleton 25
blackening 191
Blacklock, W.J. 38
Bouth 39
Bradley, Richard 102
Bristol 28–30, 81, 142
Burnett, George 29

C

Cambridge 20, 24, 33, 37, 102
Carr, Mr 23
Charlton, Mrs 144
christening 49
Christmas 36, 42, 45, 47, 49, 51, 70, 96,
101–102, 166–167
Churn, Taylor's 152

Clarkson, Catherine 57, 152
Clary 170
    Clary Wine 170
coal 23, 34, 39–40, 42, 107
Cockermouth 9, 19–21, 188
Cockyn family 161
Coleorton 44
Coleridge
    family 37, 42, 47
    Hartley 29
    Samuel Taylor 7–8, 13–14, 28–29, 34,
        40, 42, 44–45, 47, 60, 62–63, 70,
        101, 107, 197
    Sara 30
Colwith 39
Cooks
    Bill, Mary 53
    cooks 53
    Dawson, Mary 43, 52–53, 153
    Jane 53
    Mary Anne 53, 74
Cookson
    grandparents 22, 24
    Mr 22, 24
    William 22
Cooper, Margaret 195
Crosthwaite Museum 51
Crump, Mr 48

D

Danvers, Mrs 167
Dawson, Mary. *see* Cooks
De Quincey
    Thomas 46, 197, 200
Dixon, James 178–180
Dockray, Jenny 151
Dove and Olive Bough 22, 33, 35
Dove Cottage 7–9, 13–14, 19, 22, 23, 25,
    28–30, 33, 37–42, 44–46, 49,

52–53, 57, 64, 71, 102, 107, 109,
144, 151–152, 159, 161, 165–166,
172, 178, 184, 188, 189, 191, 193,
195, 197, 199, 202
Dunmail Raise 101, 127–128, 189

E

Easedale 39, 43, 48, 57, 151, 172

F

Fenwick, Miss Isabella 179
Fisher
John 36, 38, 42–43, 159
Molly 22, 36, 42–43, 50, 107, 109, 120, 152
fishing 7, 36, 73, 161
floor 21, 34–36, 51–52
chalked 51
Fricker
Edith 8, 28–29
family 8, 13, 28, 30, 133, 165, 170
Martha 13, 28–30, 50, 53, 59, 86, 88,
96, 111, 122, 153, 184, 193,
198–199
Mary 28–29
Sara 8, 28–30
fuel 34, 38, 48, 53, 99, 112

G

Gallow Hill 25, 63, 152, 192
Grasmere 5, 7–9, 13, 19–20, 22–23, 25, 28,
33–34, 36, 39, 41, 43–44, 47–49,
51, 53, 57, 107, 127–128, 153, 159,
161, 165, 179, 195, 197, 199
Church 49
Rectory 19, 51, 153
Grassy Nook 153
Green
George 39
Sally 43
Sarah 39
Greta Hall 29, 30, 47, 49, 197
Grey, Barbara 119–120

H

Halifax 20–22, 41, 125

Hawkshead 19, 37, 39, 75, 198
High Bakestones 127
High Broadrain 161
Hindwell 28, 152, 153
Hollins, The 161
Hugessen, Mrs 184
Hutchinson
family 23, 28
George 23, 25
Henry 23, 25, 73
Joanna 8, 13, 15, 19, 23, 25–28, 30, 44,
53, 60–62, 66–67, 69, 72–73,
76–77, 81, 87, 98, 108, 117, 121,
126, 140, 143, 146, 154, 162,
164, 168, 184–185, 188–190,
193, 198–199
John 195
Mary 7, 24
Sara 2, 13, 19, 23, 43–44, 48, 50–53,
63, 73, 107–108, 128, 199
Thomas 23, 24, 70

I

Ibbotson family 161
Ingleton 40

J

Jackson
Jim 159
Mr 51, 159

K

Kendal 20, 23, 39, 40, 57, 98, 119–120,
161, 180, 197–198
Keswick 8, 20, 29, 30, 37, 40, 51, 53, 101,
151, 161, 165, 189
King
Mrs 108–109, 170
Mr Thomas 169
King's Head 49, 101–102, 151, 161, 165
Kirk Ulpha 49
kitchen 20–21, 34–36, 40, 43, 50–51, 53,
57–58, 63, 68, 70, 83, 107, 127,
154, 161

L

Langdale 36, 38, 43, 179
Lloyd family 161
Lovell, Robert 28, 29
Lowther, Sir James 20
Lucock, John 20

M

Marshall
    Jane 41, 58
    John 58
Martindale 127, 177
Maryport 177
Mathew, Mrs 103
Monkhouse
    Elizabeth 23
    John 24, 163
    Margaret 24, 195
    Mary 152
    Thomas 73
    William 195

N

Nanny Patty 26
Newton, Matthew 120
Nunwick Hall 24

O

Oliff family 161
oven 14, 21, 23, 34–35, 38, 42, 58, 63–64,
    68, 71–72, 75, 90–91, 99–102,
    107, 110–116, 119, 121–125, 141,
    146

P

Pace eggs 177–180
Pantisocracy 28, 60
Park House 44
Patrick, James 23
peat 36, 38–39, 127
Penrith 22–24, 28
Powell
    Mr 155
    Mrs 168

Q

Quillinan, Edward 167

R

Racedown 22, 29
Raven Crag 49
Rawnsley
    Canon 41
    Eleanor 33, 36, 159
Rawson
    Elizabeth 20
    William 20
Richardson, Margaret. *See* Monkhouse
Rydal
    Mount 19, 26, 48–49, 51–53, 58, 155,
        163, 178–179
    Rydalwater 36, 48, 161

S

Saline Draught 184
salting 70
Seathwaite (Duddon) 49, 73
Sebergham 24
Simpson
    Miss 192
    Mr 23, 98
    Mrs 37, 43
Sockburn 22, 24–25, 28–29, 62, 95, 152, 192
Southey, Robert 8, 13, 28, 29
Stanley
    John 49, 102, 151, 161
    Peter 49
Stickle Tarn 45
Sykeside 38

T

Thirlmere 36, 171
Thirlspot 49, 101–102, 151, 161, 165
Threlkeld, Miss Elizabeth 125
Tongue Gill Mill 127
Towers, Betty 159
Twining, Mr Richard 159, 161
Tyson
    Ann 19, 37
    John 75

W

water 33–34, 38, 50, 159, 165
Whitehaven 40, 171
Whitwell, Rachel 98, 102, 120
Wigan 40
Windy Brow 20, 22, 60
Wordsworth
    Ann 19
    Christopher 19
    Dora 45, 52, 152, 153
    Dorothy 7–8, 13, 19–26, 28–30, 33,
          35–38, 40–45, 47–48, 50–53,
          57–58, 60, 62, 64–65, 69,
          71, 95, 97–98, 101–102, 107–
          109, 115, 120, 125, 127–128,
          139, 151–153, 159, 161, 165–167,
          171–172, 183–188, 192–193
    household 28, 30, 152
    John (brother) 159
    John (father) 19–20
    John (son) 43–44, 47, 64, 187
    Mary 8, 13–15, 27, 30, 33, 41, 53, 60,
          81, 90, 140, 143, 162, 192–193,
          195
    Richard 19
    Thomas 26, 47
    William 2, 13, 19, 22–26, 28–29, 33,
          35–38, 40, 42–47, 49–50, 52,
          60, 62, 71, 75, 95, 101–102, 107,
          127, 197, 198
    William (son) 45
Wrangham, Rev. Francis 33
Wythburnwater 36

Y

Young
    Arthur 24
    Mary 26

FOOD & RECIPE INDEX

A

ale 21, 33, 34, 49, 76–77, 108, 165,
    165–166, 171, 177
Ale Mearnce 166
apples 24, 45, 49, 59, 100–102, 145
apricots 88, 100
    to preserve 140

B

bacon 30, 34, 36, 50, 57, 66–69
    Egg & Bacon Pie 68
Barm 110
bass 36
batter 71, 95, 95–96, 98–99, 110, 112
beans 37, 126, 161
beef 15, 24, 36, 59, 64–65, 68, 70–71, 102
    Stewed 61
beer 33, 38, 76, 162, 165, 180
    Excellent Household 165
    Ginger Beer 163–165, 168
    to fine 165
blackcurrant vinegar 172
blancmange 15, 25, 83–86
bread 33, 36, 45–49, 57, 59, 66, 71, 76–77,
    90, 99, 104, 107–108, 110,
    120–121, 141, 151, 165, 168
    Diet bread 115
broccoli 37
butter 15, 26, 43, 45–47, 49–50, 57,
    60–63, 67, 69, 71–73, 75–77,
    82, 84, 96, 97, 97–101, 110–118,
    121–127, 133, 142, 151–153

C

Cakes 23, 28, 30, 43, 47, 111–121, 127, 133, 179
    icing for 113
    Cheesecakes 126, 142

Queen Cakes 117
    sponge 30, 113, 115
Calf's Feet 28, 62, 81, 83, 151, 153
carrots 37, 145
Char 49, 73–75
cheese 44, 47, 49, 57, 121, 125–126, 142,
    151, 154–155
    Lancashire 121, 152, 156
    Stilton 155
chicken 28, 62–64, 83
clary 170
    Clary Wine 170
coffee 15, 38, 49, 145, 161–162, 172
cowslip 167
    Cowslip Wine 170
cream 15, 28, 38, 43, 49–50, 57, 63–65,
    77, 81, 84, 86–91, 95, 98–101,
    104, 112–117, 122, 124, 126,
    140–142, 146, 151–152, 154–155,
    161–163, 188, 193
curds 125, 151, 155
currants 96, 99, 102–103, 111–114, 117,
    125, 142–143, 172
custard 85, 89–90, 98, 141

D

damsons, preserved 15, 45, 84, 140, 141

E

eels 72–73
    to collar 73
eggs 14, 45, 47, 49, 62–63, 68–69, 71,
    76, 81–82, 85–87, 89–90,
    95–101, 104, 110–119, 121–122,
    125–126, 142, 155, 170, 177–180
    & Bacon Pie 68
elderflower 166, 193
    Elderflower Wine 170

F

fish 15, 22, 36, 45, 70–73, 75–77, 83
Flummery 85

G

giblets 64–65
   Giblet Pie 65, 201
ginger
   Artificial 143
   ginger 121–123, 143, 145, 147–148,
      163–164, 168–169
   Gingerbread nuts 124
   Gingerbread [Snaps] 123, 124
gooseberries 37, 45, 51, 57, 98–100, 139,
      166, 170
   Gooseberry Pudding 99
   Gooseberry Wine 26, 167–168

H

hams 26, 30, 34, 69, 70
hare 45, 66, 67
   Hare Pie 66
honey 37–38, 47, 186

I

Imperial Water 162

J

jellies 30, 81, 83
   Calf's Feet Jelly 82
   Currant Jelly 143
   Jelly 59, 82–83, 133–134, 142–143
   Orange Jelly 83
   Shank broth or Jelly 59
   Strengthening Jelly 133–134
jumbles 117

L

lemons 82–83, 119, 133–134, 142,
146–147,
      154, 162–164, 166, 168–171, 191
   To pickle 147

M

macaroons 118
marmalade 90–91, 141
Meat Balls 62
Minc'd pies 103
mince 66, 101–102
mushrooms 61–62, 77, 146
   Pickled Mushrooms 146
   Stewed Mushrooms 77

O

Onions 37, 59–64, 71–74
oranges 84, 88, 100, 103
   Candied Orange 88
   Orange Jelly 83, 88, 141

P

parkins 125
pears 45, 91, 140
peas 34, 36–37, 57, 60–61
peat 36, 38–39, 127
pickle 15, 26, 69, 73, 144–148
   pickled lemons 146–147
   pickled mushrooms, 146
pies 64–67, 73, 101–102, 141
   Christmas Pie 102
   Egg & Bacon Pie 68
   Giblet Pie 65, 201
   Hare Pie 66
   Minc'd pies 103
   Rice [& Fruit Pie] 101–102
pig 28–29, 64, 68–69, 153
pigeons, jugged 61
pike 36, 57, 71–72, 161
plum 30, 47, 96, 99, 111–112, 141
port 112–113, 134, 171, 190
Portuguese Vegetable Soup 60
potatoes 20, 22, 24, 33, 36–37, 45, 51, 57,
      60–61, 65, 95, 108–109, 178
potted fish 24, 57, 73
potted meat 49
puddings
   black pudding 95
   cold
      Blancmange 83–86

Cream curds 155
Cream puddings 81, 84, 87–90
jaunemange 25, 85
Jellies. *See* jellies
Lemon Pudding 45
Rice pudding 90, 101
Stone Cream 88
Swiss Cream 88
hot
    Apple, Apricot 100
    Baked Batter Pudding 99
    Boiled batter pudding 95
    Custard Pudding 98
    German Puffs 99–100
    Gooseberry Pudding 99
    Hasty 97
    Plum Pudding 96
    Raspberry Fritters 104
    Roasted Apples 101

R

radishes 37
raisins 96, 103, 111–113, 166, 169–170, 184
    Raisin Wine 169
Rhubarb 37, 102, 184
rice 26, 34, 60–61, 63, 86, 90–91,
101–102, 114, 118, 125–126
roast 24, 35, 37, 47, 57, 64, 68, 95
rum 15, 49, 161, 171–172

S

salting 70
sandwiches 49
Satin Biscuits 116
sauce 57, 62, 64, 69, 72, 76–77, 95–96,
98, 100, 142, 146
    Chicken Sauce 63
    Pig Sauce 69
seed 23, 37, 51, 141, 143, 145, 147, 188
    Caraway seeds 110–111, 115–116,
    121–122, 124
shrub 144, 171–172, 190
Smyrna Wine 169
soup 25, 26, 45, 60, 62
spinach 37
Stilton cheese 155

strawberries 37
sweets
    Sponge Cream 134
    Strengthening Jelly 134

T

tea 159, 161, 179
thyme 37, 67
toast 38, 46–47, 59, 77, 110, 184
toffee 133
trout 24, 45, 73, 75–76
turnips 37, 60–61, 145

V

Veal Patties 66
vegetables 22, 30, 36–37, 45, 60, 61, 63–64,
77, 139, 144–145
vinegar 70, 73, 76–77, 139, 144–148, 154,
161, 170, 172–173, 187–188,
191–192
    Blackcurrant vinegar 172
    (Mrs Charlton's) 144
    Sugar Vinegar 144

W

walnuts 147–148
    to pickle 148
Water, Hungary 188

Y

yeast 107–108, 110–111
    Potatoe Yeast 108
    To make 108

HOUSEHOLD & REMEDIES INDEX

A

Appetite, to create 183

B

blackening 191

C

Chilblains 185
cold cream 188–189, 193
Cough Mixture 186

E

Eye Water 190

M

mahogany, to clean 192

O

Oliver's Oil 188

P

Pills
    Mrs Hugesson's 184

R

rheumatism 188

S

Saline Draught 184
Scouring Spirit 191
sore eyes 50, 179, 189
    Sore Eyes 190

W

wash-balls 28, 193
warts & Corns 188

Excellent Press
Ludlow

OTHER EXCELLENT PRESS PUBLICATIONS

Traditional Food in Shropshire

by Peter Brears

In Shropshire, the largest and most fertile of England's inland counties, the quality of locally-produced food is second to none. This book, the first major study of the subject, draws on the widest range of local evidence to show how kitchens were designed and equipped, and various foods cooked, in cottages, halls and baker's shops, either for everyday meals, or for special celebrations. There are also over a hundred traditional Shropshire recipes, each having been cooked in order to present them in modern form for anyone wishing to accurately re-create them today, including the histories and method for those great local specialities, the Shrewsbury Cake and the Shrewsbury Simnel.

Illustrated with many colour plates and line drawings by the author.

ISBN 1 900318 39 3   216pp   £19.95

Excellent Press
Ludlow

Reminiscences of an Old West Country Clergyman

by W.H.Thornton

Privately printed on the author's retirement in 1897 and recently rediscovered, this is a classic account of country life in Exmoor and Dartmoor during the Victorian period. Mr Thornton was a hard-riding outdoorsman whose clerical duties and love of the chase brought him into close contact with Devonshire characters of every stripe, from the squire and the bishop to the poorest cottagers, smugglers, thieves and murderers. The feats of riding and long distance walking described will amaze modern readers. Packed full of colourful stories, brilliantly told.

ISBN 1 900318 38 5   240pp in soft covers   £12.99

Excellent Press
Ludlow

LUDLOW FOOD SERIES

A popular series of delicious pocket books in hardcover from Shropshire's home of good food and local produce.

A Sausage Book

by Helen Saberi

A feast of sausages, from Cumberland traditional to Pigs in Blankets and Dublin Coddle, by this well known food writer.

ISBN 1 900318 31 8   60pp   £6.99

A Pudding Book

by Helen Saberi

All kinds of puddings are featured, including Apple Brown Betty, Poor Knights of Windsor, Drowned Baby, Sticky Toffee and Chocolate with pears and brandy. No concessions are made to calorie-watchers.

ISBN 1 900318 30 X   60pp   £6.99

Excellent Press
Ludlow

Good Cookery from Wales

by Lady Llanover

Anyone interested in British cookery will be fascinated by this selection from her famous book of 1867 containing some of the best traditional Welsh dishes. Lady Llanover was a famous hostess and cultural pioneer in Wales. Her cookery shows a sensitive appreciation of local produce in her descriptions of classic, but simple Welsh fare, like oatbreads and toasted cheese, along with the occasional grander dishes, such as Salt Duck and Chicken & Leek pie.

ISBN 1 900318 32 6   60pp   £6.99

Oct Ginger bread

1½ lb Treacle ½ lb Sugar 9 oz Butter
Ginger to your taste — a few cloves & a
little lemon skin — Rub the butter &
as much flour as will make the paste
stiff adding flour till it is so when
you knead it — when the butter &
treacle are stiff with cold set them
within the air of the fire to soften
in warm weather this is not
necessary —

Blacking

4 oz Ivory black 2 oz Course Sugar
mixed well with a quart of vin-
-gar — add carefully ½ oz Oil of
vitriol stirring very well with
a stick in a deep earthenware vessel
last of all add two large spoonfuls
of sweet oil —

To preserve fruit of any kind
Gather the fruit when dry & to
a pint of fruit take ¼ lb Loaf
Sugar (or fine soft will do) — put
the fruit & Sugar into Jars or

EIN
»MEISTER DER DRUCKKUNST«
IN HEIDELBERG

CHRISTOPH ROTH

Ein »Meister der Druckkunst« in Heidelberg

Das Heidelberger
Publikationsprogramm
des Inkunabeldruckers
Heinrich Knoblochtzer
1485–1495/1500

Universitätsverlag
WINTER
Heidelberg

Bibliografische Information der Deutschen Nationalbibliothek

Die Deutsche Nationalbibliothek verzeichnet diese Publikation
in der Deutschen Nationalbibliografie;
detaillierte bibliografische Daten sind im Internet
über *http://dnb.d-nb.de* abrufbar.

ISBN 978-3-8253-4800-7

© 2021 Universitätsverlag Winter GmbH Heidelberg
Imprimé en Allemagne · Printed in Germany
Umschlaggestaltung: Klaus Brecht GmbH, Heidelberg
Druck: Memminger MedienCentrum, 87700 Memmingen

Gedruckt auf umweltfreundlichem, chlorfrei gebleichtem
und alterungsbeständigem Papier

Den Verlag erreichen Sie im Internet unter:
www.winter-verlag.de

Vorwort

Die Arbeit, eine Art Bibliographie raisonnée, ist geleitet von dem Wunsch, eine kleine Auswahl aus der riesigen Datenmenge, die der *Gesamtkatalog der Wiegendrucke* (*Gw*) unter [https://www.gesamtkatalogderwiegendrucke.de/] bereitstellt, zum Sprechen und zur Anschauung zur bringen. Die abgerufenen Daten betreffen den Heidelberger Inkunabeldrucker Heinrich Knoblochtzer. Durch die Auswahl und zielgerichtete Verknüpfung der Informationen wird die Geschäftsstrategie einer mittelgroßen (Wiegen)Druckoffizin nachvollziehbar. Zugleich sollte – in wichtiger Ergänzung der bisher schon erschienen Arbeiten zur Kultur- und Literaturgeschichte Heidelbergs (Skizze dazu vgl. Einleitung) – ein plastisches Bild vom Beitrag der Druckerzeugnisse zum kulturellen Leben der von Kurfürstenhof, Universität, Franziskanerkloster und stadtbürgerlichem Leseinteresse geprägten Neckarstadt in den letzten Jahrzehnten des 15. Jahrhunderts entstehen. Dass diese Daten aus dem Gw auch zur Anschauung gebracht werden können, ist den vielen Bibliotheken und anderen Einrichtungen zu verdanken, die in großzügiger Weise Digitalisate aus den Wiegendrucken zur Verfügung stellen (in alphabetischer Reihenfolge):

Staatsbibliothek BAMBERG / Deutsches Historisches Museum BERLIN / Staatsbibliothek BERLIN Preußischer Kulturbesitz / Universitäts- und Landesbibliothek BONN / Universitäts- und Landesbibliothek DARMSTADT / Universitäts- und Landesbibliothek DÜSSELDORF / Universitätsbibliothek FRANKFURT / Universitätsbibliothek FREIBURG I. BR. / Forschungsbibliothek GOTHA der Universität Erfurt / Universitätsbibliothek HEIDELBERG / Thüringische Universitäts- und Landesbibliothek JENA / Bayerische Staatsbibliothek MÜNCHEN / Germanisches Nationalmuseum NÜRNBERG / Scheide Library, Princeton University, PRINCETON (New Jersey) / Württembergische Landesbibliothek STUTTGART / Lessing J. Rosenwald Collection, Library of Congress, WASHINGTON D. C. / Universitätsbibliothek WIEN / Herzog August Bibliothek WOLFENBÜTTEL / Zentralbibliothek ZÜRICH.

Die Quellen der Abbildungen[1] werden dem Leser stets mit vollständiger Adresse zum leichten Wiederaufruf und weiteren Studium der Materialien angegeben. Nur weniges Anschauungsmaterial musste aus lizenztechnischen Gründen ausgeklammert bleiben.

Dass die Arbeit nun in die vorliegende Publikation mündete, dafür danke ich herzlich allen Mitarbeiterinnen und Mitarbeitern des Winter-Verlags, die auf den unterschiedlichen organisatorischen, technischen und gestalterischen Ebenen so engagiert bei der Realisierung des Projektes mitgewirkt haben.

---

[1] Wenn nicht anders vermerkt, zuletzt eingesehen am 24.4.2021.

KVnst der truckerey [...] *dardurch die*
kostpern schetze schrifftlicher kunst und
weißheit, so in den alten bůchern langzeit
als der werlt unbekant in dem grabe der
unwissenheit verborgen gelegen sind, herfůr
in das liecht gelangt haben.

Buch der Croniken vnd Geschichten (‚Schedelsche Weltchronik‘), Nürnberg 1493, Bl. 252[r]

Inhalt

Einleitung: Knoblochtzer in Heidelberg... 9

A Unterschiedliche Themenblöcke, unterschiedliche Einflüsse,
  unterschiedliche Interessenten, Kunden, Initiatoren............................... 15
  1 Theologische Werke aus dem Umfeld des Franziskanerklosters......... 17
  2 Theologische Werke aus dem Umfeld der Universität...................... 24
  3 Schule und Grundstudium der Artistenfakultät 29
  4 Juridica 51
  5 Humanismus... 63
  6 Memento-mori-Thematik... 80
  7 Beichtlehren 85
  8 Sonstige Volksfrömmigkeit und Marienverehrung............................ 88
  9 Belehrung und Information (überwiegend *utilitas*) 97
    A) Prognostik, Komputistik, Astronomie/Astrologie...................... 97
    B) Politische, gesellschaftliche Information/Amtssachen................ 112
  10 Erzählende Literatur (überwiegend *delectatio*) 119
  11 Was nicht gedruckt wurde 132

B Statistik.. 137

C Fazit... 139

D Abgekürzt zitierte Literatur 141

E Register.. 143

Einleitung: Knoblochtzer in Heidelberg

Heidelberg, genauer gesagt die Bibliothek der drittältesten Universität im deutschsprachigen Raum, ist prominenter Standort von Handschriften, deren berühmteste die Große Heidelberger Liederhandschrift, der *Codex Manesse*, darstellt. Weniger bekannt ist Heidelberg als Druckort von Inkunabeln (Drucke mit beweglichen Lettern bis 1500),[2] und die sonst so opulent bestückte Universitätsbibliothek hat nicht sonderlich viele Textzeugen aus Heidelberger Druckoffizinen aufzuweisen, einige befinden sich auch im Heidelberger Stadtarchiv.[3] Der relativ geringe Bestand an Heidelberger Inkunabeln an ihrem Herkunftsort dürfte nicht darauf zurückzuführen sein, dass die Bibliotheca Palatina diese ursprünglich nicht enthielt. Vielmehr wurden die Wiegendruckbestände schon bei der Einverleibung der Kriegsbeute in die Bibliotheca Vaticana im Jahre 1622 weit weniger sorgfältig, und im Gegensatz zu den Handschriften nicht als geschlossene Fonds behandelt und dadurch weit verstreut.[4]

Eine Vorstellung davon, wie eine Heidelberger Druckwerkstatt/Offizin um 1490 ausgesehen haben könnte, gibt das in diesem Kontext mangels echter Alternativen immer wieder zitierte Bild[5] aus einem französischen Totentanz-Text, der *grant danse macabre des hommes et des femmes,* aus Lyon 1499/1500 (Gesamtkatalog der Wiegendrucke, Nr. 7954, Bl. 7r):[6] Die Memento-mori-Thematik (‚Gedenke Mensch, dass Du sterblich bist') wird hier so zum Ausdruck gebracht, dass auch in einer Druckwerkstatt, so wie in allen Berufssparten, alle vom Tod bedroht sind: a) Der Setzer (links) vor seinem Setzkasten (*les capses* heißt es im französischen Redetext des Todes an die *impremeurs*) mit der aufgesteckten Halterung für die Textvorlage (‚Tenakel'), b) derjenige, der den gesetzten Text mit Hilfe eines Lederballens einfärbt

---

[2] Das Jahr 1500 stellt nach weitverbreiteter Auffassung die hintere Grenze des Mittelalters dar. Bücher, die von der Erfindung des Buchdrucks mit beweglichen Lettern kurz nach 1450 bis zu diesem Jahr 1500 gedruckt wurden, nennt man ‚Inkunabeln' oder ‚Wiegendrucke': Die Erfindung dieses Buchdrucks in Europa (in Asien früher) ist mit dem Namen Johannes Gutenberg verbunden.

[3] Vgl. SCHLECHTER/RIES (2009). Verzeichnet sind 27 Exemplare Heidelberger Inkunabeln (ein Titel dreifach, drei doppelt), davon 22 in der UB, fünf im Stadtarchiv.

[4] Vgl. dazu kurz und aufschlussreich: WALTER BERSCHIN: *Die Palatina in der Vaticana*, Stuttgart/Zürich 1992, im Abschnitt „Die Druckschriften [...]", S. 158 f.

[5] Z. B. auch bei FERDINAND GELDNER: *Inkunabelkunde. Eine Einführung in die Welt des frühen Buchdrucks (Elemente des Buch- und Bibliothekswesens 5)*, Wiesbaden 1978, Tafel XX.

[6] Zwei Exemplare dieser Inkunabel haben sich in öffentlichen Einrichtungen erhalten, vom Exemplar Princeton University Library, Treasures of the Scheide Library, steht ein Digitalisat zur Verfügung (s. Abb. 1).

(Mitte, Hintergrund), c) der eigentliche Drucker (Mitte, Vordergrund, man beachte die Ähnlichkeit des Druckmechanismus mit einer Weinpresse und seine Verstrebung mit dem umgebenden Gebälk), und d) der ‚Buchführer‘ (so wird der nicht selten durch die Lande ziehende Buchverkäufer im Mittelalter genannt), der im Laden (im vorliegenden Fall rechts, unmittelbar neben der Werkstatt) die fertigen Bände an die Kundschaft bringen soll.[7]

Abb. 1: *Grant danse macabre des hommes et des femmes*, Lyon: Mathias Huss, 18 Feb. 1499 [/1500?], Princeton, Treasures of the Scheide Library 43.2 [https://dpul.princeton.edu/scheide/catalog/ms35td33q], 7ʳ (Bild 19, Ausschnitt).

Übergangen sind in der Abbildung zwei wichtige Arbeitsschritte, die während der Inkunabelzeit beide noch in der Hand der Druckoffizin lagen: Die diffizile Herstellung der geeigneten Farbe (‚die schwarze Kunst‘) sowie diejenige Vorarbeit, die eigentlich

---

[7]   Singulär innerhalb des Zyklus wird bei diesem Bild den beiden Berufsgruppen, die jeweils pro Seite zur Darstellung kommen, hier *les impremeurs* (links) und *le libraire* (rechts), nicht gleich viel Platz eingeräumt.

die zentrale Erfindung Gutenbergs ausmachte – der Guss der einzelnen Bleilettern.[8] Dazu kam noch die Holzschnittkunst, die für den Buchschmuck, Illustrationen und Zierinitialen, sorgte. Was von außerhalb, von Papiermühlen, von denen lange Zeit die besten in Italien angesiedelt waren, zugekauft werden musste und einen wesentlichen Kostenfaktor ausmachte, war das Papier. Nicht genuine Aufgaben der Druckoffizin waren auch das Rubrizieren, Illuminieren und Binden der Bücher, so dass die Möglichkeit bestand, dass der Leser die Texte recht günstig und schmucklos erwarb, und erst später, dem eigenen Geschmack und Geldbeutel entsprechend, für das endgültige Erscheinungsbild seines Buches sorgte.

Kurz nach 1450 war der Buchdruck mit beweglichen Lettern in Mainz von Johannes Gutenberg erfunden worden, und in den folgenden Jahren verbreitete sich die Kunst in ganz Europa, innerhalb des deutschen Sprachraums zuerst in Bamberg (1458), Straßburg (1458/9), Köln (1464/5), Eltville (1467), Basel 1468), Augsburg (1468), Konstanz (1468/9), Nürnberg (1469), … Speyer (1471). In dieser Reihe der deutschen Druckorte erscheint Heidelberg erst auf dem 40sten Platz um 1485.[9]

Von den ca. 95 Titeln, die im Zeitraum von ca. 10–15 Jahren (1485–1495/1500)[10] in Heidelberg erschienen (manche in mehreren Auflagen), gehen ca. 85 auf den Drucker Heinrich Knoblochtzer zurück. Diese Titel sind bis heute in 1204 Exemplaren an öffentlichen Bibliotheken erhalten, die kleineren meist nur in geringer Stückzahl (hier ist auch mit einer Verlustquote von Werken zu rechnen, von denen gar kein Exemplar überlebt hat), die umfänglicheren in Knoblochtzers Fall in einer Stückzahl von bis zu 166 Exemplaren. Die Zahlen sind den Verzeichnissen des großartigen Projektes *Gesamtkatalog der Wiegendrucke* (künftig *Gw*) entnommen, ohne dessen Listen, Verzeichnisse und Verlinkungen die vorliegende Arbeit gar nicht möglich gewesen wäre.[11]

Heidelberg ist ein eher ‚kleiner‘ Druckort mit relativ wenigen Ausgaben und gerade auch deshalb interessant, weil wenige Drucker (ich konzentriere mich hier auf Heinrich Knoblochtzer) alle Sparten bedienen mussten und unter verschiedenen Einflüssen agierten, während in ‚größeren‘ Druckorten wie Augsburg, Basel, Köln, Nürnberg, Ulm Spezialisierungen zwischen den zahlreichen Mitbewerbern stattfanden.

---

[8] Eigentlich eine komplexe Mischlegierung aus Blei, Zinn und Antimon. Vor und neben der Etablierung dieser Technik gab es im 15. Jahrhundert auch Versuche, mit Hilfe von Holzschnitttafeln zu einer Vervielfältigung von Text und dazugehörigen Bildern zu kommen: die sogenannten Blockbücher.

[9] GELDNER: *Inkunabeldrucker*, Inhalt, S. 7.

[10] Für die letzten fünf Jahre des Jahrhunderts ist die Drucktätigkeit Knoblochtzers nicht sehr gut gesichert, dazu später mehr. ‚Circa‘-Angaben sind angebracht, weil nahe verwandte Ausgaben desselben Titels mit nur geringen Abweichungen bisweilen doppelt gelistet werden.

[11] https://www.gesamtkatalogderwiegendrucke.de/

Aus den biographischen Daten zu Heinrich Knoblochtzer, die am ausführlichsten zuletzt von FERDINAND GELDNER zusammengestellt wurden, ergibt sich nur ein sehr schemenhaftes Bild seines Lebens und Wirkens:[12] Er wäre demnach um 1445 in Ettenheim im Ortenaukreis, zwischen Offenburg und Freiburg, geboren worden und hätte eine grundlegende Ausbildung in den Sieben Freien Künsten in der naheliegenden Benediktinerabtei Ettenheimmünster erhalten können (so ROTH: *Geschichte* [1901], S. 197). Ab 1475/76 bis 1484 war er als Buchdrucker neben einigen Mitkonkurrenten in Straßburg tätig. Akademische Titel und Bürgerrecht sind für ihn nicht nachgewiesen. Für Straßburg verzeichnet der *Gw* 72 Drucktitel vom Einblattdruck bis zu umfangreichen Codices. Aktenkundig ist nur seine Frau durch eine Entlassurkunde aus einem Pflegeheim in Schiltigheim 1479 und er selbst durch eine Schuldurkunde gegenüber dem Basler M. Tischmacher 1483. Vielleicht liegt in dieser Verschuldung auch der Grund für den Weggang aus Straßburg nach 1484. Aber auch wachsende Konkurrenz könnte die Ursache für den Ortswechsel gewesen sein. Vergleichbares lässt sich auch andernorts beobachten: Johannes Zainer, der seinerseits die Technik des Buchdrucks in Straßburg erlernt hatte, kam an seinem neuen Wirkungsort Ulm 1483 durch konkurrierende Unternehmen in so große Bedrängnis, dass er Zierinitialen und Randleisten veräußern musste, wovon dann wieder Knoblochtzer in Heidelberg profitierte, der das Material dort weiterverwendete (s. u. passim).[13] Dass es Knoblochtzer ausgerechnet nach Heidelberg zog, lag möglicherweise auch daran, dass die dortigen Kurfürsten Interesse hatten, die neue („schwarze') Kunst in ihrer Residenzstadt zu etablieren. Sie hatten das Gewerbe in Straßburg offenbar beobachtet, was wiederum durch die Tatsache belegt ist, dass der Straßburger Drucker Heinrich Eggestein schon 1466 einen Schutzbrief von Kurfürst Friedrich I. von der Pfalz ausgestellt bekam.[14] 1486 wurde Knoblochtzer dann jedenfalls (pro forma?) an der Heidelberger Universität immatrikuliert. Wahrscheinlich hat er gleichzeitig seine Drucktätigkeit in Heidelberg aufgenommen, voll firmierte, d. h. mit Ort, Jahr, Druckernamen versehene Drucke liegen aber erst seit 1489 vor (dazu Näheres im folgenden Abschnitt). In nur 15 Heidelberger, bevorzugt deutschsprachigen Inkunabeldrucken nennt er seinen Namen, ein einziges Mal bezeichnet er sich in der Schlussschrift eines eher kleinen, lateinischen Werkes (12 Bll.) als *impressorie artis magister* („Meister der Druckkunst', Gw 11597: Guarinus, Baptista: *De ordine docendi ac studendi*, s. Kap. 3). Ansonsten gibt es alle Abstufungen an Informationsgehalt innerhalb der Kolophone (Schlussschriften) von vollkommenem Ausbleiben über Angabe nur des Jahres, von Ort und Jahr, von Druckername und Jahr, von Ort und

---

[12] GELDNER: *Inkunabeldrucker* (1968). S. 66 f. und S. 265–267, sowie GELDNER: *Knoblochtzer* (1979), S. 195 mit Hinweis auf weitere Literatur, u. a. K. SCHORBACH und M. SPIRGATIS (1888), E. VOULLIÉME (²1922 und 1925), dazu FERDINAND W. E. ROTH: *Geschichte* (1901), S. 197–224.

[13] Vgl. dazu AMELUNG: *FDSW*, S. 23 sowie die Abb. der entsprechenden Initialen S. 62 f. und 67 f.

[14] GELDNER: *Inkunabeldrucker* (1968), S. 60.

Druckername bis hin zu den wenigen schon genannten voll firmierten Inkunabeln. Knoblochtzers besondere Bedeutung wurde in der Forschung immer wieder auch in der Ausstattung seiner Straßburger wie auch seiner Heidelberger Drucke mit ziervollen Initialen und Holzschnittillustrationen gesehen.[15] Wer sie anfertigte (evtl. Knoblochtzer selbst?) ist ganz unklar. Gesichert ist seine Drucktätigkeit in Heidelberg dann bis ca. 1495, GELDNERS Vermutung, dass Knoblochtzer „nicht vor 1501" gestorben sei, ist schon vom Autor selbst mit Fragezeichen versehen worden.

---

[15] Dazu später mehr. Einen guten Überblick zu diesem Aspekt bekommt man bei SCHRAMM: *Bilderschmuck 19*, Leipzig 1936, online als Digitalisat der UB Heidelberg zugänglich. SCHORBACH und SPIRGATIS (1888) weisen Knoblochtzer einen „Ehrenplatz in der Geschichte der Buchillustration" zu. Zitiert nach GELDNER: *Knoblochtzer* (1979), o. S.

A Unterschiedliche Themenblöcke, unterschiedliche Einflüsse, unterschiedliche Interessenten, Kunden, Initiatoren

Die exemplarische Beschreibung von Knoblochtzers Druckprogramm in einer mittelgroßen, vom Sitz der Pfalzgrafen und einer bereits hundert Jahre alten Universität geprägten Stadt dient zugleich der Auffüllung einer Lücke bei der Beschreibung des literarisch kulturellen Lebens in Heidelberg zum Ende des 15. Jahrhunderts: Innerhalb der Münsterschen Mittelalter-Schriften (Band 67: *Wissen für den Hof*, 1994 herausgegeben von JAN-DIRK MÜLLER) wird *der spätmittelalterliche Verschriftlichungsprozess am Beispiel Heidelberg im 15. Jahrhundert* in mehreren Beiträgen von verschiedenen AutorInnen anhand des Buchbesitzes des Hofkaplans, Kirchenrechtlers und Chronisten Mathias von Kemnat (†1476), anhand von Albertus-Magnus-Übersetzungen, anhand von Kriegskunst-Traktaten und anderen Sachtexten, anhand eines zum Wissensbuch ausgeweiteten Gebetbuchs und anhand anderer Detailuntersuchungen allesamt *vor* Knoblochtzers Zeit beschrieben.

Auch aus den zahlreichen kleingliedrigen Einzelbeiträgen in den 1986, zum Gründungsjubiläum der Universität herausgegebenen Katalogbänden *Bibliotheca Palatina* (Text- und Bildband) ergibt sich ein mosaikartiges, allerdings sehr auf die Universität zentriertes Bild des Heidelberger literarischen Lebens im Mittelalter. Das Hauptinteresse liegt naturgemäß bei den zur Ausstellung vorübergehend zurückgekehrten, vor allem lateinsprachigen Beständen der Palatina (v. a. Artes liberales, Theologie, Reformation, Zimelien, Einbände usw.), die Druckgeschichte der Stadt spielt aber keine Rolle. Dies ist ebenso wenig der Fall in der älteren Arbeit von GERHARD RITTER, der im III. Abschnitt „Zwischen alter und neuer Zeit [...]" innerhalb seiner Studie *Die Heidelberger Universität im Mittelalter (1386–1508)* die Umbrüche dieser Jahrzehnte im Lehrbetrieb der Hochschuhle, in die auch Knoblochtzers Wirkungszeit fällt, ansonsten anschaulich beschreibt.[16]

Im großen Stadtbuch *Heidelberg. Geschichte und Gestalt*, das (wie schon die *Bibliotheca-Palatina*-Bände auch) ELMAR MITTLER 1996 herausgegeben hat, findet sich eine Überblicksdarstellung von Michael Buselmeier zu *Heidelberg und die Literatur* (S. 242–267, excl. 250–253 und 257–261), in der das Mittelalter ganz peripher erwähnt wird. Mehr relevante Informationen für den hier zu betrachtenden Zeitraum bietet der Beitrag von RUDOLF KETTEMANN: *Loblied auf Heidelberg. Peter Luders Enkomion aus dem 15. Jahrhundert* (S. 321–324) und ELMAR MITTLER: *Bibliothek*

---

[16] GERHARD RITTER: *Die Heidelberger Universität im Mittelalter (1386–1508). Ein Stück deutscher Geschichte.* Heidelberg 1936, ND ebd. 1986, v. a. S. 411–491.

im Wandel. Die Universitätsbibliothek in Vergangenheit und Zukunft (S. 326–361, excl. 348 f. fürs Mittelalter v. a. 326–337). Dass auch hier die früheste Druck-geschichte Heidelbergs keine Berücksichtigung findet, belegt schon das Fehlen eines Knoblochtzer-Eintrags im Register, (obwohl der Inkunabeldrucker S. 245 einmal kurz erwähnt ist).

Die Darstellung von MARTINA BACKES: *Das literarische Leben am kurpfälzischen Hof* (1992) berücksichtigt das Ende des Jahrhunderts durchaus in instruktiven Ab-schnitten, doch fehlt die Einbeziehung der in Heidelberg erstellten *Drucke* weitge-hend. Der Abschnitt über „Die Buchdrucker", S. 66–73, bleibt recht skizzenhaft und ermangelt der Verknüpfung mit dem Abschnitt „Philipp der Aufrichtige" (S. 136–171), in dessen Regierungsjahre, 1476–1508, Knoblochtzers Wirken fällt. Die von BACKES genannten älteren Werke zum Thema von H. WIRTH und W. E. ROTH sind, was in Anbetracht der seinerzeit unendlich mühevollen Recherche nicht zu verwun-dern braucht, ganz unvollständig, bieten trotzdem hie und da brauchbare Details.[17]

Wieder ganz aus bibliotheksgeschichtlicher Sicht wird das literarisch kulturelle Leben der zweiten Hälfte des 15. Jahrhunderts in KARIN ZIMMERMANNS Beitrag *Die Anfänge der Bibliotheca Palatina bis zu Friedrich I. dem Siegreichen und Philipp dem Aufrichtigen* beschrieben.[18]

HENRIKE LÄHNEMANN vertieft 2002 nochmals einen Teilaspekt der Arbeit von MARTINA BACKES, indem sie den Fokus auf *Margarethe von Savoyen in ihren litera-rischen Beziehungen* legt.[19]

Nicht zuletzt möchte die hier vorgelegte Bibliographie raisonnée als eine Er-gänzung und Fortsetzung zu PETER AMELUNGS hervorragendem Katalogband *Der Frühdruck im deutschen Südwesten 1473–1500* fungieren, der anlässlich einer Aus-stellung der Württembergischen Landesbibliothek Stuttgart 1979 herausgebracht wurde. Das Unternehmen war auf mehrere Bände angelegt, berücksichtigt aber im publizierten Sektor nur den Ulmer Inkunabeldruck, sporadisch finden sich auch schon Hinweise auf die geplanten Folgebände, die dem Frühdruck in Esslingen, Konstanz, Freiburg, Urach u. a., und eben auch Heidelberg (kurzer Überblick S. XX) gewidmet werden sollten, aber nie erschienen sind und (nach Auskunft von entspre-chender Stelle) in absehbarer Zeit auch nicht erscheinen werden.

Von den vielen Fragen, die an die Tätigkeit Knoblochtzers in Heidelberg zu stellen wären (wo könnte seine Werkstatt angesiedelt gewesen sein, woher bezog er das not-wendige Papier, mit welchen Partnern kooperierte er, wie agierte er markttechnisch),[20]

---

[17] HERMANN WIRTH: *Geschichte der Buchdruckerkunst in Heidelberg*, in: *Archiv für die Ge-schichte der Stadt Heidelberg* 1868, S. 21–25 sowie ROTH: *Geschichte* (1901).

[18] Relevant hier v. a. die Abschnitte: „Das Anwachsen der Bibliotheksbestände unter Philipp" und „Bücher aus dem Besitz der Margarethe von Savoyen".

[19] Margarethe von Savoyen, †1479, in zweiter Ehe verbunden mit Kurfürst Ludwig IV., Mutter von Philipp dem Aufrichtigen, 1448–1508.

[20] Mit diesen und anderen Fragen mehr beschäftigen sich eingehend z. B. bezogen auf den Augsburger Inkunabeldruck die Arbeiten von HANS-JÖRG KÜNAST: ‚*Getruckt zu Augsburg*'

will ich mich hier zuerst einmal auf den Versuch konzentrieren, das Material unter inhaltlichen Gesichtspunkten zu sichten, zu gliedern, Gebrauchszusammenhänge zu eruieren, indem ich exemplarisch *alle* vertretenen Themenblöcke betrachte, was bislang für Heidelberg noch nie unternommen wurde.[21] Die gedruckten Werke dienen mal mehr der Unterrichtung (*utilitas*), mal mehr der Unterhaltung (*delectatio*) der Leser, Lateinisches ist ebenso vertreten wie Volkssprachliches, kleine Flugschriften ebenso wie umfangreiche Codices. Bisweilen sind die Themenblöcke und Rezeptionskreise (wie schon gesagt) nicht klar zu trennen, so dass Mehrfachnennungen unvermeidbar sind.[22]

1   Theologische Werke aus dem Umfeld des Franziskanerklosters

Knoblochtzer war also schon knapp zehn Jahre in Straßburg als Drucker tätig gewesen, bevor er aus Gründen, über die man nur spekulieren kann, von dort wegzog. Auch was ihn bewog, ausgerechnet in Heidelberg eine neue Offizin einzurichten, ist vollkommen unbekannt, immerhin scheint es hier so gut wie keine Konkurrenz gegeben zu haben. Vielleicht wurde er aber auch von einem der mutmaßlichen Heidelberger Akteure im kulturellen Betrieb, dem kurfürstlichen Hof, Theologen der Universität oder dem Franziskanerkloster angeworben oder zumindest angezogen. Nur ein Teil der Drucke ist firmiert, andere weist man Knoblochtzer auf Grund des Vergleichs des zum Druck verwendeten Typenmaterials zu.[23] Zwölf der 85 Titel aus der *Gw*-Liste über Knoblochtzer, die sich über einen Zeitraum von 1485–1489 datieren lassen, sind ihm nicht direkt zuzuordnen. Man hat sie früher einem Anonymus ‚Drucker des Lindelbach' zugerechnet.[24] Sie werden ihm aber seit einiger Zeit, wiederum auf der Grundlage der Analyse des verwendeten Typenmaterials und anderer ein-

---

Buchdruck und Buchhandel in Augsburg zwischen 1468 und 1555, Tübingen 1997 (*Studia Augustana 8*) und bezogen auf den Frühdruck allgemein: UWE NEDDERMEYER: *Von der Handschrift zum gedruckten Buch. Schriftlichkeit und Leseinteresse im Mittelalter und in der frühen Neuzeit. Quantitative und qualitative Aspekte*, 2 Bände, Wiesbaden 1998.

[21] Derartig literarhistorisch zentrierte Studien für andere Druckorte sind z.B.: ROMY GÜNT-HART: *Deutschsprachige Literatur im frühen Basler Buchdruck (ca. 1470–1510)*, Münster/ München u.a. 2007, sowie Barbara Weinmayer: *Studien zur Gebrauchssituation früher deutscher Druckprosa. Literarische Öffentlichkeit in Vorreden zu Augsburger Frühdrucken*, München/Zürich 1982.

[22] Vgl. MÜLLER: *Wissen für den Hof* (1994), z.B. S. 11: „Allerdings zeigen diese Beispiele letztlich nur, wie wenig sinnvoll es für das Spätmittelalter schon ist, mit streng gegeneinander abgeschlossenen Rezeptionsgemeinschaften zu rechnen." Ähnlich BACKES (1992), S. 170.

[23] Von unschätzbarem Wert dabei: Das *Typenrepertorium der Wiegendrucke* der Staatsbibliothek in Berlin, https://tw.staatsbibliothek-berlin.de

[24] Benannt nach den Drucktypen, mit denen Gw M18384: Michael Lindelbach: *Praecepta latinitatis*, 15. XII. 1486, gedruckt wurde. Vgl. die entsprechenden Einträge in *Tw* und unten Kapitel 3: Schule und Grundstudium der Artistenfakultät.

schlägiger Beobachtungen, zugeschrieben. Unter ihnen sind zahlreiche Werke, die dem Umfeld der Universität angehören (dazu später mehr in Kap. 2 und 3) und etliche, sehr opulente Drucke, die für eine erstaunliche Leistungsfähigkeit der neu gegründeten Werkstatt sprechen und dem monastischen Bereich nahestehen, so dass hier die Hypothese gewagt sei, dass diese Heidelberger Druckerzeugnisse mit dem Franziskanerkloster unterhalb des Schlosses in Verbindung zu bringen sind.

Dieses war, um 1250 gegründet, unter „besondere[r] Förderung durch die kurfürstliche Familie" 1320 auf das Areal, das heute der Karlsplatz einnimmt (seit 1807), verlegt worden und diente vielfach als Grablege der kurfürstlichen Familie.[25] Auch der Humanist Rudolf Agricola ließ sich dort bestatten (vgl. Kap. 3). Die Klosterkirche war der Gottesmutter Maria geweiht (vgl. Kap. 8). Den engen Kontakt zum Fürstenhaus im 15. Jahrhundert belegen einige erhaltene lateinische und volkssprachliche Predigten.[26] 1803/1807 wurde das Kloster aufgelöst und in der Folgezeit abgebrochen.

Wenn die besagten Inkunabeln auch nicht vom Franziskanerkloster beauftragt wurden, so könnten sie doch zumindest von dort angeregt worden sein, oder der ‚Drucker des Lindelbach' (künftigt auch abgekürzt DdL) alias Heinrich Knoblochtzer hat sich Distributionsmöglichkeiten über das Franziskanernetzwerk erhofft. Dieser Neuanfang in Heidelberg ist allemal ein enormer Kraftakt gewesen, denn es handelt sich – wie gesagt – um sehr umfangreiche Werke, die einen enormen Ankauf von Papier und kompetente, lateinkundige Mitarbeiter in der Werkstatt erforderten. Möglicherweise haben Franziskanische Mönche hier selbst mitgewirkt und sich somit eine eigene Klosterdruckerei erspart, wie sie die Fratres vitae communis in Marienthal, die Fratres ordinis Eremitorum in Nürnberg oder die Benediktiner in Augsburg, St. Ulrich und Afra, betrieben.

[Gw 06548: CHAIMIS, BARTHOLOMAEUS DE: *Confessionale* (DdL)]: Das *Confessionale* des zeitgenössischen Minoriten Bartholomäus de Chaimis, laut Angaben in *Gw* (ohne Quelle) ein Franziskaner „aus vornehmer Mailänder Familie" und „berühmter Prediger" („†um 1496") stellt eine lateinsprachige, theologisch fundierte Abhandlung zu den Rechten, Pflichten, geforderten Kompetenzen und der Vorgehensweise des Beichtigers (*confessor*) beim Abnehmen der Beichte dar und passt somit auch zum Themenschwerpunkt der Beichtlehre, die in Knoblochtzers Programm später auch noch in der Volkssprache fortgesetzt wurde, dann aber natürlich nicht den Beichtvater sondern den Beichtenden als Leser anvisierte (s. Kap. 7). Eine genaue

---

[25] ANNELIES SEELIGER-ZEISS: *Heidelberger Kirchenbaukunst*, in MITTLER: *Heidelberg* (1996), S. 202–227, hier 207.

[26] Vgl. dazu CHRISTOPH ROTH: *Lateinische und deutsche Predigten im Umfeld von Universität und Hof in Heidelberg um 1420*, in: KNAPP/MIETHKE/NIESNER (Hg.): *Schriften im Umkreis mitteleuropäischer Universitäten um 1400: Lateinische und volkssprachige Schriften aus Prag, Wien und Heidelberg: Unterschiede, Gemeinsamkeiten, Wechselbeziehungen*, Leiden 2004, S. 197–230.

Datierung des in der Heidelberger Ausgabe[27] zweispaltig gedruckten, 104 Blätter umfassenden und im Darmstädter Exemplar mit Rubrizierung versehenen Werkes, wird in *Gw* nicht vorgenommen, immerhin wird es auf „nicht nach 1485" taxiert.

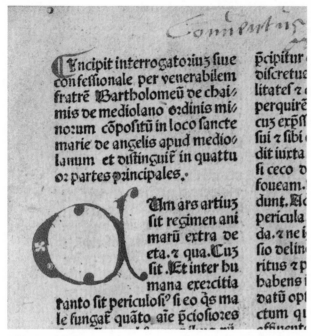

Abb. 2: ULB Darmstadt, Inc. II 637 [http://tudigit.ulb.tu-darmstadt.de/show/inc-ii-637/0001], 2ʳ (Ausschnitt).

Ein Exemplar dieses Werkes befindet sich in der UB (SCHLECHTER/RIES 218). Einen ganz ähnlichen Druck dieses Titels (im Darmstädter Exemplar wohl sogar vom selben Rubrikator überarbeitet wie Gw 06548) finden wir mit Gw 06550 vor, der vormals ebenfalls dem ‚Drucker des Lindelbach' zugerechnet wurde, heute aber in die Hagenauer Offizin von Heinrich Gran, „um 1489" lokalisiert wird. Gran hatte für seinen Drucksatz etwas mehr Papier benötigt (und damit höhere Investitionen tätigen müssen) als der Heidelberger Frühdrucker.

[Gw 0948920: EVRARDUS DE VALLE SCHOLARUM: *Sermones de sanctis* (DdL)]: Ebenfalls eine Herkulesleistung stellt gleich das zweite, nun genauer, auf „21.1.1485", datierte, vormals auch dem ‚Drucker des Lindelbach' zugeordnete Werk dar, das sogar 286 Bll. umfasst.

---

[27] Weitere Inkunabelausgaben (nach *Gw*): Mailand (2), Venedig (2) Nürnberg (2, davon eine aus der eben schon erwähnten Klosterbibliothek), Basel, Straßburg, Mainz, Hagenau und Augsburg.

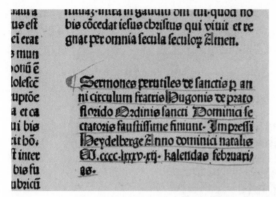

Abb. 3: ULB Düsseldorf, Pr.Th.I.379 (Ink.) [https://digital.ub.uni-duesseldorf.de/ink/content/pageview/8357396], 274ʳ (Ausschnitt).

Das Exemplar der Universitäts- und Landesbibliothek Düsseldorf, aus dem die vorstehende Abbildung stammt, wurde vom ursprünglichen Besitzer (laut zeitgenössischem Eintrag auf dem Vorsatzblatt), dem Kreuzherrenkloster Marienfriede bei Xanten (auch dies ein Bettelordenkloster) sehr hoch geschätzt: Man ließ den Druck nämlich mit relativ aufwendigen Initialen versehen. Das Exemplar der UB Heidelberg, das vormals dem Kloster Benediktbeuren gehörte, ist immerhin „durchgehend rubriziert" (vgl. SCHLECHTER/RIES 627). Die Zuschreibung der Sammlung von Musterpredigten De sanctis „per totum annum" (also für die besonderen Messen an den Heiligenfesten übers ganze Jahr, als Gegenstück zu den de-tempore-Sammlungen, die auf die Sonn- und Festtage des Kirchenjahres hin geordnet sind) an EVRARDUS ist modern,[28] im Mittelalter, auch in der hier vorliegenden Druckausgabe, lief sie unter dem prominenten Namen des Dominikaners HUGO DE PRATO FLORIDO (†1322).

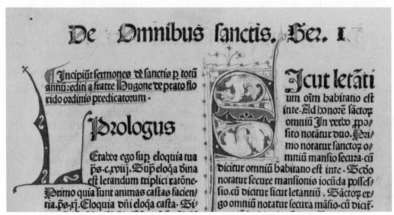

Abb. 4: ULB Düsseldorf, Pr.Th.I.379 (Ink.) [https://digital.ub.uni-duesseldorf.de/ink/content/pageview/8356852], 2ʳ (aijʳ, Ausschnitt).

---

[28] Bezieht sich auf einen französischen Prediger aus dem Augustinerorden.

Ein umfangreiches Register machte die Predigtsammlung auch als theologisches Nachschlagewerk brauchbar. Außer in Heidelberg wurde das Werk nur noch in Ulm gedruckt, dort von den Dominikanern (also auch einem Bettelorden) beauftragt.[29]

Eine bemerkenswerte Beobachtung nebenbei: Diese Inkunabel zeigt, wie derartig frühe Drucke heute auch zu Spekulationsobjekten werden können: Ein Exemplar des Heidelberger Wiegendrucks, ebenfalls aufwendig rubriziert, zudem mit einem soliden alten Ledereinband und handschriftlichen Fragmenten im Vorsatz versehen, wurde 2014 in einem Hamburger Kunsthaus für 16.800 € versteigert, ist seither im Amerikanischen Handelshaus *fine books & medieval manuscripts* für 35.000 $ angeboten worden.[30]

Einen weiteren Kraftakt vollbrachte Knoblochtzer ebenfalls in dieser frühen Heidelberger Zeit mit dem Druck eines *Vocabularius Ex quo* (*Gw*: „1485" aber nicht DdL zugewiesen), von dem kein Exemplar erhalten ist, das aber in Rückschluss von seiner Straßburger Ausgabe um die 150 Bll. umfasst haben dürfte (s. Kap. 2).

[Gw 03411: Bartholomaeus Anglicus: *De proprietatibus rerum* (DdL)]: Drei Jahre später („21.V.1488") entsteht dann die 326 Bll. umfassende, ebenfalls durch umfangreiche Register erschlossene Enyklopädie *De proprietatibus rerum*, die sich im wahrsten Sinne des Wortes mit ‚Gott und der Welt' beschäftigt:

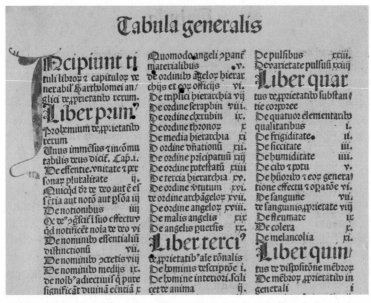

Abb. 5: ULB Düsseldorf, E. u. Ak. W. 83 (Ink.) [http://digital.ub.uni-duesseldorf.de/ink/content/pageview/3664313], 2ʳ (Ausschnitt).

---

[29] Vgl. Amelung: *Fdsw*, Nr. 107, S. 202, 205, 210.

[30] In *Gw* sind immer nur die Exemplare „in öffentlichen Einrichtungen" verzeichnet, d. h. hie und da kann man mit einer gewissen ‚Dunkelziffer' an tatsächlich erhaltenen Textzeugen rechnen.

Deren Druckausgabe dürfte auch durch franziskanisches Umfeld motiviert sein: Hier ist der Autor selbst Franziskaner gewesen, was die Schlussschrift ausdrücklich hervorhebt:

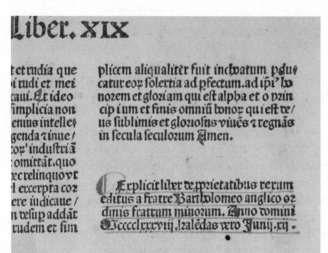

Abb. 6: ULB Düsseldorf, E. u. Ak. W. 83 (Ink.) [http://digital.ub.uni-duesseldorf.de/ink/content/pageview/3664961], 326ʳ (*DD8ʳ*, Ausschnitt).

Druckausgaben dieses Werks waren freilich nicht auf franziskanisches Umfeld beschränkt, laut Einträgen im *Gw* waren in der Inkunabelzeit mindestens elf Editionen erstellt worden, eine in Basel, drei in Köln, drei in Lyon, zwei in Nürnberg und zwei in Straßburg. Das Exemplar, das sich heute in der Uʙ Heidelberg befindet, war ursprünglich im Besitz des Zisterzienserinnenklosters Lichtenthal in Baden-Baden (Sᴄʜʟᴇᴄʜᴛᴇʀ/Rɪᴇs 206).

Für eine weitere Edition möchte ich die These wagen, dass ihr Zustandekommen durch die Franziskaner in Heidelberg zumindest begünstigt wurde:

[Gw 10786: Gᴇʀsᴏɴ, Jᴏʜᴀɴɴᴇs: *Opus tripartitum*, deutsch von Gabriel Biel]: Bei der deutschen, 30 Bll. umfassenden Ausgabe des *Opus tripartitum* des berühmten Pariser Theologen Johannes Gerson (1363–1429, „nicht nach 1488“, das einzige Werk in diesem Kapitel, das nicht dem ,Drucker des Lindelbach' zugewiesen wird) veranlasst mich der Umstand, dass dieses Werk während der Inkunabelzeit sonst nur noch in der allerältesten Klosterdruckerei, nämlich derjenigen der Fratres vitae communis (,Brüder vom Gemeinsamen Leben') in Marienthal, Geisenheim (im Rheingau-Taunus-Kreis/Hessen) zum Druck kam („um 1475“ Gw 1078550N), zur Vermutung, dass die Entstehung der hier besprochenen Edition von den Heidelberger Franziskanern motiviert, zumindest unterstützt wurde. Auch gilt Gerson als ein Theologe, der sich überaus eingehend mit dem Werk des Franziskaners Bonaventura (†1274) beschäftigt hatte. Der Übersetzer des *Opus tripartitum* ins Deutsche ist der zeitweise in Heidelberg tätige Theologe und Prediger Gabriel Biel, der 1477 auch auf Wunsch Graf Eberhards I. im Bart an der Gründung eines Hauses ,Vom Gemeinsamen Leben‘ in Urach mitwirkte.[31] Das Werk mag der Laienseelsorge, gedient haben, welcher sich die Franziskaner verschrieben hatten. Die beiden Themen ‚Memento mori‘ (*von der kůnst zů sterben*) und Beichte (*Von der bijcht*), die zwei der drei Kapitel des *drigedeilt werck* bilden, stellen natürlich auch eine starke Brücke zu den Themenblöcken des 6. und 7. Kapitels dar. Der Kolophon am Ende des Werkes lautet:

Hye endet sich diß drigedeilt werck. von dē tzehen
gebodē. Von der bijcht. Vnd von der künst zů sterben.
Dorch dē vßmelige lerer der heylgen schrifft. Meyster
Johan von Gerson Cantzler der heylgē hohen schulen
zů Parijs.

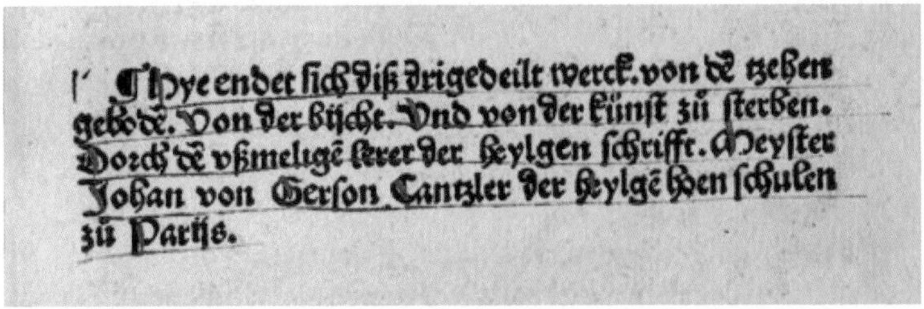

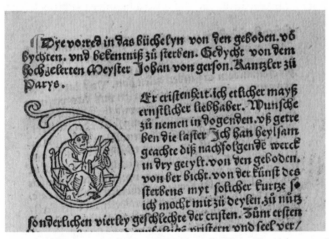

Abb. 7: ULB Darmstadt, Inc II 575 [http://tudigit.ulb.tu-darmstadt.de/show/inc-ii-575/0057], 29r (Ausschnitt).

Während an den einzelnen Abschnitten des Drucks lediglich Platz für den Eintrag von Initialen durch einen Rubrikator gelassen wurde, ist das Werk zu Beginn mit minimalem Schmuck insofern versehen, als Knoblochtzer eine schlichte Holzschnittinitiale eindrucken ließ, die er auch im berühmten *Totentanz* (s. u. Kap. 6) verwendete. Ein Teil dieser Initialen war von Johann Zainer in Ulm übernommen worden.[32] Das Motiv war hier sicher passend erschienen, weil es die gelehrte Abkunft des Autors unterstreicht:

Hye vorred in das büchelyn von den geboden. vō
bychten. vnd bekentniß zů sterben. Gedycht von dem
hochgelerten Meyster Johan von gerson. Kantzler zů
Parys.
Er cristenheit. ich etlicher mayß
ernstlicher liebhaber. Wunsche
zů nemen in dogenden. vß getre
ben die laster Jch han heylsam
geachte diß nachfolgendē werck
in dry geteylt. von den geboden.
von der bicht. von der künst des
sterbens myt solicher kurtze so
ich mocht mit zů deylen. zů nütz
sonderlichen vierley geschlechte der cristen. Züm ersten

Abb. 8: ULB Darmstadt, Inc II 575 [http://tudigit.ulb.tu-darmstadt.de/show/inc-ii-575/0003], 2r (Ausschnitt).

[31] Ulrich Bubenheimer: *Biel, Gabriel*, in: ²*VL* 1 (1978), Sp. 853–858.

[32] Zur Übernahme des Typenmaterials aus Ulm vgl. Geldner: *Inkunabeldrucker* (1968), S. 267 und Amelung: *FDSW*, S. 20 und 66.

2   Theologische Werke aus dem Umfeld der Universität

Knoblochtzers Druckwerke mit theologischer Thematik haben oft enger oder weiter mit Heidelberg verbundene Personen zu Autoren: Gabriel Biel (vgl. das zuletzt genannte Werk von J. Gerson) etwa oder Johannes de Lambsheim (s. u. in diesem Kapitel und Kap. 8). Einige von ihnen sind zugleich dem Umfeld des Heidelberger Humanismus zuzurechnen (Rudolf Agricola, Jodocus Gallus, s. Kap. 5) oder/und stehen dem Umfeld der Franziskaner nahe (vgl. Kap. 1). Wie schon gesagt: Die Abgrenzung zwischen den einzelnen Themen-/Interessenblöcken ist nicht sicher zu treffen, sie behält immer einen Anstrich von Künstlichkeit der Rückschau aus der Distanz von über 500 Jahren.

[Gw M51056: *Vocabularius Ex quo*]: Der lateinisch-deutsche *Vocabularius Ex quo* erschien in unzähligen Ausgaben innerhalb des deutschen Sprachraums (vgl. Liste im *Gw*). Er diente „als praktisches Hilfsmittel zum Verständnis der Bibel und [...] anderer lat. Texte" und „richtet sich an Benutzer mit elementaren Lateinkenntnissen (*pauperes scolares*)".[33] Von der Heidelberger Ausgabe, „um 1485", die somit zu den ersten an seinem neuen Wirkungsort entstandenen Inkunabeln Knoblochtzers zählt, ist leider kein Exemplar erhalten, man wird sie sich aber hinsichtlich des Umfangs (150 Bll.) und der Ausstattung ähnlich wie Knoblochtzers Straßburger Edition (Gw M51119, „nicht nach 1482", neben weiteren 14 Druckausgaben in Straßburg) vorstellen dürfen. Dort ist vom ganzen Alphabet nur das *A* durch eine 17 Zeilen hohe, die Fußwaschungsszene darstellende Initiale hervorgehoben. Für Querverbindung zum klösterlichen Kontext, der freilich schon in Straßburg bestanden haben müsste, spricht, dass der Apostel, der sich von Jesus die Füße waschen lässt (Petrus?), mit Mönchstonsur dargestellt ist:[34]

---

[33]   Klaus Grubmüller: *Vocabularius Ex quo*, in: ²*Vl* 10 (1999), Sp. 469–473, hier 470.

[34]   Denselben Holzschnitt (ohne Beschriftung des Spruchbandes) verwendete Knoblochtzer für die Ausgabe der lat. Predigtsammlung *Sermones dominicales super epistolas S. Pauli* (*Pars hiemalis*) von Thomas Ebendorfer, Straßburg 1478, Bl. 15r.

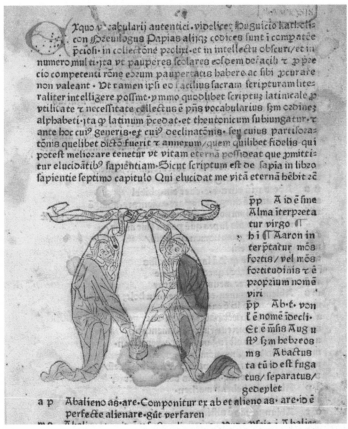

Abb. 9: BSB München, 2 Inc. s. a. 1229 [Ink V-311] [http://daten.digitale-sammlungen.de/bsb00032646/image_4], 2^r (*aij^r*, Ausschnitt).[35]

Der Eintrag zu *Abalieno* zeigt exemplarisch die Struktur der einzelnen Artikel mit Nachweis der Flexionsformen, Skizze der Komposition, lateinischer Definition und deutscher Übersetzung, hier *gût verfaren*, was nhd. so viel wie „Besitz entfremden" oder „rauben" bedeutet.

Vom Titel her legt der ebenfalls nach dem Incipit benannte *Vocabularius Curia palatium* [Gw M51289] einen ähnlichen Gebrauchszusammenhang nahe wie der *Vocabularius Ex quo*, doch muss man sich den Einsatz dieses Werkleins weit eher im Kontext Schule (s. Kap. 3) als in gelehrtem theologischem Betrieb vorstellen.

In der ersten Hälfte der 90er Jahre finden sich zwei Werke, die sich mit der Ausübung und Wirkung der heiligen Messe beschäftigen:

---

[35] Bei dieser und allen im Folgenden aus dem Bestand der B_SB_ München verwendeten Abbildungen findet die CC-Lizenz CC BY-NC-SA 4.0 (https://creativecommons.org/licenses/by-nc-sa/4.0/deed.de) Anwendung. Etwaige Änderungen bzw. Bearbeitungen des verwendeten Materials sind im Folgenden jeweils vermerkt.

[Gw M10884: Jacobus de Jüterbog: *De valore et utilitate missarum pro defunctis.*[36] Johannis de Mechlinia: *Determinatio utrum perfecta Dei opera possint impediri daemonis malitia*] datiert aus dem Jahr 1493:

vel suffragijs sacerdotis ipsius parrochic. Non ta
men oportet quot sit melius simpliciter quia forte
ipsemer in gratia proficit et plura Bonu facit in
parrochia magna quaз in parrochia parua/

Et sic est finis huius operis.
Anno. M. CCCC. XC. III.

Abb. 10: ULB Darmstadt, Inc. II 596 [http://tudigit.ulb.tu-darmstadt.de/show/inc-ii-596/0028], 14ᵛ (*Ciij*ᵛ, Ausschnitt).

Das Inhaltsverzeichnis auf der Versoseite des Titelblatts im Darmstädter Exemplar gibt Auskunft über den Inhalt des ersten enthaltenen Textes, eines *Opusculum* des Jacobus von Paradies (der auch noch mit vielen anderen Beinamen versehen erscheint) von 14 Bll.: Fragen über die Wirksamkeit von Messen, je nachdem von wem, in welcher Zahl und welcher Weise diese für Verstorbene abgehalten werden:

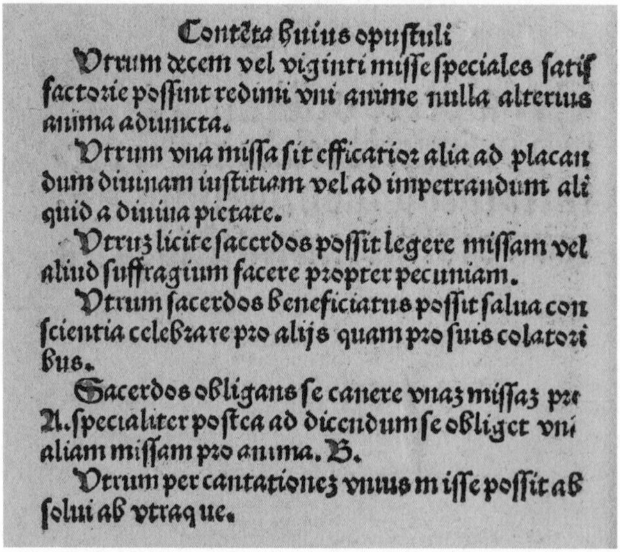

Conteta huius opusculi
Utrum decem vel viginti misse speciales satis
factorie possint redimi vni anime nulla alterius
anima adiuncta.
Utrum vna missa sit efficatior alia ad placan
dum diuinam iustitiam vel ad impetrandum ali
quid a diuina pietate.
Utruз licite sacerdos possit legere missam vel
aliud suffragium facere propter pecuniam.
Utrum sacerdos Beneficiatus possit salua con
scientia celebrare pro alijs quam pro suis colatori
Bus.
Sacerdos obligans se canere vnaз missaз pre
A. specialiter postea ad dicendum se obliget vni
aliam missam pro anima. B.
Utrum per cantationeз vnius m isse possit aB
solui aB vtraq ue.

Abb. 11: ULB Darmstadt Inc. II 596 [http://tudigit.ulb.tu-darmstadt.de/show/inc-ii-596/0002], 1ᵛ (*Aj*ᵛ, Ausschnitt).

---

[36] Die Wirkungsstätten des Autors (1381–1465), sind v. a. Krakau und Erfurt (Kartause), vgl. Dieter Mertens: *Jakob von Paradies*, in: ²*VL* 4 (1983), Sp. 478–487, zum hier genannten Werk Sp. 483.

Innerhalb dieses Werkes verwendet Knoblochtzer zur Aufwertung des sonst unscheinbaren Faszikels fünf Initialen aus verschiedenen Serien, die nicht extra für diesen Text angefertigt worden waren, und die teilweise wieder aus Johann Zainers Ulmer Werkstatt übernommen worden waren (s. o. zu Gersons *Opus tripartitum deutsch*), z. B. das *Q* im Stil der Initialen des Totentanzes von 1488/89 (vgl. Kap. 6), das für das hiesige Kleinformat im Grunde zu ausladend ist:[37]

Q Veritur primo an ille la
ijcus sapienter et ordina
te desiderauerit et pecierit
Secundo an isti fratres
recte sibi negauerint Ha/
buerint etiaȝ idē fratres
consuetudinem qȝ plures
persone missas redimerīt
oēs in vnum numerū as/
sociandi et pecunias mul
tas recipiendi. verbi gratia hodie post prandium
venit quidam petens triginta missas pro anima
patris sui iam defuncti Exhinc post horam venit
secundū petens totidem pro aīe sue uxoris Item

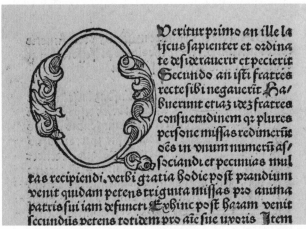

Abb. 12: ULB Darmstadt, Inc. II 596 [http://tudigit.ulb.tu-darmstadt.de/show/inc-ii-596/0004], 2v (*Aij*v, Ausschnitt)

Auf Bl. 19r: findet sich abschließend der Nachweis, dass der Text des ‚Anhangs', einer *determinatio* (‚Abgrenzung') des *johannes de mechilinia* ursprünglich einem Vortrag in der Artistenfakultät der Universität Köln zugrunde gelegen hatte:

tur ut sic nullū bonū ē irremuneratū sic nullū ma
lū maneatur impunitū. A quo nos punicīe malo
preseruet deus vt cum electis semper feliciter gau
deamus.
Explicit determinacio Eximij et desertissi/
mi doctoris sacre theologie Magistri johā
nis de mechilinia habita in vniuersitate co/
lonieñ. in scolis artistarum in quotlibet

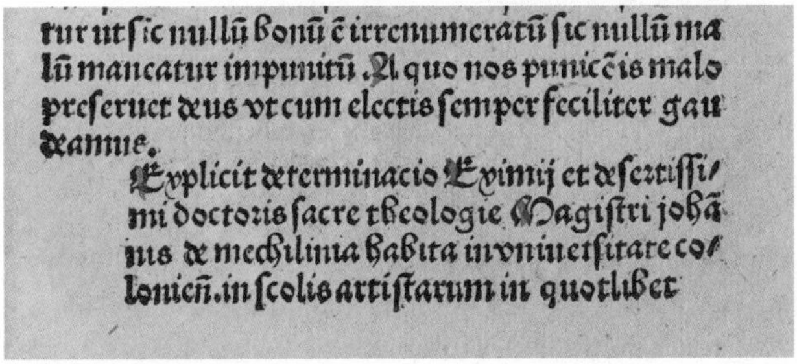

Abb. 13: ULB Darmstadt, Inc. II 596 [http://tudigit.ulb.tu-darmstadt.de/show/inc-ii-596/0037], 19r (Ausschnitt).

Ein Exemplar des Werkes besitzt die UB Heidelberg (SCHLECHTER/RIES 1006).

[37] Zur Übernahme des Typenmaterials aus Ulm vgl. Fußnote 32, hier *Q* im von AMELUNG: *FDSW*, S. 66, so genannten ‚Rokoko-Alphabet'.

[Gw M14225: JOHANNES DE LAMBSHEIM: *Speculum officii missae expositorium*]: Eine zweijährige zeitliche Lücke ergibt sich zum hier noch zu nennenden Werk („29. VI.1495") von 30 Bll. des Johannes de Lambsheim, eines „regulierte[n] Augustiner-chorherr[n] in Kirschgarten bei Worms", der evtl. mit einem *Johannes Ronp de Lamszhem* in der Heidelberger Matrikel zu identifizieren ist.[38] Es handelt sich um das *Speculum officii missae expositorium*, das „eine vorwiegend allegorische Auslegung der Messe" sowie eine *mystica expositio* enthalte.[39] Es ist mit einer präzisen Datierung mittels der Regierungszeit von Kaiser Maximilian, Pfalzgraf Philipp und dem Wormser Bischof Johannes (= Johann II. von Dalberg) im Kolophon versehen, und die tragende Rolle des ‚umsichtigen und ehrenwerten Heidelberger Druckers Heinrich Knoblo[ch]tzer‘ für die Erstellung des Textes explizit hervorgehoben:

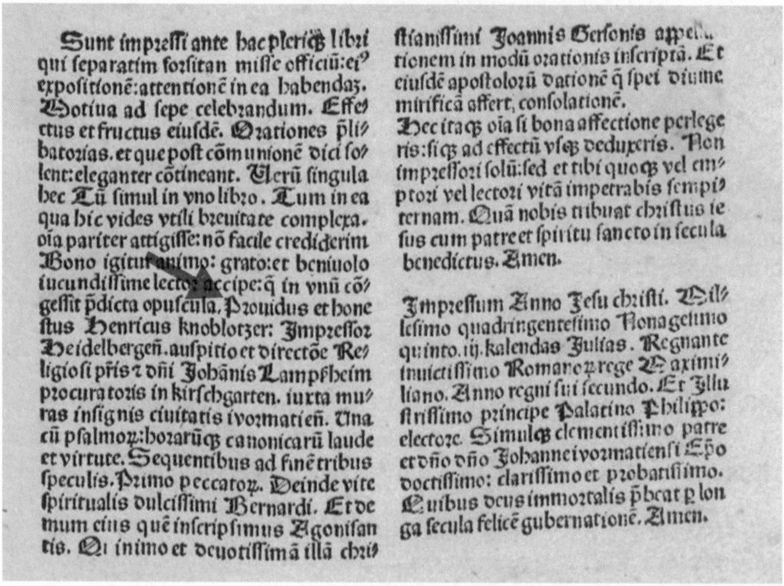

Abb. 14: ULB Bonn, Inc 1017 [https://digitale-sammlungen.ulb.uni-bonn.de/content/pageview/ 1562812], 30ʳ (Ausschnitt, Hervorhebung durch Hinzufügen eines blauen Pfeils, C. R.).

Die starke Berücksichtigung von Texten des hl. Bonaventura lässt auch Brückenschlag zu Kap. 1 denkbar erscheinen. Für dieses Werk des Johannes von Lambsheim ist Knoblochtzers Druck die einzige Ausgabe innerhalb der Inkunabelzeit, es ist in 65 Exemplaren an öffentlichen Einrichtungen erhalten. Der Theologe hatte es sich auch zur Aufgabe gemacht, die Marienverehrung zu propagieren, was ebenfalls Niederschlag in einem Heidelberger Druckwerk fand (vgl. Kap. 8: Gw M14221, JOHANNES DE LAMBSHEIM: *Libri tres perutiles de confraternitatibus rosarii et psalterii B. Mariae virginis*).

---

[38] Auf Lebensdaten legt sich F. J. WORSTBROCK: *Johannes von Lambsheim*, in: ²VL 4 (1983), Sp. 663–668 nicht fest, zuletzt bezeugt sei er 1495.

[39] Ebd. Sp. 665.

3   Schule und Grundstudium der Artistenfakultät

Neben einigen Titeln, die im 1. Kapitel (Theologische Werke aus dem Umfeld des Franziskanerklosters) zu besprechen waren, und anderen, die dann im 5. Kapitel (Humanismus) zu nennen sind, gibt es hier zunächst eine größere Gruppe von Drucken, die wieder der ‚Drucker-des-Lindelbach'-Sektion zuzuordnen sind:

Wenn auch nicht alle Ausgaben zu datieren sind, so scheinen doch die Editionen von Werken des Johannes de Garlandia (um 1195–um 1272),[40] eines Klassikers des Grammatikunterrichts, am Beginn von Knoblochtzers Heidelberger Zeit zu stehen. Es war mit diesem Autor in der Universitätsstadt wohl sicherer Absatz zu erwarten, obwohl er Humanisten wie Erasmus von Rotterdam, Jakob Wimpfeling u. a. als veraltet galt.[41] Aber kombiniert mit den Kommentaren des Niederländischen Fraterherrn Johannes Synthen (Deventer, Ende 15. Jh.), mit denen die Ausgaben in Heidelberg ausgestattet wurden, und von dem die (nieder)deutschen Einsprengsel herrühren (s. u. Abb. 15), schien der alte Schulbuchklassiker doch noch brauchbar zu sein.[42] Das Ringen um eine Neuformierung des akademischen Unterrichts zwischen Scholastik und Humanismus, das sich auch in den hier vorzustellenden Druckwerken niederschlägt, beschreibt anschaulich GERHARD RITTER im 3. Abschnitt des 3. Buches seiner Geschichte der Heidelberger Universität im Mittelalter: „Zwischen alter und neuer Zeit. Verdämmern der scholastischen Bildungsideale".[43]

[Gw M13909: JOHANNES DE GARLANDIA: *Verba deponentialia* (DdL)]: Das Werk, das sich mit dieser lateinischen Klasse von Verben beschäftigt, die in passivischer Form auftretend doch aktivische Bedeutung aufweisen, umfasst 24 Bll., ist nur vage „um 1486/87" datierbar. Deutsche Einsprengsel erleichtern den Gebrauch des Werks zur Unterrichtung von Publikum mit nicht sehr fortgeschrittenen Lateinkenntnissen. Von den fünf erhaltenen Exemplaren steht das der UB Frankfurt als Digitalisat zur Verfügung, es ist sorgfältig rubriziert, zeigt aber keine Gebrauchsspuren:

---

[40] Vgl. F. J. WORSTBROCK: *Johannes de Garlandia*, in: ²VL 4 [1983], Sp. 612–623.
[41] Ebd. Sp. 615.
[42] Vgl. F. J. WORSTBROCK: *Synthen, Johannes*, in: ²VL 9 (1995), Sp. 559–561.
[43] GERHARD RITTER: *Die Heidelberger Universität im Mittelalter (1386–1508). Ein Stück deutscher Geschichte*, Heidelberg, 1936, ND ebd. 1986, S. 411–491.

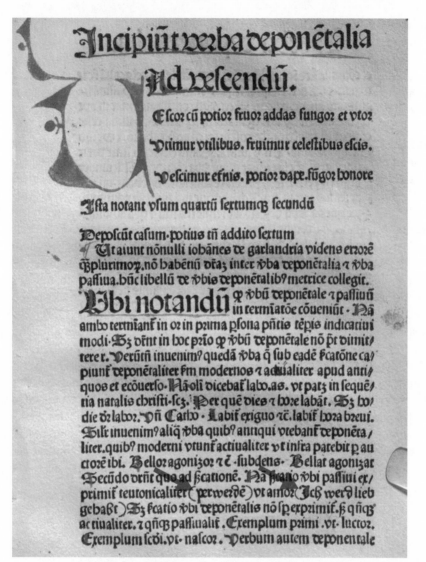

Abb. 15: UB Frankfurt, Ms. Leonh. 14, Nr. 3 [http://sammlungen.ub.uni-frankfurt.de/msma/content/pageview/5105156], 2ʳ (Ausschnitt, Hervorhebung durch Hinzufügen blauer Pfeile, C. R.).

Ein weiteres Werk des Johannes de Garlandia, *Composita verborum*, ebenfalls mit dem Kommentar des Johannes Synthen versehen, ist in *Gw* mit gleich drei Nummern von Heidelberger Inkunabeldrucken verzeichnet, die alle ursprünglich dem ‚Drucker des Lindelbach' zugeordnet worden waren:

    [Gw M13692: Johannes de Garlandia: *Composita verborum*, (DdL)] „um 1485/86": Das Münchner Exemplar steht als Digitalisat zur Verfügung (von insgesamt vier erhaltenen), der Textbeginn (*aijʳ*) lässt den Schulgebrauch von Merksprüchen und Erklärungen mit eingestreuter deutscher Übersetzung erahnen:

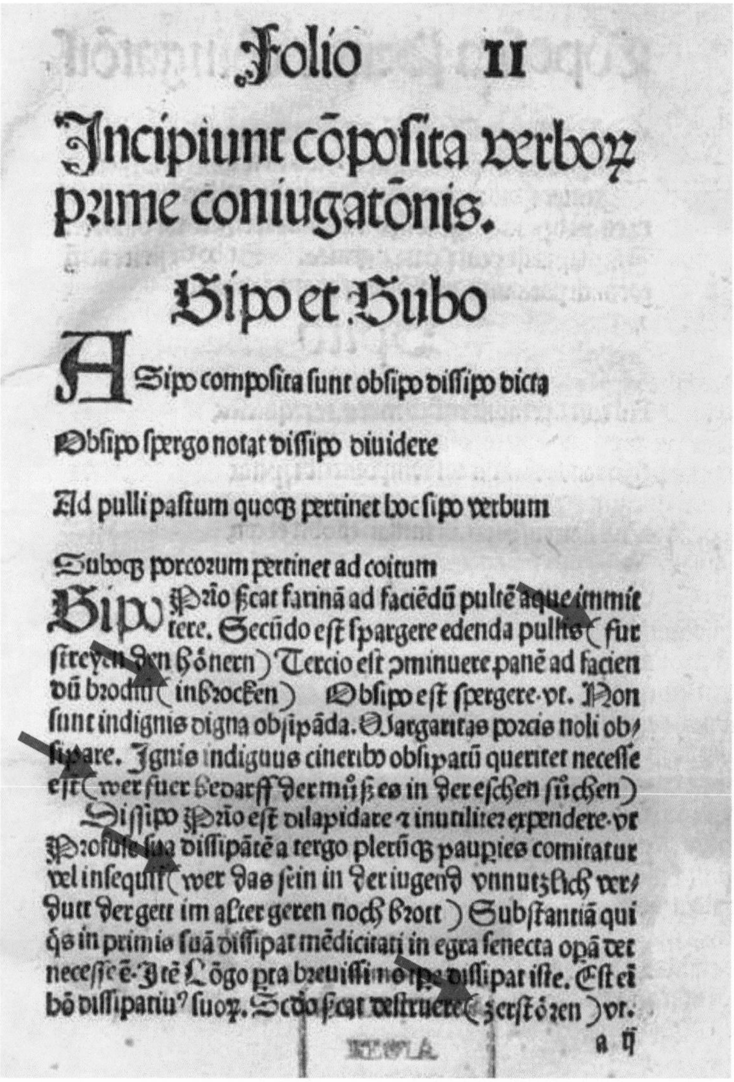
Folio II
Incipiunt cōposita verbor
prime coniugatōnis.
Sipo et Subo
A Sipo composita sunt obsipo dissipo dicta
Obsipo spergo notat dissipo diuidere
Ad pulli pastum quoqz pertinet hoc sipo verbum
Suboqz porcorum pertinet ad coitum
Sipo Pmo scat farinā ad faciēdū pultē aque immittere. Secūdo est spargere edenda pullis (fur streyen den hönern) Tercio est cōminuere panē ad faciendū brodiū (inbrocken) Obsipo est spergere. vt. Non sunt indignis digna obsipāda. Margaritas porcis noli obsipare. Ignis indiguus cineribꝰ obsipatū querit necesse est (wer fuer bedarff der muß es in der eschen süchen) Dissipo Pmo est dilapidare ꝛ inutiliter expendere. vt Profusus sua dissipātē a tergo plerūqz paupies comitatur vel insequit (wer das sein in der iugend vnnutzlich verdutt der gett im alter geren noch brott) Substantiā qui qs in primis suā dissipat mēdicitati in egra senecta opā det necesse ē. Itē Lōgo pra breuissimo tpe dissipat iste. Est ei bō dissipatiuꝰ suor. Scdo scat destruere (zerstören) vt.
a ij

Abb. 16: BSB München, 4 Inc. s. a. 1667 c [Ink I-401]; [http://daten.digitale-sammlungen.de/bsb00039571/image_7], 2r (Ausschnitt, Hervorhebung durch Hinzufügen blauer Pfeile, C. R.).

Auf Bl. *XXI* weist das Werk (in Übereinstimmung mit den folgenden Inkunabelausgaben, aber nicht textgleich) den Eintrag *censeo* auf, hat aber keine Schlussschrift und dürfte, da bei Gw 13696 noch 50 Bll. folgen, im Münchner Exemplar defekt sein.

[Gw M13694 und M13696: JOHANNES DE GARLANDIA: *Composita verborum* (DdL)] „nach 6.VII.1486": Im aufwendig zweifarbig rubrizierten Exemplar[44] der ULB Darmstadt ist der Abschiedsgruß an den *ingeniosissime adolescens* (den ‚überaus begabten Jüngling') aus der ‚Stadt der nicht nur blühenden sondern auch auf das angenehmste zu vollziehenden Studien' zu lesen: *Vale ex Heydelbergensi non minus florido quam amenissimo studio Pridie nonas Julias Anno ab incarnatione dominicale Mcccc.lxxxvj*

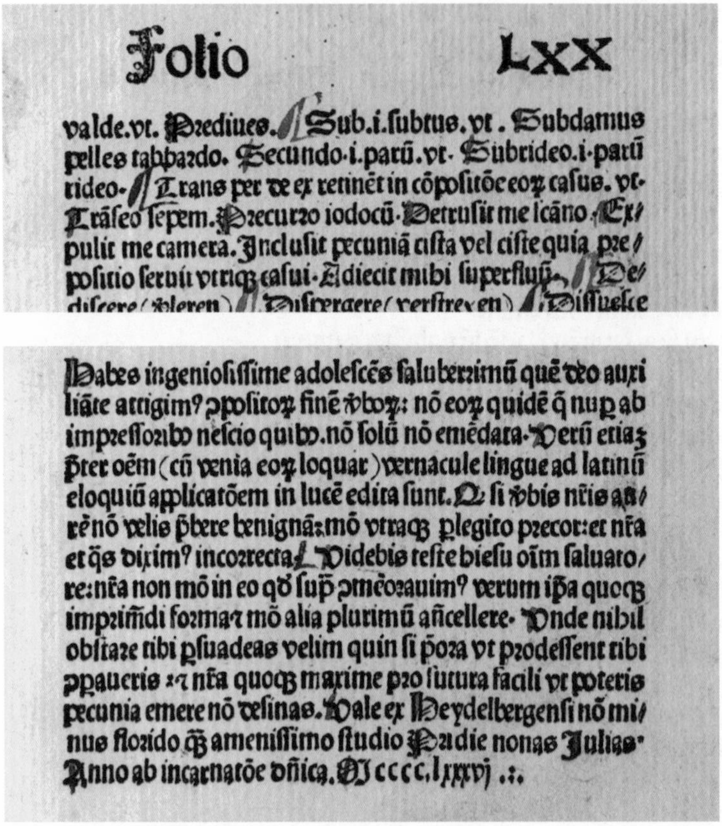

Abb. 17: ULB Darmstadt, Inc II 47 [http://tudigit.ulb.tu-darmstadt.de/show/inc-ii-47/0139], 70ʳ (Ausschnitt mit Auslassung).

Auch zur Schulliteratur zu zählen ist das Werk selbst, nach dem diese Typengruppe benannt ist:

---

[44] Ein von neun erhaltenen Exemplaren von M13696 in der UB Heidelberg: SCHLECHTER/RIES 1071.

[Gw M18384: LINDELBACH, MICHAEL: *Praecepta latinitatis* (DdL)] „15. XII. 1486“:
Precepta latinitatis, ex diuersis orator[um] atq[ue] poetarum codicibus tracta lautet
der vollständige Titel des 72 Bll. umfassenden Werks des Michael Lindelbach, der in
den 80er Jahren des 15. Jahrhunderts in Tübingen lehrte.

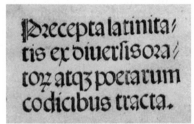

Abb. 18: BSB München, 4 Inc. c. a. 466 da [Ink L-179]; [http://daten.digitale-sammlungen.de/
bsb00039893/image_5]; 1ʳ (Ausschnitt).

Es bezieht sich in der Ordnung des Materials zwar ausdrücklich auf die alte Grammatik des Donat (*secundum ordinem donati*, Prolog, 2ᵛ), zeigt in seiner Anlage mit
den zahlreichen Belegstellen aus lateinischen Klassikern aber humanistische Ambi-
tionen.[45] Am Schluss verabschiedet sich derjenige, der den Druck des Werkes in
Heidelberg verwirklicht hat (*heydelberge Impressimus*) mit einer ausführlichen,
motivierenden Schlussrede vom Leser, dem *studiosissime lector*:

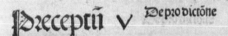

Abb. 19: BSB München, 4 Inc. c. a. 466 da [Ink L-179]; [http://daten.digitale-sammlungen.de/
bsb00039893/image_145], 71ʳ (Ausschnitt, Hervorhebung durch Hinzufügen eines blauen
Pfeils, C. R.).

In 18 Exemplaren ist der Druck aus Heidelberg überliefert, eine weitere Inkunabel-
ausgabe erschien im selben Jahr in Reutlingen, einige Jahre später dann noch einmal
bei Konrad Hist in Speyer (Gw M18386).

---

[45] Vgl. F. J. WORSTBROCK: *Lindelbach, Michael*, in: ²*VL* 5 (1985), Sp. 839 f.

Auch noch zur ‚Drucker-des-Lindelbach'-Gruppe zu zählen ist [Gw 8126: Datus, Augustinus: *Elegantiolae* (DdL)] „nach 21.VIII.1486" von 38 Bll.: Zum wiederum zeitgenössischen Autor dieser Stilkunde *De varijs loquendi regulis siue poetarum praeceptis tractatulus* (2r) hat der *Gw* die Daten zusammengetragen, dass er 1420 in Siena geboren, später ein Richteramt in Massa begleitet habe und 1478 gestorben sei. Das Werk verabschiedet sich in der Schlussschrift, ähnlich wie bei den *Composita verborum* des Johannes de Garlandia (s. o. M13696), wiederum mit einem *Vale ex heydelberga*, diesmal von einem *studiosissimus adolescens* (einem „überaus eifrigen Jüngling"):

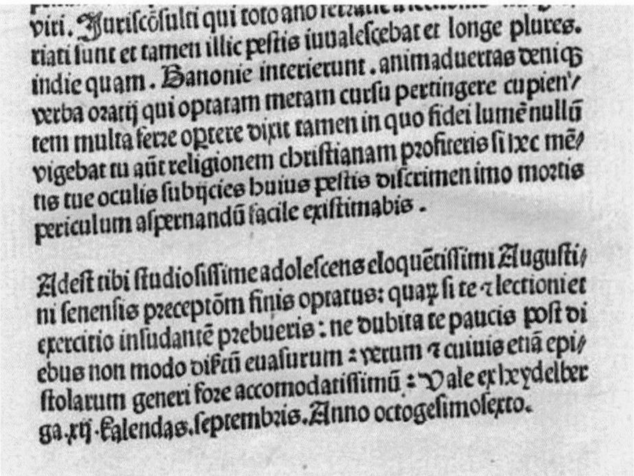
viri. Iuriscõsulti qui toto āno ...
riati sunt et tamen illic pestis inualescebat et longe plures.
indie quam. Banonie interierunt. animaduertas deniq3
verba oratij qui optatam metam cursu pertingere cupien/
tem multa ferre oportere dixit tamen in quo fidei lumē nullū
vigebat tu aūt religionem christianam profiteris si hec mē/
tis tue oculis subijcies huius pestis discrimen imo mortis
periculum aspernandū facile existimabis.

Adest tibi studiosissime adolescens eloquētissimi Augusti/
ni senensis preceptōm finis optatus: quaꝫ si te 7 lectioni et
exercitio insudantē prebueris: ne dubita te paucis post di
ebus non modo dictū euasurum: verum 7 cuiuis etiā epi/
stolarum generi fore accomodatissimū: Vale ex heydelber
ga.xij. kalendas. septembris. Anno octogesimosexto.

Abb. 20: BSB München, 4 Inc. c. a. 451 m [Ink D-23]; [http://daten.digitale-sammlungen.de/bsb00041786/image_77], 37r (Ausschnitt).

Auch hier gibt es eine gewisse humanistisch orientierte Aufbereitung des Werkes: Der Datus-Text, der auf Blatt 28v nach der Thematisierung von Anreden und Verabschiedungen sowie der Datierung von Texten in einer *Conclusio opusculi* endet, wird in einem Anhang ab Bl. 29r (*e iij*) mit einigen *Regule* für *orationes* (darunter auch Trostschreiben) *pro maiori autem exercitatione* vertieft. Diesen Abschnitt weist die Beschreibung der Inkunabel in der Bsb München dem zeitweise in Heidelberg, noch unter Kurfürst Friedrich I. (†1476) tätigen Peter Luder zu (1456–1460).[46] Luder hatte sich die Verbreitung der in Italien kennengelernten *Studia humanitatis* auf die Fahnen geschrieben.[47] Es wird sich um Teile der im *²Vl*-Artikel gelisteten (Sp. 957), stets anonym überlieferten *Ars oratoria* oder den *Modus epistolandi* handeln. Der etwas lokalpatriotisch anmutende *Vale-ex-heydelberga*-Gruß dieser Werkgruppe

[46] Lehrer des Matthias von Kemnat (†1472?), der seinerseits später pfälzischer Hofkaplan war und sich für Lorscher Klassikerhandschriften interessierte, vgl. Birgit Studt und F. J. Worstbrock: *Matthias von Kemnat*, in: *²Vl* 6 (1987), Sp. 194.

[47] Zu Luder s. Artikel von Frank Baron in: *²Vl* 5 (1985), Sp. 954–959.

würde sich auch gut in die Tradition des Städtelobs von Peter Luder fügen.[48] In der UB Heidelberg ist eines von 13 erhaltenen Exemplaren dieses Werkes vorhanden (SCHLECHTER/RIES 148).

Noch ein Werk aus der ‚Drucker-des-Lindelbach'-Gruppe liegt vor mit [GW M51289: *Vocabularius de partibus indeclinabilibus* (DdL)], mit 12 Ausgaben im *GW* gelistet (Schwerpunkt bei Hist in Speyer). Das Werk von 69 bedruckten Bll., das in alphabetischer Reihenfolge unflektierbare lateinische Lexeme auflistet, kurz erklärt und bisweilen mit Beispielen ihren richtigen Gebrauch veranschaulicht, richtet sich diesmal nicht an *adulescentes* (‚Jünglinge'), sondern an ‚Schulkinder' (*filioli* und *pueri*), versäumt – wie so oft in diesem Zusammenhang – nicht die Mahnung, neben Lerneifer auch eine fromme Haltung an den Tag zu legen: *et memoriter ceteris commenda te ad dei laudem diueque virginis gloriam et honorem Amen.*

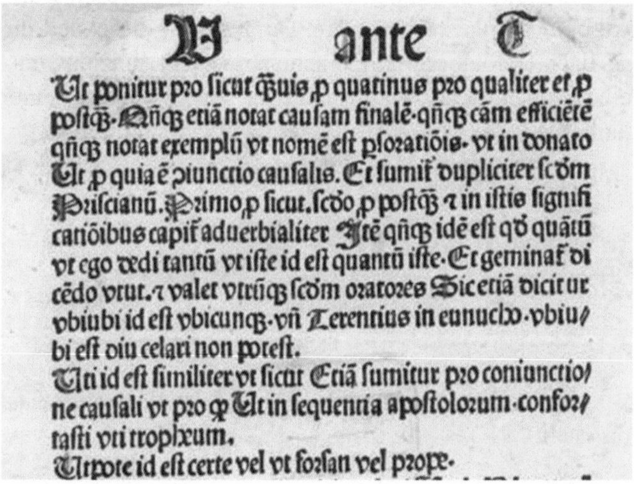
V ante C
Ut ponitur pro sicut q̃uis ꝓ quatinus pro qualiter et ꝓ
postq̃ȝ. Q̃nq̃ȝ etiã notat causam finalẽ. q̃nq̃ȝ cãm efficiẽtẽ
q̃nq̃ȝ notat exemplũ vt nomẽ est ꝓ oratiõis. vt in donato
Ut ꝓ quia ẽ ꝯiunctio causalis. Et sumit̃ dupliciter scd̃m
Priscianũ. Primo ꝓ sicut. scd̃o ꝓ postq̃ȝ ꝛ in istis signifi
catiõibus capit̃ aduerbialiter Itẽ q̃nq̃ȝ idẽ est qđ quãtũ
vt ego vedi tantũ vt iste id est quantũ iste. Et geminat̃ di
cẽdo vtut. ꝛ valet vtrũq̃ȝ scd̃m oratores Sic etiã dicitur
vbiubi id est vbicunq̃ȝ. vñ Terentius in eunucho. vbiubi est diu celari non potest.
Uti id est similiter vt sicut Etiã sumitur pro coniunctio-
ne causali vt pro q̄ Ut in sequentia apostolorum. confor-
tasti vti trophæum.
Utpote id est certe vel vt forsan vel prope.

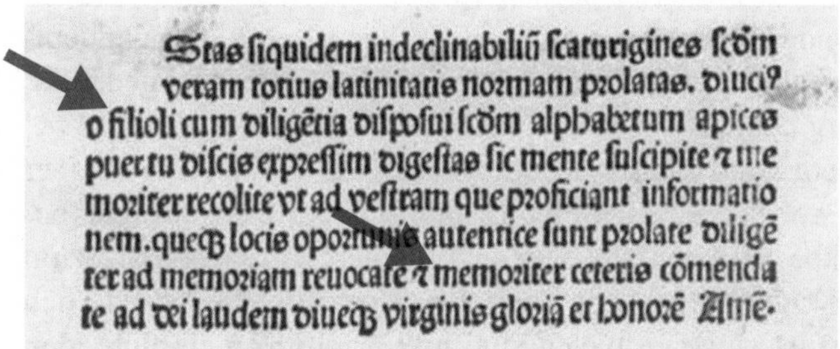
Stas siquidem indeclinabiliũ scaturigines scd̃m
veram totius latinitatis normam prolatas. dilecti
o filioli cum diligẽtia disposui scd̃m alphabetum apices
puer tu discis expressim digestas sic mente suscipite ꝛ me
moriter recolite vt ad vestram que proficiant informatio
nem. queq̃ȝ locis oportunis autentice sunt prolate diligẽ
ter ad memoriam reuocate ꝛ memoriter ceteris cõmenda
te ad dei laudem diueq̃ȝ virginis gloriã et honorẽ Amẽ.

Abb. 21: BSB München, 4 Inc. s. a. 1985 [Ink V-300 mit Datierungsvorschlag „ca. 1485/89"]; [http://daten.digitale-sammlungen.de/bsb00040470/image_141], 69r (Ausschnitt mit Auslassung, Hervorhebung durch Hinzufügen blauer Pfeile, C. R.).

48 Vgl. RUDOLF KETTEMANN: *Ein Loblied auf Heidelberg. Peter Luders Enkomion aus dem 15. Jahrhundert* (mit Textabdruck und Übersetzung) in: MITTLER: *Heidelberg* (1996), S. 321–324.

[Gw M15394: Ps.-Isocrates: *Praecepta ad Demonicum.* Übers. Rudolphus Agricola]: Auch dieses Werk schlägt eine Brücke zwischen dem 1. und dem 5. Kapitel unserer Aufstellung. Der Übersetzter Rudolf Agricola (eigentlich Huysmann, *1444 bei Groningen) ist einerseits durch die Schule der Fraterherren gegangen und andererseits ist er, allerdings eine Generation später als Peter Luder, durch Studienjahre in Italien stark vom Humanismus inspiriert worden.[49] Und auch sein Weg führte ihn, in diesem Fall über die Freundschaft mit dem kurpfälzischen Kanzler und Bischof von Worms, Johann von Dalberg, 1484 nach Heidelberg, wo seit 1476 Philipp der Aufrichtige regierte. Sehr bezeichnend ist auch, dass er nach seinem plötzlichen Tod auf der Rückreise von Rom in einer Franziskanerkutte am hiesigen Kloster (mit Marienpatrozinium, vgl. Kap. 8) unterhalb des Schlosses bestattet wurde.[50]

Man darf annehmen, dass sein Einfluss auf den Studienbetrieb und vielleicht auch auf das Druckprogramm in Heidelberg noch erheblich größer gewesen wäre, wenn er nicht schon im Oktober 1485 gestorben wäre. Da genau in diese Zeit die Übersiedlung Knoblochtzers nach Heidelberg fällt, erscheint es nicht ganz unwahrscheinlich, dass Agricola einen wesentlichen Katalysator für die Etablierung einer Druckoffizin hier vor Ort darstellte.

Abb. 22: BSB München, 4 Inc. s. a. 1115 [Ink I-648]; [http://daten.digitale-sammlungen.de/bsb00039687/image_5], 1ʳ (Ausschnitt).

Die Übersetzung der *Precepta* des griechischen Rhetors Isocrates (436–338) in Form eines Briefes an Demonicos ins Lateinische, die schon aus Agricolas italienischer Zeit stammte (1478), wurde innerhalb der Inkunabelzeit nur vier Mal gedruckt, in Siena (o. J.), in Nürnberg „um 1497" (*Gw*), in Deventer „nicht vor 30.III.1498" (*Gw*) und eben in Heidelberg von Heinrich Knoblochtzer „um 1495" (*Gw*) in einer 4°-Ausgabe von 12 Bll., (wobei die Zuschreibung an ihn in der Literatur teils bezweifelt wird). Die Ausgabe ist jedenfalls sehr ambitioniert: Im Gegensatz zum Nürnberger Druck, wo ein Durchschuss mit Leerzeilen einem Bearbeiter lediglich Platz für handschriftliche Eintragungen bietet, sind hier bereits vorgefertigte, den Kerntext erläuternde Interlinearglossen in kleinerer Type eindruckt:

---

[49] F. J. Worstbrock: *Agricola, Rudolf,* in: ²Vʟ 1 (1978), Sp. 84–93.
[50] R. Stupperich: *Agricola, Rudolf,* in: *Lexikon des Mittelalters,* Band 1, Lachen 1999, Sp. 220.

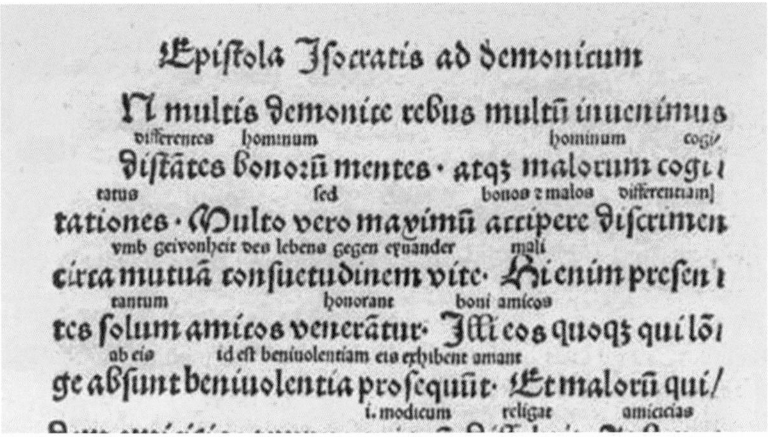

Abb. 23: BSB München, 4 Inc.s.a. 1115 [Ink I-648]; [http://daten.digitale-sammlungen.de/bsb00039687/image_7], 2^r (Ausschnitt).

An einer Stelle scheint der Setzer von diesem aufwendigen Verfahren aber überfordert gewesen zu sein: Auf Bl. 3^r bleibt am Seitenende mitten im Satz (ohne Textverlust zur Fortsetzung auf Bl. 3^v) ein Leerraum von eineinhalb Zeilen (gegenüber den sonst meist 18 Zeilen einer Seite):

[…] *Hoc quoque cognitu perfacile est, quae gloria certaminum herculis, operumque a theseo gestorum prestantia, tantum laudis insigne operibus adiecit, vt omnis temporum* ....
....
<3^v>
posteritas, rebus quas gesserunt effundere nequiuerit obliuionem.

[Gw M50208: VERSOR, JOHANNES: *Super Donatum*] „nicht nach 1491“. Johannes Versor (OP, † nach 1482),[51] von dem auch Kommentare zur Logik des Petrus Hispanus und zu Werken des Aristoteles als Inkunabeln erschienen,[52] ist hier mit einem grammatischen Werk *Super Donatum* vertreten. Das im Digitalisat aus München gezeigte Exemplar aus Knoblochtzers Offizin[53] stammt aus der Benediktinerabtei in Tegernsee:

[51] *Wikipedia*-Artikel [https://de.wikipedia.org/wiki/Johannes_Versor], 15.9.20, mit Verweis auf Artikel von MAX HEINZE in *Allgemeine Deutsche Biographie* (*ADB*) 39 (1895).
[52] Ein Verzeichnis der Digitalisate findet man in der *Digitalen Bibliothek des Münchner Digitalisierungszentrums*: https://www.digitale-sammlungen.de/index.html?c=autoren_index&l=de&ab=Johannes+%26lt%3BVersor%26gt%3B
[53] Nach Angabe der BSB München in Straßburg lokalisiert.

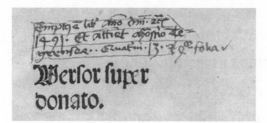

Abb. 24: BSB München, 4 Inc. s. a. 1917 [Ink V-150]; [http://daten.digitale-sammlungen.de/ bsb00072884/image_5], 1ʳ (Ausschnitt).

Weitere 15 Exemplare haben sich bis heute in öffentlichen Einrichtungen erhalten. Das Werk wurde innerhalb der Inkunabelzeit auch je zweimal in Köln und Leipzig sowie einmal in Straßburg (bei Johann Prüss) gedruckt. Und kurz vor Knoblochtzers Druck erschien eine Ausgabe in Heidelberg bei einem Drucker Friedrich Misch (Gw M50207). Von ihm sind nur acht Inkunabeln nachweisbar.[54] Wie Knoblochtzer hatte er sich in der Universität in Heidelberg eingeschrieben (schon 1483), doch vergingen bei ihm ganze fünf Jahre bis zu seinem ersten Druck.[55] GELDNER hält es für möglich, dass Misch schon 1490 gestorben ist, so dass Knoblochtzer mit seiner Edition möglicherweise ein Desiderat des universitären Heidelberger Marktes nach einem Nachdruck erfüllte, doch müsste er auch auf überregionalen Absatz gezielt haben. Einen direkten Nachdruck von Mischs Ausgabe kann Knoblochtzers Druck nicht darstellen, denn während jener 69 Bll. in 2° benötigte, sind es bei Knoblochtzer 81 Bll. in 4°. Die Kolophone zeigen aber doch auch wieder eine gewisse Verwandtschaft:

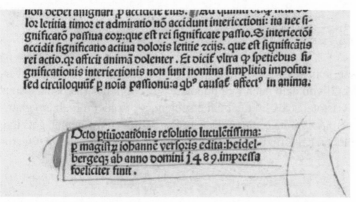

Abb. 25: Misch: BSB München, 4 Inc. c. a. 702 [Ink V-148]; [http://daten.digitale-sammlungen. de/bsb00040463/image_141], 69ʳ (Ausschnitt).

---

[54] Überwiegend zum Trivium: Neben Johannes Versor: *Super Donatum* (Grammatik) zwei Werke zur Logik eines Johannes de Magistris (ob der nicht Johannes Versor gleichzusetzen ist?), zwei Briefformel-Bücher (also Rhetorik), zwei Almanache auf das Jahr 1489 (ein lateinischer, ein deutscher) und ein Titel Medizinisches, was bei Knoblochtzer gar nicht in Erscheinung tritt.

[55] Vgl. FERDINAND GELDNER: *Inkunabeldrucker*, S. 268.

nō accidunt interiectioni, ita nec significacio passiua co[r]
q est rei significate passio. Sz interiectioni accidit signifi
cacio actiua doloris leticie z sic de aliis, q est significantis
rei actio, qz afficit animā dolenter. Et dr vltra q specie
bus significationis interiectionis nō sunt nomina simpli
cia imposita, sed circumloquunt per nomina passionum,
a quibus causatur affect9 in anima.

Octo ptium orationis resolutio luculentissima:
p mgrm iohannez versoris edita. feliciter finit.

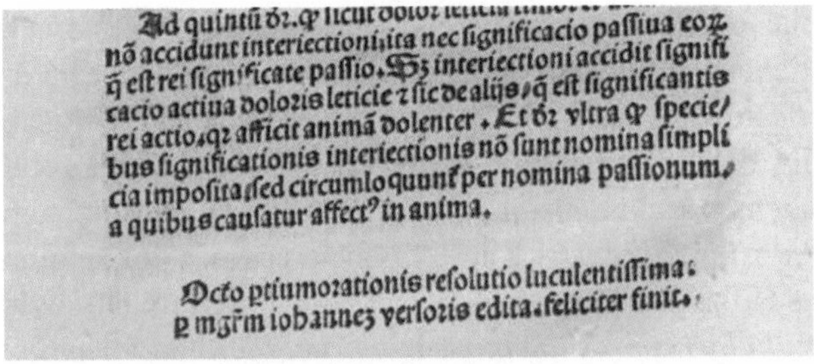

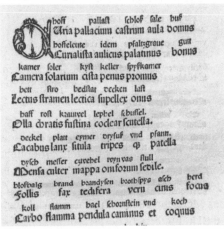

Abb. 26: Knoblochtzer: BSB München, 4 Inc.s.a. 1917 [Ink V-150]; [http://daten.digitale-sammlungen.de/bsb00072884/image_166], 81v (Ausschnitt).

Außer Auszeichnungstype und Freiraum für je eine Initiale bei den Kapitelincipits[56] *(P)artes orationes quot sunt* … (3v), *(N)omen quid est pars oracionis* … (5v), *(M)agister nomen appellativum* … (21r), *(P)ronomen quid est pars oracionis* … (23v) *(V)erbum quid est pars oracionis* … (37v), usw.[57] sieht der Knoblochtzer-Druck keinen weiteren Schmuck vor. Der Druck einer Donat-basierten Grammatik würde sich auch mit dem Interesse der Kurfürsten an dieser Grammatik treffen, die in der mit kurpfälzischen Wappen versehenen prächtigen Handschrift Cpl 1811 ihren Niederschlag fand.[58]

[Gw M51243: *Vocabularius Curia palatium*, lat.-dt.]: Der *Vocabularius Curia palatium* (vgl. das Incipit) kommt in seiner Heidelberger, nicht datierbaren Ausgabe (wohl nicht aus Knoblochtzers Anfangsjahren, nicht in der Type des DdL) von nur 8 Bll. ziemlich unscheinbar daher:

hoff pallast schlos sale huß
Curia pallacium castrum aula domus
hoffeleute idem pfaltzgraue gutt
Curialista aulicus palatinus bonus
kamer soler kyst keller spyßkamer
Camera solarium cista penus promus
bett stro bedstat decken last
Lectus stramen lectica supellex onus
haff rost krauwel lepfel schussel.
Olla cratis fuscina coclear scutella.
deckel platt eymer dryfuß vnd pfann.
Cacabus lanx situla tripes et patella
dysch messer czwebel wyn vas stull
Mensa culter mappa omforum sedile.
blosbalg brand brandysen brotspys asch herd
Follis fax tedifera veru cinis focus
koll flamm bael schornstein vnd koch
Carbo flamma pendula caminus et coquus

Abb. 27: BSB München, 4 Inc. c. a. 1466 b [http://daten.digitale-sammlungen.de/bsb00008346/image_3], 2r (Ausschnitt).

56 Im vorliegenden Exemplar vom Rubrikator rot ausgeführt.

57 Einzig im Kapitel über die Adverbien finden sich im vorliegenden Exemplar handschriftliche Anmerkungen.

58 Beschreibung und Abb. In *Bibliotheca Palatina* (1986), S. 192 f. (Textband), S. 141 (Bildband).

Neben dem Münchner Exemplar, das in einem größeren Sammelcodex eingebunden ist, sind acht weitere in öffentlichen Bibliotheken erhalten. Der Text war in der Inkunabelzeit weit verbreitet (19 Einträge in *Gw* allein der lat.-deutschen Fassungen, ohne die lat.-niederländischen), der Kölner Druck „um 1501" (Gw M51252) zeigt besonders deutlich den Gebrauchskontext des Schulunterrichts (im Gegensatz zum theologisch zentrierten *Vocabularius Ex quo*, s. Kap. 2), indem sowohl vor Beginn wie auch nach Ende des Textes Holzschnitte eingestellt sind, die das Umfeld Schule zum Gebrauch nahelegen (*Vocabularius pro Juuenibus* bzw. *Vocabula Puerorum*):

Abb. 28a (links) und 28b (rechts): BSB München, 4 Inc. s. a. 1989 w [Ink V-297] [http://daten.digitale-sammlungen.de/bsb00005223/image_5 und …/image_16], 1ʳ (28a) und 6ᵛ (28b) (jeweils Ausschnitt).

In eben dieser Ausgabe erleichtern am Rand ausgestellte Themenblöcke, die die Heidelberger Ausgabe nicht aufweist, den Gebrauch der Vokabelsammlung erheblich: *Nomina habitaculorum* (‚Bezeichnungen von Wohnstätten')/ *Nomina habitatorum* (‚Bezeichnungen der Bewohner')/ […] *Utensilia domus* (‚Utensilien im Haus')/ […] *Membra totius hominis* (‚Alle Körperteile des Menschen') usw. Es handelt sich also um eine Art lat.-dt. Grundwortschatz für den Schulunterricht des Triviums (Fächerkanon des ‚Dreiwegs': Grammatik, Rhetorik, Logik). Die Endreimbindung des lateinischen Grundtextes diente wohl der besseren Memorierbarkeit.

  [Gw 09401: *Es tu scholaris?*]: Ähnlich gelagert wie der *Vocabularius Curia palatium* ist der Gebrauchszusammenhang eines ebenfalls massenhaft gedruckten Werkes, des *Es tu scholaris*. Hier werden im ersten Teil (ähnlich wie im *Cato* [s. u. Gw 06323 und 06324] grammatische und moralische Fragen miteinander verknüpft und im zweiten Teil deutsch-lateinische Redensarten zusammengestellt (vgl. die Beschreibung in *Gw*). Das Heidelberger Exemplar „um 1494/95" von 16 Bll. Umfang ist nur einmal erhalten, und zwar in Innsbruck, ein Digitalisat steht hier noch nicht zur Verfügung. Eine gute Vorstellung vermittelt der vermutlich ähnlich aufgemachte Wiegendruck von Schäffler, den der Ulmer Drucker als ‚Gastspiel' in Freising herausbrachte.[59] Am Ende des Werkes, das ähnlich wie die Kölner Ausgabe des *Vocabularius Curia palatium* von zwei Holzschnitten mit Schulszenen eingerahmt ist, werden ohne Angabe eines Datums Druckort und Drucker genannt: *Impreſſum Heidelberge per Heinricum knobloczer.*

[Gw 11144: *Grammatica. Regula Dominus quae pars*] „um 1486/90", 16 Bll. Für deutlich jüngeres Publikum als die oben gezeigten „großen" Grammatiken, die ihre Leserschaft mit *adolescens* ansprechen, ist das massenhaft gedruckte, in zahlreichen namhaften Inkunabelstädten erschienene Werklein gedacht, das seine Leserschaft mit *puer* anspricht, in einem lateinischen Spruch, der ungefähr dem deutschen ‚Was Hänschen nicht lernt, lernt Hans nimmermehr' entspricht:

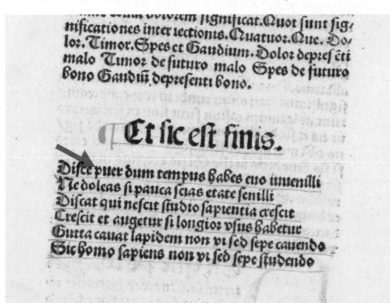

Abb. 29: WLB Stuttgart Inc.qt.13819b [http://digital.wlb-stuttgart.de/purl/bsz347866654], 14ᵛ (Ausschnitt, Hervorhebung durch Hinzufügen eines blauen Pfeils, C. R.).

Die Attraktivität des Schulbuchs, das im vorliegenden Exemplar der WLB Stuttgart sorgfältig rubriziert ist, aber keine Gebrauchsspuren aufweist, ist durch eine Holzschnittinitiale mit Jahreszeitenmotiv ‚Bauer mit Harke' (=Juni-/Brachmonat-Bild in Kalendern?) ein wenig gesteigert[60]:

---

59 AMELUNG: *FDSW*, Nr. 169, S. 386 f. mit Abb. 274 auf S. 378.
60 Nicht verzeichnet bei SCHRAMM: *Bilderschmuck 19*, auch nicht in Knoblochtzers Initialenrepertoire aus Straßburg, ebd., Tafel 18.

Abb. 30: WLB Stuttgart Inc.qt.13819b [http://digital.wlb-stuttgart.de/purl/bsz347866654], 1ʳ (*aj*, Ausschnitt).

[Gw 11219: *Grammatica Regulae congruitatum, constructiones et regimina. Constructionarius*] „um 1490“ ist mit seinen 12 Bll. Umfang der vorherigen Nummer vergleichbar. Zwar im *Gw* als Auftragsarbeit von Knoblochtzers Offizin „für Jakob Köbel“ bezeichnet, aber doch eine „Massenware“, die in der vorliegenden Fassung im *Gw* mit 23 Einträgen aus unterschiedlichen Druckorten (v. a. Basel, Straßburg, Speyer, Nürnberg, Leipzig) verzeichnet ist. Eine Ausgabe von Hist in Speyer „ca. 1495“ dürfte ein direkter Nachdruck der Heidelberger Ausgabe sein, denn hier wie dort schließt der Text mit dem Verdecknamen *Subocai Lebök* (= Jacobus Köbel, vgl. *Tischzucht* in Kap. 5). Der Heidelberger Druck ist zweifach, der Speyrer (Gw 1121910N) nur einmal in öffentlichen Bibliotheken nachzuweisen, Digitalisate von diesen Inkunabeln stehen leider nicht zur Verfügung.

[Gw 06323 und 06324: *Cato* (vulgo *Disticha Catonis*) deutsch]: Selbstverständlich hatte Knoblochtzer auch den überall massenhaft gedruckten Hybrid von sprachlicher und moralischer Belehrung, den *Cato* im Programm. Er umfasste in seinen beiden Ausgaben „um 1490“ 18 Bll., und war in einer Variante [Gw 06324] mit einem Holzschnitt, wahrscheinlich der auch in diesem Werk weit verbreiteten Schulszene (vgl. oben zum *Vocabularius Curia palatium*) versehen. Zwei bzw. drei Exemplare haben sich laut Angaben des *Gw* erhalten, ein Digitalisat (BSB München) steht nur zur ersten Fassung (ohne Holzschnitt), zur Verfügung. Die deutschen Interpretamente lateinischer Vokabeln, die ein Schüler auf dem Titelblatt eingetragen hat, verraten durch ausgebliebene Monophthongierung (*sichtůch*) und Diphthongierung (*huß* für ‚Haus‘ und *fig* für ‚Feige‘) seine alemannische Herkunft:

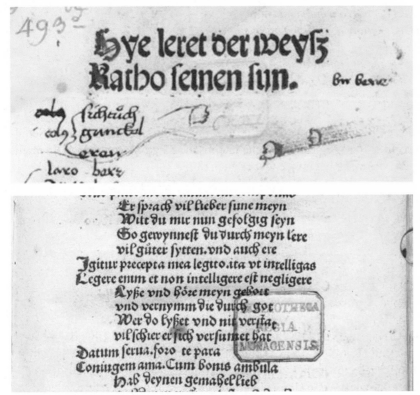

Abb. 31a (oben) und 31b (unten): BSB München, 4 Inc. s. a. 493 d [Ink D-199] [http://daten. digitale-sammlungen.de/bsb00034338/image_5 und …/image_7], 1ʳ (31a) und 2ʳ (31b) (jeweils Ausschnitt).

[Gw M37407: *Regimen scholarium*, lat. und deutsch]: Auch dieses Werk gehört zum Themenblock Schule, ist ganz nah verwandt zum *Cato*, ist, wie dieser auch, auf grammatisch-moralischer Ebene angesiedelt. Gut ein halbes Dutzend Ausgaben weist der *Gw* für diesen Titel nach, der teils auch unter der Bezeichnung *Statuta vel praecepta scolarium* läuft. Die Ausgabe aus Augsburg [Gw M37405, Digitalisat München, zit.], entstanden etwa sieben Jahre nach dem Heidelberger Druck „um 1490", und ist wiederum mit einem Holzschnitt der weit verbreiteten Schulszene versehen, wie sie sich auch am Ende des Kölner Exemplars des *Vocabularius Curia palatium* findet (s. o.). Die Belehrungen im Wechsel von lateinischen paarigen Langzeilen und je vier deutschen Vierhebern konzentrieren sich im Gegensatz zum *Cato* hier ganz auf das Thema Schule (1ʳ)[61]:

---

[61] „geistlich und moralisch ausgerichtete[] Didaxe", vgl. N. HENKEL: *Scolaris*, in: ²*Vl* 8 (1992), Sp. 954 f.; vier Handschriften nachgewiesen im *Handschriftencensus*: http://www. handschriftencensus.de/werke/3920 (25. 3. 2021).

SCholaris qui uis prouehi culmen et honoris
Preceptum meum tibi sit gratum omnibus horis
    Wiltu schůler von lere
    Erkriegen gůtt vnnd ere
    So volge disem bůchlein nach
    Nach seiner lere sei dir gach

Mit Hilfe dieses Textes sollte die Motivation zum Schulbesuch befördert, die Schulordnung vermittelt und zugleich einfache lateinische Sätze erlernt werden. In ähnlichem Ton, wie das Werk beginnt, endet es auch (8[r]):

Hic libellus explicit cuius serues leges
Quas si tu seruaueris te honore reges
    Hie hat dis bůchlein ein ende
    zů der lere dich fleissigklich wende
    Behalt des bůchleins lere wol
    So wirstu gůtes und ere vol
        Deo gracias.

[Gw 11597: GUARINUS, BAPTISTA: *De ordine docendi ac studendi*]: Über dieses Werk des Guarino Battista (1434–1513, Sohn des bekannten Humanisten Guarino da Verona, †1460)[62] schreibt der *Wikipedia*-Eintrag (eingesehen am 15.4.2020) „Seine[!] 1459 abgeschlossenes Werk *De ordine docendi et studendi* (‚Über die Ordnung des Lehrens und Lernens') gehört zu den richtungsweisenden pädagogischen und bildungstheoretischen Schriften des Renaissancehumanismus." Insofern könnte es für Heidelberg im Druckjahr „1489" die Bedeutung gehabt haben, die Bestrebungen des 1485 in Heidelberg verstorbenen Rudolf Agricola fortzusetzen, der seinerseits an einer Reform der universitären Ausbildung interessiert war, was sich bei ihm z.B. explizit in einem Brief *De reformando studio* niedergeschlagen hat.[63] Somit haben wir auch hier wieder ein Werk, das zugleich im 5. Kapitel hätte verzeichnet werden können.

Die kleine Programmschrift umfasst nur 11 Bll., 49 Exemplare sind in öffentlichen Bibliotheken erhalten, zwei davon in der UB Heidelberg.[64] Am Anfang ist der Wiegendruck mit drei Initialen geschmückt, deren erste (*B*) ALBERT SCHRAMM für Knoblochtzer in Straßburg verzeichnet.[65]

---

[62]   Zu diesem Guarino da Verona siehe den Eintrag in *Tusculum Lexikon griechischer und lateinischer Autoren des Altertums und des Mittelalters*, München/Zürich ³1982, S. 309 f.

[63]   F. J. WORSTBROCK: *Agricola, Rudolf*, in: ²VL 1 (1978) Sp. 84–93, hier Sp. 92.

[64]   SCHLECHTER/RIES 829 und 830.

[65]   SCHRAMM: *Bilderschmuck 19*, Tafel 18, Bild 116.

Abb. 32: BSB München, 4 Inc. s. a. 521 m [Ink G-425]; [http://daten.digitale-sammlungen.de/bsb00006899/image_1], 1ʳ (Ausschnitt).

Die beiden anderen ähneln sehr denjenigen Holzschnittinitialen, die sich ursprünglich einmal im Besitz von Zainer in Ulm befanden und bei Knoblochtzer teils auch im *Totentanz* (s. u. Kap. 6) Verwendung fanden.

Eine ursprünglich wohl als *M* gemeinte Ziermajuskel aus dem von AMELUNG so genannten „Rokoko-Alphabet" wird hier in einem bei Knoblochtzer öfter zu beobachtenden, ökonomisch geschickten Manöver durch eine 90°-Drehung zu einem *E* umfunktioniert[66]:

Abb. 33: BSB München, 4 Inc. s.a . 521 m [Ink G-425]; [http://daten.digitale-sammlungen.de/bsb00006899/image_3], 2ʳ (Ausschnitt).

Druckgeschichtlich gesehen ist aber der Kolophon am Ende das interessanteste Faktum an diesem Wiegendruck: Knoblochtzer weist sich darin erstmals in seiner Heidelberger Zeit als Drucker namentlich aus, zudem in einer sehr selbstbewussten, einmalig nur hier in Erscheinung tretenden Form, als ‚Meister der Druckkunst'

---

[66] Vgl. AMELUNG: *FDSW*, Abb. 34, S. 67 und Text S. 66.

(*impressorie artis magister*). Dazu kommt noch der Umstand, dass es m. W. das einzige Werk Knoblochtzers ist, das über die Jahreszahl hinaus eine direkte genaue Datumsangabe macht: *xv. kal. Januarias* (= 18. Dezember).[67]

ris: vt quã de te spem nobis tua indoles pollicet. z quam
tui ingenij opinionẽ cõcitasti / nõ mõ sustinere z tueri / ve
rum etiam superare possis: Verone. xv. kal. Martij. M.
cccc. lviij.

Finit modus z ordo docendi ac discedi Guarini bapti
ste / impressus heydelberge. per Henricum knoblochtzer
impressorie artis magistrum Anno salutis nostre Mille
simo quadringentesimo octogesimo nono. xv. kl. Januarias

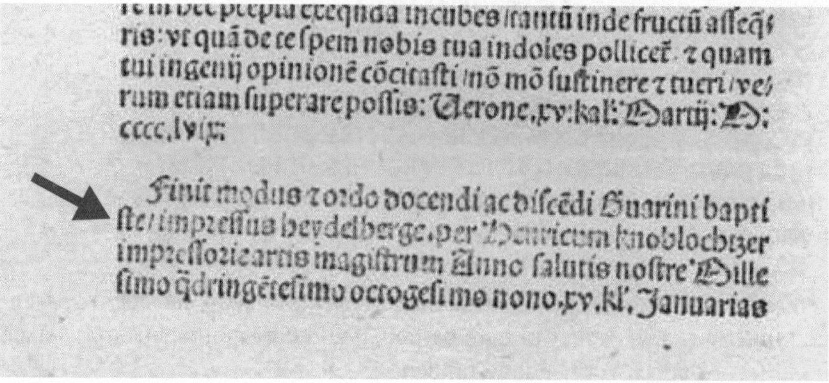

Abb. 34: BSB München, 4 Inc. s. a. 521 m [Ink G-425]; [http://daten.digitale-sammlungen.de/bsb00006899/image_22], 11v (Ausschnitt, Hervorhebung durch Hinzufügen eines blauen Pfeils, C. R.).

[Gw M20717: *Manuale scholarium*] „um 1490“: *Manuale* (‚Handbuch‘) ist ein weit verbreiteter Titel, er tritt u. a. in den Varianten *Manuale divinum* und *Manuale parochialium sacerdotum* innerhalb des Inkunabeldrucks in Erscheinung. Beim *Manuale scholarium*, das auch in Deventer (3), Köln (4), Speyer (Konrad Hist) und Straßburg (Martin Flach) gedruckt wurde, muss es sich also im Gegensatz zum vorherigen Titel, der sich programmatisch mit universitärer Ausbildung befasste, hier um ein praktisches Handbuch für die Studierenden selbst handeln. Das Werk endet im Heidelberger Druck auf Bl. 26r, nach einem Katalog der Anreden durch die Studenten an die *Magistri* der Universität, um diese zum Essen einzuladen, in einem (gelehrten Anstrich vermittelnden) griechischen *TELOS* (‚Schluss‘)[68] und einer Drucker(?)-Marke,[69] die an Herrscher- oder Marienmonogramme erinnert, aber schwerlich mit Knoblochtzers Namen zu tun hat, viel eher mit *Litterae* (‚Gelehrsamkeit, Studien, Wissenschaft‘) assoziiert werden könnte:

[67] Einige wenige weitere Inkunabeln gibt es, aus denen man aus der Nennung der einschlägigen Namenstage o. ä. auf das Datum schließen kann, vgl. z. B. Johannes von Tepl: *Der Ackermann von Böhmen* (Kap. 6).

[68] Im Kölner Druck von ca. 1493: *Et sic est finis deo laus et gloria trinis*. Ohne Marke.

[69] Als Druckerzeichen verzeichnet bei Ernst Weil: *Die deutschen Druckerzeichen des XV. Jahrhunderts*, München 1924, S. 68. „Die Verlegermarke […] aus dem *Manuale scholarium* […] ist noch nicht gedeutet.“ So Geldner: *Inkunabeldrucker* (1968), S. 267.

[Abbildung eines Textausschnitts in gotischer Schrift]

vvvib onoctte poſſes nut ynotic pei juen juvivi qin/

Optime magiſter audiui a voßis libros eſencozuz
peto nunc vt recognitoez dare nõ recuſetis pro quo
iuxta cõſuetudineDignitati vrẽ ſatiſfaciaz .

Dilectiſſime magiſter puto dominatõez veſtram
memorie tradidiſſe ac vos contentũ feciſſe tẽpoze ta/
ve medievento itaqz reuerẽtiã veſträ precaturus qua
tenus mißi recognicionem aſſignetis .

Honorãde magiſter audineriz a voßis exerciciũ
veteris artis peto nomine magiſtri mei teſtimoniuz
cirograpßo veſtro velitis tribuere pro quo magiſter
meus vos contẽtum faciet.   TELOS.

[Druckerzeichen/Signet mit Buchstaben]

Abb. 35: BSB München, 4 Inc. s. a. 1213 a [Ink M-146 (hier „ca. 1493")]; [http://daten.digitale-sammlungen.de/bsb00039878/image_55], 26ʳ (Ausschnitt).

Das Handbuch soll einem Studienanfänger den Eintritt ins Studium (*universitates aggredi*) erleichtern und das Fortkommen befördern (*ac postea in eis proficere*), indem es Musterdialoge zwischen Studierenden (*Bartoldus* und *Camillus*) notiert, oder – so der Beginn des Werkes – das Aufnahmegesuch des Studenten beim Magister vorentwirft. Soweit konkreter Ortsbezug hergestellt wird, ist Ulm als Herkunftsort des Studierwilligen (s. Abb. 37) und Heidelberg als sein Zielort eingesetzt.

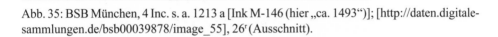

[Abbildung eines Textausschnitts]

Capitulũ. VII. alter alteruz de itinere in/
terrogat   Ca.

De venis Bar. De erfozdia. Ca.
que noua ducis inap
v   pertiũ.Bar.nulla.Ca.nulla prorſus.Bar.pe
nitus nulla Ca.arbitratus ſuz erfozdie veſuti poztũ
eſſe nouozũ omniũ.Bar.res iſta me fugit et vt veruz
fateoz ñ delectoz in nouitatibus audiedis.Ca.quo/
ſuz ẽiter tuũ.Bar.Heidelßergaz verſus.Ca.quid tuuz
ißidẽ negociũ ẽ.Bar.multociẽs ad me delatũ eſt opti/

Abb. 36: BSB München, 4 Inc. s. a. 1213 a [Ink M-146 (hier „ca. 1493")]; [http://daten.digitale-sammlungen.de/bsb00039878/image_27], 12ʳ (Ausschnitt, Hervorhebung durch Hinzufügen eines blauen Pfeils, C. R.).[70]

---

[70] Und nochmals 12ᵛ, jeweils mit Unterstreichungen eines lokalhistorisch interessierten Lesers, der auch den Namen eines genannten Professors (*Conradus Schuitzer*, 9ᵛ; auch andere Namen werden genannt) sowie die Angabe der Heilig-Geist-Kirche (*ecclesie sancti spiritus* 7ᵛ) mit Bleistift markiert hat.

Diese Angaben übernehmen auch die Drucke, die bei Heinrich Quentell in Köln hergestellt wurden, obwohl sie früher als der Heidelberger Druck datiert sind, so dass man annehmen muss, dass eine frühere, heute nicht mehr erhaltene Auflage eines Knoblochtzer-Drucks die Vorlage für die Kölner Wiegendrucke gebildet haben müsste.[71]

Knoblochtzer hat das Handbuch mit einer wohl aus Johannes Zainers Fundus stammenden (nicht aber im *Totentanz* verwendeten) *R*-Initiale aufgewertet. Sie und die Titelzeile erscheinen im Münchener, nicht rubrizierten Exemplar in Rot, im Züricher, von einem Rubrikator überarbeiteten Exemplar in Schwarz:

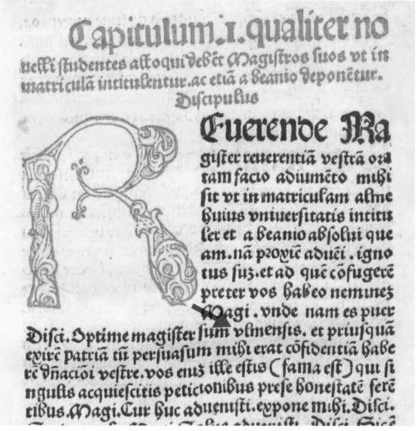

Abb. 37: BSB München, 4 Inc. s. a. 1213 a [Ink M-146 (hier dat. „ca. 1493")]; [http://daten. digitale-sammlungen.de/bsb00039878/image_7], 2ʳ (Ausschnitt, Hervorhebung durch Hinzufügen eines blauen Pfeils, C. R.).

---

[71] Für die Deventer-Drucke konnte dies mangels Digitalisat nicht überprüft werden.

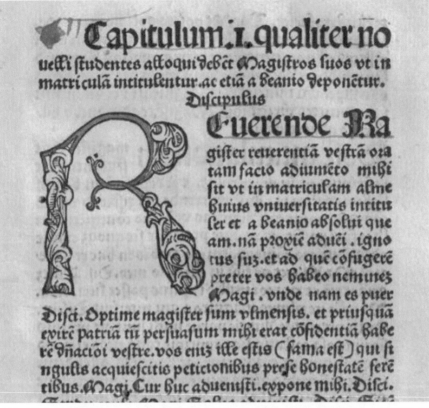

Abb. 38: Zentralbibliothek Zürich, Raa 53,4 [https://doi.org/10.3931/e-rara-45041], 2ʳ (Ausschnitt).

Exkurs: Amtlich, gesellschaftlicher Funktion der Universität, aber nicht sicher Knoblochtzer zuzuordnen ist:

[Gw M42895: SPANGEL, PALLAS: *Oratio ad universitatem Heidelbergensem.* Mit Beig. von LEONARDUS PELICANUS und JOHANNES VOLMANNIUS]

Dem aktuellen Eintrag im *Gw*, der undatiert bleibt, ist der Inhalt der Rede nicht zu entnehmen, aber der alte handschriftliche Eintrag im *Gw*-Register, der dankenswerterweise mitdokumentiert wird, spricht dafür, dass es sich um diesen Druck handelt:

Abb. 39: [https://commons.wikimedia.org/wiki/File:Pallas_Spangel_verbessert.jpg]

Die Rede hielt also der 1460 in Heidelberg immatrikulierte, seit 1477 mehrfach zum Rektor der Heidelberger Universität bestellte, aus Neustadt an der Weinstraße stammende Pallas Spangel (†1512, Schüler Wimpfelings, Lehrer Melanchthons), anlässlich des Todes von Margarethe von Bayern-Landshut (1456–1501), Gemahlin von Kurfürst Philipp d. Aufrichtigen (1448–1508). Der Druck wurde wohl in Heidelberg (evtl. mit Typenmaterial von Knoblochtzer, aber nicht mehr von ihm selbst) erstellt.[72]

---

[72] Vgl. die entsprechenden Stellen nach Registereintrag in GERHARD RITTER: *Die Heidelberger Universität im Mittelalter (1386–1508). Ein Stück deutscher Geschichte*, Heidelberg 1936, ND 1986, S. 531. und. HARTFELDER, KARL: *Spangel, Pallas*, in: *Allgemeine Deutsche Biographie (ADB)* 35 (1893), S. 32–33 [Online-Version: https://archive.org/details/allgemeine deutsc35lili/page/32/mode/2up?q=Spangel]. Vgl. auch die Ausführungen zum *Nosce te ipsum* (Gw M13471) im 5. Kapitel.

4   Juridica

[Gw 1708, 1709 und 1721: ANDREAE, JOHANNES: *Super arboribus consanguinitatis et affinitatis et cognationis spiritualis [...] cum exemplis*]: Wie im Schulsektor Johannes de Garlandia, so ist hier der italienische Kirchenrechtler Johannes Andreae (†1348) mit seinem Standardwerk *Super arboribus consanguinitatis* mehrfach vertreten: Drei Auflagen druckte Knoblochtzer in den beiden Jahren „um 1494" (Gw 1708 und 1721) sowie „um 1495" (Gw 1709). Dasselbe Werk hatte der Drucker auch in den letzten Straßburger Jahren (1483) herausgebracht (Gw 1707). Die Wiederaufnahme des Titels in Heidelberg dürfte ihm den Start an neuer Wirkungsstätte erheblich erleichtert, wenn nicht überhaupt erst ermöglicht haben. Von Gw 1708 zu Gw 1709 behält der Drucker die zehn Holzschnitte, bekannte Baumgraphiken und andere z. T. im Querformat gedruckte Schemata bei,[73]

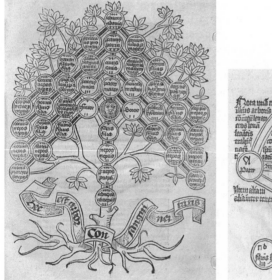
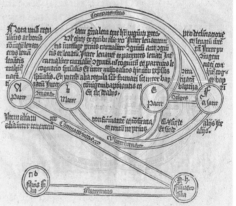

Abb. 40a (links) und 40b (rechts): Gw 1708: BSB München, 2 Inc. s. a. 59 a [Ink I-303]; [http://daten.digitale-sammlungen.de/bsb00017900/image_7] 2ʳ (40a) und [http://daten. digitale-sammlungen.de/bsb00017900/image_23] 10ʳ (40b) (jeweils stark verkleinert).

erhöht aber von der einen zur anderen Auflage die Zeilenzahl von 42 (einspaltig) auf 64 (zweispaltig), so dass er den Papieraufwand (und damit Kosten) von 14 auf 10 Bll. reduzieren kann. Von Gw 1708 befinden sich zwei, von Gw 1709 ein Exemplar in der UB (SCHLECHTER/RIES 1049–1051).

---

[73] Alle leicht in fast voller Größe einsehbar als Digitalisat der UB Heidelberg bei SCHRAMM: *Bilderschmuck 19*, Tafel 22–25.

Abb. 41: Gw 1708 „um 1494": BSB München, 2 Inc. s. a. 59 a [Ink I-303]; [http://daten.
digitale-sammlungen.de/bsb00017900/image_8], 2ᵛ (Ausschnitt).

Abb. 42: Gw 1709 „um 1495": BSB München, 2 Inc. s. a. 351 [Ink I-304]; [http://daten.digitale-
sammlungen.de/0002/bsb00029207/image_5], 2ᵛ (Ausschnitt).

Ökonomisches Handeln kann man schon in den beiden Ausgaben von „um 1494"
beobachten, wo der Drucker die *D*-Initiale von *Des ersten* […] der deutschen Ausgabe (Gw 1721) in der lateinischen Ausgabe einfach umdreht und dem Leser abver-
langt, diese nun als *C* von *Circa* zu lesen.[74]

Abb. 43a (links) und 43b (rechts): Gw 1721: BSB München, 2 Inc. s. a. 61 [Ink I-315]; [http://
daten.digitale-sammlungen.de/bsb00032023/image_7] (43a) und Gw 1708: BSB München,
2 Inc. s. a. 59 a, [http://daten.digitale-sammlungen.de/bsb00017900/image_8], 2ᵛ (43b) (jeweils
Ausschnitt).

Die Baumdiagramme hingegen mussten für die sprachverschiedenen Ausgaben in
Blockbuchmanier (Zeichnung und Beschriftung in Holz geschnitten) je separat angefertigt werden, das zeigen auch die unterschiedlichen Gesichter im Zentrum:

Abb. 44a (links) und 44b (rechts): Gw 1721: BSB München, 2 Inc. s. a. 61 [Ink I-315];
[http://daten.digitale-sammlungen.de/bsb00032023/image_6], 1ᵛ (44a) und Gw 1708: BSB
München, 2 Inc. s. a. 59 a [Ink I-303]; [http://daten.digitale-sammlungen.de/bsb00017900/
image_7], 2ʳ (44b) (jeweils Ausschnitt).

---

[74] Als *D* abgebildet in SCHRAMM: *Bilderschmuck 19*, Abb. 116, Tafel 18.

Von der lateinischen Fassung des Werks sind über 30 Inkunabelausgaben nachgewiesen, Friedrich Creussner in Nürnberg ist dabei über zehn Mal vertreten. An Druckorten werden weiterhin Köln, Mainz, Memmingen, Wien, mehrfach Leipzig aber auch Paris, Perugia und Löwen genannt. Knoblochtzers zahlreiche Straßburger Editionen in lateinscher und deutscher Fassung waren, z. T. sparsamer illustriert, mit einem Gesamtumfang von nur 8 Bll. erschienen. Die Diagramme konnte er in Heidelberg wiederverwenden. Das Werk, das sich mit den kirchen- und zivilrechtlichen Implikationen von Verwandtschaftsgraden (*zûgehörde*) befasst, die man von Geburt her ‚erbt‘ (*consanguinitas*) oder durch geschlechtlichen Umgang ‚erwirbt‘ (*affinitas* = dt. *mogschaft*) oder durch Patenschaften ‚gewinnt‘ (*cognatio spiritualis* = dt. *gevatterschafft*), war offensichtlich sowohl bei lateinkundigen Lesern wie auch bei Laien immer wieder ein gefragter rechtlicher Leitfaden.[75]

[Gw 10187: *Formulare und deutsch Rhetorica*], ein Werk von 90 Bll., seinem Titel nach stilistisches Handbuch, seinem Gebrauch nach eher Formel- und Mustersammlung für Urkunden und Amtsbriefe. Der *Gw* kennt eine niederdeutsche Fassung aus Rostock (Gw 10177), sechs Drucke einer Augsburg-/Ulmer Tradition (Gw 10178–10183 sowie 9 Sp. 34a), und eine Fassung, die man als ‚Rheinische Fassung‘ bezeichnen könnte, mit Drucken aus Straßburg (Gw 10184–10186 von Johann Prüss 1483, Heinrich Knoblochtzer 1483 und Johann Grüninger 1486), Heidelberg (Gw 10187 von Knoblochtzer 1488), Speyer (Gw 10188 von Konrad Hist 1492) und Köln (Gw 10189 von Johann Koelhoff d. J. „nicht vor 11. VIII. 1492“), wobei die letztgenannte Inkunabel wiederum eine kürzende, ins Niederdeutsche umgesetzte Bearbeitung von 144 Bll. darstellt, die zugleich die einzige in 4° gegenüber den anderen 2°-Ausgaben ist. Die Rheinischen Fassungen zeigen ihre Verwandtschaft schon durch den Nachschnitt (oder Wiederverwendung?) des Titelholzschnitts, wobei Knoblochtzer in seiner Heidelberger Fassung (nicht aber schon im Straßburger Druck) wiederum, wie so oft, eine Initiale aus dem Typenfundus verwendet, der dem Stil nach dem von J. Zainer in Ulm ererbten Repertoire angehört[76]:

---

[75] „Darstellung der Grade der Blutsverwandtschaft [...] die für das kirchliche Eherecht wichtig sind und auch im Erbrecht Beachtung erlangten“, so HELKO EIS: *Andreae, Johannes*, in: *²VL* 1 (1978), Sp. 336 f.
[76] AMELUNG: *FDSW*: Abb. 34, S. 67 und Text S. 66: ‚Rokoko-Alphabet‘.

Abb. 45: Prüss, Straßburg 1483: SBB Berlin PK, Ink. 365/7a [https://digital.staatsbibliothek-berlin.de/werkansicht?PPN=PPN881354120&PHYSID=PHYS_0003&DMDID=], 1ʳ (Ausschnitt).

Abb. 46: Knoblochtzer, Straßburg 1483: UB Heidelberg, G 225 A qt. INC: [1]; [https://digi.ub.uni-heidelberg.de/diglit/if00245000/0005], 1ʳ (Ausschnitt).

Abb. 47: Grüninger, Straßburg 1486, ULB Darmstadt, Inc. IV-19 [http://tudigit.ulb.tu-darmstadt.de/show/inc-iv-19/0001], 1ʳ (Ausschnitt).

Abb. 48: Knoblochtzer, Heidelberg 1488: ULB Darmstadt Inc IV-169 [http://tudigit.ulb.
tu-darmstadt.de/show/inc-iv-169/0177], 1ʳ (Ausschnitt).

Abb. 49: Hist, Speyer 1492: BSB München, 2 Inc. c. a. 2711 [Ink F-200]; [http://daten.digitale-
sammlungen.de/bsb00082272/image_5], 1ʳ (Ausschnitt).

Im Text folgt Knoblochtzers Heidelberger Druck von 1488 bemerkenswerterweise
nicht seiner Straßburger Fassung, sondern fast zeilengetreu dem Vorläufer von Grüninger 1486 (hier im Vergleich die letzte Seite, Bl. 85 der gezählten Blätter ohne Titelblatt und vorgeschaltetem Register):

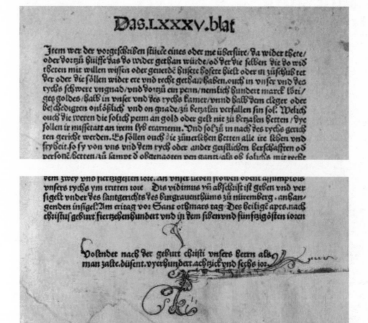

Abb. 50: Grüninger, Straßburg 1486: ULB Darmstadt, Inc. IV-19 [http://tudigit.ulb.tu-darm
stadt.de/show/inc-iv-19/0177], 85ʳ (Ausschnitt mit Auslassung).

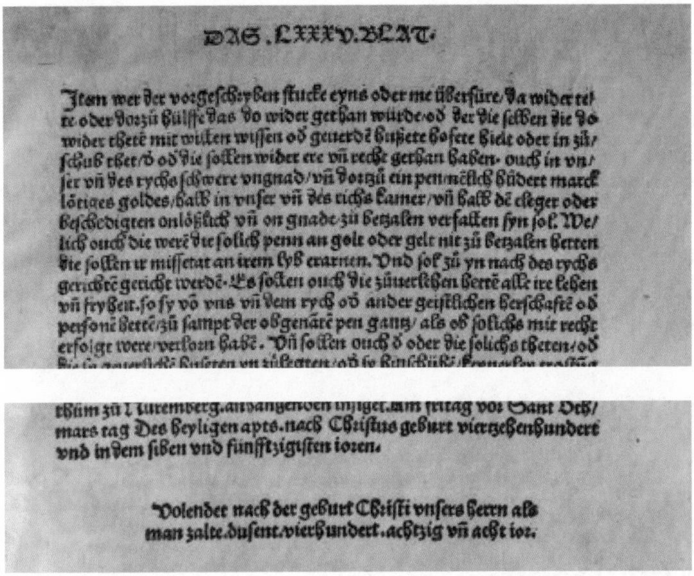

DAS . LXXXV. BLAT.

Item wer der vorgeschryben stucke eyns oder me übersüre/ da wider tet te oder dorzü hülffe das do wider gethan würde/ od der die selben die do wider thetē mit wilken wissen od geuerdē husete hosete hielt oder in zü/ schub thet/ d od die sollen wider ere vñ recht gethan haben. ouch in vn/ ser vñ des rychs schwere vngnad/ vñ dorzü ein pen/ nēlich hūdert marck lötiges goldes/ halb in vnser vñ des richs kamer/ vñ halb dē cleger oder beschedigten onlößlich vñ on gnade zü betzalen verfallen syn sol. We/ lich ouch die werē die solich penn an golt oder gelt nit zü betzalen hetten die sollen ir missetat an irem lyb erarnen. Vnd sol zü yn nach des rychs gerichtē gericht werdē. Es sollen ouch die züuerlichen herrē alle ire lehen vñ fryheit. so sy vō vns vñ dem rych od ander geistlichen herschaftē od personē hettē/ zü sampt der obgenātē pen gantz/ als ob soliche mit recht erfolgt were/ verlorn habē. Vñ sollen ouch ō oder die solichs theten/ od

thüm zü Lutzemberg. anhangenden insigel. am fritag vor Sant Oth/ mars tag Des heyligen apts. nach Christus geburt viertzehenhundert vnd in dem siben vnd funfftzigisten ioren.

Volendet nach der geburt Christi vnsers herrn als man zalte. dusent. vierhundert. achtzig vñ acht ior.

Abb. 51: Knoblochtzer, Heidelberg 1488: ULB Darmstadt, Inc IV-169 [http://tudigit.ulb.tu-darmstadt.de/show/inc-iv-169/0353], 85r (Ausschnitt mit Auslassung).

Die UB in Heidelberg weist sowohl ein Exemplar des Straßburger wie auch des Heidelberger Knoblochtzer-Druckes auf (SCHLECHTER/RIES 669 und 670, s. o. Abb. 46). Die Rheinischen Fassungen zeigen verschiedene sprachgeographische Einflüsse, indem sie nur sporadisch Diphthongierung der mhd. Langvokale aufweisen. Die Einleitung zum Werk enthält einerseits eine Ankündigung auf die besprochenen rhetorischen Mittel und die gebotenen Briefmuster (*koufbrief, lehenbrief* …), andererseits wird ausdrücklich vor der unreflektierten Übernahme der Muster gewarnt und zu einer gewissenhaften Anpassung auf den je aktuellen Einsatz aufgefordert, eine Art Warnung vor unkontrolliertem Copy-and-Paste-Verfahren: *Ob ouch die nachgesetzten brief gantz yn glycher form alwegen nit dienende sind/ sol der leser syn vernunfft vfthůn vnd dy artickel vnd puncten (nitt on groß müg*[77] *vnd arbeit*[78]*) zůsamensůchen/ vnd sy mit flyß setzen. Wann*[79] *von künfftigen handeln vnd sachen mag nit eygenlich vnd gewißliche als von vergangen dingen (die hier ynn exempla sind) geschriben werden.*

In demjenigen der 16 erhaltenen Textzeugen des Heidelberger Drucks, der digitalisiert zur Verfügung steht (ULB Darmstadt, s. o. Abb. 48) ist der Text des deutschen *Formulare* aus unerfindlichen Gründen mit einem lateinischen Druck der *Historia Trojana* nach Guido de Columnis (Husner, Straßburg 1483, von ähnlichem Umfang wie das *Formulare*) zusammengebunden!

[77] Nhd. ‚Können'.
[78] Nhd. ‚Mühe'.
[79] Nhd. ‚Denn'.

[Gw M16365 und Gw M16367: *Ordo iudiciarius*, deutsch]: Während Knoblochtzer vom *Arbor consanguinitatis* (s. o.) sowohl lateinische wie auch deutsche Ausgaben herausbrachte, ist für den *Ordo iudiciarius* aus Heidelberg allein eine deutsche Inkunabel erhalten.[80] Diese volkssprachige Variante war eigentlich eine Domäne der Augsburger Offizinen, aus denen nicht weniger als elf Inkunabelausgaben dieses Titels hervorgingen. Sie waren oft, wie auch ein Teil von Knoblochtzers beiden Ausgaben von 1490 mit dem Zusatz *Wie man Höfe, Zehnte und Mühlen verleihen soll* ergänzt. Innerhalb dieser Ausgabe gibt es verschiedene Varianten: Die beiden Digitalisate aus München [Gw M16365] und Berlin [Gw M16367] enthalten beide diesen Zusatz, umfassen jeweils 14 Bll., weisen das gleiche Titelblatt auf:

Ein oꝛdnung vnnd vn
derweisunge. Wie sich
ein ieglicher halten soll
voꝛ dem rechten.

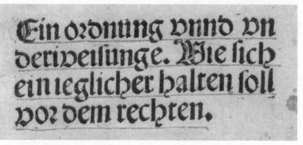

Abb. 52: BSB München, 4 Inc. c. a. 772 a [Ink O-76]; [http://daten.digitale-sammlungen.de/bsb00034564/image_5], 1r (Ausschnitt).

Ein oꝛdnũg vnnd vn
derweisunge Wie sich
ein ieglicher halten soll
voꝛ dem rechten.

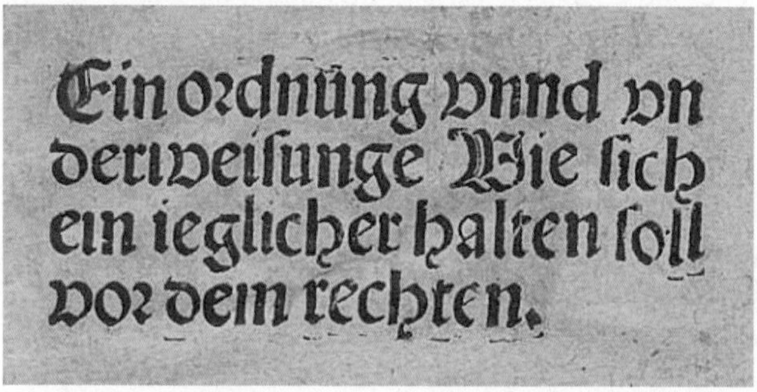

Abb. 53: SBB Berlin PK, Inc. 1201, [https://digital.staatsbibliothek-berlin.de/werkansicht?PPN=PPN894047345&PHYSID=PHYS_0005&DMDID=], 1r (Ausschnitt).

Im Detail zeigen sie dann aber geringfügige Satzunterschiede, die Knoblochtzers Versuch dokumentieren, zu einem orthographisch, satztechnisch oder/und ästhetisch optimalen Ergebnis zu gelangen. Die *I*-Initiale aus dem von Amelung so genannten ‚Rokoko-Alphabet', das von Zainer in Ulm übernommen wurde,[81] nutzt er für beide Lösungen:

[80] Für dessen lateinische Variante verzeichnet *Gw* elf Ausgaben aus der Inkunabelzeit (mehrfach Köln und Paris, je einmal Poitiers und Reutlingen).

[81] Amelung: *Fdsw*: Abb. 34, S. 67 und Text S. 66.

Abb. 54: BSB München, 4 Inc. c. a. 772 a [Ink O-76]; [http://daten.digitale-sammlungen.de/bsb00034564/image_7], 2ʳ (Ausschnitt, Hervorhebung durch Hinzufügen eines blauen Pfeils, C.R.).

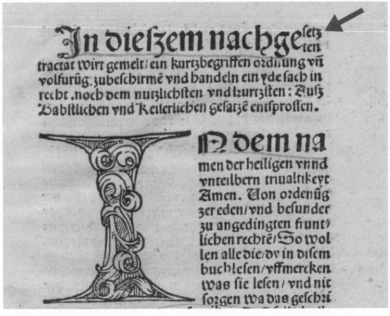

Abb. 55: SBB Berlin PK, Inc. 1201, [https://digital.staatsbibliothek-berlin.de/werkansicht?PPN=PPN894047345&PHYSID=PHYS_0007&DMDID=], 2ʳ (Ausschnitt, Hervorhebung durch Hinzufügen eines blauen Pfeils, C.R.).

Sogar die Kolophone der beiden Varianten unterscheiden sich geringfügig, immerhin in der Namensform des Druckers, wobei man die zweite wohl für die korrigierte halten darf:

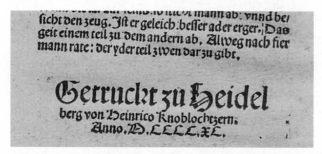

Abb. 56: BSB München, 4 Inc. c. a. 772 a [Ink O-76]; [http://daten.digitale-sammlungen.de/bsb00034564/image_30], 13ᵛ (Ausschnitt).

Abb. 57: SBB Berlin PK, Inc. 1201, [https://digital.staatsbibliothek-berlin.de/werkansicht?PPN=PPN894047345&PHYSID=PHYS_0030&DMDID=], 13ᵛ (Ausschnitt).

Für die Vermutung, dass Jakob Köbel, von dem später noch öfter die Rede sein wird (dezidiert in Kap. 5 *Tischzucht*, Kap. 8 *Fußpfad zur Seligkeit* und 9.A *Sybillen Weisagung*), auch der Autor dieses *Ordo* ist (so die Darstellung im *Gw*), gibt das Kolophon keine Bestätigung. Ganz unwahrscheinlich scheint die Vermutung andererseits nicht, da Köbel später, nachdem er sich in Oppenheim niedergelassen hatte, wo er auch als Stadtschreiber fungierte, eine *Gerichtsordnung* verfasst haben soll.[82] Inhalt des Heidelberger *Ordo iudicarius* von nur 10 Bll. Umfang sind die Anleitung zur Abfassung einer Gerichtsrede, eine Auflistung der Anredeformeln für Personen von verschiedenem Stand (insofern eine Art Kurzfassung des *Formulare und deutsch Rhetorica*, Gw 10187), die Regeln der Zeugenladung und -vernehmung, die Dokumentation des Verfahrens usw. Der Anhang von 3 Bll. *Wie man Höfe, Zehnte und Mühlen verleihen soll* wird wiederum mit einer Initiale *Z* aus dem schon genannten, Ulmer Typenrepertoire eröffnet.[83]

---

[82] GRIMM, HEINRICH: *Köbel, Jakob*, in: *Neue Deutsche Biographie* 12 (1979), S. 289–290, Online-Version: [https://www.deutsche-biographie.de/pnd118724142.html#ndbcontent]

[83] Dieses *Z* selbst ist in Abb. 34 des Zainerschen ,Rokoko-Alphabets' nicht vertreten, vgl. AMELUNG: *Fdsw* S.66–68, mit Abb. 34.

Wie mann hoef.ze henden.vnnd mulen verleyhen soll.
Zvm ersten ist ze mercken / ob der hof vnuogtber/vnsteu erber vngerichtber/vn zehentber/ vñ vndinst ber sei/vnd ob er allein lige. So leihet mann den einem meyer / das er im burgschafft oder gewerschaft thu trew iar gewisser vnd wes

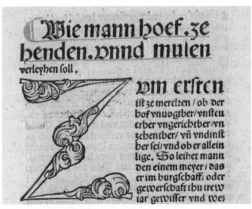

Abb. 58: BSB München, 4 Inc.c.a. 772 a [Ink O-76]; [http://daten.digitale-sammlungen.de/bsb00034564/image_25], 11r (Ausschnitt).

Von der ersten der beiden 1490 gedruckten Ausgaben des Werkes liegt ein Exemplar im Heidelberger Stadtarchiv (Schlechter/Ries 1370).

[Gw M25075: *Modus vacandi beneficiorum. Modus acceptandi*]: Die Werke mit dem Titel *Modus* könnte man als ‚Ratgeber' bezeichnen: *Modus disponendi se ad mortem* (‚Ratgeber zur Vorbereitung auf den Tod'), *Modus epistolandi* (‚Ratgeber, Briefe zu schreiben'), *Modus perveniendi ad summam sapientiam* (‚Ratgeber, zu höchster Weisheit zu gelangen'), *Modus praedicandi* (‚Ratgeber, eine Predigt zu halten'), *Modus redimendi animas in purgatorio existentes* (‚Ratgeber, wie man den Seelen im Fegefeuer helfend beistehen könnte'), *Modus studendi* (‚Ratgeber für ein erfolgreiches Studium') usw. sind gängige Titel in der Inkunabelzeit (s. *Gw*-Liste unter *Modus*).

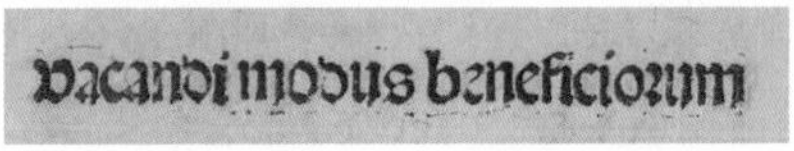

vacandi modus beneficiorum

Abb. 59: HAB Wolfenbüttel, A: 202.32 Quod. (17) [http://diglib.hab.de/inkunabeln/202-32-quod-17/start.htm?image=00001], 1r (Ausschnitt).

Der hier vorliegende, schmale Ratgeber von 4 Bll.[84] handelt davon, wie man sich von Pfründ-/ und Lehenspflichten befreien oder befreit werden könnte. Die einzelnen Abschnitte beginnen mit einer *Si quis possidet/habuerit/habet*-Formel und zählen dann die Bedingungen für die Befreiung auf. Am Ende befindet sich bei den meisten Ausgaben (wie auch hier) ein kurzer Abschnitt *Modus acceptandi*, der die notariellen

[84] Die Abb. stammt aus der Herzog August Bibliothek Wolfenbüttel, dort wird die Inkunabel, abweichend von Angaben im *Gw*, Hist in Speyer 1497 zugeordnet. Bei dieser und allen im Folgenden aus dem Bestand der HAB Wolfenbüttel verwendeten Abbildungen findet die CC-Lizenz CC BY-SA 3.0 (https://creativecommons.org/licenses/by-sa/3.0/de/) Anwendung. Etwaige Änderungen bzw. Bearbeitungen des verwendeten Materials sind im Folgenden jeweils vermerkt.

Usancen und Notwendigkeiten beim Erwerb eines Beneficiums beschreibt. Das kleine Werk wurde außer in Heidelberg auch in Basel, Mainz, Passau, Toulouse, Venedig je einmal und in Rom allein 24 mal während der Inkunabelzeit gedruckt, was die kirchenrechtliche Relevanz deutlich unterstreicht. Der Knoblochtzer-Druck („um 1490") ist, für ein so schmales Bändchen ungewöhnlich, in 15 Exemplaren erhalten, wohl auch deshalb, weil es, wie in Wolfenbüttel, mit anderen Juridica zusammengebunden war. Deutlich wird auch, dass Knoblochtzer für diesen Text keinen zusätzlichen Kaufanreiz bieten musste, hier lässt er nämlich jedes Schmuckelement wie Initialen und dergleichen weg, und die Versoseite des Titelblattes bleibt ganz großzügig unbedruckt (Im Gegensatz etwa zum *Pfaffen von Kalenberg*, s. d. Kap. 10).

[Gw M45623: *Termini causarum et Festa in Romana Curia servari soliti in causa beneficiali*. Daran: *Festa palacii Apostolici*]: Bei diesem Werk ist die Zentrierung im Kirchenrecht noch deutlicher: Außer der Ausgabe aus Heidelberg „nicht nach 14. IV.1491", von der 20 Exemplare erhalten sind, verzeichnet *Gw* weitere 13 Drucke, die allesamt (ohne kalendarischen Zusatz) seit 1470 in Rom angefertigt wurden. Die in der Römischen Kurie üblicherweise eingehaltenen (*in Romana curia servari soliti*) *Termini causarum* werden nicht nur für die *causa beneficiali* sondern auch für *causae prophanae*, *super grauamine*, […] *super excommunicatione* usw. in je verschiedenen *instantiae* aufgelistet. Abschließend folgt noch der *stilus es modus observandi et practicandi terminorum predictorum* und (nur in der Heidelberger Ausgabe!) ein kalendarischer Zusatz, der auf 10^r (von insgesamt 11 Bll.) beginnt, Orientierung innerhalb der Terminierung schafft und so dem Rezipienten den Gebrauch des Kerntextes erleichtert.

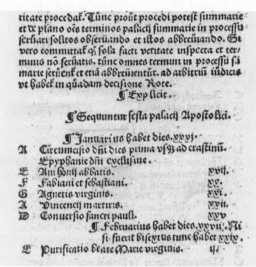

Abb. 60: BSB München, 4 Inc. s. a. 1751 [Ink T-117] [http://daten.digitale-sammlungen.de/bsb00040290/image_23], 10^r (Ausschnitt).

(Einzelne kürzere Juridica, Urkunden und Amtssachen werden unten, in Kap. 9.B noch besprochen.)

5 Humanismus

Gewissermaßen handelt es sich hier nicht nur der Anordnung nach, sondern auch inhaltlich um ein zentrales, aber auch oszillierendes Kapitel mit Verflechtung zu vielen anderen Themenbereichen. Denn vielfach finden sich in den sonstigen Abschnitten, wie schon unter den Schulbüchern zu beobachten, humanistisch inspirierte Titel oder doch solche, die notdürftig aus der alten Zeit in die neue Ära hinein adaptiert worden waren (vgl. Kap. 3, Anfang). Andererseits lässt sich an dieser Stelle aber auch unterstreichen, was MARTINA BACKES in ihrer Studie *Das literarische Leben am kurpfälzischen Hof zu Heidelberg im 15. Jahrhundert* zu diesem Thema bemerkt: „Das Etikett ‚humanistisch‘ erweist sich vielfach durchaus als problematisch, vor allem, wenn man den Lesern […] literarische Interessen und Erwartungshaltungen unterschiebt, die sich aus den Konnotationen des Begriffs für heutige Ohren ergeben."[85]

[Gw M4978110: VERGILIUS MARO, PUBLIUS: *Opera*]: Die Vergil-Ausgabe von 1495 scheint auf den ersten Blick nur zufällig in Heidelberg entstanden zu sein und nicht als Zeugnis verstärkten Interesses des humanistischen Kreises an antiker Literatur in der Universitätsstadt ins Felde geführt werden zu können, da es sich um den belegbaren Fall einer Auftragsarbeit einer anderen Druckerei, der Offizin Peter Drachs d.M. (†1504) in Speyer, handelt.[86] Dann zeigt sich aber bei genauerem Hinsehen, dass Knoblochtzers Druckausgabe dermaßen viele Detailübereinstimmungen hat mit der berühmten Vergil-Handschrift Vat. Pal. lat. 1632,[87] dass man nicht von einem Zufall ausgehen kann: Im Gegensatz zu den meisten Vergil-Ausgaben ist in dieser Handschrift und in Knoblochtzers Inkunabeldruck der Kerntext nicht vom Servius-Kommentar gerahmt. Besagte Handschrift und der Heidelberger Druck bieten gleichermaßen zur *Georgica* (Inkunabel ab 26ʳ) und zur *Aeneis* (ab 90ʳ) den Ps.-Ovid-Kommentar, beide weisen als *Argumentum in libros Eineidum* die *Anthologia latina* 634 auf.[88] Um sich die Übereinstimmung vor Augen zu führen, betrachte man das

---

[85] BACKES (1992), S. 171.

[86] Kurz erwähnt bei GELDNER: *Inkunabeldrucker* (1968), S. 192. Näheres bei: MÄKELER, HENDRIK: *Das Rechnungsbuch des Speyerer Druckherrn Peter Drach d. M. (um 1415–1504)*, [*Sachüberlieferung und Geschichte 38*], Sankt Katharinen 2005, v.a. S. 54. und P.W. SCHWEITZER-MARTIN in seiner Heidelberger Zulassungsarbeit von 2017: *Das Druckprogramm der Speyerer Werkstatt ‚Peter Drach‘ (1475–1504)*, die ich dankenswerterweise einsehen durfte. Auch der vielfach mit Knoblochtzer in unterschiedlicher Weise zusammenarbeitende Jakob Köbel findet in diesem genannten Rechnungsbuch Erwähnung, hier als ‚Buchführer‘, vgl. GRIMM, HEINRICH: *Köbel, Jakob*, in: *Neue Deutsche Biographie* 12 (1979), S. 289–290, Online-Version: [https://www.deutsche-biographie.de/pnd118724142.html#ndb content]. Und CHRISTOPH RESKE: *Die Buchdrucker des 16. Und 17. Jahrhunderts im deutschen Sprachgebiet. Auf der Grundlage des gleichnamigen Werkes von Josef Benzing*, Wiesbaden 2007, S. 761.

[87] Auftragsarbeit für den Pfalzgrafen Philipp den Aufrichtigen zu dessen Hochzeit mit Margarete von Bayern-Landshut 1474.

[88] Das ist zwar nicht ganz singulär, stellt aber insgesamt doch die Ausnahme dar.

Digitalisat von Bl. 63ʳ des Codex Pal. Lat. 1632 aus der Bibliotheca Vaticana Rom [https://doi.org/10.11588/diglit.9861#0133], aus dem leider keine Kopien gezogen werden dürfen,[89] und vergleiche die Übereinstimmungen im Text mit der entsprechenden Stelle in der Heidelberger Inkunabel:

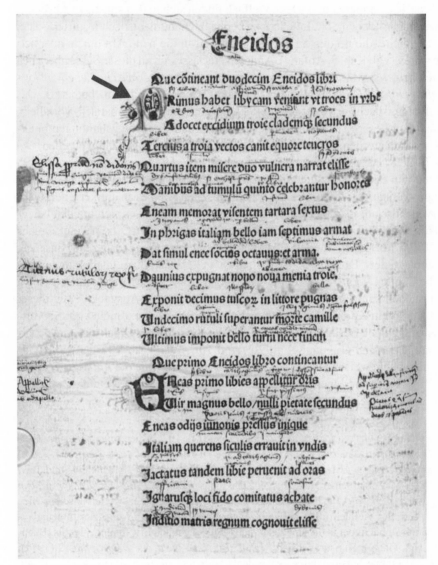

Abb. 61: BSB München, 4 Inc. c. a. 1253 m [Ink V-132]; [http://daten.digitale-sammlungen. de/bsb00044396/image_182], 89ᵛ (Ausschnitt, Hervorhebung durch Hinzufügen eines blauen Pfeils, C. R.).

---

[89] Näheres zu diesem Codex vgl. WALTER BERSCHIN: *Die Palatina in der Vaticana. Eine deutsche Bibliothek in Rom*, Stuttgart/Zürich 1992, S. 126–128.

So erscheint es wahrscheinlich, dass Knoblochtzer in Heidelberg den von Peter Drach initiierten und finanzierten Druck nicht (oder jedenfalls nicht nur) aus wirtschaftlich-technischen Gründen (etwa wegen mangelnder Kapazität der Speyer Offizin) übernahm. Vielleicht liegt der Grund eher darin, dass in Heidelberg der Druck in der Nähe der prominenten Vorlage aus der Palatina erstellt werden konnte, die das Fürstenhaus nicht einmal vorübergehend nach Speyer verleihen wollte. Eine Kooperation zwischen den beiden Offizinen lässt sich aber auch bei einem Inkunabeldruck von Johannes Virdungs *Practica* beobachten (vgl. unten Kapitel 9.A). Im Kolophon stellt sich die Inkunabel ganz als Werk des Heidelberger Druckers dar:

Abb. 62: BSB München, 4 Inc. c. a. 1253 m [Ink V-132]; [http://daten.digitale-sammlungen.de/bsb00044396/image_742], 369ᵛ (Ausschnitt).

Von Umfang (369 Bll.), Inhalt und Anspruch sowohl an den Produzenten wie den Rezipienten haben wir hier ein Werk von ganz anderem Kaliber vor uns als die Texte aus der *Cato*-Gruppe (vgl. Kap. 3), dieses Opus magnum ist viel eher mit den großen franziskanisch motivierten Kompendien zu vergleichen, die im 1. Kapitel beschrieben wurden. Die Heidelberger Vergil-Ausgabe von 1495 ist in 6 Exemplaren überliefert, das Münchner Exemplar ist voll von handschriftlichen Anmerkungen eines Lesers (*Magister Georgius Sch….[?]*), der diesen Klassiker der lateinischen Literatur offensichtlich (laut handschriftlicher Anmerkung 1504) nicht nur eifrig gelesen, sondern durchgearbeitet und diese Arbeit am Tag der Auffindung des heiligen Kreuzes (*in die inventionis sancte crucis*) beendet hat.

Abb. 63: BSB München, 4 Inc. c. a. 1253 m [Ink V-132]; [http://daten.digitale-sammlungen.de/bsb00044396/image_742], 369ᵛ (erweiterter Ausschnitt der vorherigen Abb., Hervorhebung durch Hinzufügen eines blauen Pfeils, C. R.).

Für solch einen Leser, der in einigen handschriftlichen Nachträgen zu Beginn des Codex, in denen er auch sporadisch ungelenke griechische Schrift benutzt,

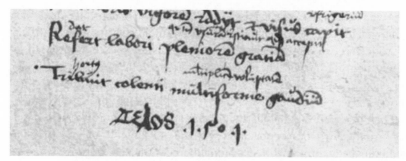

Abb. 64: BSB München, 4 Inc.c.a. 1253 m [Ink V-132]; [http://daten.digitale-sammlungen.de/bsb00044396/image_6], 1ᵛ (Ausschnitt).

um damit vermutlich seine humanistische Bildung unter Beweis zu stellen, ist diese Ausgabe gedacht gewesen, denn der Text ist durchwegs mit Leerzeilen durchschossen, die Platz für Interlinearglossen boten.

Abb. 65: BSB München, 4 Inc. c. a. 1253 m [Ink V-132]; [http://daten.digitale-sammlungen.de/bsb00044396/image_7], 2ʳ (Ausschnitt).

[Gw M13471: JOHANNES DE DEO CARTUSIANUS: *Nosce te ipsum*. Mit Beig. von JODOCUS GALLUS und GABRIEL BRUNUS (DdL)]: In diesem und dem folgend genannten Werk haben wir die jüngsten, dem ‚Drucker des Lindelbach‘ zugeordneten Inkunabeln vor uns (hier „6.VII.1489", knapp 100 Bll.). Das *Nosce te ipsum* des nicht näher zu identifizierenden Autors Johannes[90] passt auch inhaltlich zu den in Kapitel 1 besprochenen monastisch zentrierten Werken, hier wohl in der Tradition der *Collationes patrum* des Johannes Cassianus (4. Jh.), die im Rahmen der Devotio moderna ins Niederländische übersetzt wurden[91] und zudem dem Dominikaner Johannes Nider (ca. 1380–1438) zur Grundlage für sein in der Klosterreform des 15. Jh. s wichtiges Werk *Die 24 goldenen Harfen* diente. Stichwörter sind entsprechend die *diuini amoris scintilla* ('Das Fünklein göttlicher Liebe' 3[r]), die *reformatio in fide et sensatione* ('Erneuerung von Glaube und Geist' 5[v]); *vita activa* und *contemplativa* werden in einem allegorischen Verfahren den Fischen beim neutestamentlichen Wunder der Fischvermehrung zur Speisung der Viertausend (Mt 15, 32 ff.) verglichen usw. Wenn das Publikum vom Autor apostrophiert wird, ist von *dilectissimi fratres* die Rede (6[v]), der Titel *Nosce te ipsum* wird mit der Absicht begründet, die Entscheidung über die Wahl des Standes *cuiuscumque mentis* (6[v], kontemplativ oder aktiv) überaus klar darstellen zu wollen. Noch näher an Cassians *Collationes* (s. o.) rückt die Textzusammenstellung mit der Anfügung eines *Liber qui intitulatur Corona senum* ('Versammlung der Alten' 54[v]). Der Ausgabe ist sowohl in der Editio princeps aus Venedig 1480 wie auch in der Heidelberger Inkunabel ein Bündel von Inprimatur-Urteilen von namhaften Theologen vorgeschaltet (ab 2[r]), dessen letztes wiederum von einem Minoriten, Gabriel Brunus, stammt.[92] Dieses Werk, das im Kern also rein monastisch geprägt ist, wird nun in der Ausgabe von Knoblochtzer äußerlich humanistisch überformt, indem er eine Art Motto in Form eines nicht eben genialen Vierzeilers (*Tetrastichon iodoci galli rubiacensis*) in antikischem Versmaß dem eigentlichen Text (werbewirksam?) voranstellt:[93]

---

[90] Das Lexikon des Mittelalters kennt einen Johannes de Deo, 13. Jh., doch ist dieser Kanonist und kommt als Autor für das *Nosce te* nicht in Frage (N. Höhl: *Johannes de Deo*, in: *Lexikon des Mittelalters* 5 [1999], Sp. 569). Besser passt das Werk in das Spektrum von Jacobus Carthusiensis/Jakob von Paradies (1381–1465), vgl. den entsprechenden Artikel von D. Mertens in ²*VL* 4 (1983), Sp. 478–487, v. a. Sp. 482.

[91] Vgl. Klaus Klein: *Johannes Cassianus*, in ²*VL* 4 (1983), Sp. 567–570. Nähe zur Devotio moderna war ja auch in dem Werkrepertoire des 1. Kapitels zu beobachten.

[92] Diesem Beispiel früher 'Zensur' verdankt der Titel einen ausführlichen Eintrag mit Abdruck zahlreicher Passagen bereits in: J. N. Weislinger: *Armamentarium catholicum perantiquae, rarissimae ac pretiosissimae bibliothecae, quae asservatur Argentorati* […], Straßburg 1749, S. 505–508.

[93] Nicht vorhanden in der einzigen weiteren Inkunabel, die der *Gw* verzeichnet, der editio princeps aus Venedig 1480.

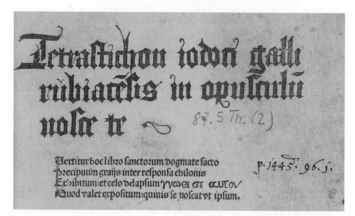

Abb. 66: HAB Wolfenbüttel, Ink. 87.5. theol. (2) [http://diglib.hab.de/inkunabeln/87-5-theol-2/
start.htm?image=00001], 1ʳ (Ausschnitt).

Sein Autor ist Jodocus Gallus, seinerseits Franziskaner (vgl. Kap. 1), stammend aus
Ruffach im Elsaß 1459, gestorben zu Speyer 1517. Er wird zusammen mit dem oben
schon erwähnten Pallas Spangel (Ende 3. Kapitel) von GERHARD RITTER zum „Geschlecht jüngerer ‚scholastischer Humanisten' […], die ihre Kenntnis altrömischer Literatur […] an der Universität selber empfangen haben," gezählt.[94] Es scheint hierbei
aber das ‚Nosce te ipsum' nur ein Reizwort gewesen zu sein, das die Möglichkeit bot,
das ganze Werk mit einem von Knoblochtzer wohl extra in ungelenken griechischen
Lettern zu schnitzenden γνωθι σε αυτον in Motto (s. o.) und Kolophon einzuspannen:

Abb. 67: HAB Wolfenbüttel, Ink. 87.5. theol. (2) [http://diglib.hab.de/inkunabeln/87-5-theol-2/
start.htm?image=00198], 99ᵛ (Ausschnitt, Hervorhebung durch Hinzufügen eines blauen
Pfeils, C. R.).

---

[94] GERHARD RITTER: *Die Heidelberger Universität im Mittelalter (1386–1508). Ein Stück
deutscher Geschichte*, Heidelberg 1936/ND ebd. 1986, S. 463. Näheres dazu auch im
Artikel von BIUNDO, GEORG, in: *Neue Deutsche Biographie* 6 (1964), S. 55, Online-Version:
[https://www.deutsche-biographie.de/pnd102501726.html#ndbcontent]

Das nimmt unmissverständlich auf den bekannten Spruch des Orakels von Delphi Bezug, erweitert den Adressatenkreis (im Werk selbst war ja von *dilectissimi fratres* die Rede) unversehens über die Ordensschranken zum *studiosissime lector* im Allgemeinen.[95] Allerdings muss dieser Leser doch einer den *contemptus mundi* stützenden theologisch-mystischen Betrachtung (*maxime deuotionis vtilitatisque opusculum*, vgl. Abb. 67, Z. 1/2) zugänglich sein. Es entbehrt nicht ganz einer gewissen Ironie, dass dieses Werk, während es mit griechischen Buchstaben antikisiert wird, bei seinem Transfer aus Venedig an den Neckar zugleich aus der lateinischen Antiqua in die deutsche gotische Schrift umgesetzt wird. Aus dem Lokalkolorit wird kein Hehl gemacht, indem dem Leser ein *Optime vale Ex Heidelberga* (Z. 12) geradezu zugerufen wird. In diesem Kontext wird er (auch wieder nach Art der Grammatiken aus der DdL-Gruppe), noch zum häufigen Gebrauch (*cottidiana lectio*) ermahnt, denn der Kauf allein nütze nur dem Drucker: *Fac igitur, persuade tibi non modo vt eum emas, quod impressori pergratum est, sed et tibi velut enchiridion* [wörtl. ‚das zur Hand Seiende‘] *et cottidiana lectione frequentandum vsurpes*.

Das Heidelberger Netzwerk dieser Tage um Kurfürst Philipp (1448–1508), seinen Kanzler und Bischof von Worms, Johannes von Dalberg (1455–1503), seinen Hofastrologen, Mathematiker und Mediziner Johannes Virdung (1463– um 1538, s. u. Kap. 9.A), den Theologen, Juristen und Prinzenerzieher Adam Wernher von Themar (1462–1537), Jodocus Gallus (1459–1517) und Jakob Köbel (um 1462–1533)[96] zur produktivsten Zeit der Knoblochtzerschen Drucktätigkeit in Heidelberg,[97] gewinnt an Kontur durch den Umstand, dass das einzige deutsche Werk des Jodocus Gallus, sein *Ewangelisch Abc* eben jener Jakob Köbel später in seiner eigenen Druckerei in Oppenheim 1517 herausgegeben hat,[98] der zuvor als Verleger und Autor einige Drucke in Knoblochtzers Offizin initiiert hatte (s. u. in diesem Kapitel u. ö.).[99] Über Adam Wernher von Themar, von dem bekannt ist, dass er viele Mariengedichte verfasst hat,[100] und diesen Jodocus Gallus ergibt sich nun wiederum eine Verbindung zur

---

[95] Vgl. die Anrede an den *ingeniosissime adolescens, studiosissime adolescens* u. ä. in einigen DdL-Inkunabeln in Kap. 3, Gw M13696: Johannes de Garlandia, Gw 8126: Augustinus Datus u. ö.

[96] Bis auf Virdung alle Mitglieder der *Sodalitas litteraria Rhenana*, ebenso wie Gallus' Lehrer Wimpfeling und auch Trithemius, Reuchlin, Peutinger u. a. m., vgl. auch oben zum Vergil-Druck.

[97] Und auch etwas später. ‚Produktivste‘ Zeit 1489/90, hinsichtlich der Zahl der Werke, nicht hinsichtlich der gesetzten Blätter, s. Abschnitt B: ‚Statistik‘.

[98] Vgl. Erich Kleinschmidt: *Gallus, Jodocus*, in: *VL Deutscher Humanismus 1480–1520*, Bd. 1 (2006), Sp. 862–870.

[99] „Bei […] zahlreichen […] Drucken bedarf die Frage nach der Verfasserschaft Köbels noch der Absicherung", so G. Keil im ²*VL*-Artikel, Band 4 (1983): *Köbel, Jakob*, Sp. 1276–1278, hier 1277.

[100] Hartfelder, Karl: *Werner von Themar, Adam*, in: *Allgemeine Deutsche Biographie (ADB)* 42 (1897), S. 39–41, Online-Version: [https://www.deutsche-biographie.de/pnd122162358.html#adbcontent]

Marienfrömmigkeit (s. u. Kap. 8), da auch Letzterer als Verfasser eines lateinischen Traktat-Dialogs zwischen Teufel und Maria in Erscheinung tritt.[101] So ist seine Vita (wie auch die des Rudolf Agricola, s. u.) ein Zeugnis für die Tatsache, dass sich humanistischer Impetus und tiefe Frömmigkeit innig miteinander verbinden konnten.[102] Ein Exemplar des Werkes findet sich in der UB (SCHLECHTER/RIES 1042).

[Gw M22814: *Mensa philosophica* (DdL)]: Eine weitere, hier unterdrückte Angabe des *Gw*: „Hrsg. Jakob Köbel und Johannes Wacker" gibt die Sachlage wohl nicht zutreffend wieder und wurde in den bibliographischen Angaben zum Münchner Exemplar schon korrigiert. An den ‚ihm engstens verbundenen Heidelberger Bruder und Freund' (*coniunctissimo sibi fratri et amico*, s. Abb. 69) Jakob Köbel ist vielmehr das vorangestellte Anschreiben des Jodocus Gallus in der Heidelberger, 50 Bll. umfassenden Ausgabe dieser „Stoff- und Exempla-Sammlung, die [...] über Inhalt und Art von Tischgesprächen belehren will", gerichtet.[103]

Abb. 68: BSB München, 4 Inc. c. a. 667 [Ink M-330]; [http://daten.digitale-sammlungen.de/ bsb00039888/image_5], 1ʳ (Ausschnitt, Hervorhebung durch Hinzufügen eines blauen Pfeils, C. R.).

---

[101] ERICH KLEINSCHMIDT: *Gallus, Jodocus*, in: *VL Deutscher Humanismus 1480–1520*, Bd. 1 (2006), Sp. 867.

[102] Ähnliches ist zu beobachten bei Sigsimund Gossembrot (1417–1493), der, Humanist und Bürgermeister in Augsburg, sich im Alter in ein wiederum von der ‚Devotio moderna' inspiriertes geistliches Stift nach Straßburg zurückzog.

[103] W. J. WORSTBROCK: *Mensa philosophica*, in: ²*VL* 6 (1987), Sp. 395–398; man beachte auch die interessante Wirkungsgeschichte u. a. auf den *Ulenspiegel* und auf Fischart (Sp. 397).

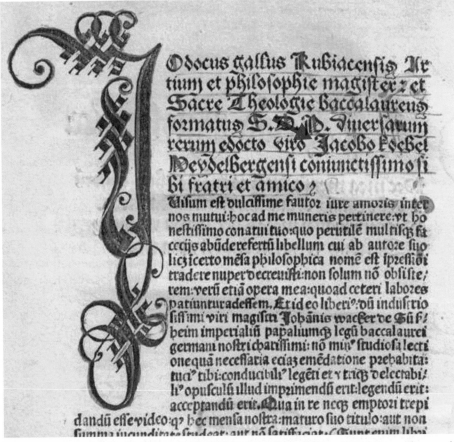

Abb. 69: BSB München, 4 Inc. c. a. 667 [Ink M-330]; [http://daten.digitale-sammlungen.de/
bsb00039888/image_6], 1ᵛ (Ausschnitt, Hervorhebung durch Hinzufügen eines blauen Pfeils,
C.R.).

Der Absender der ‚Grußadresse' ist derselbe Jodocus Gallus, der 1489 bei dem zuletzt genannten Titel, dem *Nosce te ipsum* [Gw M13471], mitgewirkt hatte und für
die *Mensa philosophica* bisweilen als Herausgeber genannt wird. Es dürfte sich also
wiederum nicht um ein ‚Gewächs' des Heidelberger Humanistenkreises handeln,
sondern dort nur auf sehr wohlwollenden Zuspruch gestoßen sein. *Gw* datiert das
Werk „1489" (vgl. auch Abb. 71 Kolophon), im Münchner Exemplar ist nach dem
Explicit des Werkes, das um Nachsicht mit evtl. gemachten Fehlern oder ungebühr-
lichen Scherzen bittet (*Parcite queso mihi ...*), handschriftlich vom Rubrikator das
Jahr *1491* (als Nachweis der Beendigung seiner Arbeit?) eingetragen:

fectus foret,lentus recessit ad ciuitatem in domum solitam,conti-
nuans suos labores letius q̄ꝫ consueuerat

Parcite queso mihi si non sint omnia vera
Vel non digna ioco: parcite queso mihi

Finit feliciter

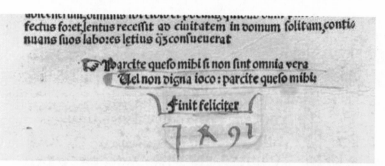

Abb. 70: BSB München, 4 Inc. c. a. 667 [Ink M-330]; [http://daten.digitale-sammlungen.de/bsb00039888/image_103], 50r (Ausschnitt).

Während sich das erste Buch mit den Speisen selbst, das zweite mit dem ‚Wesen und den Sitten derer, die sich mit uns am Tisch versammeln' (*de natura et moribus eorum cum quibus in mensa sumus*, 2v Register), das dritte mit den ‚Tischgesprächen' (*de quaestionibus mensalibus*, ebd.) beschäftigt, sammelt das umfangreichste vierte Buch ehrbare Scherzreden und tröstende Unterhaltungen (Schwänke und Faszetien), mit denen ‚wir uns das Mahl angenehm gestalten können' (*de honestis iocis et solacijs quibus in mensa iocundamur*, 4r Register und der Kolophon, 48v):

Presens liber quē mensam philosophicā vocant:
vnicuiqʒ perutilis: ꝯpendiose pertractā si primis
quid in ꝯuiuijs pro cibis et potibus sumendū est.
deinde qui sermões illis ſm exigentiaʒ personarū
habēdi sunt: et que questiones discutiēde que insu-
per facetie siue ioci interserēdi Feliciter explicit.
Impressum heidelberge Anno. M.cccc.lxxxix.

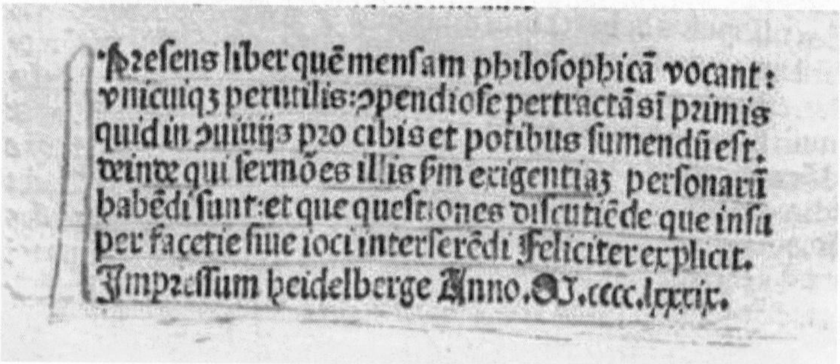

Abb. 71: BSB München, 4 Inc. c. a. 667 [Ink M-330]; [http://daten.digitale-sammlungen.de/bsb00039888/image_100], 48v (Ausschnitt).

Von den drei längeren Schwänken, die Gallus beigegeben habe,[104] und die oft Anstoß erregt haben und in einigen Exemplaren deshalb entfernt worden sind, wird der letzte wohl zur Steigerung der Komik (*apta ioco* „Scherzen zugetan", vgl. Titelblock, Abb. 68) dem deutsch benannten „langnasigen Pedell" zugeschrieben:[105]

[104] W. J. Worstbrock: *Mensa philosophica*, in: ²*VL* 6 (1987), Sp. 395–398, Sp. 397.

[105] Zur Rolle des Pedells bei Drucken, die in der Universität hergestellt werden, vgl. Konrad Haebler: *Schriftguss und Schrifthandel* 1924, zitiert bei Wolfgang Schmitz: *Grundriss der Inkunabelkunde. Das gedruckte Buch im Zeitalter des Medienwechsels*, Stuttgart 2018, S. 12 mit Anm. 47.

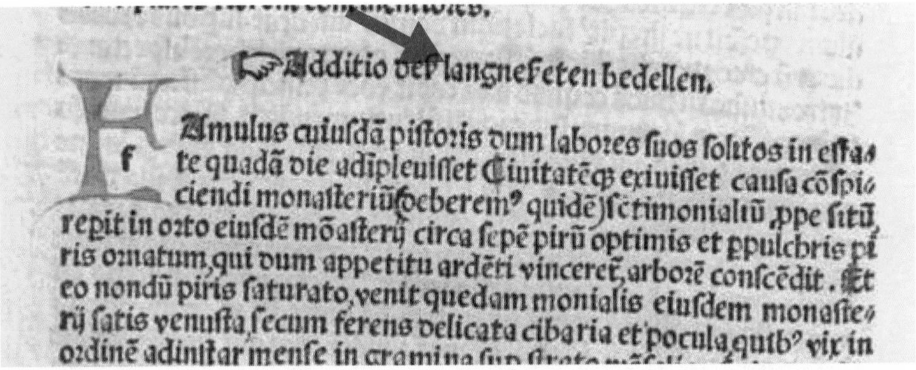

Abb. 72: BSB München, 4 Inc.c.a. 667 [Ink M-330]; [http://daten.digitale-sammlungen.de/bsb00039888/image_102], 49ᵛ (Ausschnitt, Hervorhebung durch Hinzufügen eines blauen Pfeils, C. R.).

Der drittletzte Schwank wird als Beigabe des Korrekturlesers (*Additio correctoris* 49ʳ), der vorletzte gar als Zutat des Druckers (*Additio impressoris*, 49ᵛ) deklariert. Der Text, von dem knapp zehn Inkunabelausgaben publiziert wurden (die meisten davon, so auch die Erstausgabe, in Köln, sonst auch Löwen und 1512 dann Paris), dürfte einen nicht unerheblichen Teil seiner Wirkung daraus beziehen, dass er in seiner Diktion nebenher sowohl die klösterliche Tischlesung als auch die gelehrte universitäre Quästion (*quaestiones* werden die Abschnitte häufig ausdrücklich genannt) parodiert. Zu einem Text im Spannungsfeld zwischen Universität, humanistisch ambitioniertem Kurfürsten und Kloster passt zuletzt auch der Umstand, dass für die Entstehungsgeschichte der Minorit Johannes von Düren ins Spiel gebracht wird (²VL 6, Sp. 395) und eine der Kölner Ausgaben *Apud praedicatores* erschien [vgl. *Gw* zu M22813]. Vom Heidelberger Druck sind 40 Exemplare an öffentlichen Einrichtungen erhalten, drei allein auch in Heidelberg selbst, zwei in der Uʙ, eines im Stadtarchiv (Sᴄʜʟᴇᴄʜᴛᴇʀ/Rɪᴇs 1266–1268).

[Gᴡ M16371 Köʙᴇʟ, Jᴀᴋᴏʙ: *Tischzucht*]: Während Jakob Köbel als *diversarum rerum edoctus vir* (‚in verschiedenen Künsten hochgelehrter Mann' vgl. den Widmungsbrief der *Mensa philosophica*) Adressat der in lateinischer Prosa abgefassten, von humanistischem Interesse an antiken Textsammlungen eingefärbten Tischlehre war, tritt er *XCij* (also [14]92) nun selbst als Autor und Herausgeber (er selbst nennt sich *diß buchs ein angeber*, s. u. Abb. 75) auf. Es handelt sich um eine volkssprachige *Tischzucht*, eine Art *Mensa philosophica* für Laien zur Unterrichtung ihrer Kinder. Das in Reimpaaren abgefasste Buch stellt sich dem Leser/Hörer selbst vor:

> TIschzucht/ also bin ich genant
> In allen landen wol erkant.
> Wer mich mit züchten üben thůt
> Der wirt vor schanden wol behůt.

Abb. 73: BSB München, 4 Inc. c. a. 914 m [Ink K-38]; [http://daten.digitale-sammlungen.de/bsb00029631/image_4], 1ʳ (Ausschnitt).

Ob wohl mit dem direkt angesprochenen Adressaten der Prosa-Vorrede (der Autor habe sich entschlossen, *zůsammen zereymen dir diß buchlein*, 1ᵛ) Pfalzgraf Philipp d. A. selbst gemeint ist, der in der Schlussrede indirekt angesprochen ist (s. u. Abb. 75)? Immerhin ist nach dieser Vorrede ein nicht weiter ausgestaltetes ritterliches Wappen eingedruckt[106]:

---

[106] SCHRAMM: *Bilderschmuck 19*, Tafel 80, Abb. 575.

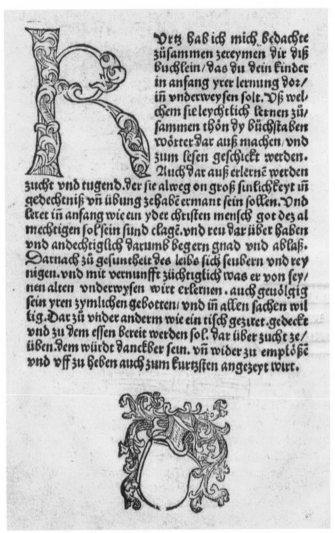

Abb. 74: BSB München, 4 Inc. c. a. 914 m [Ink K-38]; [http://daten.digitale-sammlungen.de/
bsb00029631/image_5], 1ᵛ (Ausschnitt).

Aus demselben, schon öfter angesprochenen Typenrepertoire wie hier das *K*, erscheinen auf Bl. 2ʳ und 2ᵛ noch die Initialen *G* und *I*.[107] Die Unterweisung in den
richtigen Tischmanieren sind eher nur Vorwand, *seine kinder mit grossem ernst vnd
fleyß zucht vnd tugend zu leren* (2ʳ). Nebenbei könnten die Zöglinge (*zucht/*,Erzie-
hung' gehört zu den häufigsten Lexemen des Textes) noch *leychtlich lernen zůsammen
thôn dy bůchstaben, wôrter dar auß machen vnd zum lesen geschickt werden.* Diese

---

[107] Das *K* passt vom Typus her zu dem Zainerschen Alphabet, ist aber in AMELUNG: *Fᴅsᴡ*, S. 67
nicht nachgewiesen.

Mischung von Erstlese-/Erstschreibunterricht mit ethischer Unterweisung erinnert auch wieder an den *Cato*-Werkkomplex (s. o. Kap. 3). Der Text ist von A. Schirokauer und Th. P. Thornton 1957 dankenswerterweise ediert worden,[108] die Einreihung unter „Grobianische Tischzuchten", die die Materie persiflieren oder zumindest ironisch brechen, dürfte allerdings, wie man schon gesehen hat, nicht zutreffen. Immer wieder wird innerhalb des Textes neben Benimmregeln, die an der Oberfläche wirken, auch eine tiefergehende Moral vermittelt (hier V. 163–166):

Fleuch böß geselschafft, ere die weisen,
Gib almusen, wiltu mit eren greisen (‚würdig alt werden').
Du solt alczeit früm leut eren,
Als dich die meister leren.

Der Heidelberger Jakob Köbel (1462–1533), der solange er noch in seiner Heimatstadt wirkte, wo sein Haus „Sammelpunkt der Heidelberger, Wormser und Speyrer Humanistenkreise" war,[109] nimmt intensiv die Dienste von Knoblochtzers Druckwerkstatt in Anspruch, bevor er später, ab 1499 in Oppenheim eine eigene Offizin betreibt. 1494 wird sogar in einem Knoblochtzer-Druck schon die Druckermarke verwendet, die Köbel später in Oppenheim gebrauchte (s. u. Kap. 8: *Fußpfad zur ewigen Seligkeit*). Bei seiner *Tischzucht* tut er alles dafür, dass das Büchlein nicht moralinsauer daherkommt. Diesen ‚augenzwinkernden' Vortrag der Belehrung unterstreicht der Kolophon durch das schon bekannte Versteckspiel mit dem Namen des Autors incl. Lösungsanweisung[110] wie auch das (wohl fingierte) Datum der Ausgabe zu diesem ‚närrischen' Termin (*Vff aller mann fastnacht volendet gering/ Morgens vor fantasei, ee man butzen ging*).[111]

Die mittels der Datierung *In zeiten, als Philps regirt, der tugenthaft*[112] hergestellte Nähe zum Fürstenhaus will wohl die Affinität des Autors zum Heidelberger Humanistenzirkel, zu dem sich auch Philipp der Aufrichtige zugehörig fühlte, unterstreichen.[113]

---

[108] A. Schirokauer/Th. P. Thornton: *Grobianische Tischzuchten (Texte des späten Mittelalters 5)*, Berlin 1957, Köbels *Tischzucht* darin S. 24–32. Manche der Texte seien „zumindest grobianisch angehaucht" relativiert Thornton in der Einleitung, S. 7. Überblick über die Gattung gibt Dieter Harmening: *Tischzuchten*, in: ²VL 9 (1995), Sp. 941–947, zu Köbels Bearbeitung Sp. 945.

[109] Grimm, Heinrich: *Köbel, Jakob*, in: *Neue Deutsche Biographie* 12 (1979), S. 289–290, Online-Version: [https://www.deutsche-biographie.de/pnd118724142.html#ndbcontent].

[110] Vgl. oben Kap. 3. [Gw 11219: *Grammatica. Regulae congruitatum*].

[111] Daraus hat man den 3. Februar 1492 errechnet.

[112] Vgl. den Kolophon zu Johannes de Lambsheim: *Speculum officii missae expositorium*, Kapitel 2.

[113] Vgl. dazu M. Folkerts/G. Keil: *Köbel, Jakob* in: ²VL 4 (1983), Sp. 1276–1278, hier v. a. 1276 und (auch zum Oppenheimer humanistischen Netzwerk um Köbel): Grimm, Hein-

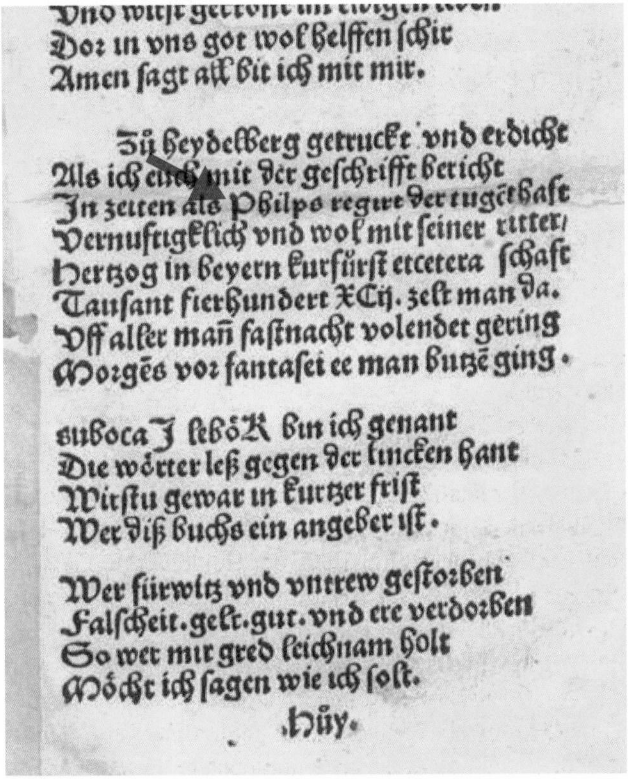

Vnd wirst gekront im ewigen leben
Dor in vns got wol helffen schir
Amen sagt all bit ich mit mir.

Zů Heydelberg getruckt vnd erdicht
Als ich eins mit der geschrifft bericht
In zeiten als Philps regirt der tugenthaft
Vernunftigklich vnd wol mit seiner ritter/
Hertzog in beyern kurfürst etcetera schaft
Tausent fierhundert XCij. zelt man da.
Vff alter man faßnacht volendet gering
Morgēs vor fantasei ee man butzē ging.

suboca J lebö K bin ich genant
Die wörter leß gegen der lincken hant
Wirstu gewar in kurtzer frist
Wer diß buchs ein angeber ist.

Wer fürwitz vnd vntrew gestorben
Falschheit.gelt.gut.vnd ere verdorben
So wer mir gred leichnam holt
Möcht ich sagen wie ich solt.

.Hüy.

Abb. 75: BSB München, 4 Inc. c. a. 914 m [Ink K-38]; [http://daten.digitale-sammlungen.de/bsb00029631/image_14], 6r (Ausschnitt, Hervorhebung durch Hinzufügen eines blauen Pfeils, C. R.).

Denkbar erscheint auch, dass diese Inkunabel mit der Rolle des (im Bezug auf Köbel) etwa gleichaltrigen Adam Wernher von Themar als Prinzenerzieher der Söhne Philipps des Aufrichtigen, vor allem des späteren Ludwig V. (geb. 1478), zu tun hat. Der Druck der *Tischzucht* und die damit anvisierte weitere Verbreitung mag genau den Punkt markieren, als Hofkunst in „bürgerlich-städtische Rezeption" gerät.[114] Nur drei Exemplare dieser schmalen Inkunabel von 6 Bll. sind in öffentlichen Bibliotheken erhalten.

Ganz anders verhält es sich beim folgenden Werk, [Gw M31621 Petrarca, Francesco: *De remediis utriusque fortunae*], von dem mindestens 71 Exemplare nachweisbar sind.

rich: *Köbel, Jakob*, in: *Neue Deutsche Biographie* 12 (1979), S. 289–290, Online-Version: [https://www.deutsche-biographie.de/pnd118724142.html#ndbcontent].

114 Peter Assion: *Siebentes Kapitel. Fachliteratur*, in: Ingeborg Glier: *Die deutsche Literatur im späten Mittelalter. 1250–1370, Zweiter Teil: Reimpaargedichte, Drama, Prosa* (*Gesch. d. dt. Lit. von den Anfängen bis zur Gegenwart III/2*), S. 371–395, hier S. 381.

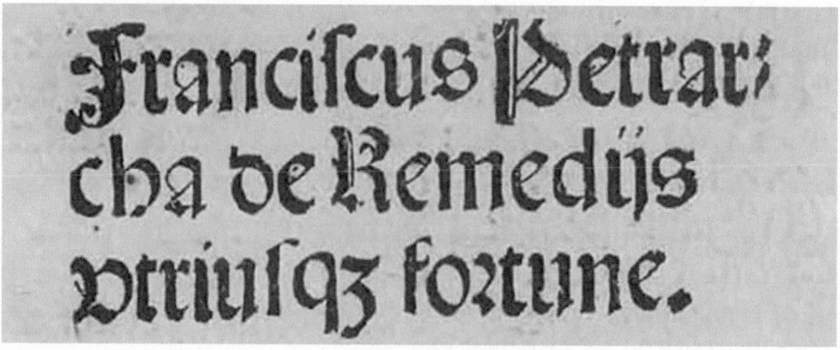

Franciscus Petrar/cha de Remedijs vtriusq3 fortune.

Abb. 76: HAB Wolfenbüttel, 82. 19. quodl. 1 [http://diglib.hab.de/inkunabeln/82-19-quod-1/start.htm?image=00001], 1ʳ (Aussschnitt).

Es kommt wiederum nicht ausschließlich humanistischem Interesse entgegen. Da schon eine klösterliche, explizit franziskanische Rezeption gerade dieses Werkes festzustellen ist,[115] ergibt sich auch hier eine Affinität zu den Texten des 1. Kapitels. Für die Platzierung im Humanismus-Abschnitt innerhalb der Heidelberger Geistesgeschichte spricht aber der Umstand, dass Petrarca „auf niemanden [...] eine ähnliche Anziehung ausgeübt haben [dürfte] wie auf Rudolf Agricola".[116] Eine weitere Heidelberger Tradition ergibt sich für dieses Werk aus dem Umstand, dass „Adam Werner (von Themar) [1462–1537], Erzieher der Söhne Pfalzgraf Philipps [...]", der „zum Übersetzerkreis des Heidelberger Humanismus" zu zählen ist, Teile daraus übersetzt hat.[117] Diese wurden aber nicht schon von Knoblochtzer in Heidelberg, sondern erst von Jakob Köbel in Oppenheim 1516 zum Druck gebracht. Knoblochtzers *Remedia*-Druck wird von *Gw* „nicht nach 1490" datiert und umfasst 130 Bll. Das Werk wurde vor 1500 nicht allzu oft gedruckt (lokalisierte Ausgaben nur aus Cremona und Straßburg), ist aber später durch die äußerst kunstvollen Illustrationen des ‚Petrarca-Meisters' zu einiger Berühmtheit gelangt.[118] In der Heidelberger Ausgabe erscheint es noch erstaunlich schmucklos:

---

[115] F. J. WORSTBROCK: *Petrarca, Francesco*, in: ²VL 7 (1989), Sp. 471–490, hier 480 f.

[116] Ebd. Sp. 482. Vgl. auch Agricolas Übersetzung von Ps.-Isocrates: *Praecepta ad Demonicum*, die auch bei Knoblochtzer herauskam, s. o. Kapitel 3.

[117] F. J. WORSTBROCK: *Petrarca, Francesco*, in: ²VL 7 (1989), Sp. 471–490, hier Sp. 484 f.

[118] Faksimiles der Holzschnitte bietet WALTHER SCHEIDIG: *Die Holzschnitte des Petrarca-Meisters. Zu Petrarcas Werk ‚Von der Artzney bayder Glück des guten und widerwärtigen'* (Augsburg 1532), Berlin 1955.

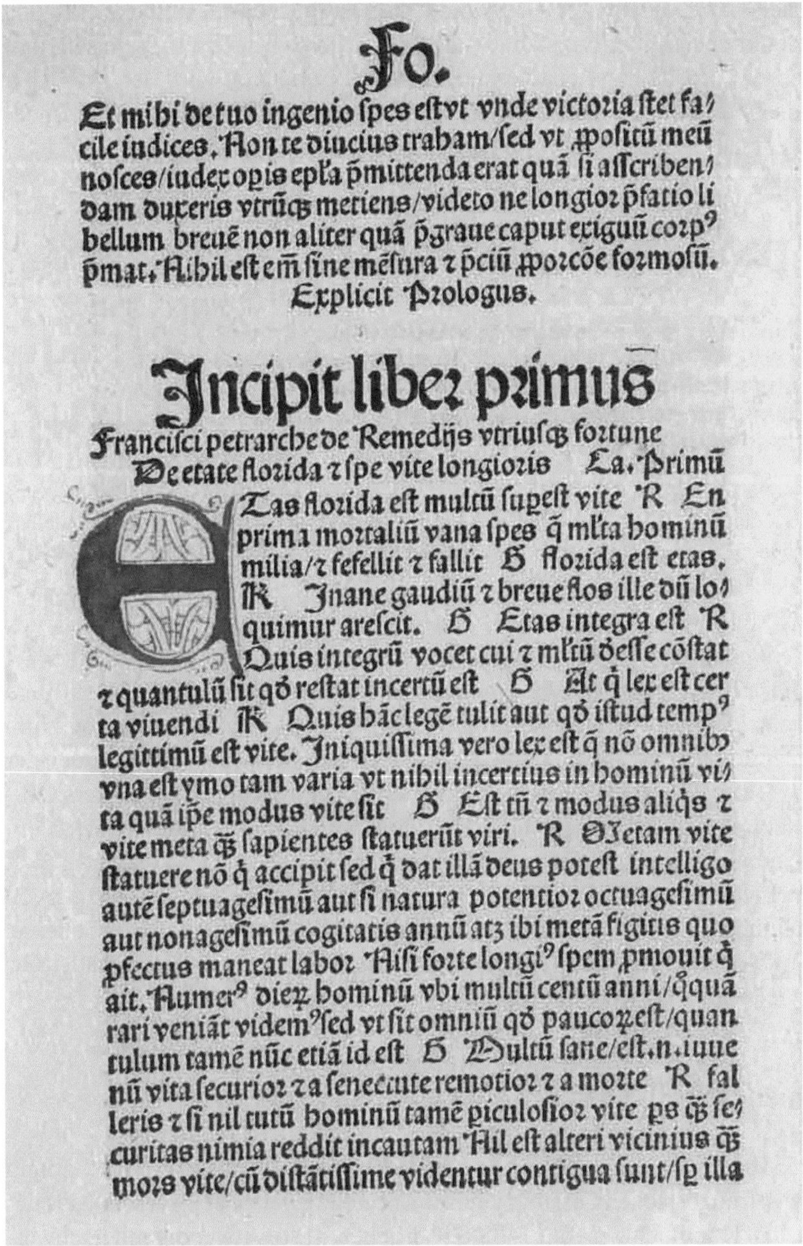
Fo.
Et mihi de tuo ingenio spes est vt vnde victoria stet facile iudices. Non te diucius trabam/sed vt ꝓpositū meū
nosces/iudex opis epl'a pmittenda erat quā si asscriben-
dam duxeris vtrūqꝫ metiens/video ne longior pfatio li
bellum breuē non aliter quā pgraue caput exiguū corp⁹
pmat. Nihil est em̄ sine mēsura z pciū ꝓporcōe formosū.
Explicit Prologus.
Incipit liber primus
Francisci petrarche de Remediis vtriusqꝫ fortune
De etate florida z spe vite longioris Ca. Primū
Etas florida est multū supest vite R En
prima mortaliū vana spes q̄ ml'ta hominū
milia/z fefellit z fallit G florida est etas.
R Jnane gaudiū z breue flos ille dū lo-
quimur arescit. G Etas integra est R
Quis integrū vocet cui z ml'tū deesse cōstat
z quantulū sit qđ restat incertū est G At q̄ lex est cer
ta viuendi R Quis hāc legē tulit aut qđ istud temp⁹
legittimū est vite. Jniquissima vero lex est q̄ nō omnib⁹
vna est ymo tam varia vt nihil incertius in hominū vita quā ipe modus vite sit G Est tn̄ z modus aliqs z
vite meta q̄s sapientes statuerūt viri. R Metam vite
statuere nō q̄ accipit sed q̄ dat illā deus potest intelligo
autē septuagesimū aut si natura potentior octuagesimū
aut nonagesimū cogitatis annū atꝫ ibi metā figitis quo
pfectus maneat labor Nisi forte longi⁹ spem ꝓmouit q̄
ait. Numer⁹ dierꝫ hominū vbi multū centū anni/q̄quā
rari veniāt videm⁹ sed vt sit omniū qđ paucorꝫ est/quan
tulum tamē nūc etiā id est G Multū sane/est. n. iuue
nū vita securior z a senectute remotior z a morte R fal
leris z si nil tutū hominū tamē piculosior vite ps q̄s se-
curitas nimia reddit incautam Nil est alteri vicinius q̄s
mors vite/cū distātissime videntur contigua sunt/sz illa

Abb. 77: HAB Wolfenbüttel, 82. 19. quodl. 1 [http://diglib.hab.de/inkunabeln/82-19-quod-1/start.htm?image=00018], 8v (4v der nummerierten Blätter, Ausschnitt).

Und auf Bl. 130r endet es in einem schlichten *Laus deo* (‚Gott sei Dank'), ein Kolophon fehlt. Eines der zahlreich in öffentlichen Bibliotheken erhaltenen Textzeugen besitzt die UB in Heidelberg (SCHLECHTER/RIES 1439).

Die Frage nach dem Umgang mit Glück und Unglück, die hier mit Berücksichtigung aller nur erdenklichen Lebensumstände (körperlich, geistig, seelisch, materiell, moralisch) nach Art einer Enzyklopädie philosophisch betrachtet wird, ist unter eher lebenspraktischen Aspekten auch Thema der Prognostiken, wie der des Johannes Lichtenberger (s. u. Kapitel 9.A; Gw M18242):

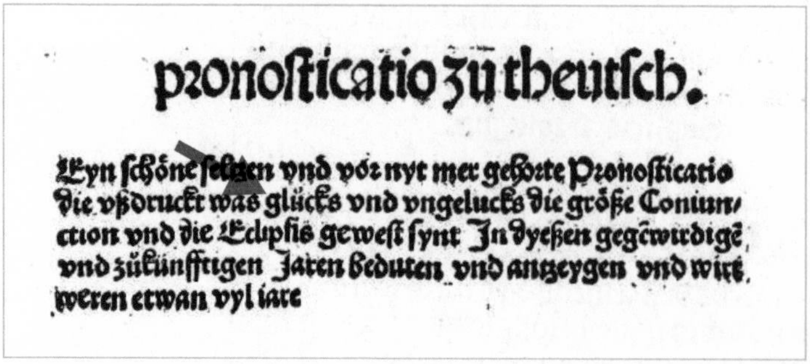
pronosticatio zů theutsch.

Eyn schöne seltzen vnd vor nyt mer gehörte Pronosticatio die vßdruckt was glücks vnd vngelucks die größe Coniunction vnd die Eclipsis gewest synt In dyeßen gegēwirdigē vnd zůkünfftigen Jaren beduten vnd anzeygen vnd wirt weren etwan vyl iare

Abb. 78: BSB, München, 2 Inc. s. a. 790 [Ink L-168]; [http://daten.digitale-sammlungen.de/bsb00008265/image_5], 1r (Ausschnitt, Hervorhebung durch Hinzufügen eines blauen Pfeils, C. R.).

[Gw M31605: Petrarca, Francesco: *Psalmi poenitentiales*] wird im *Gw* als Druck Knoblochtzers noch evtl. in Betracht gezogen (mit Fragezeichen versehen), der *Incunabula Short Title Catalogue* (*ISTC*) ordnet den Wiegendruck aber „Paris: Pierre Poulhac, about 1500" zu. Thematisch würde das Werk in Knoblochtzers Programm nicht nur unter dem Aspekt der humanistisch inspirierten Schriften, sondern auch der Beichtlehren (Kap. 7) passen, aber das Erscheinungsjahr macht Knoblochtzers Offizin als Entstehungsort unwahrscheinlich, bestenfalls wurde um diese Zeit noch mit seinem Typenmaterial in Heidelberg gedruckt.

Den Druck von Petrarcas *Epistola de Historia Griseldis* in der Übersetzung von Heinrich Steinhöwel, ansonsten eines der am häufigsten gedruckten Inkunabeltexte, den auch Knoblochtzer reich illustriert in Straßburg 1478 herausgebracht hatte (Gw M31581), wiederholt er in Heidelberg nicht.

6 Memento-mori-Thematik

[Gw M4725510 und M47257 *Totentanz*]: Ein *Totentanz*, (wir kennen die Gattung bereits in einer französischen Fassung von der Abbildung der Druckwerkstatt aus der Einleitung), den Knoblochtzer „um 1488/89" druckte, ist so aufwendig mit hochwertigen Illustrationen, dazu noch mit aus Ulm stammenden Zierinitialen geschmückt,[119] dass er zu den berühmtesten Inkunabeln des Druckers gezählt wird und als eine Fassung des *Mittelrheinischen Totentanzes* Eingang in die Literaturgeschichte fand.[120]

[119] Geldner: *Inkunabeldrucker* (1968), S. 266 f.

[120] Hellmut Rosenfeld: *Mittelrheinischer Totentanz*, in: ^{2}*Vl* 6 (1987), Sp. 625–628.

Um die ‚Tanzsituation' erkennbar zu halten, seien hier mehrere kleine Abbildungen zusammengestellt:

Abb. 79a–f: BSB München, Im. mort. 1 [Ink T-398]; [http://daten.digitale-sammlungen.de/bsb 00001856/image_9, …/image_13, …/image_32, …/image_34, …/image_43 und …/image_44], Eröffnung: Totentanz mit Flöten und Posaunen (79a); Der Bischof (79b); Das junge Kind (79c); Der Spieler (79d); Der Schreiber (79e); Die Nonne (79f).

Den Genuss der artifiziellen Holzschnitte in voller Größe ermöglicht der Blick auf die leicht erreichbaren Heidelberger und Münchener Digitalisate dieses außerordentlich berühmten Artefakts, von dem MANFRED LEMMER 1991 im Inselverlag (*Insel-Bücherei 1092*) unter dem Titel *Der Heidelberger Totentanz von 1485*, in sehr kleinem Format auch schon eine wohlfeile moderne Druckausgabe besorgt hat. Zu sehen ist, dass keine Berufsgruppe ausgespart bleibt, kein Geschlecht, keine Altersgruppe, dass sich der Tod nicht um Moral oder Unmoral kümmert, und – dass dieser Totentanz vor dem Druckzeitalter entstanden sein muss, da ein Schreiber, nicht wie in der

Danse macabre aus Lyon ein Drucker, vom Tod geholt wird (Abb. 79e). Die Holzschnitte übernahm später offensichtlich Jacob Meydenbach in Mainz, denn dort
wurde das Werk um 1492 mit identischem Bildmaterial, allerdings in neuem Satz
und ohne die entsprechenden Initialen nochmals aufgelegt [Gw M47259].[121] Seltsam
ist, dass gerade diese überaus aufwendigen, ästhetisch anspruchsvollen Ausgaben in
Heidelberg und auch in Mainz ohne Kolophon geblieben sind. Wenn man „die Holzschnitte des *Totentanzes* [...] dem gleichen Holzschneider zuschreiben [kann] wie
die des von Peter Drach gedruckten *Spiegels menschlicher Behaltnis*",[122] dann er-
gäbe sich (nach der Vergil-Ausgabe oben) ein weiterer Beleg für die Zusammenarbeit der Heidelberger und der Speyrer Offizinen.

[Gw 202: *Ackermann von Böhmen*]: Ebenfalls der Memento-mori-Thematik ist
der ursprünglich schon um 1400 entstandene *Ackermann von Böhmen* des Saazer
Juristen Johannes von Tepl zuzuordnen. Dieses Streitgespräch zwischen einem ver-
witweten Amtsschreiber und dem Tod, der vom Kläger wegen des Verlustes seiner
geliebten Ehefrau Margarete angeklagt wird, hatte Knoblochtzer schon 1477 in
Straßburg einmal auf 32 Bll. gedruckt (Gw 198, Abb. 80b). Dabei stand er, das zeigt
ein Vergleich der Titelholzschnitte, eindeutig unter dem Einfluss des Basler Drucks
von Flach 1474 (Gw 196, Abb. 80a).

Abb. 80a (links) und 80b (rechts): ThULB Jena, Bibliotheca Electoralis [Konvolut: Sign. 4
Jur. XXV,1] [https://collections.thulb.uni-jena.de/rsc/viewer/HisBest_derivate_00004671/BE_
1414_0159.tif], 1ʳ (80a) und GNM Nürnberg, Inc. 8° 90508 a [http://dlib.gnm.de/item/
4Inc90508a/9], 1ʳ (80b) (jeweils Ausschnitt).[123]

---

[121] So auch Lichtenbergers *Prognosticatio* (s. u. Kap. 9.A); GELDNER: *Inkunabeldrucker*
       (1968), S. 42.

[122] So W. L. SCHREIBER 1910, zit. bei GELDNER: *Inkunabeldrucker* (1968), S. 267.

[123] Bei diesen und allen im Folgenden aus dem Bestand der ThULB Jena und des GNM Nürn-
       berg verwendeten Abbildungen findet die CC-Lizenz CC BY-NC-SA 4.0 (https://creative

Während die Straßburger Ausgabe nur mit dem Druckjahr versehen worden war, weist eine weitere Ausgabe dieses Titels aus Heidelberg (Gw 202) dann auch einen Kolophon mit Knoblochtzers Namen auf: *Gedrůckt vnd volendet durch Heinrich knobloczer zů Heydelberg am dunerstag vor sant Margarethen tag in dem Lxxxx iar.* (das wäre, wenn man die Angabe für bare Münze nehmen darf, der 8. VII. 1490). Zur Verzierung des Textanfangs greift er nun aber nicht auf seine eigene Straßburger Ausgabe zurück, sondern lässt diesmal den Titelholzschnitt einer Ulmer Ausgabe von Lienhart Holl um 1483/84 (Gw 199, vgl. Abb. 214, in: AMELUNG: *FDSW*, S. 290) sehr detailgetreu, und nicht einmal seitenverkehrt, nachschneiden. Außerdem gelingt es ihm, den Papieraufwand (und damit die Investitionskosten) auf 20 Bll. zu reduzieren.

Abb. 81a (oben) und 81b (unten): BSB München, 4 Inc. c. a. 714 [Ink I-600]; [http://daten. digitale-sammlungen.de/bsb00045025/image_4], 1ᵛ (81a) und [http://daten.digitale-sammlungen. de/bsb00045025/image_41] 20ʳ (81b) (jeweils Ausschnitt).

Die Ausgabe dieses Textes trifft sich aber auch mit dem Interesse der pfalzgräflichen Familie: Philipp der Aufrichtige (1448–1508) hatte eine handschriftliche Fassung des *Ackermann* nämlich als Erbschaft von seiner 1479 verstorbenen Mutter Margaretha (von Savoyen), bekommen, die zuletzt selbst in dritter Ehe mit Ulrich V. von Württemberg verheiratet gewesen war und in Stuttgart die Schreibstube von Ludwig Henfflin mit der Herstellung mehrerer meist überaus reich illustrierter Handschriften, u. a. dem ‚Ackermann' (im Schnitt mehr als eine Miniatur pro Blatt), beauftragt hatte:[124]

Abb. 82: UB Heidelberg, Cpg 76 [https://digi.ub.uni-heidelberg.de/diglit/cpg76/0011], 2^r (Ausschnitt)

Das Druckdatum der Inkunabel *vor sant Margarethen tag* (s. o. Kolophon) ist sicher nicht zufällig gewählt, wenn nicht überhaupt fingiert.[125] Dadurch wird nämlich ein vielfaches Anspielungsgeflecht hergestellt: ‚Margarethe' ist sowohl der Name der Protagonistin des Textes (also der verstorbenen Frau des ‚Ackermanns'), als auch der Auftraggeberin der Handschrift, Philipps des Aufrichtigen Mutter Margarethe von Savoyen (s. o.), wie auch dessen Frau: Margaretha von Bayern-Landshut (1456–1501).

---

[124] Zu dieser Werkstatt und ihrer Beziehung zu Margarete von Savoyen vgl. die Internet-Seite der UB Heidelberg: https://digi.ub.uni-heidelberg.de/de/bpd/glanzlichter/oberdeutsche/henfflin. html (23.9.2020)

[125] Eine genaue Datierung kennen wir sonst aus Knoblochtzers Drucken nur vom Guarinus: *De ordine docendi* […], s. o. Kap. 3.

7   Beichtlehren

Das Thema Beichte ergibt sich aus dem ‚Memento mori' wie von selbst. Es hat (natürlich nicht nur) im Heidelberg der 1480er Jahre eine enorme Rolle gespielt: Von Johann
von Soest (1448–1506, Sängermeister unter Kurfürst Friedrich I. [1449–76] und
Philipp dem Aufrichtigen [1476–1508]) nimmt man an, dass er 1483 eine Beichtlehre
in Reimen dem Kurfürsten Philipp gewidmet hat (Cpg 730, 51r–74v),[126] und auch das
Opus tripartitum des Johannes Gerson, das Knoblochtzer in der deutschen Übersetzung von Gabriel Biel „nicht nach 1488" im Druck herausgebracht hatte, bestand zu
einem wesentlichen Teil aus einer Beichtlehre (vgl. Kap. 1: […] *diß drigedeilt werck.*
Von den tzehen geboden. Von der bijcht. Vnd von der künst zů sterben. […]).

[Gw 3780: *Beichtbüchlein*]: Von den 16 Ausgaben im *Gw* unter diesem Titel sind
acht durch das gemeinsame Initium ‚Es sind viel Menschen' miteinander verbunden,
die anderen sind voneinander unabhängig, so auch die Heidelberger Edition von
„1494", die mit ihren 64 Bll. das umfangreichste unter den verzeichneten gedruckten
Büchlein (!) darstellt. Es ist wieder eines der wenigen Heidelberger Inkunabeln mit
ausführlichem Kolophon:

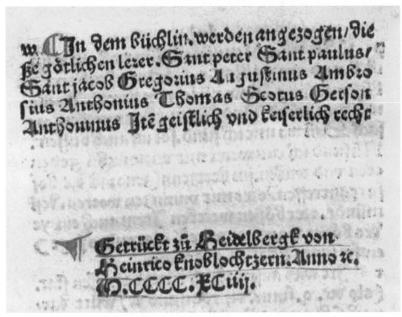

Abb. 83: BSB München, 4 Inc. c. a. 1123 [Ink B-262]; [http://daten.digitale-sammlungen.de/
bsb00034113/image_132], 64ᵛ (Ausschnitt).

---

[126] Gesa Bonath: *Johann von Soest*, in: ²VL 4 (1983), Sp. 744–755, Zu *Dy gemeyn bicht* v. a.
Sp. 748 f.; dazu auch Backes (1992), S. 163.

Das erste Blatt des schlichten Druckes, der bis auf Auszeichnungstypen in den Überschriften ohne Verzierung auskommt, aber im Münchner Exemplar immerhin sorgfältig rubriziert wurde, weist als Causa scribendi des Textes aus, dass er ‚einfachen,
wenig gebildeten‘ Pfarrern als Hilfsmittel in der Seelsorge dienen sollte (*den
schlechten pfarrern nit gar on not, die es auch alle jare jren vnderthonen verkünden
solten*), und es zeigt durch die Beigabe eines Registers den Charakter als Findbuch:

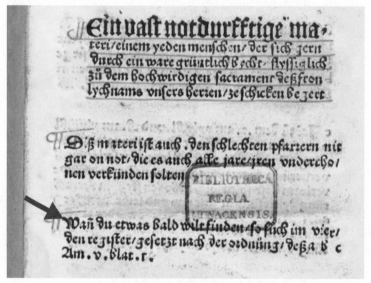

Abb. 84: BSB München, 4 Inc. c. a. 1123 [Ink B-262]; [http://daten.digitale-sammlungen.de/
bsb00034113/image_5], 1ʳ (Ausschnitt, Hervorhebung durch Hinzufügen eines blauen Pfeils,
C. R.).

Der als sehr unbedarft dargestellte Laienrezipient wird über die katechetischen
Grundgebete an die Materie herangeführt (2ʳ): <u>*Die wyl*</u>[127] *der gemein ley in/ weltlichen
sachen spitz-/ fündig*[128] *(luce xvj.) Aber in dingen die seel antref-/ fend*[129], *leider
vast grob*[130] *dann gar lützel, recht verstan/ den das pater noster, Aue maria, den
gloûbenn*[131] [und andere Texte, welche die Vorbereitung auf die Beichte erleichtern]
darumb volget hie nach Item züerst das pater noster [...]. Neben der Erklärung
der katechetischen Grundgebete, der Erztugenden und Sünden (incl. der üblichen,
ausführlichen Aufzählung derselben) wird auch auf ein vertieftes Verständnis der
Liturgie hingewirkt (4ᵛ): *Die wyl man ettliche ding teglichen thůt in messz vnd vesper*

---

[127] ‚Weil‘.

[128] ‚schlau‘.

[129] ‚betreffend‘.

[130] ‚sehr unwissend‘.

[131] ‚so dass sie (selbst) das *Vater unser*, das *Gegrüßest seist du Maria* und das *Glaubens-
bekenntnis* kaum richtig verstehen‘.

etc. brŭchen, ist billich (vmb grŏsser andacht willen) das der ley auch verstande die meynŭng der selben dinge. Immerhin zwei der erhaltenen 15 Exemplare, die in *Gw* verzeichnet sind, befinden sich in Heidelberg, eines in der UB und eines im Stadt-archiv (SCHLECHTER/RIES 234, 235).

[Gw 13746 (vormals Gw n0448) *Hymni. Hymnarium*, deutsch u. lat.] „1494" 22 Bll.: Eines der merkwürdigsten Werke aus Knoblochtzers Presse segelt unter falscher Flagge, hat mit den üblichen Hymnaren (die neun lateinischen Inkunabelausgaben unter diesem Titel *Hymni. Hymnarium* in *Gw* weisen meist Notenmaterial auf) nichts gemein, ist auch die einzige deutsche Variante des Titels und beinhaltet eigentlich eine Beichtlehre, wie schon der Titel verrät:

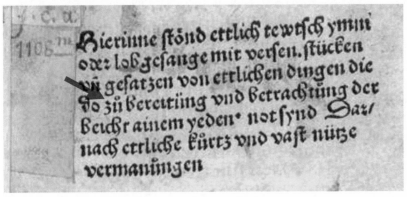

Abb. 85: BSB München, 4 Inc. c. a. 1108 m [Ink D-101] [http://daten.digitale-sammlungen. de/bsb00034235/image_5], Erstes Blatt recto vor den nummerierten Bll. (Ausschnitt, Hervor-hebung durch Hinzufügen eines blauen Pfeils, C. R.).

Eine genaue Analyse des Inkunabeltextes, vor allem der enthaltenen *Ave-praeclara*-Kompilation aus der Fassung des Mönchs von Salzburg und einer anderen verbreite-ten Übersetzung der alten Sequenz (ursprünglich Hermann von Reichenau 1013–1054), zuzüglich eigenen Zusätzen von einem Anonymus legte BURGHART WACHINGER vor.[132] Die drei von ihm gesichteten Exemplare weisen eine je verschiedene Anord-nung der teils nicht bezeichneten Blätter auf. Die Beichtlehre wird durch poetische Texte untermauert, die allerdings teils in Prosa aufgelöst wurden, da nach altem Topos gereimte Texte schon lange unter dem Verdacht standen, Zugeständnisse an den Wahrheitsgehalt machen zu müssen (*oft würt der recht sine der wort zerstŏrt, wann man es allenthalb vnderstet ze rewmen*):

---

[132] BURGHART WACHINGER: *Der Mönch von Salzburg. Zur Überlieferung geistlicher Lieder im späten Mittelalter*, Tübingen 1989, S. 145–158: *Anhang II: ‚Ave praeclara' in zwei Über-tragungen.* Kurz dazu auch WALTHER LIPPHARDT: *Ave praeclara maris stella (deutsch),* in: ²*VL* 1 (1978), Sp. 568–570.

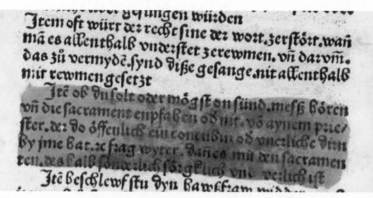

Abb. 86: Verso-Seite der vorherigen Abb.: [http://daten.digitale-sammlungen.de/bsb00034235/
image_6] (Ausschnitt).

Es handelt sich also gleichsam um eine Mischung von Johanns von Soest gereimter
Beichtlehre (Cpg 730) und dem allzu prosaischen Beichtbüchlein von 1494 (Gw
3780). Gemeinsam ist ihnen eine „Neigung zu Zahlensystematiken",[133] welche für
die zu Quantifizierung tendierende Frömmigkeit des ausgehenden Mittelalters typisch
ist,[134] die Texte aber nicht eben ‚schmackhaft‘ macht und das Protestpotential, das
zur Reformation führte, ebenso stark gesteigert haben dürfte wie der unsittliche
Lebenswandel der Priesterschaft. Diesen verschweigt auch die Textausgabe nicht,
ein kritischer Leser aber hätte ihn wohl gerne verschwiegen gesehen (s. Abb. 86).
Das Werk ist insgesamt (teils fragmentarisch) in 7 Exemplaren an öffentlichen Einrichtungen erhalten, eines davon befindet sich in der UB Heidelberg (SCHLECHTER/
RIES 964).

8   Sonstige Volksfrömmigkeit und Marienverehrung

[Gw: M38921: *Rosarium deutsch. Rosenkranz unserer lieben Frau*]: Unter diesem
Titel kamen Inkunabeln im gesamten deutschen Sprachgebiet heraus: Zwei in Augsburg, eine in Basel, eine in Köln, eine (niederdeutsche) in Magdeburg, eine in Würz-
burg. Und Knoblochtzer selbst hatte den Text schon in zwei Auflagen in Straßburg
gedruckt (Gw M38915 und M38918). Dort hatte er allerdings andere Holzschnitte
verwendet als in der Heidelberger Ausgabe „1495" (18 Bll.):[135]

---

[133] BURGHART WACHINGER: *Der Mönch von Salzburg*, wie vorherige Fußnote, S. 156.
[134] Zum ganzen Komplex „Gezählte[r] Frömmigkeit" s. den gleichnamigen Abschnitt in
ARNOLD ANGENENDT: *Geschichte der Religiosität im Mittelalter*, Darmstadt 1997, S. 581–
584.
[135] Die Straßburger Ausgaben hatten mehr Holzschnitte aufzuweisen als der Heidelberger
Druck: vgl. SCHRAMM: *Bilderschmuck 19*, Tafel 44, Nrr. 251 und 252, sowie Tafel 85,
Nr. 616.

Abb. 87: ForschB Gotha, Mon.typ 1495 4° 00005 [https://dhb.thulb.uni-jena.de/rsc/viewer/ufb_derivate_00011756/Mon-typ-1495-4-00005_000005.tif], 1ʳ (Ausschnitt).

Das Blatt 1ᵛ bietet eine Inhaltsangabe, *die tafel der Capittel disz büchlins* [...]: [1.] *Wer marie brůderschaft gestift und gelert hat*: [1475 in Köln *durch vil doctores der heiligen geschrift prediger ordens*, 2ʳ],[136] [2.] *Wie du den Rosenkrantz betten vnd opffern solt*, [3.] *Was die pater noster vnd ave maria betütten.* Hier trifft sich die Intention dieses Werkes mit dem katechetischen Grundprogramm des *Beichtbüchleins* (vgl. Kap. 7). Das siebte Kapitel beinhaltet dann u. a. *Vil schóner exempel von dem Rosenkrantz vnd psalter marie.* Ein Exempel, das sich auf Bl. 14ʳ findet, ist eben das, welches Knoblochtzer als Dreingabe auf dem letzten Blatt seiner Heidelberger *Sigenot-*

---

[136] Das trifft sich mit dem heutigen Kenntnisstand, vgl. K. KÜPPERS: *Rosenkranz*, in: *Lexikon des Mittelalters* 7, Lachen 1999, Sp. 1035.

Ausgabe (ein Heldenepos!) von 1490 schon angefügt hatte (vgl. unten Kap. 10): *EYn man het die gewonheit das er allen tag vnser liebenn frawenn macht eynen rosenkrantz [...]*. Dieser Zusatz mag auch durch die enge Verbindung des Fürstenhofes und der Heidelberger Humanisten zum Franziskanerkloster mit seinem marianischen Patrozinium motiviert gewesen sein. Vom Heidelberger Druck des deutschen *Rosariums* sind in *Gw* drei erhaltene Exemplare nachgewiesen.

Beim folgenden Titel, [Gw M14221: JOHANNES DE LAMBSHEIM: *Libri tres perutiles de confraternitatibus rosarii et psalterii Beatae Mariae virginis*], handelt es sich gewissermaßen um das lateinische Pendant zum deutschen *Rosarium*. Das Datum der Ausgabe ist mit „1485–94" nur sehr vage anzugeben,[137] der Umfang beträgt wiederum 18 Bll. Dass auch studierte Theologen sich um die Beförderung der Marienverehrung bemüht hatten, war schon bei Jodocus Gallus (s. o. Kap. 5 zum *Nosce te ipsum*) zu beobachten. Das hier zu betrachtende lateinische Textkonglomerat von Predigten (*Sermones*), Gebeten (*Orationes*) und Liedern (*Carmina*) zur Verehrung der Gottesmutter ist nun bezeichnenderweise, abgesehen von der gotischen Auszeichnungstype der Überschriften, in der italienischen Antiqua gedruckt, und weist (wiederum in Übereinstimmung mit dem *Nosce te ipsum*) auch wieder lateinische Metren auf:

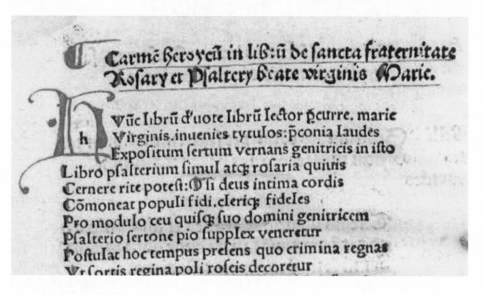

Abb. 88: BSB München, 4 Inc. s. a. 559 [Ink I-464]; [http://daten.digitale-sammlungen.de/bsb00029412/image_6], 1ᵛ (Ausschnitt).

---

[137] So der Eintrag im Nachweis der BSB München und in *Incunabula Short Titel Catalogue* [ISTC], *Gw* gibt (wohl fälschlich) 1500 an.

Auch für dieses lateinische Werk hatte Knoblochtzer den dann im *Rosarium* wieder eingesetzten Titelholzschnitt verwendet:

Abb. 89: BSB München, 4 Inc. s. a. 559 [Ink I-464]; [http://daten.digitale-sammlungen. de/bsb00029412/image_5], 1ʳ (Ausschnitt).

Diese Darstellung war im Spätmittelalter weit verbreitet, man vergleiche nur das berühmte Volkacher Rosenkranz-Schnitzwerk von Riemenschneider in *Maria im Weingarten* bei Volkach (1521–1524). Auf den Blättern 7ʳ und 13ʳ (Abb. 90) findet sich dann zudem ein Holzschnitt mit der ebenfalls im Spätmittelalter überaus weit verbreiteten Anna-Selbdritt-Darstellung:

Abb. 90: BSB München, 4 Inc. s. a. 559 [Ink I-464]; [http://daten.digitale-sammlungen.de/
bsb00029412/image_29], 13ʳ (Ausschnitt).

Der auf dem Titelbild handschriftlich annotierte Verfasser, Johannes de Lambsheim,
Augustiner-Chorherr in Christgarten bei Worms, ist auch Autor einer Messlehre,
die mindestens ein Jahr später (1495) ebenfalls bei Knoblochtzer zum Druck kam
(s. Kap. 2).[138] Seine Verbindung mit Johannes Trithemius zeigt wiederum Affinität zu
Humanistischen Kreisen (wie bei Jodocus Gallus, s. o.).

[Gw 10429: *Fußpfad zur ewigen Seligkeit*; Knoblochtzer für Jakob Köbel]: Im
Jahr „1494" druckte Knoblochtzer ein Werk von 29 Bll., das im Gegensatz zu vielen
seiner Editionen eine Rarität in der Inkunabellandschaft darstellt. Nur der Heidelberger Drucker hat den in zwei Handschriften unter dem Titel *Die Ritterschaft* über-

---

[138] Zum Autor F. J. WORSTBROCK: *Johannes von Lambsheim*, in: ²VL 4 (1983), Sp. 663–668,
zum hier genannten Werk v. a. Sp. 666 f.

lieferten Text vor 1500, wohl in Jakob Köbels Auftrag, als Wiegendruck herausgebracht.[139] Über die Manuskriptfassungen hinaus wurde die Druckausgabe mit Abbildungen versehen, welche die ritterlichen Ausrüstungsgegenstände zeigen, die allegorisch im Sinne geistlichen Rüstzeugs ausgelegt werden, so *Dye vorrede disz büchleins, in welcher die geystlich ritterschafft/ der werltlichen verglichen wirt/* [...]):

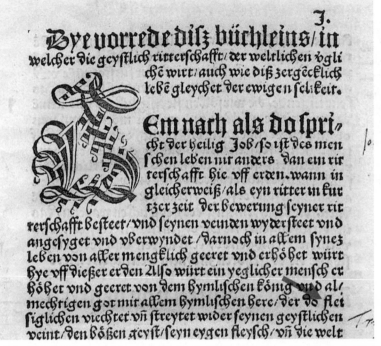

Abb. 91: UB Freiburg i. Br., Ink. K 3361, f [http://dl.ub.uni-freiburg.de/diglit/fusspfad1494/0009], 5ʳ (Ausschnitt, Hervorhebung durch Hinzufügen eines blauen Pfeils, C. R.).

Nach einem kurzen Leben werde mit der ewigen Seligkeit belohnt, wer auf Erden *fleisiglichen viechtet und streytet wider seynen geystlichen veint/ den bôsen geyst/ seyn eygen fleysch/ vnd die welt* [...]. Die herangezogenen Gegenstände sind u. a. das Pferd, der Sattel, der Stegreif, der Gurt, der Panzer, das Schwert:[140]

---

[139] Vgl. FRANZJOSEF PENSEL: *Die Ritterschaft,* in: ²VL 8 (1992), Sp. 104–106. PENSEL war 1992 nur eine handschriftliche Überlieferung bekannt (LB Dresden), seither wurde ein weiterer Textzeuge (UB Gießen) aufgefunden, vgl. Handschriftencensus: http://www.handschriften census.de/werke/1638 (29.9.2020).

[140] Abbildungen aller Holzschnitte bei SCHRAMM: *Bilderschmuck 19,* Tafeln 83 und 84. Die ganze Inkunabel ist auch digital ediert in *DTA* (*Deutsches Textarchiv*), allerdings mit falscher Lokalisierung nach Nürnberg: http://www.deutschestextarchiv.de/book/view/nn_fusspfad_ 1492?p (28.3.2021).

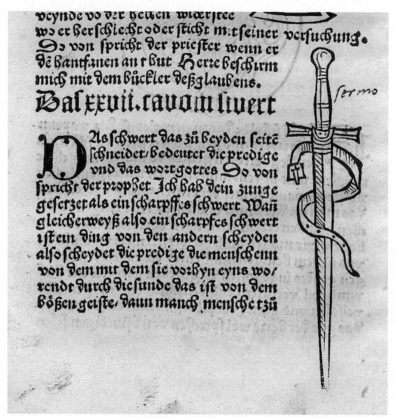

Abb. 92: UB Freiburg i. Br., Ink. K 3361, f [http://dl.ub.uni-freiburg.de/diglit/fusspfad1494/0052], 26ᵛ (Ausschnitt).

Die Idee ist freilich nicht neu, ganz ähnlich hatte schon in Rudolfs von Ems *Barlaam und Josaphat* (ca. 1225) der Asket gegenüber seinem Schützling, dem Königsohn, das geistliche Rüstzeug mit dem weltlichen verglichen:[141]

Dîn halsperc rehtiu güete sî,
diu machet dich von übele vrî.
diu wârheit sî dîn gürtel dîn,
gotes minne sol dîn helm sîn,
das gotes wort daz sî dîn schilt. [...]

Der Titel des Drucks zeigt ein sinnfälliges Bild des ‚Miles christianus':

---

[141] Ed. FRANZ PFEIFFER, Leipzig 1843, V. 7676–7680.

Abb. 93: UB Freiburg i. Br., Ink. K 3361, f [http://dl.ub.uni-freiburg.de/diglit/fusspfad1494/
0001], 1ʳ (Ausschnitt).

So wie für die Fürsten am Heidelberger Hof eine bis zwei Generation(en) zuvor
Fechtbücher erstellt wurden,[142] so wird nun für in ritterlicher Tradition stehende und
auch bürgerliche Laien dieses Lehrbuch für das Gefecht gegen die Gefahren, die die
Seele bedrängen, gedruckt. Das hier zum Schluss des Werkes eingebrachte Wappen
ist dasselbe, das Jakob Köbel später in seiner Oppenheimer eigenen Offizin als

---

[142] Vgl. THERESIA BERG und UDO FRIEDRICH: *Wissenstradierung in spätmittelalterlichen Schriften zur Kriegskunst: Der ‚Bellifortis' des Konrad Kyeser und das anonyme ‚Feuerwerks-
buch'* in: MÜLLER: *Wissen für den Hof.* (1994), S. 169–232.

Druckermarke verwendet.[143] Das Motiv geht wohl auf Köbels Wohnhaus in Heidelberg ‚Zur Schleiereule‘ zurück:[144]

Abb. 94: UB Freiburg i. Br., Ink. K 3361, f [http://dl.ub.uni-freiburg.de/diglit/fusspfad1494/
0058], 29ᵛ (Ausschnitt).

Interessant ist auch, dass die Dresdner Handschrift daneben Texte mitüberliefert, die
uns aus Knoblochtzers Druckprogramm schon bekannt sind: die *Ulmer Hofzucht*
(vgl. Knoblochtzers *Tischzucht*), Kalendertafeln und die *Sybillenweissagung* (s. fol-
gendes Kapitel). Und weiterhin interessant, dass der Endredaktor der Inkunabel
(Köbel?), der wohl nach Vollendung des Druckes dem Werk ein *registerleyn* voran-
gestellt hat (2ʳ–4ʳ), gleich zweimal Korrekturen anbringen musste: *Das zweyt Capitel
(da der trücker geirt vnnd das drit gesettzt hat) sagt* […] und *Das xxvj. Capitel (da
der trücker geirt vnnd xxvij. gesetzt hat) herinnert vns* […].[145] Wenn damit nicht nur
der Setzer angesprochen ist, sondern Knoblochtzer selbst, dann wäre das eine ziem-
liche Blamage für den Leiter der Offizin, der ja 1489 mit dem Anspruch angetreten
war, *impressorie artis magister*, also ‚Meister der Druckkunst‘ zu sein (vgl. oben
zum Guarinus, Kap. 3).

---

143 GRIMM, HEINRICH: *Köbel, Jakob*, in: *Neue Deutsche Biographie* 12 (1979), S. 289–290, Online-
    Version: https://www.deutsche-biographie.de/pnd118724142.html#ndbcontent (29.9.2020).
    Noch nicht richtig zuordnen konnte die Marke ERNST WEIL: *Die deutschen Druckerzeichen
    des XV. Jahrhunderts*, München 1924, S. 68: „Es ist nicht ganz sicher, ob dies nicht nur
    eine Schlußvignette darstellt.“
144 GELDNER: *Inkunabeldrucker* (1968), S. 290. Vgl. auch die Angabe in Köbels *Sibyllen-
    weissagung*, diese sei *zů der schlaireylen* entstanden, unten Kap. 9 A.
145 2ʳ und 3ᵛ. Eine pauschale Druckerschelte findet sich auch, wiederum von J. Köbel in der
    Vorrede zu seiner Edition der *Sibyllenweissagung*, auch hier Näheres unten innerhalb des
    Kapitels 9 A.

9 Belehrung und Information (überwiegend *utilitas*)

In diesem Segment von Knoblochtzers Druckerzeugnissen sind überproportional oft kleine, nur ein Blatt umfassende Werke (Einblattdrucke) enthalten, die sicherlich oft nicht konservierenswert erschienen, da die Brauchbarkeit ihres Informationsgehaltes nur einen kurzen Zeitraum umfasste. Daher wurden sie gerne als Makulaturmaterial verwendet oder gänzlich vernichtet. Die ‚Dunkelziffer' ist also hoch, man darf über das erhaltene Material hinaus von weitaus mehr Drucken dieser Art ausgehen.

9 A) Prognostik, Komputistik, Astronomie/Astrologie

Auffällig ist hier ein Themenschwerpunkt um Prognostik und Komputistik aus der Grauzone zwischen Astronomie und Astrologie, wie er in vielen Wiegendruckorten stark vertreten ist:[146]

Die Angaben aus dem *Gw* zu Nr. [Gw 0139920: *Almanach auf das Jahr 1486*, deutsch], der nur in einem fragmentarischen Exemplar erhalten ist, von dem kein Digitalisat zur Verfügung steht, vermitteln einen Eindruck von der Machart und dem Gehalt dieser Almanache: Betont wird die Kompetenz der Urheber: *Nach rat vnd beſchluß der meiſter,* der Informationsgehalt: *des geſtirns vnd auch der artzney* [meist günstige Aderlasstermine], genauer spezifiziert: […] *geſetzt vff dē geworen lauff der ſunnen vnd des mones Mit abſcheydung der böſſen planeten,* der Zeitraum der Gültigkeit: *Des iores Criſti vnſers herren geburt Viertzehenhundert vnd vi. vnd achtzig ior.* Und aufgeführt werden die wichtigen Kennzahlen und -buchstaben zur Bestimmung der beweglichen Feiertage: *vnd iſt . U. Sontagbůchſtab Vnd fünff die gemein zahl Vnd ſechs wochen zwyſchen winacht vnd der pfaffen faſtnacht* [= Sonntag Estomihi].[147]

Da auch zahlreiche lateinische Exemplare dieser Gattung erhalten sind, ist klar, dass diese Einblattdrucke durchaus nicht nur auf ungebildetes Publikum abzielten. Aus Heidelberg ist [Gw 01419: *Almanach auf das Jahr 1487*, lat.] „um 1487" erhalten. Auf Grund des Typenmaterials, das Knoblochtzer von Johann Zainer aus Ulm übernommen hatte (s. o. Einleitung u. ö.), war der Druck auch schon einmal diesem zugeschrieben worden. Es ist wiederum nur ein Fragment (in Stockholm) erhalten, ein Digitalisat steht nicht zur Verfügung, dafür eine ausführliche Beschreibung bei *VE 15*, A-295/10.

Im Gegensatz zu Gw 0139920, *Almanach auf das Jahr 1486*, deutsch (s. o.), beschränkt sich [Gw M4474030: *Tafel zur Bestimmung der beweglichen Feste für die*

---

[146] Zur Bedeutung der Astronomie für die Kriegsstrategie: THERESIA BERG und UDO FRIEDRICH: *Wissenstradierung in spätmittelalterlichen Schriften zur Kriegskunst*, in: MÜLLER: *Wissen für den Hof* (1994), S. 199.

[147] Einlässliche Beschreibung eines Almanachs auch bei AMELUNG: *FDSW*, Kat. Nr. 89, S. 76, der konkret hier vorliegende bei *VE 15*, A-281.

Jahre 1488–1507] „um 1488" ganz auf die Komputistik, ordnet die Daten aber in einem gefälligen Gesamtbild an, geschmückt mit Figuren, wie sie dann in ähnlicher Art in den Sibyllenbüchern von Jakob Köbel und Jodocus Eichmann (s. u.) wieder erscheinen.[148]

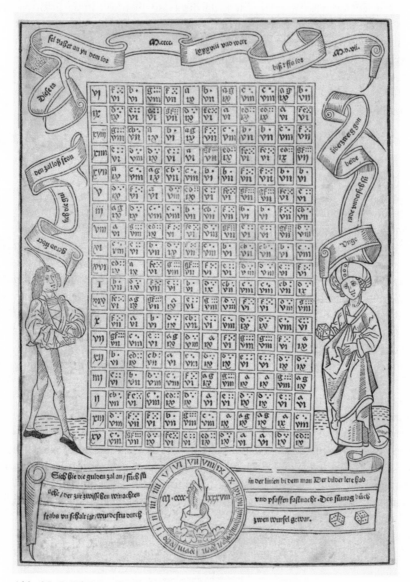

Abb. 95: DtHistMus Berlin, RB 17/305 [http://daten.digitale-sammlungen.de/bsb00083148/image_1], (verkleinert), unter Anwendung der CC-Lizenz CC BY-NC-SA 4.0 (https://creative commons.org/licenses/by-nc-sa/4.0/deed.de).

[148] Weitere Beschreibung, Transkription und Lit. bei *VE 15*, T-3.

Die Beschreibung von [Gw 01454: *Almanach auf das Jahr 1491*, deutsch] „um 1491", von dem wiederum kein Digitalisat zur Verfügung steht,[149] ist fast gleichlautend mit der vom Almanach von 1486 (s. o.) und belegt den stereotypen Charakter dieser Drucke. Sie waren sicher relativ leicht herzustellen und bildeten wohl eine verlässliche Einnahmequelle für die Offizinen. Auf die Gattung Almanach ist unten bei der Zusammenstellung der Werke von Johann Virdung nochmals zurückzukommen.

Eine spekulativere Art der Zukunftsprognose bietet ein Werk, das Knoblochtzer in kurzer Folge in einer lateinischen und in einer deutschen Ausgabe herausbrachte: Zuerst, „um 1488", erschien die an ein gebildetes Publikum gerichtete lateinische Inkunabel: [Gw M18217: Lichtenberger, Johannes: *Prognosticatio*].

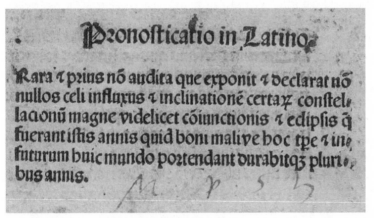

Abb. 96: Lessing J. Rosenwald Collection, Library of Congress, Rare Book and Special Collections Division, Washington D. C. [https://www.loc.gov/resource/rbc0001.2015rosen0122/?sp=5], 1ʳ (Ausschnitt).

Man merkt schon am etwas marktschreierischen Ton des Titels *Rara et prius non audita* (,rar und nie dagewesen'), dass hier die Frage nach Glück und Unglück (*quid boni malive* [...]) ganz anders gestellt wird als bei Petrarca (s. o. Kap. 5: *De remediis utriusque fortunae*). Der himmlische Einfluss, aus dem gegenwärtige und zukünftige, auch politische Ereignisse abgeleitet werden, bezieht sich auf eine besondere Planeten- und Sternbildkonstellation (*nonnulli celi influxus et inclinatio certarum constellationum magne videlicet coniunctionis et eclipsis*), die im Jahr 1484 eingetreten war.[150] Auch in der Schlussschrift der deutschen Ausgabe [Gw M18242, s. u.] gibt sich das Ganze einen numinosen Anstrich: *Gegeben In der fenstern gaszen vnderm gespeneten eychbaům.*

---

[149] Verzeichnet auch bei *Ve 15*, A-348.
[150] Genaueres dazu Dietrich Kurze: *Lichtenberger, Johannes*, in: ²*Vl* 5 (1985), Sp. 770–776, hier Sp. 773.

¶ Loß vnd ere sage ich got in ewigkeyt
der nyt leßt vnbelônet eynge gude arbeyt.
Gegeben In der fenstern gaßen vnderm gespeneten eychbaum Im iar. M.cccc
lxxxviij. am ersten tage des Apprills durch dem pylgrin Rüch der in welden
verborgen lyt. des augen syn dünckel worde. der griffel zidderet vonn alter. Got
wolle wol den güden vnd den swetzern als sie verdyenen.

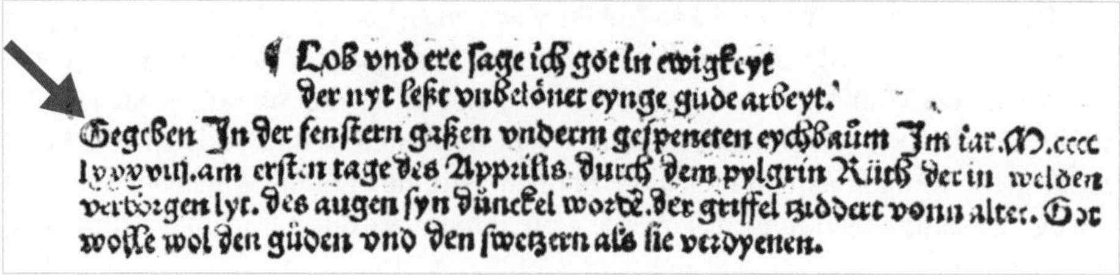

Abb. 97: BSB München, 2 Inc. s. a. 790 [Ink L-168]; [http://daten.digitale-sammlungen.de/bsb00008265/image_93], letztes bedrucktes Bl., recto (Ausschnitt, Hervorhebung durch Hinzufügen eines blauen Pfeils, C. R.).

Ein solches Werk musste natürlich von großer politischer Brisanz sein, weswegen der Autor hier unter einem Pseudonym als *peregrinus Ruth* (‚Pilger Ruth‘) auftritt.[151] Seine Arbeit war durchaus fragwürdig, kam ins Visier der Inquisition, wurde von den Autoren der ausgeschriebenen, oft nicht genannten Quellen angegriffen, und hatte doch ungeheuren Erfolg bis ins 19. Jahrhundert.[152] Hinter dem Verdecknamen verbirgt sich der aus Grünbach zwischen Kaiserlautern und Idar-Oberstein stammende, um 1440 geborene Astronom/Astrologe („Sterndeuter und Prophet“ Kurze, Sp. 770) Johannes Lichtenberger (ca. 1440–1503). Als *astrorum iudex sacri imperii* (Zitat Kurze, Sp. 771) versuchte er, sich als Akteur auf großer politischer Bühne zu gerieren. Das Opus magnum von 36 Bll. in Folio, versehen mit zahlreichen großformatigen Holzschnitten[153] erschien zuerst bei Knoblochtzer in Heidelberg,[154] der damit ein gutes Gespür für den Geschmack und Bedarf des lesenden Publikums zum Ende 15. Jahrhunderts bewies. Später folgten noch Ausgaben in Köln und Straßburg, im frühen 16. Jahrhundert in Augsburg, noch in der Inkunabelzeit sogar auf Italienisch in Brescia, Mailand, Modena und Venedig. Jakob Meydenbach, der um dieselbe Zeit auch die Totentanz-Holzschnitte von Knoblochtzer übernommen hatte, druckte 1492 unter Verwendung der Illustrationen aus der Heidelberger Offizin (zu einer Zeit, da Knoblochtzer nachweislich noch in Heidelberg tätig ist),[155] ebenfalls eine lateinische und eine deutsche Ausgabe.

[151] Unter Lichtenbergers wirklichem Namen erst ab 1525 erschienen, vgl. Dietrich Kurze: *Lichtenberger, Johannes*, in: ²*VL* 5 (1985), Sp. 770–776, hier Sp. 773.

[152] Dietrich Kurze: *Lichtenberger, Johannes*, in: ²*VL* 5 (1985), Sp. 770–776, hier Sp. 771 und 773 f.

[153] Weshalb sie als „grobgeschnitten“ abgewertet werden in Geldner, *Inkunabeldrucker* (1968), S. 42, zitatweise nach Schreiber, ist m. E. nicht ganz nachvollziehbar.

[154] Im *Gw* 34 erhaltene Exemplare gelistet.

[155] Vgl. nur unten das Kolophon von 1493 zu Jodocus Eichmann: *Sibyllenweissagung* [Gw 09255]. Derselbe Vorgang lässt sich beim *Totentanz* (s. Kap. 6) beobachten. Geldner: *Inkunabeldrucker* (1968), S. 42 (im Abschnitt Mainz, Meydenbach) bezeichnet die Mainzer Ausgaben als „Nachdrucke“.

Abb. 98a (links) und 98b (rechts): Heidelberg 1488: Lessing J. Rosenwald Collection, Library of Congress, Rare Book and Special Collections Division, Washington D. C. [https://www.loc. gov/resource/rbc0001.2015rosen0122/?sp=8], 2ᵛ (98a) und Mainz 1492: BSB München, 2 Inc. c. a. 2729 [Ink. L 164]; [http://daten.digitale-sammlungen.de/bsb00033583/image_8], 2ᵛ (98b) (jeweils verkleinerter Ausschnitt).

Dass Knoblochtzer mit seiner Editio princeps ganz nahe am Enstehungsprozess des Werkes handelt, zeigt sich auch in den Bildüberschriften, die noch wie redaktionelle Anweisungen des Autors formuliert sind, z. B. *Hic debet stare Saluator* (lat. Ausgabe, 6ʳ) / *Hye sal steen der saluator* (dt. Ausgabe, 6ʳ, der folgende Holzschnitt 6ᵛ hat die lateinische Beschriftung beibehalten), was dann schon bei Meydenbach zu *Der saluator am iungsten gericht spricht* umformuliert wird. Die Illustrationen selbst zeigen teils Allegorien, teils historische Szenen. Der Text gibt sich in der Vorrede einen durchaus wissenschaftlichen Anstrich, indem über die drei Möglichkeiten der Vorhersage der Zukunft Rechenschaft abgelegt wird: 1. Beobachtung, 2. Sterndeutung, 3. Prophezeiungen von Personen mit seherischen Fähigkeiten. Als Kronzeugen für die drei Kategorien werden ins Feld geführt: Aristoteles, Ptolemäus, Sibylle, Brigitta, Bruder Reinhard (s. Abb. 98a und b). Innerhalb der Kapitel erfolgen Vorhersagen über zu erwartende Ereignisse in Politik, Kirche und Gesellschaft, alles versetzt mit reichlichen Ratschlägen.

Bartholomäus Kistler verwendet für seine Ausgaben 1499 und 1500 (Gw M18229, M18233 und M18236) ein kleineres Format und dementsprechend neues, auch ganz anders geartetes, ‚moderner‘ wirkendes Bildmaterial mit Holzschnitten, die an die *Schedelsche Weltchronik* erinnern. Von der lateinischen Variante der Heidelberger Inkunabel besitzen die Uʙ und das Stadtarchiv in Heidelberg je ein Exemplar (Sᴄʜʟᴇᴄʜᴛᴇʀ/Rɪᴇs 1177 und 1178).

[Gw M18242: LICHTENBERGER, JOHANNES: *Prognostikon*, deutsch] „um 1490": Die deutsche Ausgabe aus Heidelberg weist immer noch das schon bekannte, nun einge-deutschte Pseudonym Lichtenbergers *pylgrin Rüth* auf (s. o. Abb. 97). Nicht einge-deutscht werden hingegen (wie schon erwähnt) die Beschriftungen der Holzschnitte. Ein handschriftlicher Textzeuge aus Philadelphia (Pennsylvania), Univ. of Pennsyl-vania, Rare Book & Manuscript Libr. Collections, LJS 445[156] ist wohl eine Abschrift vom Druck.

   [Gw M50711: VIRDUNG, JOHANNES: *Almanach auf das Jahr 1498*, deutsch] „um 1498": Ganz im Zentrum des schon bekannten Heidelberger (Humanisten-)Kreises befinden wir uns mit den Werken des Johann Virdung von Haßfurt (1463–ca. 1535). Seine Werke wurden vielfach gedruckt, zwei davon auch in Heidelberg. Von den Ausmaßen und dem gesamten Erscheinungsbild seines Almanachs auf das Jahr 1498 kann man sich einen einigermaßen realistischen Eindruck nur machen, wenn man zwei erhaltene Fragmente zusammennimmt. Der untere Rand fehlt den Exemplaren in Boston und Bamberg (allein die Ausmaße des Fragments belaufen sich auf 40,5 × 27,5 cm), die obere Hälfte im Münchener Exemplar:

Abb. 99: SBB Bamberg, VI F 63 [https://nbn-resolving.org/urn:nbn:de:bvb:22-dtl-000008 6465], (Ausschnitt, Hervorhebung durch Hinzufügen eines blauen Pfeils, C.R.), unter An-wendung der CC-Lizenz CC BY-SA 4.0 (https://creativecommons.org/licenses/by-sa/4.0/ deed.de).

---

[156] Nachweis im *Handschriftencensus* [http://www.handschriftencensus.de/werke/7227], (2.10.2020).

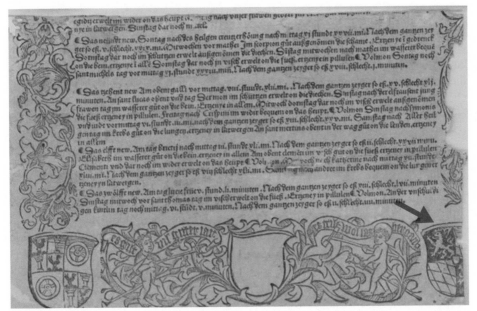

Abb. 100: BSB München, Einbl. Kal. 1498 eb [Ink V-229]; [http://daten.digitale-sammlungen.de/bsb00101515/image_1], (Ausschnitt, Hervorhebung durch Hinzufügen eines blauen Pfeils, C. R.).

Der Autor stellt sich vor als: *den hochberümpten meister hansen virdung von haßfurt des durchleüchtigen fürsten vnd herren hern Philippen pfaltzgrauen by rhein etc. mathematicum vnd Astronomum:*[157]

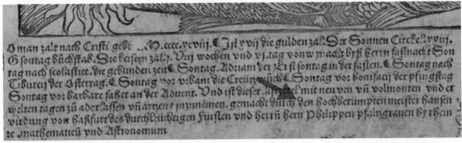

Abb. 101: Vergrößerter Ausschnitt von Abb. 99, Hervorhebung durch Hinzufügen eines blauen Pfeils, C. R.

Die enge Verbindung mit dem Pfalzgrafen wird dann nochmals durch das entsprechende Wappen am rechten unteren Rand untermauert (s. Abb. 100). Inhaltlich kann man diesen Almanach am ehesten den heute noch gebräuchlichen Mondkalendern

---

[157] Ab 1494 „im Dienst des Kurfürsten Philipp des Aufrichtigen von der Pfalz (1476–1508) als Hofastrologe und ‚Bombardist'": FRANCIS B. BRÉVART: *Virdung, Johann, von Haßfurt*, in: ²*VL* 10 (1999), Sp. 372–375, hier 372.

vergleichen. Es werden für jeden Monat die Neu- und Vollmonddaten angegeben, sowie sonstige astronomische Konstellationen und die daraus abzuleitenden, zu empfehlenden Tätigkeiten zur Gesundheitspflege. Bei diesen Einblattdrucken ist mit einer hohen Verlustrate zu rechnen. Von den neun in *Gw* nachgewiesenen Drucken dieses Werkes (fünf lateinische Varianten, vier deutsche) sind acht bei Konrad Kachelofen in Leipzig erschienen, sogar die Ausfertigungen, die explizit auf Heidelberg zugeschnitten waren (1494 und 1495, je lat. und dt.). Das heißt wohl, dass die Heidelberger Presse nicht von vornherein für die Anfertigung dieser Werke mit dem ungewöhnlich großen Format geeignet war. Und bei den drei erhaltenen Exemplaren, von denen Digitalisate zur Verfügung stehen, herrscht Uneinigkeit in der Zuschreibung: In Bamberg wird der Einblattdruck Grüninger in Straßburg, in Boston J. Zainer in Ulm (wahrscheinlich wegen der aus Ulm stammenden Bordüre) zugeschrieben, nur in München wird die Ausgabe in Heidelberg lokalisiert. Von Knoblochtzer ist auch hier nicht die Rede. Die Köbelsche(?) Eule (s. Abb. 99) könnte ein Indiz dafür sein, dass diesen Druck nicht mehr Knoblochtzer selbst, sondern Köbel mit dessen Typenmaterial in Heidelberg oder evtl. schon in Oppenheim zur Ausführung brachte.

[Gw M50739: VIRDUNG, JOHANNES: *Prognostikon auf das Jahr 1495*, deutsch] „um 1495": Häufiger als die Almanache sind die Prognostiken/Praktiken des Johannes Virdung erhalten, 28 Nachweise gibt es allein für die Zeit bis 1500 im *Gw*, die Mehrzahl in lateinischer Sprache, 13 davon auch auf Deutsch, teils Niederdeutsch. Einige Exemplare sind wieder auf einzelne Jahre oder Zeiträume oder bestimmte Orte gemünzt (Leipzig und Krakau). Die Mehrzahl der Drucke stammt wiederum aus der Offizin von Konrad Kachelofen in Leipzig, ansonsten sind Druckorte im ganzen deutschen Sprachraum vertreten, 1500 erschien gar eine Ausgabe bei Köbel in Oppenheim (Gw M50750). Der Zusammenhang mit dem Heidelberger (Humanisten-) Kreis (vgl. oben Kap. 5) wird verschiedentlich deutlich z. B. durch eine Vorrede an Wimpfeling in Gw M50749:[158] *Dem wirdigen hochgelerten hern Jacoben Wimpfeling von Sletstat, poetischer gedicht erfarner, heidnischer lere bewerter*[159]*, vnd heiliger cristlicher geschrifft ergrunter [...] Enbüt meister hans virdung von haßfurt synen gruß.* (2ᵛ) Oder auch durch das vorangestellte ‚Carmen' des oben (Kap. 5) schon erwähnten, als Prinzenerzieher bekannten Adam Wernher von Themar in Gw M50742 aus Leipzig: *Ad illustrissimi Prinicipis Philippi Comitis palatini Rheni etcetera Mathematicum et bombardistam insignem liberalium arcium Magistrum Johannem Uirdungum Hassfordensem Carmen Ade Wernheri Temarensis lincentiati iurium vt prognosticon in annum domini M.cccc.xcvij. scribat [...]* (1ᵛ).

Während der zuvor erwähnte Druck Gw M50749, „um 1499/1500" kaum noch aus Knoblochtzers eigener Druckerei stammen dürfte, ist dies für die Ausgabe auf das Jahr 1495 (Gw M50739) durchaus wahrscheinlich: Diese Ausgabe eröffnet nun

---

[158] Diesen Druck ordnet *Gw* um „1499/1500" mit Fragezeichen wohl zu Unrecht noch „Knoblochtzer(?)" zu (s. Eintrag unten).

[159] Heißt: ‚in Studien der klassischen Antike erfahren'.

mit einer Widmung an Pfalzgraf Philipp. Umso erstaunlicher ist die nicht eben sorg-
fältige Machart des Druckes, die immerhin einen großen Titelholzschnitt (Mars im
Sternbild Skorpion?) trägt:

Deütsch practica Cracouiensis magistrij Johan
nis virdung von hasfart gemacht czů ereun[160] *dem*
durchletichtig(e)n[161] *fürsten vnd herren herren philip-*
sen pfaltzgraffen by Rheyn (et)c(etera) Vff das Tausent
vierhundert vndfünffvndneüntzigistes Jare

Abb. 102: WLB Stuttgart, Inc. Qt .8373b [http://digital.wlb-stuttgart.de/purl/bsz348658990]
= Titel (Ausschnitt).

[160] Wahrscheinlich Druckfehler mit verdrehtem ersten *n* für richtig *erenn*.
[161] Gemeint ist nhd. ‚durchlauchten‘.

Von diesem Werk, das zu Beginn noch eine Holzschnitt-Initiale *D* in raffiniertem Flechtwerkornament aufweist,[162] ist nur ein Exemplar in der Württembergischen Landesbibliothek Stuttgart, dieses zudem nur fragmentarisch, erhalten, so dass man sich vom Umfang keine genauen Vorstellungen machen kann. Immerhin ist im Erhaltenen von neun Kapiteln die Rede (es können natürlich auch mehr gewesen sein). Der Autor zeigt in der Vorrede an, dass er zu seiner Darstellung durch gewissenhafte Beobachtung *mit flisiglich(e)n*[!] *ansehen/ der figuren desz himelsz nach lere der weysen* gekommen sei. Ziel sei es, unglückliche und glückliche Ereignisse vorauszusehen, die uns Sterblichen (*vnsz doettliche[n] yrdischen menschen*) widerfahren können. In Betracht kommen einerseits Krieg (*streydt*), Tod (*dŏttlikeyt*), Teuerung, Regengüsse, große Kälte und furchterregende Donnerschläge, andererseits *gůt lufft, Gesuntheyt der corper fruckbarkeyt vnd derglychen.*

Gw M50741, eine lateinische Ausgabe auf das Jahr 1496, die wieder das Carmen des Adam Wernher von Themar aufweist (s. o.), erfährt in *Gw* gar keine Zuordnung zu einer Offizin, der *Inka*-Eintrag nimmt Bezug auf die verwendeten Typen und kommt zu der hochinteressanten Aussage: „Heidelberg: Heinrich Knoblochtzer [teilw. mit dem Typenmaterial des Peter Drach in Speyer]".[163] Das passte natürlich bestens zu der Kooperation der beiden Werkstätten, die oben bei der Vergil-Ausgabe von 1495 u. ö. schon zu beobachten war.

Die gedruckten Ausgaben ‚für's Volk' haben prunkvolle Pendants in handschriftlichen Wahrsagebüchern innerhalb der Bibliothek der Kurfürsten: Virdungs *Tabulae resolutae de supputandis siderum motibus* (Vatikan, Bav, Stamp. Pal. IV 489; lat. 566c), seine *Practica Vom XLIII. Iar an biß man zelt LXIIII* (ebd. Stamp. Pal. IV 146; ted. 3194k)[164] und das berühmte *Heidelberger Schicksalsbuch* (Cpg 832, ca. 1490).[165]

[Gw M50749: Virdung, Johannes: *Prognostikon auf das Jahr 1500,* deutsch] „um 1499/1500":

---

[162] Ähnlich der vom *Fußpfad zur ewigen Seligkeit* (s. o. Kap. 8), vgl. Schramm: *Bilderschmuck 19*, Tafel 83, Abb. 589.

[163] *Inkunabelkatalog deutscher Bibliotheken*: [http://www.inka.uni-tuebingen.de/?inka=2300 3772] (3.10.2020); vgl. auch Backes (1992), S. 156–158: Weiteres zur Rolle Virdungs in Heidelberg.

[164] Vgl. die beiden Einträge von Joachim Telle in: *Bibliotheca Palatina* (1986), S. 106–108.

[165] Eintrag von Karin Zimmermann: A15, in: *Kostbarkeiten gesammelter Geschichte*, S. 149 f. mit Farbtafel 3, S. 289.

Abb. 103: SBB Berlin, PK, 8° Inc 1208.9 [https://digital.staatsbibliothek-berlin.de/werkansicht?
PPN=PPN1015971687&PHYSID=PHYS_0003&DMDID=], 1ʳ (Ausschnitt).

Dieser Druck dürfte, wie oben schon dargelegt, kaum noch in Knoblochtzers eigener
Regie erstellt worden sein.

[Gw M16375: KÖBEL, JAKOB: *Sibyllen Weissagung*]: Das Werk, das im 14. Jh. entstanden sein dürfte, ist in unterschiedlich langen Redaktionen (zwischen 672 und
1024 Versen) handschriftlich vielfach überliefert.[166] Der Heidelberger Wiegendruck
hat prominente Vorgänger: Eine nur fragmentarisch erhaltene Inkunabel dieses Titels
von Gutenberg gilt „als der älteste bezeugte, mit beweglichen Lettern gedruckte Text
in dt. Sprache".[167] Jakob Köbel (vgl. oben Kap. 5: *Mensa philosophica* und *Tischzucht*, Kap. 8: *Fußpfad zur Seligkeit*, Kap. 9: Virdungs *Almanach auf das Jahr 1498*)
legte für ‚seine' Ausgabe, der er eine Widmung an seinen Vater Klaus Köbel, *burger
zů heydelberg* und *aller liebster vatter* (1ᵛ der Heidelberger Ausgabe) vorausschickt,
die 830 Verse umfassende Redaktion zu Grunde. Und wie seine *Fußpfad*-Ausgabe

---

[166] In 37 Handschriften lt. B. SCHNELL/N. F. PALMER: *Sibyllenweissagungen* (deutsch), v. a. Abschnitte III: *Sibyllen Buch* und IIIa: *Drucküberlieferung des SB*, in: ²*VL* 8 (1992), Sp. 1140–
1152, v. a. 1145–1149, hier Sp. 1145 und 1148.
[167] Ebd. Sp. 1149.

auch (s. d.) erschließt er den Inhalt durch eine beigefügte Kapitelübersicht, ein *regis-terlin* (4ʳ des Ulmer Drucks). Klaus Köbel habe seinen Sohn schon seit langem da-rum gebeten (*ermant*), *etwas vß den alten Coronickschreibern zusammen ze raspeln* (1ᵛ der Heidelberger Ausgabe, *ze klauben* 2ʳ der Ulmer Ausgabe), was die Zuver-lässigkeit des *buchlin genant die Sibyllen weyssagung* prüfen solle. Der Redaktor konzentriere sich von den zehn nachgewiesenen auf die *Sibylla Erythrea/Erethrea* (beide Schreibungen 1ᵛ der Heidelberger Ausgabe), die König Salomon begegnet sei. Dies Begegnung wird auf dem Titelholzschnitt dargestellt (s. u.). Im Inkunabel-zeitalter wurde diese Köbelsche Redaktion zwei Mal gedruckt, wobei der Druck von Schäffler in Ulm (Gw M16377) lt. AMELUNG (*Fᴅsᴡ*, S. 382) „eine genaue Kopie der Heidelberger Vorlage"[168] sein dürfte[169]:

Abb. 104a (links) und 104b (rechts): Heidelberger Ausgabe: GNM Nürnberg, Inc. 8° 14765 [http://dlib.gnm.de/item/8Inc14765/3], 1ʳ (104a) und Ulmer Druck: SBB Berlin, PK, 8° Inc 2667.5 [https://digital.staatsbibliothek-berlin.de/werkansicht?PPN=PPN788612867&PHY SID=PHYS_0006&DMDID=], 1ʳ (104b) (jeweils Ausschnitt).

---

[168] AMELUNGS Angaben: *Fᴅsᴡ* (1979), Nr. 164, S. 381–383, sind äußerst gehaltvoll, im Detail teils durch B. SCHNELL/N. F. PALMER: *Sibyllenweissagungen* (deutsch), v.a. Ab-schnitte III: *Sibyllen Buch* und IIIa: *Drucküberlieferung des SB*, in: ²Vʟ 8 (1992), Sp. 1140–1152, v.a. 1145–1149, überholt.

[169] Zu Köbels deutscher Ausgabe aus seiner eigenen Druckerei in Oppenheim von 1516 s. N. F. PALMER, wie vorherige Anm. IIIa: *Drucküberlieferung des SB*, Sp. 1150.

Freilich benötigt der Ulmer Drucker für die Edition in 8° 27 Bll. Papier, während die Heidelberger Ausgabe in 4° nur 16 Bll. umfasst. Wenn der Titel auch verspricht, dass der Leser in die Lage versetzt werden sollte, *warlich kunfftig ding [zu] sagen* (s. o.), so sind die Sibyllen-Passagen doch von einem starken heilgeschichtlichen Rahmen eingefasst (*Die vorred diß bůchlins thůt anzaigen die almechtikayt gotes. Schöpfung himels vnd der erden des paradiß vnd der menschen betrůgung des teuffelischen schlangen* [...] *Das ix. Capitel sagt wie gott das iungst gericht besitzt vndd gůt vnd böß vervrtailen wirt etc.* 4r und 5v der Ulmer Ausgabe) und münden in ein Memento mori und den Appell zur rechtzeitigen Umkehr vom sündigen Leben. Die Redaktion der Textgrundlage in Heidelberg verschweigt auch der Ulmer Druck nicht (3v), wir begegnen wieder einmal, diesmal nicht in bildlicher, sondern in sprachlicher Form dem schon bekannten Haus „Zur Schleiereule". Vielleicht ist die *eyl* im Diktum *hab ich dir in ainer eyl zůsamen geklaubt*, auch schon doppeldeutig als ‚Eile' und ‚Eule' zu verstehen:

dye ich zů disem bůchlin hab dir in
ainer eyl zů samen geklaubt in aller
vndertänigkait Damit so spar dich
got gesund. Datum haidelberg zů
der schlaireylen. Anno domini Tau
sent Vierhundert Vnd in dem zwai
vnd neünzigisten iar Auff dē Esch
er mitwoch.

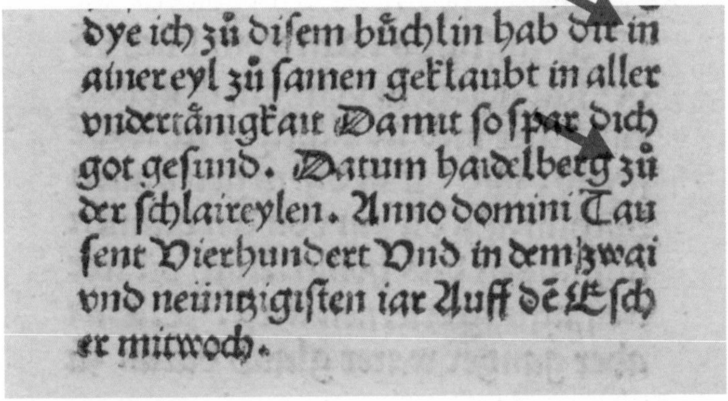

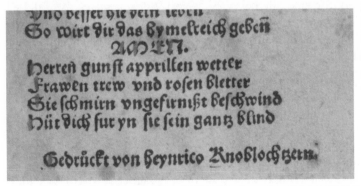

Abb. 105: SBB Berlin PK, Ink 2667, 5 [https://digital.staatsbibliothek-berlin.de/werkansicht?PPN=PPN788612867&PHYSID=PHYS_0010&DMDID=], 3v (Ausschnitt, Hervorhebung durch Hinzufügen blauer Pfeile, C. R.).

Der Druck selbst ist dann eindeutig Knoblochtzers Werkstatt zugeordnet.

So wirt dir das hymelreich geben
AMEN.
Herren gunst apprillen wetter
Frawen trew vnd rosen bletter
Sie schmirn vngefirnißt beschwind
Hüt dich fur yn sie sein gantz blind
Gedrückt von heynrico Knoblochtzern.

Abb. 106: Heidelberger Ausgabe: GNM Nürnberg, Inc. 8° 14765 [http://dlib.gnm.de/item/8Inc14765/27], 16r (Ausschnitt).

Überaus interessant ist in diesem Zusammenhang, dass die von Köbel vorgeschaltete Vorrede wiederum eine (im Vergleich zum *Fußpfad*, wo ja auf konkrete Fehler des Druckers verwiesen wird), nun pauschale Druckerschelte enthält, indem in einer editionsphilologisch modern anmutenden textkritischen Anmerkung darauf hinge-wiesen wird, dass über mehrere Stationen tradierte Texte von *vil schreybern* und *vnfleißigen truckern* [...] *offt geergert*[170] *vnd selten gebessert werden* (3ᵛ der Ulmer Ausgabe) und man also bei der Lektüre immer mit Verderbnissen zu rechnen hätte, weshalb kein *gantzer warer glaub daran zů haben sey* (3ʳ/ᵛ der Ulmer Ausgabe). Da-mit stellt Jakob Köbel natürlich auch höchste Ansprüche an sein künftiges Gewerk in Oppenheim, wo er später eine eigene Offizin betreibt.

[Gw 09255: EICHMANN, JODOCUS: *Weissagungen der 12 Sibyllen über die jungfräu-liche Geburt Christi*]: Dieses Werk kommt äußerlich so ähnlich daher wie das vor-herige, hat einen vergleichbaren Umfang (hier 18 Bll. dort 16 Bll.) und wird vom selben Titelblatt geschmückt. Und doch verbirgt sich dahinter ein völlig anderer Text. Es ist gleichsam die wissenschaftlich-theologische Variante des Themas in Prosa im Gegensatz zur persönlich motivierten Darstellung des Themas durch Köbel in Versen. Das Werk geht von 12 (statt 10) Sibyllen aus und hat seinen Ursprung in einer Predigt des um eine Generation älteren Theologen und Humanismusförderer der ersten Stunde Jodocus Eichmann (ca. 1420–1489 oder 1491).[171] Obwohl ein Digitalisat der beiden erhaltenen Exemplare nicht zur Verfügung steht, kann man sich dank der Beschreibung im *Gw* eine recht gute Vorstellung vom Konzept des Werkes machen: Es war betitelt als: *Bewerung*[172] *der menſchwerdung chriſti / von einer iungfrawen / mit gezugknuſſe zwölffer nachbenanten Sybillen von doctor Ioſt eychman etwan prediger zů Heydelberg gepredigt.*

Auf Bl. 1ᵇ wird das Programm entworfen: *Diß buchlin von zwölff Sybillen zu er-kennen gibt / was ein ygklich derſelben / von chriſto von der mutter gottes marie / vnd andern gotlichen dingen geweiſſagt vnd geoffenbart / auch was geſtalt geberde weſen vnd kleidung ygklich Sybil getragen vnd gehabt hat.*

Die Attraktivität der Publikation wurde wohl erheblich durch Holzschnitte aller 12 Sibyllen gesteigert. Sie sind alle bei A. SCHRAMM, *Bilderschmuck 19*, Tafel 81 und 82 (Abb. 577–588) wiedergegeben, wirken in dieser Zusammenstellung wie eine spätmittelalterliche Modenschau. Auf Bl. 18ʳ endet das Werk nach der üblichen Bitte um göttlichen Beistand (*helff vns got vatter vnd ſone vnd der heilig geiſt. Amen.*) in einem ausführlichen Kolophon: *Getruckt zů Heydelberg von heinrico knob≈/lochtzern Nach chriſti vnſers herren geburt Tau-/ ſant Fierhundert Nüntzig vnd drew* [1493] *iar etc.*

---

[170] ‚ärger gemacht' also ‚verschlechtert, verderbt' werden.
[171] Der Autor ist also zur Zeit des Drucks schon verstorben, vgl. auch F. J. WORSTBROCK: *Eich-mann, Jodocus*, in: ²*VL* 2 (1979), Sp. 393–397, zum Werk kurz Sp. 396.
[172] ‚Wahrheitsgemäße Prophezeiung'.

Belehrung und Information ist bisweilen auch im Miniaturformat größeren Werken beigegeben: Eine Seite *Was zeyt vnd monat im iar ein ieglicher visch am besten sey*:

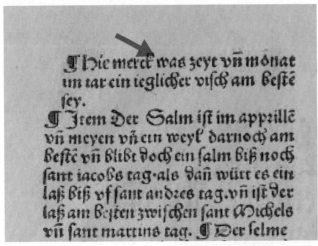

Abb. 107: ULB Darmstadt, Inc. III-29 [http://tudigit.ulb.tu-darmstadt.de/show/inc-iii-29/0002], 1ᵛᵃ (Ausschnitt, Hervorhebung durch Hinzufügen eines blauen Pfeils, C. R.).

hat wohl deshalb auf die Verso-Seite des Titels zu Philipp Frankfurter: *Der Pfaffe vom Kalenberg* (s. u. Kap. 10) gefunden, weil die Erzählung auf einem Fischmarkt beginnt:

Abb. 108: ULB Darmstadt, Inc. III-29 [http://tudigit.ulb.tu-darmstadt.de/show/inc-iii-29/0003], 2ʳᵇ (Ausschnitt).

Vom Redegestus her schließt der Text deutlich an die Kalendarien und Prognostiken an. Er dürfte, wie in anderen Druckausgaben auch, den zweiten Teil von [Gw: 0567910N: *Büchlein, wie man Fische und Vögel fangen soll*] gebildet haben. Von der Heidelberger Edition, die im *Gw* wiederum mit „Jakob Köbel (um 1493)" verbunden wird, ist leider kein Exemplar erhalten. Die anderen Auflagen innerhalb der Inkunabelzeit aus Straßburg (4), Erfurt (1), Antwerpen (1) umfassen meist 6 Bll., weisen teils auch Holzschnittillustrationen auf, z. B. die Erfurter Inkunabel:

Abb. 109: UB Wien, Inc. I 137981 [https://fedora.phaidra.univie.ac.at/fedora/objects/o:224 846/methods/bdef:Book/view], 1ʳ (= Aufnahme 5, Ausschnitt, Hervorhebung durch Hinzufügen eines blauen Pfeils, C. R.).

9 B) Politische, gesellschaftliche Information/Amtssachen

Die Informationen zum Tagesgeschehen in Stadt, Region und Reich, die meist in Form von Einblattdrucken erschienen sind, stellten ein wesentliches wirtschaftliches Standbein der meisten Druckereien in dieser frühen Zeit dar. Die Dunkelziffer an tatsächlich erschienen „Drucksachen" dieser Kategorie dürfte sehr hoch sein, da auch diese Einblattdrucke oft nicht erhalten sind (vgl. Einleitung zu Kap. 9). Aus Knoblochtzers Offizin sind gut zehn dieser tagespolitischen und/oder informierenden Kleindrucke überliefert. Zwei davon betreffen Kaiser Maximilian:

1. [Gw M22076: Maximilian I., Römischer Kaiser: *Erwählung*]: Der *Gw* verzeichnet unter Kaiser Maximilian I. (1459–1519) eine Fülle von Einblattdrucken mit ‚Ausschreiben', ‚Aufforderungen', ‚Mahnungen', ‚Geboten' und ‚Instruktionen'.[173] Im vorliegenden Fall handelt es sich um eine etwas umfangreichere Drucksache. Die Betitelung im *Gw* ist insofern irreführend, als es sich bei dem Werk im Wesentlichen um nichts weiter als ein Verzeichnis der zu Maximilians Königswahl am 16.2.1486 in Frankfurt anwesenden Personen handelt, zu einer Zeit also, da sein Vater, Friedrich III., noch die Kaiserwürde innehatte. Vom Heidelberger Exemplar (*Gw*: „nach 20.II.1486")[174] sind 3 Textzeugen erhalten, es steht aber kein Digitalisat zur Verfügung. Der Text wurde auch in mehreren anderen Orten gedruckt, so bei Schöffer in Mainz (Gw M22087), die Heidelberger Inkunabel dürfte ähnlich aussehen:

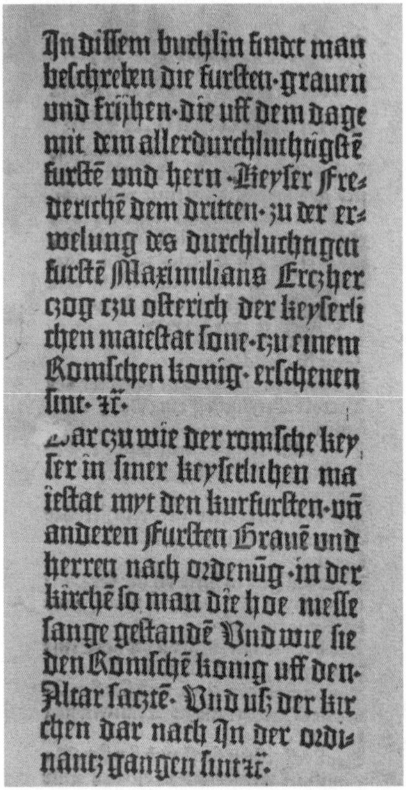
In dissem buchlin findet man
beschreben die fursten·grauen
und frijhen·die uff dem dage
mit dem allerdurchluchtigstē
furstē und hern ·Keyser Fre=
derichē dem dritten·zu der er=
welung des durchluchtigen
furstē Maximilians Erczher
czog czu osterich der keyserli
chen maiestat sone·czu einem
Romschen konig·erschenen
sint·zc·
ar czu wie der romsche key
ser in siner keyserlichen ma
iestat myt den kurfursten·vn̄
anderen Fursten Grauē und
herren nach ordenūg·in der
kirchē so man die hoe messe
sange gestandē Und wie sie
den Romschē konig uff den·
Altar sacztē· Und usz der kir
chen dar nach In der ordi=
nancz gangen sint zc·

Abb. 110: UB Frankfurt, Inc. Qu 504 [http://sammlungen.ub.uni-frankfurt.de/inc/content/pageview/5359577], 1r (Ausschnitt).

173 Vgl. auch *Ve 15*, M-17 bis M-144. Zum Memoria-Programm (*gedächtnus*) von Kaiser Maximilian I. vgl. Jan Dirk Müller: *Kaiser Maximilian I.* in: *²Vl* VI (1987), Sp. 204–236.

174 Die Zuschreibung an Knoblochtzer ist nicht unumstritten: Der *Incunabula Short Titel Catalogue* [*Istc*] folgt der Zuschreibung von *Gw* nicht, sondern nimmt Grüninger in Strassburg als Urheber der Inkunabel an.

Instruktive Information zur Textgattung und eine großformatige Abbildung bietet auch AMELUNG unter den Angaben zu einem Druck von Conrad Dinckmut aus Ulm (Gw M22088).[175]

2. [Gw M2210810: Maximilian I., Römischer Kaiser: *Handel und Vornehmen Etlicher in Flandern gegen die römische Majestät*] entstammt der Auseinandersetzung Kaiser Friedrichs III. und seines Sohnes, König Maximilians (*Gw*: „nach Februar 1488"), mit den Flandrischen Städten, mit denen dann im Oktober 1489 ein Frieden zustande kam, worin Maximilian als Regent in Vertretung seines minderjährigen Sohnes anerkannt wurde.[176] Es ist ein Text, der außer hier in Heidelberg auch bei Friedrich Creussner in Nürnberg gedruckt wurde (Gw M2211010), wovon noch vier Exemplare nachweisbar sind (davon eines in der UB Heidelberg: SCHLECHTER/RIES: 1252). Vom Heidelberger Druck ist nur ein Textzeuge bekannt, und zwar in New York, Morgan Library (vgl. Angaben im *Gw*).

[Gw 02855–02858: *Aufforderung an die Pfarrgeistlichen, für die Verbreitung des Ablasses zum Besten des Kampfes gegen die Türken mitzuwirken*]: Der sogenannte *Türkenkalender*, besser die *manung der cristenheit widder die durken* steht prominent am Beginn des Inkunabelzeitalters, da diese Flugschrift von 6 Bll. als erster Wiegendruck in deutscher Sprache gilt. Er ging aus Gutenbergs Presse in Mainz hervor, ist auf Dezember 1454 datiert (Gw M19909) und beinhaltet, kalendarisch sortiert und mit Gebeten ‚garniert', die Aufforderung an verschiedene Fürsten des Reiches, sich im Kampf gegen die ‚Türken', die 1453 Konstantinopel erobert hatten, zu engagieren. Jahrzehnte später ist das Thema noch ebenso aktuell. AMELUNG: *FDSW* verzeichnet unter Nr. 150 (S. 340, Abb. 232) einen lateinischen Ablassbrief von Raimundus Peraudi, 1488 *zum Besten des Kampfes wider die Türken*. Die erhaltenen Exemplare, oft auf Pergament gedruckt, um die Wichtigkeit des Dokuments zu unterstreichen, zeigen durch die jeweils handschriftlich annotierten Namen und Daten, wer diese Ablassbriefe erworben hat.[177] Die Komplexität der Kampagne wird durch den vorliegenden Druck deutlich, der nun seinerseits wieder die Pfarrgeistlichen dazu auffordert, die Werbetrommel für derlei Ablässe zu rühren. Im Gegensatz zum *Gw* ordnet das *VE 15* (A-140 bis A-143) diesen Druck Grüninger in Straßburg („um 1500") zu.

[Gw M25010: *Modus quem observabunt commissarii pro tuitione fidei in indulgentiarum publicatione*] entstammt dem gleichen Zusammanhang. Hier wird „um 1487" in lateinischer Sprache formuliert, welches Verfahren die Glaubenshüter (*commissarii pro tuitione fidei*) bei der Veröffentlichung von Ablässen einzuhalten hätten. *ISTC* schreibt denn den Text auch wieder Raimundus Peraudi zu (vgl. vorherigen Eintrag). Unter den zahlreichen *Modi*, die der *Gw* verzeichnet, ist dieser der einzige mit diesem Initium, in *VE 15* findet sich kein Eintrag.

---

[175] AMELUNG: *FDSW*, Nr. 114, S. 226–228 mit Abb. 172, S. 227.
[176] Vgl. K. F. HALTAUS: *Geschichte des Kaisers Maximilian I.*, Leipzig 1865, S. 77.
[177] Vgl. *VE 15*, P-62 bis P-200!

[Gw M12524 und M12528: *Instrumentum iudicum Moguntinensium*]: Es dürfte sich bei den beiden *Gw*-Nummern um denselben Frühdruck handeln, eine Arbeit von 4 Bll., die in den verschiedenen Textzeugen nicht vollständig erhalten ist (das Münchner und das Memminger Exemplar ergänzen einander wohl). Der *Gw* beschreibt den Inhalt des Dokuments so: „Es handelt sich um ein von den Richtern des Mainzer geistlichen Gerichts ausgestelltes Transsumpt [=‚Aktualisierung‘] der Ablassbulle *Thesauri sacratissimae passionis* Papst Innozenz' VIII., Rom, 10.X.1487, mit Bestätigung des Notars Johannes Fries [...] Mainz, 16.I.1488". Die Zuschreibung an Knoblochtzer erfolgt wohl nicht zuletzt wegen des Einsatzes des von ihm bekannten Initialentyps, hier eines zum *I* gedrehten *H* aus dem ‚romanischen Alphabet‘, das Knoblochtzer von J. Zainer übernommen hatte:[178]

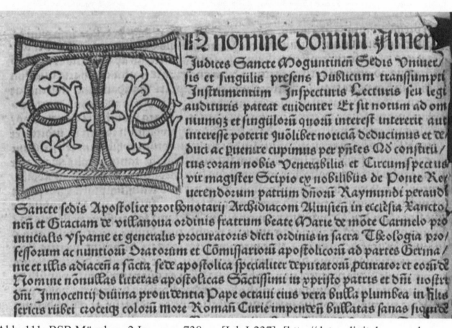

Abb. 111: BSB München, 2 Inc. s. a. 738 m, [Ink I-237]; [http://daten.digitale-sammlungen.de/bsb00039555/image_1], 1ʳ (Ausschnitt).

Bei [Gw M37153: RAUSCHNER, JÖRG: *Einladung zu einem Armbrustschießen nach Heidelberg, 18.V.1490*] handelt es sich um eine ca. 32 × 26 cm große, 62 Zeilen umfassende Einladungsurkunde zu einer Art von Kurfürst Philipp ausgerichteten oder zumindest bewilligten Schützen- und Volksfest, ausgestellt von dem Schützen- oder Zeremonienmeister Jörg Rauschner. Dass der Druck aus Knoblochtzers Werkstatt stammt, ist aus dem Umstand abzuleiten, dass die Initiale, die hier als deutsches *D* zu lesen ist, andernorts in lateinischen Texten wie z. B. bei Jacobus de Jüterbog: *De*

---

[178] Vgl. AMELUNG: *FDSW*, Abb. 31, S. 62 und Text S. 66.

valore et utilitate missarum von 1493 (Gw M10884, Kap. 2) u. ö. um 180° gedreht als *Q* verwendet wurde (s. d.):[179]

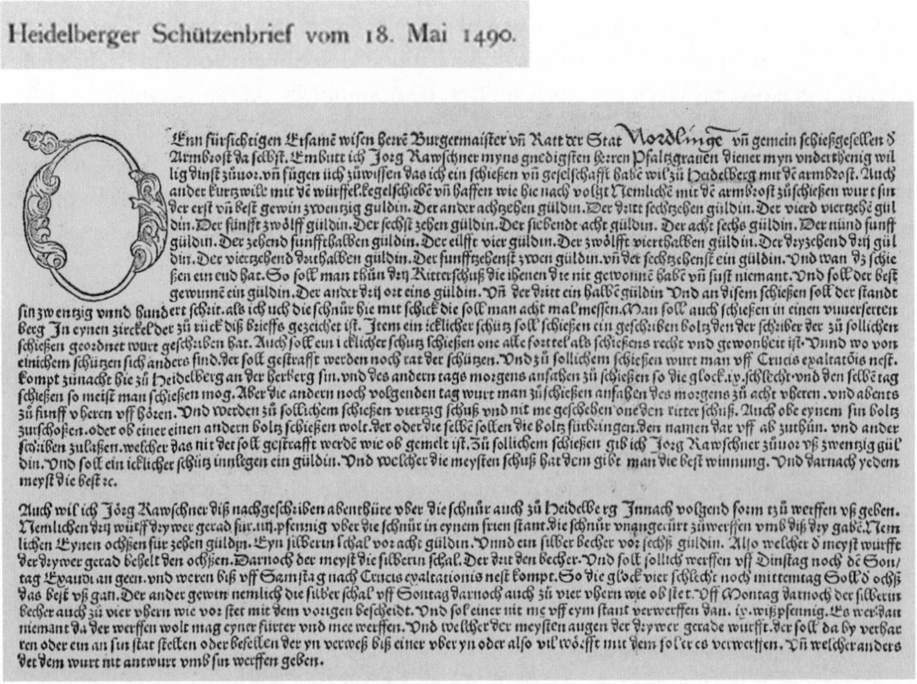
Heidelberger Schützenbrief vom 18. Mai 1490.

Enn fürsichtigen Ersamē wisen herrē Burgermaister vñ Ratt der Stat Nordlinge vñ gemein schießgesellen d Armbrost da selbst. Embutt ich Jorg Rawschner myns gnedigsten herren Pfaltzgrauen diener myn vnderthenig wil lig dinst züuor. vñ fügen üch zü wissen das ich ein schießen vñ geselschafft habē wil zü Heidelberg mit dē armbrost. Auch ander kurtzwile mit dē würffel. kegelschiebē vñ haffen wie hie nach volgt Nemlichē mit dē armbrost züschießen wurt sin der erst vñ best gewin zwentzig guldin. Der ander achtzehen güldin. Der dritt sechtzehen güldin. Der vierd viertzehē gül din. Der fünfft zwölff güldin. Der sechst zehen güldin. Der sibendt acht güldin. Der acht sechs güldin. Der nünd funff güldin. Der zehend funffthalben güldin. Der eilfft vier güldin. Der zwölfft vierthalben güldin. Der dryzehend dry gül din. Der viertzehend drithalben güldin. Der funfftzehenst zwen güldin. vñ der sechtzehenst ein güldin. Vnd wan dz schie ßen ein end hat. So soll man thün dry Ritterschuß die ihenen die nit gewonnē habē vñ sust niemant. Vnd soll der best gewinnē ein güldin. Der ander dry ort eins güldin. Vñ der dritt ein halbē güldin Vnd an disem schießen soll der standt sin zwentzig vnnd hundert schrit. als ich uch die schnür hie mit schick die soll man acht mal messen. Man soll auch schießen in einen vinnersertem berg In eynen zirckel der zü rück diß brieffs gezeichet ist. Item ein icklicher schütz soll schießen ein geschriben boltz den der schriber der zü sollichen schießen geordnet wurt geschriben hat. Auch soll ein icklicher schutz schießen one alle forttel als schießens recht vnd gewonheit ist. Vnnd wo von einichem schützen sich anders find. der soll gestrafft werden noch rat der schützen. Vnd zü sollichem schießen wurt man vff Crucis exaltatōis nest. kompt zünacht hie zü Heidelberg an der herberg sin. vnd des andern tags morgens anfahen zü schießen so die glock. ix. schlecht. vnd den selbē tag schießen so meist man schießen mog. Aber die andern noch volgenden tag wurt man züschießen anfahen des morgens zü acht vheren. vnd abents zü funff vheren vff hören. Vnd werden zü sollichem schießen viertzig schuß vnd nit me geschehen one den ritter schuß. Auch obe eynem sin boltz zurschoßen. oder ob einer einen andern boltz schießen wolt. der oder die selbē sollen die boltz fürbringen. den namen dar vff ab zuthün. vnd ander schriben zulaßen. welcher das nit det soll gestrafft werdē wie ob gemelt ist. Zü sollichem schießen gib ich Jorg Rawschner züuor vß zwentzig gül din. Vnd soll ein icklicher schütz innlegen ein güldin. Vnd welcher die meysten schuß hat dem gibt man die best winnung. Vnd darnach yedem meyst die best rc.

Auch wil ich Jörg Rawschner diß nachgeschriben abenthüre vber die schnür auch zü Heidelberg Innach volgend form tzü werffen vß geben. Nemlichen dry würff drywer gerad für. iiij. pfennig vber die schnür in eynem frien stant. die schnür vngangeürt züwerffen vmb diß dry gabē. Nem lichen Eynen ochßen für zehen güldyn. Eyn silberin schal vor acht güldin. Vnnd ein silber becher vor sechß güldin. Also welcher d meyst würfft der drywer gerad behelt den ochßen. Darnoch der meyst die silberin schal. Der drit den becher. Vnd soll sollich werffen vff Dinstag noch dē Son/ tag Exaudi an geen. vnd weren biß vff Samstag nach Crucis exaltationis nest kompt. So die glock vier schlecht noch mittemtag Soll d ochß das best vß gan. Der ander gewin nemlich die silber schal vff Sontag darnoch auch zü vier vhern wie ob stet. Vff Montag darnoch der silberin becher auch zü vier vhern wie vor stet mit dem vorigen bescheidt. Vnd sol einer nit me vff eym stant verwerffen dan. ix. wißpfennig. Es wer dan niemant da der werffen wolt mag eyner fürter vnd mee werffen. Vnd welcher der meysten augen der drywer gerade wurfft. der soll da by verhar ren oder ein an sin stat stellen oder befellen der yn verweß biß einer vber yn oder also vil wörfft mit dem sol er es verwerffen. Vñ welcher anders der dem wurt nit antwurt vmb sin werffen geben.

Abb. 112: aus Freys, Ernst: *Gedruckte Schützenbriefe des 15. Jahrhunderts: in getreuer Nachbildung*, München 1912, Digitalisat der UB Heidelberg, Tafel 24 [https://digi.ub.uni-heidelberg.de/diglit/freys1912/0071], (oberer Abschnitt).

Der Brief mit sechs Textblöcken von 21, 10, 9, 10, 4 und 8 Zeilen beginnt:

Denn fürsichtigen Ersamen wisen herren Burgermaister vnd Ratt der Stat [……..][180] *vnd gemein*[181] *schießgesellen der Armbrost da selbst. Embutt ich Jorg Rawschner myns gnedigsten herren Pfaltzgrauen diener myn vnderthenig willig dinst zůuor. vnd fůgen üch zů wissen das ich ein schießen vnd gesellschaft haben will zů heidelberg mit den armbrost. Auch ander kurtzwile mit dem würffel, kegelschieben vnd haffen.*[182]

[179] Sogenanntes, ursprünglich aus Ulm stammendes ‚Rokoko-Alphabet' vgl. Amelung: *Fdsw*, Abb. 34 und Text S. 66.

[180] In die vorgesehene Lücke ist hier von Hand *Nördlingen* eingetragen, dort, im Stadtarchiv liegt auch das einzig erhaltene Exemplar der Einladung.

[181] ‚allen'.

[182] Gemeint ist ‚Glückshafen', eine Art Lotterie. Weitere Information dazu bei *Ve 15*, R-6.

Darauf folgt dann im Weiteren die detaillierte Beschreibung von Ablauf und ausgelobten Preisen dieses *abenthüres*. Die Datierung am Schluss lautet: *Geben czů heydelberg vnder mynem Ingesigel getruckt zů endt dißer schrifft Vff Dinstag noch dem Sontag vocem iocunditatis. Anno etc. Nonagesimo*

zům ersten.zwentzig gůldin.Die ander achtzehen gůldin.Die drit sechtzehen gůldin.Die vierd viertzehen gůldin.Die fünfft zwölff gůldin.Dye sechst zehen gůldin.Die sibend acht gůldin.Die acht sechs gůldin.Die nůnd vier gůldin.Die zehend zwen gůldin.Vnd der aller erst nam vnd die des hat ein gůldin.vnnd der letzt ouch ein gůldin.Wer es aber das in dem ersten od letzten zedel eyn gab kem/so hat er den gůldin vnnd die gab dar zů.Vnd welcher inlegen wil der sol für ein iglichen namen inlegen vier heidelberger pfennig.Vnd so offt er ein namen lat schriben.so ler vt er pfennig inlegen.als offt wurt ein vngeschickter zedel auch ingeleit in ein andern haffen inleit.des nam vnd zůnam.vn von wanne er sey.oder wer für yn ingeleit hab.sol also eygtlich vff geschtibe werde.Vn wem also etwas gefelt er sy im land wo er wol.sol im getrewlich behalte werde

Vnd fürter so 3s obgemelt schiessen ein end hat.wurt man die plünde die zů heidelberg syn vn kome werde zů kurtzwillig vß geb.Temliche eyn saw vor vry gůldin.also in der gestalt man wurt mache eyn schrancken.Vnd mitten dar in eyn pfol mit eyne vmb lauffen tinck dar an dye saw an eyn strick binden.Vnd eyn iglichen blinden in synem harrnasch in dye schrancken in syn stant stellen mit eim kolben.Vnnd welcher dye saw zů vot schlecht.des ist dye saw.

Welcher auch an die schiessen vn kurtzwillung der die wer gerad kegelschiß vn haffen gewynne wurt.der sol von eym gůldin eyn wißpfennig geb den knechtren do mit 3s lonen die der ding warten werden vnd 3a mit vmb geen.Dar vmb bite ich üch mit fründlichem fliß iwer schießgesellen zů sollichem schiessen vnd kurtzwillung vertigen vnd schicken.Auch andern iwern vmbstossen vnd nachbawren edeln vnd vnedeln auch verkünden vnd mit üch pringen das wil ich willig syn alle zeit vmb üch zůuerdienen. Ich ban auch an mynem gnedigsten herren pfaltzgrauen vnd Cösür sten.erlangt.das alle schützen vnd andere zů zů schiessens 1 zů kurtzwillung gen heidelberg kommen werden fry.starck.sicher vngeuerlich ge/leit haben sollen.vßgenomen syner gnaden offen finde.vnd die isenen die vff syner gnaden schad gewest sint.das noch nit verricht oder vertra/gen ist.Auch den syner gnade landt verbotten ist Geben zů heydelberg vnder mynem Ingesigel getruckt zů endt dißer schrifft Vff Dinstag noch des Sontag Vocem iocunditatis.Anno etc.Nonagesimo.

Abb. 113: Unterer Abschnitt aus derselben Quelle wie Abb. 112, Hervorhebung durch Hinzufügen eines blauen Pfeils, C.R.

Diese Einladungsbriefe haben offensichtlich schon eine längere Tradition: Um 15 Jahre älter, aber im Grunde schon identisch strukturiert, ist die Einladung zu einem Armbrustschießen aus Ulm 1478 mit 83 Zeilen, das handschriftlich an das fränkische Allersheim adressiert ist.[183]

[Gw M50312: *Verteidigung der Rechte des Deutschen Ordens auf die Balleien Apulien und Sizilien*] „nach 25.VII.1492".[184] Die Zuschreibung an Knoblochtzer wird nach der schon bekannten, aus Ulm stammenden *D*-Initiale zu Beginn des Textes vorgenommen: *Der Teutsche orden. Ist. Als das offenbar am tage ligt/ Jnn seier ersten Stifftung gesetzt [...] Uff den Adel/ der Teutschen nacion …*[185]

Ähnlich gelagert ist [Gw 12882: HOHENLOHE, KRAFT GRAF VON: *Klage beim Schwäbischen Bund gegen die Stadt Schwäbisch Hall. Neuenstein, 29.IV.1493*]: Darin ist mehrfach auf ‚Missiven', also Sendschreiben, Bezug genommen, eine Gattung von amtlichen Schreiben, für deren Anfertigung in *Formulare und deutsch Rhetorica* (1488) eine Anweisung vermittelt wird (s. o. Kap. 4). Da ein Digitalisat von den verzeichneten drei erhaltenen Exemplaren nicht vorhanden ist, gebe ich die Inhaltsskizze aus *Gw*:

---

[183] AMELUNG: *FDSW*, Nr. 34, S. 108; Dieser Brief war ERNST FREYS 1912 noch nicht bekannt.

[184] Datum ermittelt nach dem Todesdatum Papst Innozenz' VIII., das auf der verso-Seite erwähnt wird. Vgl. auch *VE 15*, D-4.

[185] Zitiert nach dem Eintrag in *VE 15*, Typengenauigkeit leicht vereinfacht.

[1ʳ] *Den gemeinen hauptlewten des bundes zu ſwaben*

[1ᵛ] *MEin freuntlichen dinſt alles gut vnd gunſtlichen gruß zuuor Wolgeborner freuntlicher lieber Schwager vnd beſunder lieber In vergangen tagen han ich vch gemeinen hauplewten vnd auch der verſamlung des Bundes zů Swaben Die vff montag nach Conceptionis marie negſtuergangen zu Vlme bei einander geweſen ſind geſchrieben* […]

[3ᵛ, Z. 11] … *Datum Newenſtein vff Montag nach dem Sontag Iubilate Anno .M.cccc.xciij. Crafft Graue von Hohenloe vnd zů ziegennhain etc. Darnach han die von halle Nach beſchluſſe yr miſſiue etliche Clage Artickel wieder mich der ſelben yr miſſiue angehangen Darvff bitte ich mein antwort zůuerne*men […]

[4ʳ, Z. 34] … *Aber wan die zeit das erheyſchen würdet/ wyll ich dapfferer artickel vnd ſpruche dan die von halle angezeigt han noch zethůn wyſſen/ fürpryngen/ Aber die zů dieſem malen vß vrſache verhalten.*

Eine gute Vorstellung von dieser Art der Publizierung von Klagen, Drohbriefen und Beschwerden gewinnt man, wenn man das im *Gw* verzeichnete *Ausschreiben* dazu nimmt, das in diesem Fall nun vom Schwäbischen Bund ausging und sich gegen den Raubzug von Hans Lindenschmid gegen ein Mitglied des Bundes richtet.[186]

Aus den Jahren 1496–1498, kurz nachdem Knoblochtzer noch das riesige Auftragswerk für Drach in Speyer, die lateinische Ausgabe der Werke Vergils, ‚gestemmt‘ hatte, sind dann Knoblochtzers Typen nur noch in diesen kleinen Drucken nachzuweisen, die inhaltlich dem eben Beschriebenen vergleichbar sind. Das legt die Vermutung nahe, dass sie evtl. nach Niedergang der Offizin gar nicht mehr von Heinrich Knoblochtzer selbst angefertigt wurden:

[Gw M33125: KURFÜRST PHILIPP VON DER PFALZ: *Ausschreiben betr. Übernahme des Reichsvikariats*]: Einblattdrucke, die auf Kurfürst Philipp d. A. zurückgehen, sind nur sehr wenige überliefert (drei Nummern bei *VE 15*: P-220 bis P-222, zwei davon Prüss in Straßburg zugeordnet): *Philips von gots gnaden Pfaltzgraue bei Rein Hertzog in Beyern des heiligen Romischen richs Erttzdruchseß vnd Kurfurst* beginnt das einseitig bedruckte Blatt von 32 Zeilen (zitiert nach *VE 15*, P-221), die Datierung am Schluss lautet: *Datum heydelberg vff Samstag nach Bartholomej Apostoli. Anno domini Milesimo quadragentesimo Nonagesimo Sexto* (zitiert nach *VE 15*, wie zuvor). Sie gibt den Termin der Ausfertigung an, nicht des Drucks, weshalb *Gw* „nach 27.VIII.1496" datiert.

[Gw M47454 und M4745410: TRATT, HANS VON: *Ausschreiben über seinen Handel mit der Stadt Weißenburg*] „nach 17.I.1497": Mit einer Flut von Höflichkeitsfloskeln beginnt das Schreiben, mit dem sich Tratt gegen die Verleumdungen und Übergriffe der Stadt Weißenburg verwahrt:[187] *(A)llen vnd jglichen hochwirdigen durchluchtigen hoch vnd wolgebornen Erwirdigen wirdigen edeln strengen vesten Ersamen fürnemen wisen Geistlichen [...] Embiet ich hans vom dradt Ritter der pfaltz marschalck*

---

[186] Gw M40956–M40959, und auch AMELUNG: *FDSW*, Nr. 152, S. 342.

[187] Genauere Beschreibung in *VE 15*, T-23 und 24, daraus auch die folgende Transkription (im Typenrepertoire leicht vereinfacht).

Min vndertenig schuldig gehorsam willig früntlich dinst. Dass sich Hans von Tratt für die Austragung seiner Streitigkeiten und Reklamierung seiner Rechte gerne des neuen Mediums Druck bediente, belegen zwei weitere, ähnlich lautende Einträge unter seinem Namen im *Gw*, eine davon von Drach in Speyer gedruckt (M4745310).

[Gw M51378: WALBRUN, HANS UND PHILIP VON: *Beschwerde über die Ermordung ihres Vaters Hans von Walbrun durch seinen Bruder*]: Das Ausschreiben, das mit einer Flechtwerk-*A*-Initiale aus Knoblochtzers Repertoire beginnt, wendet sich an die *Gnedigsten vnd gnedigen lieben herren vnd guten fründe* (Z. 5)[188] mit der Versicherung, dass die beiden Ausfertigenden, Hans und Philip von Walbrunn, von der Ermordung ihres Vaters ausgehen: *vns zwyffelt nit der große vnmeßlich vnnatürlicher freflicher mort vnd strafwirdig vbel an hern hanßen von walbrün ritter vnserrn lieben vatter seligen durch syn brůder [...]* (Z. 5 f.). Darauf folgt eine Skizze über den Lebenslauf des mutmaßlich Ermoderten und die Aufforderung, den Mörder *Crafft des heilligen richs ordenung zů worms* (Z. 41) zur Rechenschaft zu ziehen. Ausgefertigt ist das Dokument *vff sant Symon vnd judas obent Anno domini millesimo Quadringentesimo Nonagesimo Octauo* (= 27.10.1498).[189] Der Druck selbst wird von *Gw* und *Ve 15* „vor 13.I.1499" datiert.

10   Erzählende Literatur (überwiegend *delectatio*)

Zwischen Information, Panegyrik und erzählender Literatur ist der 460 Reimpaare umfassende *hubsche spruch* angesiedelt, der nur in diesem Druck (ohne Zeilenumbruch bei den Reimpaaren) überliefert ist [Gw 09056: DRABSANFT, MATTHIAS: *Von den Schlachten in Holland*] und in dem *Mathiß Drabsanfft [...]* seinem/seinen Befehlshaber(n) und dem König Maximilian *zu dienst und zu eren* in 460 Reimpaaren teils aus eigener Anschauung die Ereignisse bei der Niederschlagung eines „Aufstand[s] der holländischen Adelspartei" schildert.[190]

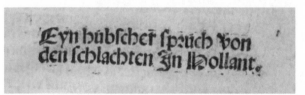

Abb. 114: SBB Berlin, PK, Inc. 1206, 8 [https://digital.staatsbibliothek-berlin.de/werkansicht? PPN=PPN818846801&PHYSID=PHYS_0005&DMDID=], 1ʳ (Ausschnitt).

---

[188]   Zitate nach Abb. 98 im ersten Band von *Ve 15*, dort auch weitere Information unter W-1, Bd. 3, S. 596.

[189]   Zitiert nach *Ve 15*, W-1 unter Korrektur der Druckfehler der Inkunabel.

[190]   FRIEDER SCHANZE: *Drabsanft, Mathis*, in: ²*Vl* 2 (1979), Sp. 220 f.

gewan ... ...
fronlichnams abent.das die frōmen lantzknecht myn
gnedigen herzen stalmeister den selben ritter her Johā
Alweg zū eyne hūth pfennig gaben
    Disse schlacht haben ir wol vernōmen.die stat roter
dam ist ritterlich vnd erlich gewunnen.Das man sie by
lijb vnnd gūt hat gelassen.des hant sie jglichem knecht
ein pfunt groß das ist ein monet solt: sie sullen habē jrē
eigenen herzē den vßerwelten Romschen kunig also
bolt so als sie das thun so mogēt sie ire stat vffricht han
    Item Matbiß drabsanfft hat dissen spruch
gedicht zu dienst vnd zu eren meim herzen
stalmeister vnd berz Jacob silberkamern
vnd allen frōmē lantzknechtē Und vnserm
aller Durchluchtigstē herren dē Romschē kunig.

Ein fehlerhafter Druck des Blattes, dessen obere Ränder nach Faltung auf 3^r und 4^v
(von insgesamt 6 Bll.) zu liegen kamen (Abb. hier 4^v), dürfte als ‚Mängelexemplar'
auch damals „um 1489" schon zu einer Wertminderung des Heftchens geführt haben:

... ...
Su bast vns bracht jn disse noit.Die da floben Sē gyng
es auch nyt wol.sie lieffen jn eyn schiff Das wart zu vol
Das es ist vnder gesuncken.Die selben.synt alle gader er
druncken.   Eyn ander Schlacht:
    was ich vch sagen Das ist war.Das ist gescheen jm

Der künstlerische Wert der Arbeit war ohnehin überschaubar, das zeigt eine Kost-
probe von Bl. 3^v: *Die slacht wol wir lassen faren. Vnd wollen von eyner frisschen
nŭwen sagen, die vff dem wasser ist geschen. Ritter vnd knecht hant das gethan man-
cher stoltzer man hat das gesehen. Do es wart am viij. tag noch vnsers heren vffartz.
Den man nent den non tag. Nŭn merckent jr herren was ich vch sag. Do gebrach den
von rotterdam. Fleisch brot wyn vnd ander profand.* Die Punkte sollen wohl überwiegend die Reime markieren.

[Gw 12795 und 12796: *Historia. Sigenot.* 1490 und 1493, erstere Inkunabel mit
Beigabe einer Exempelerzählung vom *Rosenkranz unserer lieben Frauen*, s. o. Kap. 8]:
Wie schon beim *Ackermann von Böhmen* (s. o. Kap. 6) ergab sich (wohl nicht zu-
fällig) ein Einfluss der Interessen, die sich in der kurfürstlichen Bibliothek ablesen

lassen, auf Knoblochtzers Druckprogramm bei einem weiteren Druckwerk von 1490 (und 1493), das nun eindeutig eher der *delectatio* zuzuordnen ist: Es handelt sich um die in heldenepischen Strophen abgefasste Erzählung von den abenteuerlichen Erlebnissen des Dietrich von Bern (historisch eigentlich Theoderich der Große; *Bern* = ,Verona') mit dem Riesen ,Sigenot', in dessen Gefangenschaft der Held zeitweise gerät, jedoch von seinem ,Mentor' und Meister Hildebrand wieder befreit werden kann. Der von der Germanistik etablierte Titel *Sigenot*, den auch der *Gw* übernommen hat, ist hier etwas irreführend, im Mittelalter und auch hier im Druck lief das Werk unter dem Titel *her Diethrich von Berñ,*

Abb. 117a (oben) und 117b (unten): SBB Berlin, PK, 4° Inc. 1200 [https://digital.staatsbibliothek-berlin.de/werkansicht?PPN=PPN729131610&PHYSID=PHYS_0005&DMDID=], 1ʳ (117a) und [https://digital.staatsbibliothek-berlin.de/werkansicht?PPN=PPN729131610&PHYSID=PHYS_0045&DMDID=], 21ʳ (117b) (jeweils Ausschnitt).

Auch dieser Text war (wie der *Ackermann von Böhmen*) in einer handschriftlichen Fassung aus der berühmten Henfflin-Werkstatt[191] Bestandteil der Büchererbschaft von Margarethe von Savoyen an ihren kurpfälzischen Sohn Philipp (Cpg 67).[192] Doch mag der Druck auch daher angeregt worden sein, direkt abhängig sind die Heidelberger Inkunabeln nicht von der Handschrift der kurpfälzischen Bibliothek: Mit Blick auf die Verwandtschaft der Darstellung des Eröffnungsbildes könnte man meinen, Knoblochtzer habe die Heidelberger Handschrift für seinen Inkunabeldruck zum Vorbild genommen:

Abb. 118a (links) und 118b (rechts): UB Heidelberg, Cpg 67 [https://digi.ub.uni-heidelberg. de/diglit/cpg67/0007] 1ʳ (118a) und SBB Berlin, wie oben: [https://digital.staatsbibliothek-berlin. de/werkansicht?PPN=PPN729131610&PHYSID=PHYS_0007&DMDID=], Bl. 2ʳ (118b) (Ausschnitt).

Der Text des Druckes hängt aber, so ergab eine Kollationierung der beiden Textzeugen, nicht von Cpg 67 ab.[193] Und eine weitere Umschau belegt, dass Knoblochtzers Holzschnitte vereinfachte, seitenverkehrte Nachschnitte einer Augsburger Inkunabel aus dem Jahre 1487/88 sind, von der sich nur wenige Seiten erhalten haben:

---

[191] Vgl. dazu die überaus instruktive Seite von ULRIKE SPYRA und MARIA EFFINGER von 2012: https://digi.ub.uni-heidelberg.de/de/bpd/glanzlichter/oberdeutsche/henfflin.html (6.10.2020).

[192] Vgl. BACKES (1992), S. 184, ZIMMERMANN (1999), S. 17.

[193] So auch die Neuedition des *Sigenot* von E. LIENERT/E. PONTINI/S. BAUMGARTEN, Berlin/ Boston 2020 (*Texte und Studien zur mittelhochdeutschen Heldenepik 12*), S. 47.

Abb. 119a (links) und 119b (rechts): BSB München, Rar. 317 [Ink S-382], Gw 12794, [http://daten.digitale-sammlungen.de/bsb00017547/image_4], (Fragment) (119a) und SBB Berlin, wie oben [https://digital.staatsbibliothek-berlin.de/werkansicht?PPN=PPN729131610&PHYSID=PHYS_0025&DMDID=], Bl. 11ʳ (119b) (jeweils Ausschnitt).

Für seine zweite Ausgabe dieses offensichtlich erfolgreichen Titels von 1493 [Gw 12796] verwendet Knoblochtzer die Holzschnitte nochmals.[194] Den Text aber muss er neu setzen, erreicht durch geschickteren Umbruch eine Reduzierung des Papieraufwands von vorher 22 auf jetzt 20 Bll. Von dieser zweiten Auflage ist nur ein, zudem sehr ramponiertes Exemplar erhalten (GNM Nürnberg, Inc. 4° 76786, Digitalisat vorhanden). Dass auch von zwei weiteren Drucken aus Reutlingen 1495 und Nürnberg „nach 1500(?)" [Gw 12796 und 12799] nur Fragmente überliefert sind, spricht für den intensiven Gebrauch des Textes beim mittelalterlichen Leser. Möglicherweise sind einige Auflagen auch ganz verloren gegangen. Auch noch erhalten sind zwei Exemplare einer Erfurter Ausgabe von 1499 [Gw 12798], die als Bildprogramm nur die Eröffnungsszene (Dietrich und Hildebrand im Gespräch) als größeren Nachschnitt der bekannten Muster aus Augsburg und Heidelberg in der Funktion des Titelblattes bietet.

---

[194] Die von HEITZ/RITTER übernommenen Angaben zu den Abhängigkeitsverhältnissen der Holzschnittfolgen in den beiden Heidelberger Ausgaben bei LIENERT/PONTINI/BAUMGARTEN: *Sigenot* (vgl. vorherige Fußnote), S. 22 sind etwas missverständlich. Es wurde einfach in der Ausgabe von 1493 ein Holzschnitt auf Bl. 17ʳ und 18ʳ doppelt verwendet, wo in der älteren Ausgabe (18ᵛ und 19ᵛ) noch zwei verschiedene Illustrationen eingesetzt worden waren.

[Gw 10289: Frankfurter, Philipp: *Der Pfarrer vom Kalenberg*]: Von diesem Werk, dessen Entstehung man sich um 1470 in Wien vorstellt,[195] hatte Knoblochtzer möglicherweise Kenntnis durch Mechthild von der Pfalz (*1419), die in zweiter Ehe mit Erzherzog Albrecht VI. von Österreich (†1463) verheiratet war und nach dessen Tod den ‚Musenhof' in Rottenburg unterhielt. Mit der eben (beim ‚Sigenot') schon erwähnten Margarethe von Savoyen war sie doppelt verschwägert und starb 1482 in Heidelberg.[196] Das Werk ist handschriftlich gar nicht, in Drucken nur sehr schlecht überliefert. Die beiden Ausgaben aus Augsburg 1480 und der niederdeutsche Druck aus Lübeck „nicht vor 1500" sind in keinem Exemplar vollständig überliefert, einige Inkunabelausgaben, so vermutet der *Gw*, dürften auch „verlorengegangen" sein.

Im selben Jahr wie die Heidelberger Inkunabel „[14]90", kam eine auch in Nürnberg heraus (60 Bll. in 8°, 36 Holzschnitte). Die Heidelberger Ausgabe ist mit 38 kleinen Illustrationen ausgestattet, wobei das letzte Bildchen bereits zu einer Reimpaar-Erzählung *von dem aller schonsten ritter Alexander vnnd von seiner schonen frauwen* gehört,[197] die Knoblochtzer auf frei gebliebenem Papier seiner Folioausgabe von 19 Bll. zur Steigerung der Attraktivität noch beigibt. Die Scheu, leeres Papier zu verkaufen, war offensichtlich in diesem Fall so groß, dass Knoblochtzer auf der Verso-Seite des Titelblattes:

Despfaffen geschicht vnd
histori vom kalenberg.
Auch von dem aller schon
sten ritter Alexander vnnd
von seiner schonen frauwē.

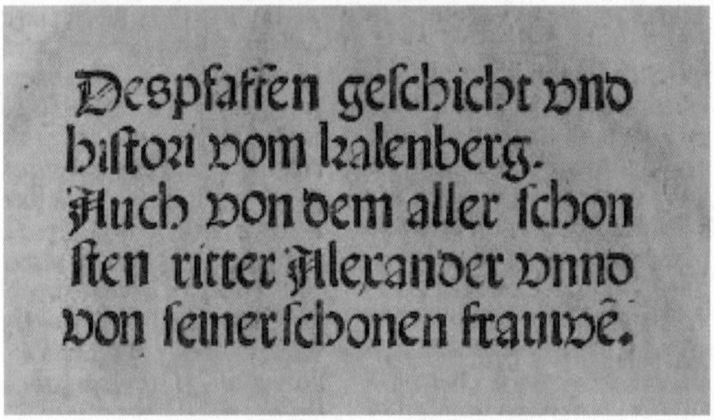

Abb. 120: ULB Darmstadt Inc. III-29 [http://tudigit.ulb.tu-darmstadt.de/show/inc-iii-29/0001/image], 1^{r} (Ausschnitt).

auch noch den informierenden Text darüber beigibt, *was zeyt vnd monat im iar ein ieglicher visch am besten sey* (s. o. Kap. 9 A).

Am Ende des Kerntextes vom *Pfarrer vom Kalenberg* ist der Autor genannt:

[195] Vgl. Hellmut Rosenfeld: *Frankfurter, Philipp*: in: ^{2}*VL* 2 (1979), Sp. 817–820.

[196] Vgl. auch das Kapitel 4.2. „Die Rolle der adligen Damen" in: Backes (1992): S. 171–191.

[197] Über das Märe, „das in ungewöhnlicher Weise eine Ehebruchsgeschichte mit dem Thema der treuen Minne" verbindet, vgl. Frieder Schanze: ‚*Ritter Alexander*', in: ^{2}*VL* 8 (1992), Sp. 94 f.

Dô selb der pfarer gestorben ist
got sy mit im zü aller frist
zu siner hochen ewekeyt
Vn maria dye reine meit
Also will ich lossen do von
wer ynder do eyn bidermann
Vn der noch wyter wer gewesen
dan ich / vn het sun mer gelesen
Der mag es wol setzen her zü
wol beyde spat vn auch frü
Blybt es von mir vnußgeschlagen
ich wolt im des danck sagen
Wänynder lebt uff erden kein man
der alle ding gantz wyssen kan
Darumb bit ich euch all gemeyn
arm reich groß vn auch klein
All dy die legend hören lesen
das sie mir wollen gnedig wesen
Mit iren worten vn schimpff
das er mir nit bring vngelimpff
Ob ich zü lützel oder zü vyl
vn nyt begriffen het das zyl
das macht das ich bin vngelert
vn sich dy kunst byn von mir kert
Darumb ist myn gemüt so schwer
so redt phillip franckfurter
Zü wien in der löblichen stat
der das zü rymen gemacht hat

Vn hört von eyner hystorien
wie eyner erlost ward vo sorgen
Der bübst ritter von bar vnd leib
vn het das aller schönst weiß
als sie in wyten landen was
ir beider schon waß an maß
Dar zü er eren halb nit ließ
der ritter alexander hieß
Vnd was von gebürt ein frantzoß
mit schilt sper zü fuß zü roß
Ward maniger helt von im verseret
vn bezwungen mit dem schwert
Deß halb sein lob erhalt gar weit
daß dort ein herolt uff ein zeit
Vn sprach got hat ye gethon
sunder gnad an disem man
Vn sinem weib mit großer schon
doch ob ir ein andere cron
Die wont zü lon in engelant
do wirt dye schönst euch bekant
Die lang geboren ward vo eine wiß
do dacht der ritter minen lieb
mag ich do bin wie es mir gee
vnd solt ich kumen nömer mer
Nicht dan ein knecht er mit im nam
vnd alß er in dye stat dort kam
Gar offt er den weg mit füßen maß
Vn alß sie einest darauß drat

Item von eynem frantz osische ritter
der dz aller schönst wyep het in siner
riter. vn wie er noch mit einer schön/
ern in einem andern land sin ee brach
da durch dy beide in den thun gelit
wurten. vn wie sin recht ee weip si
beyde erledigt von dem tod

Abb. 121: ULB Darmstadt Inc. III-29 [http://tudigit.ulb.tu-darmstadt.de/show/inc-iii-29/0034/image], 17ᵛ (Ausschnitt, Hervorhebung durch Hinzufügen eines blauen Pfeils, C. R.).

Am Ende des ganzen Druckwerkes, also nach der Geschichte *Vom Ritter Alexander* nennt sich der Drucker, eingebunden in ein letztes haarsträubendes Reimpaar, das immerhin verrät, dass man sich als Leserschaft dieses Textes hauptsächlich weibliches Publikum vorstellte:

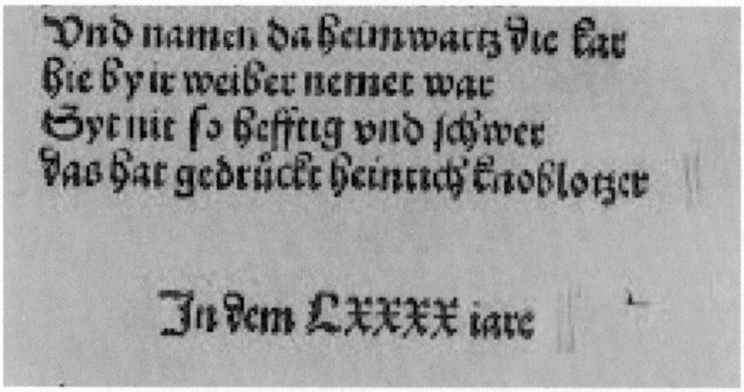
Vnd namen da heimwartz die hat
hie by ir weiber nemet war
Syt nit so hefftig vnd schwer
Das hat gedrückt heinrich knoblotzer

In dem LXXXX iare

Abb. 122: ULB Darmstadt Inc. III-29 [http://tudigit.ulb.tu-darmstadt.de/show/inc-iii-29/0037/image], 19^r (Ausschnittt).

Möglicherweise ist der Druck am Rande auch vom Interesse des Humanistenkreises motiviert, der ja ganz offensichtlich auch Einfluss auf Knoblochtzers Druckprogramm nahm. Man denke an die Schwankbeigaben im 4. Buch der *Mensa philosophica* (Kap. 5). Dann wäre ein möglicher Gebrauchszusammenhang der Schwanksammlung auch kurzweilige Tischunterhaltung, eine Art weltliche Tischlesung.

[Gw 12663 *Historia. Melusine*, deutsch]: Von einer französischen Prosafassung dieses (auch seinem Ursprung nach französischen) Stoffes von Jean d'Arras sind ebenfalls Inkunabeln erhalten (Gw 12649–12654, „1478" bis „um 1498"). Erstaunlich ist jedoch, dass dieser Text auch im deutschsprachigen Raum eine breite Rezeption fand. Sie fußt auf der deutschsprachigen Prosa des Berner Stadtbeamten Thüring von Ringoltingen,[198] dessen Bearbeitung allerdings auf die Versfassung „des poitevinischen Dichters Couldrette" zurück geht (Jan-Dirk Müller, Sp. 908). Die *delectatio* über die Wundergeschichte von Melusine, die, halb Mensch halb Meerwesen, den in Not geratenen Fürsten Raimund nicht nur rettet, sondern ihn auch heiratet, scheint den genealogischen Aspekt der Geschichte (aus den reichlich männlichen Nachkommen, die alle mit einem ‚Muttermal' versehen sind, leitet ein französisches Adelsgeschlecht seine Herkunft ab), im deutschen Sprachraum überwogen zu haben. Den eigentlichen Motivationskern für die Geschichte, nämlich, dass Melusine ihre Ehe mit Raimund davon abhängig macht, dass sie sich jeden Samstag von ihm unbeobachtet in das ursprüngliche Mischwesen zurückverwandeln darf, und ihr Mann aber eines Tages dagegen verstößt und damit eine Katastrophe auslöst, verschweigt die Vorrede der Heidelberger Inkunabel vom 13.12.1491 zugunsten einer ambitionierten Wahrheitsbeteuerung (in Übersetzung)[199]: ‚Diese abenteuerliche Geschichte erzählt uns von einer Dame namens Melusine, einer Meerfrau von königlicher Abstammung, die aus dem Berge Avalon gekommen war. Dieser Berg liegt in Frankreich. Und diese Meerfrau wurde jeden Samstag vom Nabel abwärts ein lang-

[198] Jan-Dirk Müller: *Thüring von Ringoltingen*, in: ^{2}*VL* 9 (1995), Sp. 908–914.

[199] Meiner Übersetzung liegt der kritisch edierte Text von Karin Schneider zu Grunde: *Thüring von Ringoltingen, ‚Melusine'*, Berlin 1958 (*Texte des späten Mittelalters 9*), S. 36. Die Inkunabel enthält nämlich einige Druckfehler, die eine Übersetzung schwer machen.

gestrecktes Drachenwesen, da sie zur Hälfte ein Geistwesen hatte. Es stammten von ihr auch große, mächtige Geschlechter ab mit Königen, Fürsten, Grafen, freien Rittern und Knechten, deren Nachkommen noch heute namhafte Leute dieses Standes sind, woran man erkennt, dass diese Geschichte durch eigene Erfahrbarkeit zeigt, dass sie voll und ganz der Wahrheit entspricht.'

Abb. 123: GNM Nürnberg, Inc. 4° 101382; Knoblochtzer, Heidelberg 1491 [http://dlib.gnm.de/item/4Inc101382/7], 2ʳ (Ausschnitt).

Deutsche Inkunabelausgaben sind nun sogar älter (schon ab 1474) und zahlreicher (zumindest erhalten) als die französichen. Zehn Ausgaben verzeichnet der *Gw*, neun hoch- eine niederdeutsche: Gw 12655–12664. Die ältesten stammen aus Augsburg und Basel (Gw 12655 und 12656), vier Druckausgaben gehen allein auf Knoblochtzer zurück, drei davon entstanden in Straßburg und eine in Heidelberg. In der Ästhetik der Präsentation und auch der Zahl und Art der Holzschnitte folgt Knoblochtzer in seinen Straßburger Ausgaben (Gw 12657, 12658, 12661: „um 1477"/„um 1481/83") ganz der Inkunabel aus Basel (Gw 12656: „um 1474"), doch kann er den Papieraufwand durch entsprechende Typen- und Satzwahl von 100 zunächst auf 79, dann auf 64 Bll. absenken (allesamt 2° Format).

epmõd do der dise grüſſenlich vñ frõmde geſchöp
ffet Ȼn ſinē gemahel geſach Do ward er gar ſer be
kũmbert vñ von allē ſunem gemũtte betrũbt/vñ er-
ſchrack vs der acht võ diſer geſicht/ vñ ſtund alſo
võ vozcht/m groſſen ſozge dz im der ſchweis võ nöt vs gieng/
doch er beſinte ſich vñ vmacht dis lochlin/ ſo er mit dē ſwert
gemacht hat/wider mit emē tüchlin/ vñ wachs vñ vſach ſich
mit dz es ſm gemahel befundē het/Was er geton hatte vñ ker
te do mit ſchwigēde võ danné m groſſem zozn vnd wider mũt
vber ſmē bzuder vñ er beſigelt nũ dis loch wol vñ widerumbe
das niemāt hm geſehē möcht vñ kam do wider zũ ſmē bzuder
Ȼn groſſem zozn vñ gzymikeit/do m der bzuder ſach kome do
bedũcht m wol/repmõd wer vaſt zozmg/vñ vſach ſich er hett
ſm wip meluſmē an etwas vnerlicher getätt vnd an vntruwen

Abb. 124: SBB Berlin, 4° Inc 2223; Knoblochtzer, Straßburg 1478 (Gw 12658) [https://digital.
staatsbibliothek-berlin.de/werkansicht?PPN=PPN729132951&PHYSID=PHYS_0079&
DMDID=], 38ʳ (Ausschnitt).

In der Heidelberger Ausgabe reduziert Knoblochtzer den Umfang dann auf gar nur
40 Bll. in 4°. Das war freilich nur durch den Einsatz neuer, kleinerer Holzschnitte im
spiegelverkehrten Nachschnitt der Straßburger Bilder zu erreichen:

vnd herberg an do in er dē ymes gehebt
hat an vn verbrāt vn verbarß ð virt vn
alles sein haußgesind kint vn diener·vn
sich man noch dy geübē des bauß.nū kū
ich wid an dy hystory vn füget sich auff
eine samßstag.Dz Reimōd Melusinenn
aber verlore het alß auch and samßstag
doch het er sy nit darūß versucht noch ie
nach gefragt vn sun geluß vn eið gehal
ēe dan er auch dan gūts vn nit arges ni
gedacht.vn ist ð zeit eben do wz ð graff
vom Vorst Reimōds vatter abgägen
mit dez tod.Darūß so kaz sein brūd ð elt
est ð do zū mol graff wz zū. Lusiune zū
sein brūd ð in gar schön vn erlich entpfy
eng vn dis wz zū einer hochzit Dz dy gra
ssen vn lands herrē zū Hoff zū. irez herrē
geritten warent do sprach ð graff vom
Vorst zū sein brūd.lyeber brūð geyssent
eweren gemahel her jur zū iren vn euwe
ren gesten kümen vn sy entpfohen vnd
in er an thō alß ir gezimbt. Reimōd ant
wurt vn sprach.lieber brūd laßt vch nyt
bekangen morgen soll ir sy sehen also
wart nū ð ymbiß geben erlich vn nach
dez ymbiß do nam ð graff vom Vorst
sein brūd besund vn sprach Reimōd lie
ber brūd ich besorge ir sient verzoubert
vn dz ist ein gantz lantmer.vnd spricht
menglich ir sint nit wol bedacht das ir
nit sollent noch getörent ewer gemahel
noch fragen wo sy oð wye sich halt am
samstag.vn ist ein fremde sach dz ir nyt
solt wissen wz ir gewerb thō oder kössen
sy.Vn ich müß es vch sagen ir hant sein
grosse vnere vn kind rede vil.dan etlich
meinent sy treibe bübery vnd baß ander
leut lieber dan vch etlich sprechent es sye
ein gespenste vn ein vngehür wesen vm
sy.Dis sag ich vch als meynem brüder
vnd rat vch daß ir gedenckt zū wissen wz
ir gewerb seyg daß ir nit also zū einem to
ren gemacht vn ir von ir geefft werden
Reymond do er dise mer hort do wart
er von zorn rot darnach bleich vnd kert
an mer wort von seinem brūder in groß

grimigkeit vnd in herten zorn vn ging
gar schnelle vn nam sein schwert vnnd
lieff an ein kammer vor in er vor nie kū
men was.dan.Melusyna die ie selbs zū
ir heimlichkeit gebauwen het vnd kam
an ein eisine tür do stūð er vnnð gedacht
wz im zū thō wer nach seins brūð wor/
ten also, do kaz ym zū sinnen vn geda/
chte das sein weib gegen ym vntrulich
für vn büberey tryb vnð villicht yetz an
sollichem end wer des sy laster vn vnere
het.er zoch sein schwert auß vn sucht wo
er möcht ein loch finden do durch er sins
gemahels gewerb sehe vnd do durch er
der worheit innen wart vn aiß zwiffel
kummen mocht vn macht myt seinem
schwert ein loch durch die tür.Ach wye
werckte er im selbs do so groß vbel dan
er verlor do durch alle freud vn lüst Py
ser zeyt Reymonð sach nū durch dz loch
hin in vn sach dz sein weybe inn einem
bad nacket saß vnd sy was von dem na
bel auff auß der achte ein schön weiblich
bild vo seib vn angesicht schön. aber vo
deznabel hin ab wz sy ein groser sauger
wurmß. vo blower lasur mit weisser sil
bere farwe vn dar vnd silberin tröpflin
gesprenget vndeinand als ein schlang.

Wye Reimōd melusinen im bad sa
ch vn er vbel erschrack vn in grossen zo/
ren seine brūd vō im schickt wan er im ar
ges vō Melusinē sagt Dz ab er nit sun
den het

Abb. 125: GNM Nürnberg, Inc. 4° 101382; Knoblochtzer, Heidelberg 1491 [http://dlib.gnm.de/
item/4Inc101382/44], 20ᵛ (Ausschnitt).

Gleichwohl wurde die Attraktivität des Werkes durch den Einsatz zahlreicher
Initialenholzschnitte gesteigert, von denen ziemlich alle Versionen, die wir aus
Knoblochtzers Drucken bisher schon kennengelernt hatten, hier wieder erschei-
nen:

Je watt die hoch zeit an gehabenn mit freuden vnd myt crê. vñ watt do gestochen ge/tantzet vñ kurtz/weil vil getriben Der künig stach zu mol wol vnd wert die hochzeit acht tag. darnach wolten sy von hoff scheiden vnd vrlaub fordern so kumpt ein hott schnell geritten von Behem vnd fragt nach dem künig von Elsas vnd also watt er schnelle in gelossen vñ bracht dez künig brieff do er dye auff getet vnd gelesen hett.

¶ Wye dez künig võ Elsas botschafft kam dz die Türcken seinen brüder dem künig võ Behem Prag beleget hettenn

erschrack er ser vnnd sagt yn al/ leun das ym der künig von Beße botschafft getho vnnd verschriße het. daß der keiser auß der türckey dye stat zu Prag gar mit starckem volck besessen het vnd er von niemant entschüttung noch hie lff west zu habenn dann võ ym vnnd das er ynn vmb hilff vnnd brüderlyche truwe hoch ermanet het vnnd batt der künig zu stund dye beydenn gebrüder mit grossem ernst demütigtlichen das sye vmb der gantzen cristenheyt vnnd vmb seinns brüders dienst willenn auch vmb irs truwen nammen willen wolte dar zu hilff thonn das dye Heydischenn vnnd Türckischenn diet von Behem vß dem land geschlagenn wurdenn vnnd seynn brüder entschüttet wurd. Do ant wurt Antton vnnd sprach. Lyeber her sint vnerschrockenn. Dann wissent sych er furwar meynn brüder Reinhart der soll darfarenn myt vch vnnd mit man gem türenn ritter vnnd soll do zu thon myt der hilff des der alle ding vermag. das dye Heydenn von hannenals ich zu got hoff geschlagenn vnnd vertribenn werdenn. Sollent ir euch auch myt eü/wer macht besammelen vnnd vnd wy der her kummen Als dann so zücht me ynn brüder myt euch.

danckte ym d künig gar flessig lichen vñ sprach. Ist den das vns gelingt als ich zu gott hoff. so hatt mein brüder eyn enig tochter dye ym fast lyeb yst. versprich ich vch by meinenn erenn das

Abb. 126: GNM Nürnberg, Inc. 4° 101382 [http://dlib.gnm.de/item/4Inc101382/34], 15ᵛ (Ausschnitt).

Die werbewirksame Betitelung:

Melosine geschicht.
Mit den figuren.

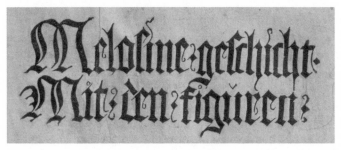

Abb. 127: GNM Nürnberg, Inc. 4° 101382 [http://dlib.gnm.de/item/4Inc101382/5], 1r (Ausschnitt).

weckt also durchaus keine falschen Erwartungen. Der Kolophon weist den maximalen Datensatz der Firmierung einer Inkunabel auf: Drucker, Druckort und genau umschriebenes Datum:

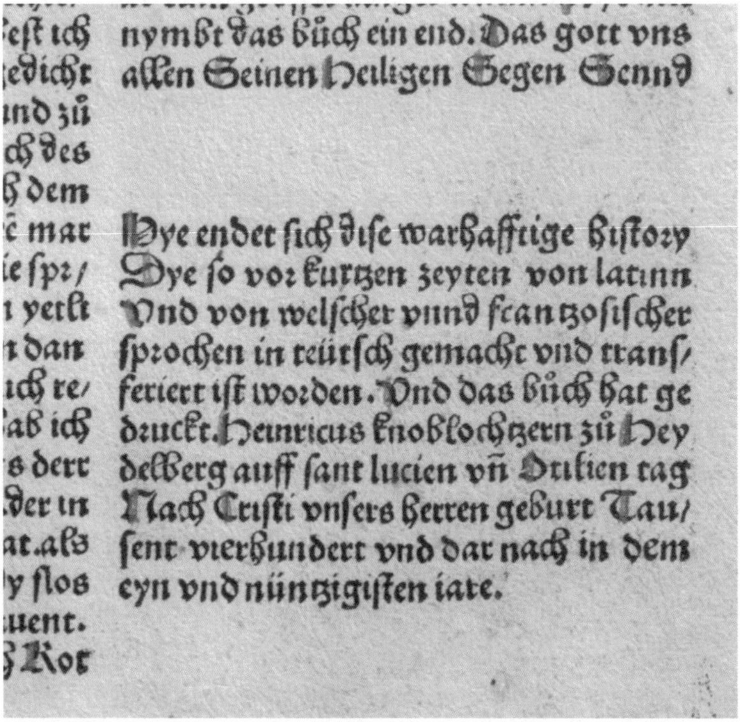
nymbt das büch ein end. Das gott vns
allen Seinen Heiligen Segen Sennd

Hye endet sich dise warhafftige history
Dye so vor kurtzen zeyten von latinn
Vnd von welscher vnnd frantzosischer
sprochen in teütsch gemacht vnd trans/
feriert ist worden. Vnd das büch hat ge
druckt. Heinricus knoblochtzern zü Hey
delberg auff sant lucien vñ Otilien tag
Nach Cristi vnsers herren geburt Tau/
sent vierhundert vnd dar nach in dem
eyn vnd nüntzigisten iare.

Abb. 128: GNM Nürnberg, Inc. 4° 101382 [http://dlib.gnm.de/item/4Inc101382/81], 39r (Ausschnitt).

Vom diesem Heidelberger Druck besitzt das Heidelberger Stadtarchiv ein (nicht ganz vollständiges) Exemplar (SCHLECHTER/RIES 1265).

11   Was nicht gedruckt wurde

An Kontur gewinnt Knoblochtzers Druckprogramm schließlich auch, wenn man es ‚von außen' betrachtet, aus der Warte der Themen nämlich, die aus verschiedenen Gründen ins Repertoire der Heidelberger Offizin hätten aufgenommen werden können. Diese ‚Negativliste' erhebt keinerlei Anspruch auf Vollständigkeit:

Am einfachsten wäre es für Knoblochtzer wohl gewesen, so müsste man denken, in Straßburg schon Gedrucktes in Heidelberg wieder in sein Publikationsprogramm aufzunehmen. Eine *Gw*-Liste, die für Knoblochtzer in Heidelberg 85 Treffer anzeigt, ergibt für Straßburg 72 Titel, das Lebenswerk ist also in etwa gleichmäßig auf die beiden Wirkungsstätten verteilt, doch ist der Umfang an eingesetzten Holzschnitten in Straßburg beträchtlich größer. Eine ungefähre Vorstellung davon vermitteln die Tafeln von A. SCHRAMM.[200] Bei einigen Heidelberger Titeln hat Knoblochtzer ja tatsächlich auf sein Straßburger Druckprogramm zurückgegriffen, wie oben beschrieben: der *Ackermann von Böhmen* hat einen Straßburger Vorläufer (Gw 198), wie auch verschiedene *Almanache* und *Kalender* (Kap. 9 A)[201] und der *Arbor consanguinitatis* des Johannes Andreae in lateinischen und deutschen Fassungen (Gw 1696, 1707, 1719, 1720). Die vielen für die Beichte relevanten Titel aus Heidelberg konnten an Antonius Florentinus: *Confessionale* anknüpfen (Gw 02098), Johannes Versors *Super Donatum* aus Heidelberg schließt an Donats *Ars minor* mit deutscher Interlinearglosse aus Straßburg an (Gw 08973). Das *Formulare und deutsch Rhetorica* wird neu aufgelegt wie auch der *Ordo iudicarius*. Gersons *Ars moriendi* aus Straßburg (Gw 10840) wird mit der deutschen Ausgabe des *Opus tripartitum* in Heidelberg wieder aufgegriffen. Der Sequenz *Unserer Lieben Frau* des Mönchs von Salzburg (Gw 12291) wird diese oben beschriebene, merkwürdige Heidelberger Ausgabe von *Hymni. Hymnarium deutsch* zur Seite gestellt. Die Heidelberger *Melusine* hatte Straßburger Vorläufer (Gw 12657, 12658, 12661), allerdings mit anderem Bildrepertoire (wie oben beschrieben), die *Rosenkranz*-Ausgaben waren ebenso in Straßburg schon im Programm (Gw M 38915 und 38918) wie der *Vocabularius Ex quo* (Gw M5119 und M 5120).

Doch überwiegen die Titel, die Knoblochtzer nicht aufnahm, obwohl sie nach Ausweis der Frühdruckgeschichte oft Erfolg versprechend waren, möglicherweise war der Markt für einige Titel schon gesättigt (vgl. z. B. die *Historia vom Herzog Ernst*). Straßburger Titel, die in Heidelberg nicht aufgegriffen wurden, sind weiterhin ¶ die Fabelsammlung *Aesop* in einer lateinischen und zwei zweisprachigen, von

---

[200] ‚Ungefähr' deshalb, weil SCHRAMM: *Bilderschmuck 19*, Tafeln 4–106 (Bild 11–424 Straßburg, 425–659 Heidelberg) noch nicht alles Material kannte und auch eine problematische Nummerierung der einzelnen Holzschnitte unabhängig von ihrer Größe und Komplexität durchführte.

[201] In Heidelberg wiederholt Knoblochtzer aber nicht den umfangreichen deutschen Kalenderdruck wie Straßburg 1483 (Gw M16012) mit einem opulenten Bildprogramm, vgl. SCHRAMM: *Bilderschmuck 19*, Abb. 83–114.

Heinrich Steinhöwel erstellten Ausgaben (Gw 348, 355, 356 von 1481–1483), die deutlich in der Tradition des berühmten ‚Ulmer Aesop'[202] standen; die drei ‚Topseller' ¶ Petrarcas *Historia Griseldis* in der deutschen Fassung von H. Steinhöwel (Gw M31581 und M31582, Straßburg 1478 und 1482) und ¶ *De duobus amantibus* von Aeneas Silvius Piccolomini (=*De Euriolo et Lucretia*; Gw M33548 und M33550, Straßburg 1477) sowie ¶ *De duobus amantibus* von Brunus Aretinus (=*De amore Guiscardi et Sigismundae*, Gw 5644 und 5645 um 1476/78 und 1482), beide Liebesgeschichten in der Übersetzung von Niklas von Wyle, ¶ die vom Schachspiel abgeleitete Gesellschaftsallegorie *Schachzabelbuch* (= Cessolis, Jacobus de: *De ludo scachorum*, deutsch), um 1478 und 1483, mit je 40 Bll. und 15 bzw. 16 Holzschnitten (GW 6528 und 6530), ¶ zwei kleinere Titel von Geiler von Kaysersberg (Gw 10586 und 10592), ¶ die riesigen Sammlungen lateinischer Sermonen des Johannes Herolt von 524 Blättern (Gw 12387, nicht nach 1477) und Jordanus von Quedlinburg mit 248 Blättern (Gw M15125, nicht nach 1479), ¶ die *Historia vom Herzog Ernst*, eine Inkunabel von 56 Bll. mit 32 Holzschnitten (Gw 12535, um 1477)[203], die in dieser Fassung später mancherorts wiederholt herausgebracht wurde, nicht mehr aber zu Knoblochtzers Heidelberger Zeit. Denkbar wäre sicher auch gewesen eine Wiederholung der ersten lateinischen Druck-Ausgaben des ¶ paradoxen Dialogs zwischen Weisheit und Schlauheit: *Salomon et Marcolfus* (14 Bll. Gw 12755) mit Zierbordüre und *S*-Initiale ‚Salomon und Marcolphus im Gespräch',[204] sowie ¶ eine deutsche Ausgabe der *Historia septem sapientum* (*Cronick vnd histori* […] *die man nempt der siben meister bůch*) mit umfangreichem Holzschnittprogramm von 52 (ungewöhnlicherweise oft rahmenlosen) Bildern unterschiedlicher Qualität, verteilt auf die ersten 41 von 76 Bll. (ab 42ʳ *geistliche vßlegung und glose*). ¶ Der *Belial*, den man als iuristische Causa (*Litigatio Christi cum Belial*) oder als Trostbuch (*Consolatio pecccatorum*) lesen konnte, kam bei Knoblochtzer in Straßburg in der deutschen Fassung 1477, 1478, 1481 und 1483 gleich vier Mal unter Wiederholung des Bilderschmucks von 33 Holzschnitten (Gw M11086, M11087, M11091 und M11096)[205] und dann noch einmal in einer lateinischen Fassung ohne Illustration (Gw M11057) heraus. ¶ Der *Liber de translatione trium regum* von Johannes von Hildesheim kam in der deutschen Fassung (*ein bůch gesetzet in eren vnsers herren Jhesu cristi vnd seiner můter mareien vnd der heiligen dryer künig wirdigkeit wie sy in die land komen vnd ander werck die sy begangen vnd volbrocht haben vntz in ir end* […] nach Ausweis des *Gw* aussschließlich in Straßburg heraus, zweimal bei Knoblochtzer (Gw M14019 und M14020),[206] einmal bei Prüss. ¶ Vom *Prebyterbrief* des ‚Priesterkönigs

---

202 Vgl. dazu AMELUNG: *FDSW*, Nr. 28 mit zahlreichen Abbildungen. Die Holzschnitte sind bei SCHRAMM: *Bilderschmuck 19*, im Gegensatz zu denen der meisten hier folgenden Werke, nicht berücksichtigt.

203 SCHRAMM: *Bilderschmuck 19*, Abb. 202–231.

204 SCHRAMM: *Bilderschmuck 19*, S. 8 mit Abbildung 424 auf Tafel 70.

205 SCHRAMM: *Bilderschmuck 19*, Abb. 11–44.

206 zum Bildprogramm SCHRAMM: *Bilderschmuck 19*, Abb. 147–200.

Johannes' (vgl. Einträge unter diesem Titel im *Handschriftencensus*) sind keine Inkunabeln der deutschen Fassung erhalten, dass es sie nicht gegeben hat, ist unwahrscheinlich. Von den vier lateinischen Fassungen dieses schmalen Werks geht eine auf
Knoblochtzer in Straßburg zurück (Gw 14515, um 1482, 9 Bll.), dabei setzt er die
Zierbordüre ein, die er auch bei der *Salomon-et-Marcolfus*-Ausgabe verwendete.
Der Kolophon gibt nur den Titel des Werkes an: *Explicit epistola de Johanne qui dicitur presbiter Indie.* ¶ Erstaunlich ist, dass der *Vocabularius praedicantium*, ein umfangreiches lateinisch-deutsches Wörterbuch, das humanistisch eingefärbt und mit
ambiotioniertem Anspruch auftretend von Johannes Melber auf der Basis des Oeuv-
res von dessen Lehrer Jodocus Eichmann (vgl. oben Kap. 9 A: Gw 09255: *Weissagungen der 12 Sibyllen*) schon in den 50er Jahren des 15. Jhs. wohl in Heidelberg
erstellt wurde,[207] von Knoblochtzer in Straßburg (als zweitälteste von über 25 Inkunabelausgaben) gedruckt wurde (Gw M22727, 1482, 234 Bll.), nicht aber in Heidelberg. Merkwürdig auch, dass Titel, die sonst zu den in der Inkunabelzeit am
häufigsten gedruckten gehören, ¶ wie die quadrivial-theologische Minimal-
enzyklopädie *Ludcidarius* (Gw M09344, Straßburg um 1481) und ¶ Hans Tuchers
bei *Gw* mit sechs Ausgaben gelistete *Reise ins gelobte Land* (Knoblochtzers Inkunabel aus Straßburg Gw M47734) in Heidelberg nicht nochmals aufgelegt wurden,
jedenfalls sind keine Exemplare erhalten. ¶ Nicht verwunderlich ist dagegen, dass
die drei Inkunabeldrucke, die sich um die Burgunderkriege (Feldzüge Karls des
Kühnen gegen Ludwig XI. seit 1465) drehen, Gw M17614: *Burgundische Legende*,
Gw M17616: Konrad Pfettisheim *Reimchronik der Burgunderkriege* und Gw
M48074: H.E. Tüsch *Burgundische Historie* (Knoblochtzer, Straßburg, soweit datiert 1477),[208] und ein Lied von Veit Weber über die Schlacht von Murten 1476 (Gw
M51444) in Heidelberg nicht wiederholt wurden. Von ihrer Machart her aber finden
diese Werke ein Pendant in der Heidelberger Inkunabel Gw 09056: M. Drabsanfts
Reimspruch Von den Schlachten in Holland (vgl. Kap. 10). ¶ Die Straßburger Inkunabel *De Turcis; De origine, potentia et gestis Turcorum* (Gw M48136, Straßburg
1481) ist im selben Kontext zu sehen wie Knolochtzers Heidelberger Drucke, die
zum Ablass für die Finanzierung des Kampfes gegen die Türken auffordern (vgl.
Kap. 9 B).

Innerhalb des Publikationsprogramms des ,Drucker des Lindelbach' sind auffall-
lend viele Titel vertreten, die dem Umfeld der Bettelorden, insbesondere der Franziskaner zuzuordnen sind (vgl. Kap. 1). Wenn wir diesen Drucker tatsächlich mit Knoblochtzer gleichsetzen dürfen, so hätte er einige Werke ins Heidelberger Programm
aufnehmen können, die z.B. auch in Ulm in vergleichbarem Kontext erschienen

---

[207] KLAUS KIRCHERT/DOROTHEA KLEIN: *Melber, Johannes aus Gerolzhofen*, in: ²*VL* 6 (1987),
Sp. 367–371, und die entsprechenden beiden Handschrifteneinträge in *Handschriftencensus* unter seinem Namen.

[208] Vgl. KURT HANNEMANN: *,Burgundische Legende'*, in: ²*VL* 1 (1978), Sp. 1131–1134 und
FRIEDER SCHANZE: *Pfettisheim, Konrad*, in: ²*VL* 7 (1989), Sp. 564–567, vgl. auch SCHRAMM:
Bilderschmuck 19, Abb. 46–53.

sind, wie ¶ die Predigtsammlungen des Franziskaners Konrad Gristsch/Grütsch (Gw 11539 und 11540: 1475/76, je 271 Bll.)[209] und ¶ des (Pseudo-) Bonaventura (Gw 4812: 1481, 288 + 140 Bll.),[210] ¶ die ebenfalls Bonaventura zugeschriebenen *Meditationes vitae Christi* (Gw 04745, 1487, 54 Bll.) oder ¶ die Rede von Octavianus de Martinis zu Bonaventuras Heiligsprechung (Gw 21356: 1482, 21 Bll.).[211]

Knoblochtzers Heidelberger Offizin ist offensichtlich auch nicht zuständig für den Druck von Liturgica, auf die sich etwa die Drachs in Speyer oder Ratdolt in Augsburg spezialisiert hatten. Nicht einmal die Ausgabe des ¶ *Plenars*, das Knoblochtzer in Straßburg „um 1482" und „um 1484" zwei Mal gedruckt hatte (Gw 34130 und 34131, 230 Bll.: *hie vaht sich an ein plenari nach ordenung der heiligen cristenlichen kirchen in dem man geschriben vindet all epistel vnd ewangeli als die gesungen vnd gelesen werdent in dem ampt der heiligen meß durch das gantz Jahre*) wird in Heidelberg wiederholt.[212]

Jacob Meydenbach in Mainz hat ab 1491 insgesamt ein knappes Dutzend Drucke hervorgebracht. Für die lateinischen und deutschen Ausgaben von Lichtenbergers *Prognosticatio* (lat. 1491, 1492 lat. und dte. Ausgabe: Gw M18222, M18225, M18244) verwendet er die Holzschnitte von Knoblochtzers Ausgaben von ca. 1488 und ca. 1490 (M18217 und M18242, vgl. oben Kap. 9 A). Ebenso greift er beim Druck des *Totentanz mit figuren* (um 1494/5; Gw M47259) auf das Material des Heidelberger ‚Druckmeisters' zurück (um 1488; Gw M47257). Daneben findet sich in seinem Publikationsprogramm u. a. schon 1491 eine riesige Ausgabe ¶ des *Hortus sanitatis* von 454 Bll. mit 1073 Holzschnitten.[213] Derartiges medizinisches Schrifttum fehlt Knoblochtzer in Heidelberg ganz, nicht einmal das sonst weit verbreitete ¶ *Regimen sanitatis*[214]oder Pestregimina[215] hat er im Programm.

Im 6. und 10. Kapitel war festzustellen, dass Knoblochtzers literarisches Repertoire u. U. von der Fürstenbibliothek, insbesondere den Titeln, die 1479 als Erbschaft der Margarete von Savoyen an ihren Sohn Philipp d. A. in Heidelberg gegangen waren, beeinflusst wurde. Parallelen, Anregungen und Einflüsse waren denkbar beim *Ackermann von Böhmen*, dem *Sigenot*, evtl. dem *Pfaffen vom Kalenberg*. Wäre dieser mutmaßliche Einfluss weiter gegangen, hätten beispielsweise noch ¶ Eleonores von Österreich *Pontus und Sidonia* (Cpg 142; 4 Inkunabelausgaben aus Augsburg Gw 12719–12722) oder ¶ Elisabeths von Nassau-Saarbrücken: *Herpin* (Cpg 152; Druck zuerst Straßburg 1514, vgl. Gw 11 Sp. 176a) bei Knoblochtzer in Heidelberg erscheinen können.

---

[209] AMELUNG: *FDSW*, Nr. 22 (fälschlich <u>Johannes</u> Gritsch).

[210] AMELUNG: *FDSW*, Nr. 43.

[211] AMELUNG: *FDSW*, Nr. 54.

[212] Zum Bildprogramm vgl. SCHRAMM: *Bilderschmuck 19*, Abb. 370–421.

[213] Vgl. neben den Angaben im *Gw* auch GELDNER: *Inkunabeldrucker* (1968), S. 42.

[214] Vgl. AMELUNG: *FDSW*, Nr. 94.

[215] Z. B. AMELUNG: *FDSW*, Nr. 95 u. ö. (Register: „Pestschriften").

Vom Werk der Humanisten, die mit Heidelberg verbunden waren, lag manches, wie Luders *Ars oratoria*, für Knoblochtzers Tätigkeit in Heidelberg ‚zu früh' anderes war ‚zu spät' wie Wimpfelings *Adolescentia* u. a. oder einige Titel aus Reuchlins Werk. Dessen ¶ *Vocabularius breviloquus*, der seit 1477 bis in die späte Inkunabelzeit unzählige Male in ganz Europa gedruckt wurde, hätte aber auch in Knoblochtzers Heidelberger Programm gut gepasst (s. die verschiedenen Vokabularien, die bei ihm erschienen sind). Jakob Köbel, der schon als Verleger die Dienste von Knoblochtzers Druckerei in Anspruch genommen hatte (s. o. allenthalben), setzte in seiner eigenen Offizin in Oppenheim Knoblochtzers Tradition insofern fort, als er manches Material von ihm verwendete, manche Titel wie Virdungs *Practica* (s. o. Kap. 9 A) wieder aufnahm. Von einigen Titeln, die Jakob Köbel in der eigenen Werkstatt herausbrachte,[216] hätten sicher manche auch schon bei Knoblochtzer erscheinen können.

Zum Themenschwerpunkt der Marienverehrung (vgl. Kap. 8) hätten auch noch Titel wie ¶ die Sequenz *Von Unserer Lieben Frau* des Mönch von Salzburg, ¶ Pseudo-Bonaventuras *Von dem großen Mit Leyden der Jungkfrawen Marie*, ¶ Alanus' de Rupe *Marienpsalter* oder das *Lob der Glieder Mariae* gepasst, die allesamt u. a. in Ulm erschienen,[217] dessen Buchdruckerszene auf Knoblochtzers Schaffen nicht nur durch die Übernahme von Zainers Initialenmaterial einen gewissen Einfluss ausgeübt zu haben scheint.

So mag manches noch denkbare Projekt bei Heinrich Knoblochtzer daran gescheitert sein, dass seine Schaffenskraft durch gesundheitliche Gründe, mangelnde wirtschaftliche Prosperität oder fehlende Aufträge versiegte.

---

[216] GELDNER: *Inkunabeldrucker* (1968), S. 290; CHRISTOPH RESKE: *Die Buchdrucker des 16. und 17. Jahrhunderts im deutschen Sprachgebiet. Auf der Grundlage des gleichnamigen Werkes von Josef Benzing*, Wiesbaden 2007, S. 761 f. mit weiterer Literatur.

[217] AMELUNG: *FDSW*, Nrr. 7, 120, 121, 124, 126.

B Statistik

Dieser Überblick in Form einer Bibliographie raisonneé sollte ein einigermaßen plastisches Bild von *dem* führenden Heidelberger Inkunabeldrucker, Heinrich Knoblochtzer ergeben. Und es lassen sich einige Korrekturen an der bisherigen Einschätzung anbringen: Die Zahl der gedruckten Werke suggeriert ein Nachlassen der Aktivität schon nach 1490:

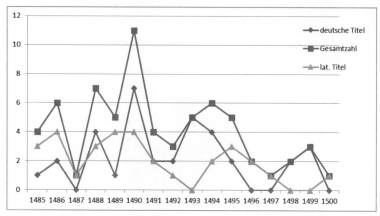

Abb. 129: Anzahl der gedruckten Titel

Betrachtet man hingegen die Anzahl der gesetzten Blätter, so kann man noch deutlicher eine zweite Tätigkeitsspitze in den Jahren 1494/5 ausmachen, bevor es dann gegen Ende des Jahrhunderts tatsächlich ‚bergab' ging:

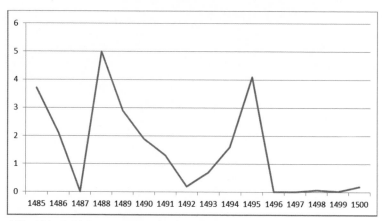

Abb. 130: Zahl der gesetzten Blätter in Tausend

Eine zweite Korrektur ergibt sich, wenn man das Verhältnis zwischen lateinischer
und deutscher Sprache nicht nur auf die Werke bezieht (dies führte bislang zur Einschätzung Knoblochtzers als einem Drucker, der vor allem Deutsches druckte), sondern die gesetzten Blätter beachtet. So zeigt sich, dass der Aufwand an Material und
Mitarbeitern für lateinische Texte weitaus größer war als für deutsche.

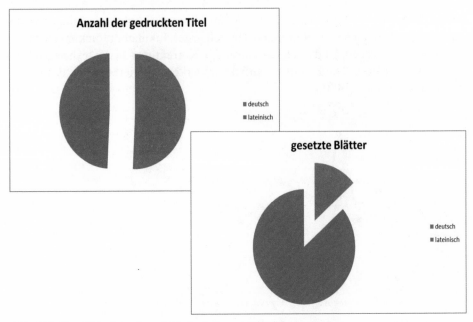

Abb. 131: Der Materialaufwand für deutsche und lateinische Texte

C Fazit

Als Fazit ergibt sich:

Knoblochtzer, aus Ettenheim stammend, zuerst Drucker in Straßburg neben vielen anderen, konkurrierenden Offizinen, wandert von dort wegen Schulden oder auf der Suche nach neuem Standort mit weniger Konkurrenz um 1484/85 nach Heidelberg aus (vgl. Einleitung).

In Heidelberg waren bis dahin keine Druckwerkstätten ansässig. Woher er das notwendige Papier bezog, wird eine genaue Wasserzeichenanalyse seiner Drucke klären können, die hier nicht zu leisten war. Vielleicht befindet sich seine Werkstatt in Wassernähe im Mühlenviertel?

Evtl. wurde sein Herzug aber auch vom Fürstenhof, den vom Hof unterstützten Franziskanern oder/und humanistischen Bestrebungen um den bis kurz zuvor hier weilenden Rudolf Agricola (†1485) befördert.

In Heidelberg bezieht Knoblochtzer (falls man ihn mit dem ‚Drucker des Lindelbach‘ gleichsetzen darf) jedenfalls erste Aufträge aus dem Franziskanerkloster unterhalb des Schlosses (am heutigen Karlsplatz) oder erhofft sich Distributionsmöglichkeiten über das Ordensnetzwerk (vgl. Kap. 1).

Knoblochtzer sucht dann auch die Nähe zur Universität, eine der ältesten im deutschen Sprachraum (seit 1386), schreibt sich 1486 hier ein, druckt Werke, die für das Studium benötigt werden, dabei bevorzugt er erkennbar hier tätige Theologen (vgl. Kap. 2).

Er publiziert Werke aus dem hier aktiven Humanistenkreis (vgl. Kap. 5), der seinerseits wieder in engem Kontakt zum Hof und zum Franziskanerkloster stand (vgl. Kap. 1) und versorgt aus gleicher Quelle gespeiste spätmittelalterliche Frömmigkeitsbewegungen (vgl. Kap. 6, 7, 8).

Eine verlässliche Säule seines Unternehmens scheint der Druck von informierenden Schriften gewesen zu sein (Kap. 9), wobei auch hier wieder in Heidelberg ansässige oder geschätzte Autoren bevorzugt werden (Köbel, Eichmann, Virdung).

Knoblochtzer setzt später sein Druckprogramm aus Straßburg hier fort, nicht ohne es in Blick auf günstigere Kalkulation technisch weiterzuentwickeln (Kap. 4, 6, 10), stellt Beziehung zum Fürstenhof und zur zunehmend gebildeten städtischen Käuferschicht her (Kap. 5, 6, 10).

Aus der Zeit, als die Produktivität seiner Offizin in Heidelberg ihren Höhepunkt erreicht (1489–1491), stammt auch sein selbstbewusstestes Kolophon als ‚Meister der Druckkunst‘ (*Impressus heydelberge, per henricum knoblochtzer impressorie artis magistrum*), wohl nicht zufällig in einem humansitisch angehauchten lateinischen Werk, das sich auf das Studium an der Universität bezieht (Baptista Guarinus: *De ordine docendi ac studendi*; Kap. 3). Aber auch später, 1495, wird in einer anderen, theologischen Inkunabel seine Bedeutung für die Texterstellung als umsichtiger, ehrenwerter Drucker (*Providus et honestus Henricus knoblotzer: Impressor Heidelbergensis*) hervorgehoben (vgl. Kap. 2, Johannes de Lambsheim: *Speculum officii missae expositorium*):

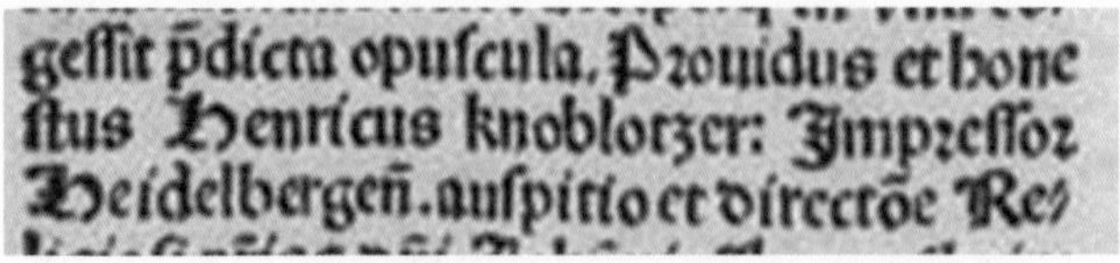
gessit p̄dicta opuscula. Prouidus et hone
stus Henricus knoblotzer: Impressor
Heidelbergeñ. auspitio et directōe Re

Abb. 132: ULB Bonn, Inc 1017 [https://digitale-sammlungen.ulb.uni-bonn.de/content/pageview/1562812], 30r (Ausschnitt).

Er kooperiert mit anderen Akteuren in der Region. Hinter manchen Drucken stehen Verleger (z. B. Jakob Köbel, Kap. 5, 9 A u. ö.) oder andere Drucker wie die Offizin Drach in Speyer. Er kooperiert auch technisch überregional, übernimmt z. B. Lettern von Johannes Zainer in Ulm, er ist letztlich ein Drucker, der vielfältige Sparten bedient, und nicht zuletzt insofern ein Pionier, als er Heidelbergs Tradition als Druck- und Verlagsstadt begründet:

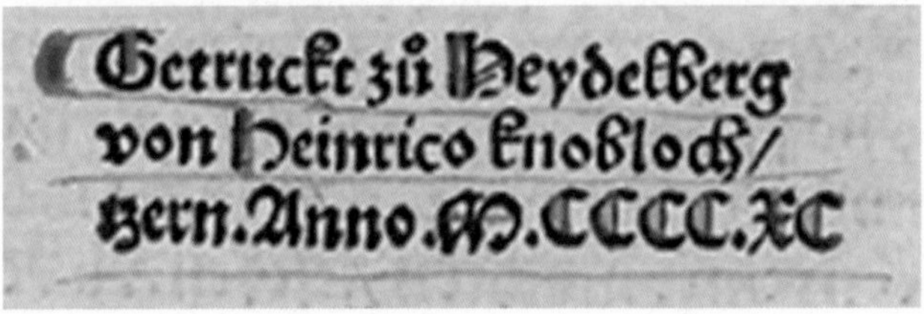
Getruckt zů Heydelberg
von Heinrico knoblochs/
zern. Anno. M.CCCC.XC

Abb. 133: aus: *Her Diethrich von Berñ/Sigenot*, vgl. Kap. 10 (mit Nachweis dort).

D   Abgekürzt zitierte Literatur

AMELUNG: *FDSW*
PETER AMELUNG: *Der Frühdruck im deutschen Südwesten 1473–1500. Band 1: Ulm. Eine Ausstellung der Württembergischen Landesbibliothek Stuttgart*, Stuttgart 1979.

BACKES (1992)
MARTINA BACKES: *Das literarische Leben am kurpfälzischen Hof zu Heidelberg im 15. Jahrhundert. Ein Beitrag zur Gönnerforschung des Spätmittelalters* (*Hermaea: Germanistische Forschungen NF 68*), Tübingen 1992.

Bibliotheca Palatina (1986)
Katalog zur Ausstellung vom 8. Juli bis 2. November 1986 in der Heiliggeistkirche Heidelberg, Textband und Bildband, hg. von ELMAR MITTLER in Zusammenarbeit mit WALTER BERSCHIN, VERA TROST u. a., Heidelberg 1986.

GELDNER: *Inkunabeldrucker* (1968)
FERDINAND GELDNER: *Die deutschen Inkunabeldrucker. Ein Handbuch der deutschen Buchdrucker des XV. Jahrhunderts nach Druckorten, Band 1: Das deutsche Sprachgebiet*, Stuttgart 1968.

GELDNER: *Knoblochtzer* (1979)
FERDINAND GELDNER: Knoblochtzer, Heinrich, in: *Neue Deutsche Biographie 12* (1979), S. 195 [Onlinefassung, o. S.].

GW
Gesamtkatalog der Wiegendrucke, herausgegeben von der Kommission für den Gesamtkatalog der Wiegendrucke, Leipzig 1925 ff.: [https://www.gesamtkatalogderwiegendrucke.de/].

INKA
Eberhard-Karls-Universität Tübingen: Der Inkunabelkatalog *INKA* ist kein abgeschlossener Katalog, sondern bietet Zugriff auf verschiedene Dateien eines Datenpools, der sich aus Exemplarbeschreibungen von Inkunabeln in verschiedenen Bibliotheken zusammensetzt. Der Datenpool wird regelmäßig aktualisiert: [https://www.inka.uni-tuebingen.de/].

ISTC
Incunabula Short Titel Catalogue: international database of 15th-century European printing created by the British Library with contributions from institutions worldwide: [http://www.bl.uk/catalogues/istc/].

LÄHNEMANN (2002)
HENRIKE LÄHNEMANN: *Margarethe von Savoyen in ihren literarischen Beziehungen*, in: *Encomia-Deutsch*, Sonderheft der Deutschen Sektion des *International Center for Language Studies*, Tübingen, S. 158–173.

MITTLER: *Heidelberg* (1996)
ELMAR MITTLER (Hg.): *Heidelberg. Geschichte und Gestalt*. Heidelberg 1996.

MÜLLER: *Wissen für den Hof* (1994)
JAN-DIRK MÜLLER (Hg.): *Wissen für den Hof. Der spätmittelalterliche Verschriftlichungsprozess am Beispiel Heidelberg im 15. Jahrhundert* (SFB 231: *Träger, Felder, Formen pragmatischer Schriftlichkeit im Mittelalter; Münstersche Mittelalter-Schriften, Band 67*), München 1994.

ROTH: *Geschichte* (1901)
FERDINAND W. E. ROTH: *Geschichte und Bibliographie der Heidelberger Buchdruckereien 1485–1510*, in: *Neues Archiv für die Geschichte der Stadt Heidelberg 4* (1901), S. 197–224.

SCHLECHTER/RIES (2009)
Universitätsbibliothek Heidelberg: *Katalog der Inkunabeln der UB Heidelberg, des Instituts für Geschichte der Medizin und des Stadtarchivs Heidelberg*, bearbeitet von ARMIN SCHLECHTER und LUDWIG RIES, Wiesbaden 2009.

SCHRAMM: *Bilderschmuck 19*
ALBERT SCHRAMM: *Der Bilderschmuck der Frühdrucke (Band 19): Die Straßburger Drucker: 1. Johann Mentelin ...*, Leipzig 1936; Digitalisat UB Heidelberg: [https://digi.ub.uni-heidelberg.de/diglit/schramm1936bd19].

Tw
Typenrepertorium der Wiegendrucke: Inkunabelreferat der Staatsbibliothek zu Berlin/Preußischer Kulturbesitz, Datenbank der im Buchdruck des 15. Jahrhunderts verwendeten Drucktypen: [https://tw.staatsbibliothek-berlin.de/].

VE 15
FALK EISERMANN: *Verzeichnis der typographischen Einblattdrucke des 15. Jahrhunderts im Heiligen Römischen Reich Deutscher Nation*, 3 Bände, Wiesbaden 2004.

²*VL*
Die deutsche Literatur des Mittelalters. Verfasserlexikon, zweite, völlig neu bearbeitete Auflage (11 Bände), herausgegeben von KURT RUH und BURGHART WACHINGER, Berlin/New York 1978–2004.

ZIMMERMANN (1999)
KARIN ZIMMERMANN: *Die Anfänge der Bibliotheca Palatina bis zu Friedrich I. dem Siegreichen und Philipp dem Aufrichtigen*, in: *Universitätsbibliothek Heidelberg: Kostbarkeiten gesammelter Geschichte. Heidelberg und die Pfalz in Zeugnissen der UB*, hg. von ARMIN SCHLECHTER, Heidelberg 1999, S. 3–17.

E   Register

Grundstock des alphabetischen Werkregisters ist die Liste, die der *Gw* bei der ma-
schinellen Suche nach den Schlagwörtern: Druckort ‚Heidelberg' und Druckername
‚Knoblochtzer' auswirft. Die Liste enthält 85 Treffer, die ich hier mit Querverweisen
versehe. Rot hervorgehoben werden die Firmierungen, soweit sie dem Druck selbst
in ganz unterschiedlichen Ausprägungen zu entnehmen sind (vgl. Einleitung). Blau
hervorgehoben sind die Angaben, die auf den früher separat geführten ‚Drucker des
Lindelbach' verweisen, der heute nach überwiegender Auffassung (aber nicht mit
letzter Sicherheit) mit Knoblochtzer gleichgesetzt wird. In eckiger Klammer bleiben,
nach Usus des *Gw*, aus dem Typenmaterial erschlossene Angaben stehen. Zahlreiche
Werktitel etwa von Knoblochtzers Drucken aus Straßburg sind im Register nicht
berücksichtigt, sind aber im entsprechenden Abschnitt des 11. Kapitels leicht auf-
zufinden. Angegeben ist immer die Seite, auf der der Eintrag beginnt, auf *f.*- und
ff.-Angaben wird verzichtet.

Ablass → *Aufforderung an die Pfarrgeist-*
lichen […]; → *Modus quem observabunt*
commissarii pro tuitione fidei in indul-
gentiarum publicatione
Ackermann von Böhmen Heidelberg:
Heinrich Knoblochtzer, 8.VII. [14]90. 4°
[Gw 00202]: **82**
Agricola, Rudolph → Isocrates
Almanach auf das Jahr 1486, deutsch.
[Heidelberg: Heinrich Knoblochtzer];
[Gw 0139920]: **97**
Almanach auf das Jahr 1487, lat. [Heidel-
berg: Heinrich Knoblochtzer, um 1487];
[Gw 01419]: **97**
Almanach auf das Jahr 1491, deutsch.
[Heidelberg: Heinrich Knoblochtzer, um
1491]; [Gw 01454]: **99**
Almanach → Virdung, Johannes
Andreae, Johannes: *Super arboribus*
consanguinitatis et affinitatis et cogna-
tionis spiritualis et legalis una cum
exemplis et enigmatibus [Heidelberg:
Heinrich Knoblochtzer, um 1494]; 2°
[Gw 01708]: **51**

Andreae, Johannes: *Super arboribus*
consanguinitatis et affinitatis et cogna-
tionis spiritualis et legalis una cum
exemplis et enigmatibus [Heidelberg:
Heinrich Knoblochtzer, um 1495]; 2°
[Gw 01709]: **51**
Andreae, Johannes: *Super arboribus*
consanguinitatis et affinitatis et cogna-
tionis spiritualis cum exemplis, deutsch
[Heidelberg: Heinrich Knoblochtzer, um
1494]; 2° [Gw 01721]: **51**
Arbor consanguinitatis → Andreae,
Johannes
Aufforderung an die Pfarrgeistlichen, für die
Verbreitung des Ablasses zum besten des
Kampfes gegen die Türken mitzuwirken
[Heidelberg: Heinrich Knoblochtzer, um
1488]; [Gw 02855, 02856, 02857 und
02858]: **114**

Bartholomaeus Anglicus: *De proprietatibus*
rerum [Heidelberg: Drucker des Lindelbach (Heinrich Knoblochtzer)], 21. V.
1488; 2° [Gw 03411]: **21**
Bartholomaeus de Chaimis → Chaimis

Beichtbüchlein. Heidelberg: Heinrich
    Knoblochtzer, 1494; 4° [Gw 03780]: **85**
Biel, Gabriel → Gerson
Brunus, Gabriel → Johannes de Deo
    Cartusianus
*Büchlein, Wie man Fische und Vögel fangen
    soll* [Heidelberg: Jakob Köbel, um
    1493]; [Gw 0567910N]: **112**

Cato, deutsch. [Heidelberg: Heinrich Knob-
    lochtzer, um 1490]; 4° [Gw 06323 und
    06324]: **42**
Chaimis, Bartholomaeus de: *Confessionale.*
    [Heidelberg: Drucker des Lindelbach
    (Heinrich Knoblochtzer), nicht nach
    1485]; 4° [Gw 06548]: **18**
Constructionarius → *Grammatica. Regulae
    congruitatum*

Danse macabre des hommes, Grant; Lyon
    [Matthias Huss] 18.2. [1499/1500];
    [Gw 7954]: **9**
Danse macabre → *Totentanz*
Datus, Augustinus: *Elegantiolae* etc.
    [Heidelberg: Drucker des Lindelbach
    (Heinrich Knoblochtzer), nach(?) 21.
    VIII.1486]; 4° [Gw 08126]: **34**
Deutscher Orden → *Verteidigung der Rechte
    des Deutschen Ordens*
Dietrich von Bern → *Sigenot*
Disticha Catonis → *Cato*
Drabsanft, Matthias: *Von den Schlachten in
    Holland* [Heidelberg: Heinrich Knob-
    lochtzer, um 1489]; 8° [Gw 09056]: **119**

Eichmann, Jodocus: *Weissagungen der 12 Si-
    byllen über die jungfräuliche Geburt
    Christi,* Heidelberg: Heinrich Knobloch-
    tzer, 1493; 4° [Gw 09255]: **110**
Einblattdruck → *Almanach;* → *Philipp,
    Kurfürst von der Pfalz;* → *Rauschner,
    Jörg;* → *Tafel zur Bestimmung der
    beweglichen Feste für die Jahre 1488–
    1507;* → Tratt, Hans von; → *Verteidi-
    gung der Rechte des Deutschen Ordens
    auf die Balleien Apulien und Sizilien;* →

Virdung, Johannes; → Walbrun, Hans
    und Philipp von.
Elegantiolae → Datus, Augustinus
Es tu scholaris? Heidelberg: Heinrich
    Knoblochtzer, [um 1494/95]; 4°
    [Gw 09401]: **40**
Evrardus de Valle Scholarum: *Sermones de
    sanctis,* Heidelberg: [Drucker des
    Lindelbach (Heinrich Knoblochtzer)],
    21.I.1485; 2° [Gw 0948920]: **19**

Formulare und deutsch Rhetorica [Heidel-
    berg: Heinrich Knoblochtzer], 1488; 2°
    [Gw 10187]: **54**
Frankfurter, Philipp: *Der Pfarrer vom Kalen-
    berg.* Davor: *Wann ein jeglicher Fisch
    am besten ist.* Daran: *Vom Ritter
    Alexander und seiner Frau.* [Heidel-
    berg]: Heinrich Knoblochtzer, [14]90; 2°
    [Gw 10289]: **111, 124**
Fußpfad zur ewigen Seligkeit, Heidelberg:
    [Heinrich Knoblochtzer für Jakob
    Köbel], [14]94; 4° [Gw 10429]: **92**

Gallus, Jodocus → Johannes de Deo
    Cartusianus
Gabriel Brunus → Johannes de Deo
    Cartusianus
Gerson, Johannes: *Opus tripartitum,* deutsch
    von Gabriel Biel. [Heidelberg: Heinrich
    Knoblochtzer, nicht nach 1488]; 4°
    [Gw 10786]: **22**
Grammatica. Regula Dominus quae pars
    [Heidelberg: Heinrich Knoblochtzer, um
    1486/90]; 4° [Gw 11144]: **41**
*Grammatica. Regulae congruitatum,
    constructiones et regimina. Constructio-
    narius.* [Heidelberg: Heinrich Knob-
    lochtzer für] Jakob Köbel, [um 1490]; 4°
    [Gw 11219]: **42**
Guarinus, Baptista: *De ordine docendi ac
    studendi.* Heidelberg: Heinrich Knob-
    lochtzer, 18.XII.1489; 4° [Gw 11597]: **44**

Historia Melusine → *Melusine*
Historia Sigenot → *Sigenot*

Hohenlohe, Kraft Graf von: *Klage bei dem Schwäbischen Bund gegen die Stadt Schwäbisch Hall*. Neuenstein, 29. IV.1493. [Heidelberg: Heinrich Knoblochtzer]; 2° [Gw 12882]: **117**

Hugo de Prato Florido → Evrardus de Valle Scholarum

Hymni. Hymnarium (*ettlich tewtsch ymni oder lobgesange* [...] *die do zů bereitung vnd betrachtůng der beicht ainem yeden not synd*) Heidelberg: Heinrich Knoblochtzer, 1494; 4° [Gw 13746]: **87**

(Ps.)-Isocrates: *Praecepta ad Demonicum*. Übers. Rudolphus Agricola. [Heidelberg: Heinrich Knoblochtzer, um 1495]; 4° [Gw M15394]: **36**

Instrumentum iudicum Moguntinensium [Heidelberg: Heinrich Knoblochtzer, nicht vor 16.I.1488]; 2° [Gw M12524 und M12528]: **115**

Jacobus de Jüterbog: *De valore et utilitate missarum pro defunctis*; daran: Johannes de Mechlinia: *Determinatio utrum dei opera possint impediri daemonis malitia*. [Heidelberg: Heinrich Knoblochtzer], 1493; 4° [Gw M10884]: **26**

Jodocus Gallus → Johannes de Deo Cartusianus, → *Mensa philosophica*

Johannes de Deo Cartusianus: *Nosce te ipsum*; mit Beig. von Jodocus Gallus und Gabriel Brunus. [Heidelberg: Drucker des Lindelbach (Heinrich Knoblochtzer), nach 6.VII.1489]; 4° [Gw M13471]: **66**

Johannes de Garlandia: *Composita verborum*. [Heidelberg: Drucker des Lindelbach (Heinrich Knoblochtzer), um 1485/86 und nach 6.VII.1486]; 4° [Gw M13692]: **30**

Johannes de Garlandia: *Composita verborum*. Mit Komm. von Johannes Synthen. [Heidelberg: Drucker des Lindelbach (Heinrich Knoblochtzer), nach 6. VII.1486]; 4° [Gw M13694 und M13696]: **32**

Johannes de Garlandia: *Verba deponentialia*. [Heidelberg: Drucker des Lindelbach (Heinrich Knoblochtzer)]; 4° [Gw M13909]: **29**

Johannes de Lambsheim: *Libri tres perutiles de confraternitatibus rosarii et psalterii B. Mariae virginis*. Mit Beigabe von Rutger Sycamber. [Heidelberg: Heinrich Knoblochtzer, um 1500]; 8° [Gw M14221]: **90**

Johannes de Lambsheim: *Speculum officii missae expositorium*. Heidelberg: Heinrich Knoblochtzer, 29.VI.1495; 4° [Gw M14225]: **28**

Johannes de Mechlinia → Jacobus de Jüterbog

Johannes Synthen → Johannes de Garlandia: *Composita verborum*.

Johannes von Tepl: → *Ackermann von Böhmen*

Kalender → Almanach

Köbel, Jakob: *Tischzucht*. Heidelberg [Heinrich Knoblochtzer], 6.III.1492; [Gw M16371]: **73**

Köbel, Jakob: *Sibyllen Weissagung*. [Heidelberg] Heinrich Knoblochtzer, [nach 1492]; 4° [Gw M16375]: **107**

Köbel, Jakob → *Büchlein, Wie man Fische und Vögel fangen soll*; → *Fußpfad zur ewigen Seligkeit*; → *Grammatica, Regulae congruitatum*; → *Mensa philosophica*

Kraft, Graf von Hohenlohe → Hohenlohe

Kurfürst → Philipp

Lichtenberger, Johannes: *Prognosticatio*. [Heidelberg: Heinrich Knoblochtzer, um 1488]; 2° [Gw M18217]: **99**

Lichtenberger, Johannes: *Prognostikon*, deutsch. [Heidelberg: Heinrich Knoblochtzer, um 1490]; 2° [Gw M18242]: **80, 99, 102**

Lindelbach, Michael: *Praecepta latinitatis*. Heidelberg: [Drucker des Lindelbach (Heinrich Knoblochtzer)], 15.XII.1486; 4° [Gw M18384]: **33**

Manuale scholarium [Heidelberg:
Heinrich Knoblochtzer, um 1490]; 4°
[Gw M20717]: **46**

Maximilian I., Römischer Kaiser: *Erwählung.* [Heidelberg: Heinrich Knobloch-
tzer(?), nach 20.II.1486]; 4°
[Gw M22076]: **113**

Maximilian I., Römischer Kaiser: *Handel
und Vornehmen Etlicher in Flandern
gegen die römische Majestät.* [Heidel-
berg: Heinrich Knoblochtzer, nach
Februar 1488]; 4° [Gw M2210810]: **114**

Melusine, deutsch, übers. u. bearb. von
Thüring von Ringoltingen, Heidelberg:
Heinrich Knoblochtzer, 13.XII.1491; 2°
[Gw 12663]: **126**

Mensa philosophica. Hrsg. Jodocus Gallus,
Jakob Köbel und Johannes Wacker.
Heidelberg: [Drucker des Lindelbach
(Heinrich Knoblochtzer)], 1489; 4°
[Gw M22814]: **70**

Misch, Friedrich: **38**

*Modus quem observabunt commissarii pro
tuitione fidei in indulgentiarum publicatione.* [Heidelberg: Heinrich Knoblochtzer, um 1487]; 2° [Gw M25010]:
114

*Modus vacandi beneficiorum. Modus
acceptandi.* [Heidelberg: Heinrich
Knoblochtzer(?), um 1490]: 4°
[Gw M25075]: **61**

Nosce te ipsum → Johannes de Deo Cartusianus

Ordo iudiciarius, deutsch. Heidelberg:
Heinrich Knoblochtzer, 1490; 4°
[Gw M16365]: **58**

Ordo iudiciarius, deutsch; daran: *Wie man
Höfe, Zehnte und Mühlen verleihen soll.*
Heidelberg: Heinrich Knoblochtzer,
1490; 4° [Gw M16367]: **58**

Petrarca, Francesco: *Psalmi poenitentiales*
[Heidelberg: Heinrich Knoblochtzer(?),
1500]; 8° [Gw M31605]: **80**

Petrarca, Francesco: *De remediis utriusque
fortunae* [Heidelberg: Heinrich Knoblochtzer, nicht nach 1490]; 4°
[Gw M31621]: **77**

Der Pfarrer vom Kalenberg → Frankfurter,
Philipp

Philipp, Kurfürst von der Pfalz: *Ausschreiben
betr. Übernahme des Reichsvikariats.*
Heidelberg, 27.VIII.1496. [Heidelberg:
Heinrich Knoblochtzer, nach 27.
VIII.1496]; [Gw M33125]: **118**

Prognosticatio/Prognostikon → Lichtenberger, Johannes; → Virdung, Johannes

De proprietatibus rerum → Bartholomaeus
Anglicus

Rauschner, Jörg: *Einladung zu einem
Armbrustschießen nach Heidelberg.*
[Heidelberg: Heinrich Knoblochtzer,
nach 18.V.1490]; [Gw M37153]: **115**

Regimen scholarium, lat. und deutsch.
[Heidelberg: Heinrich Knoblochtzer, um
1490]; 4° [Gw M37407]: 43

Ritter Alexander → Frankfurter, Philipp

Rosarium, deutsch. [Heidelberg: Heinrich
Knoblochtzer], 1495; 4° [Gw M38921]:
88

Rosenkranz unserer lieben Frauen →
Sigenot

Sibyllenweissagung: → Köbel, Jakob:
Sibyllen Weissagung, → Eichmann,
Jodocus: *Weissagungen der 12 Sibyllen*

Sigenot (*Her Diethrich von Bern̄*); daran:
Rosenkranz unserer lieben Frauen.
Heidelberg: Heinrich Knoblochtzer,
1490; 2° [Gw 12795]: **120**

Sigenot Heidelberg: Heinrich Knoblochtzer,
1493; 2° [Gw 12796]: **120**

Spangel, Pallas: *Oratio ad universitatem
Heidelbergensem.* Mit Beig. von
Leonardus Pelicanus und Johannes
Volmannius. [Heidelberg: Heinrich
Knoblochtzer]; 4° [Gw M42895]: **49**

Sycamber, Rutger → Johannes de Lambsheim: *Libri tres perutiles*

*Tafel zur Bestimmung der beweglichen Feste
  für die Jahre 1488–1507.* [Heidelberg:
  Heinrich Knoblochtzer, um 1488];
  [Gw M4474030]: **97**
*Termini causarum et Festa in Romana Curia
  servari soliti in causa beneficiali. Festa
  palacii Apostolici.* [Heidelberg: Heinrich
  Knoblochtzer, nicht nach 14.IV.1491]; 4°
  [Gw M45623]: **62**
Thüring von Ringoltingen → *Melusine*
Tischzucht → Köbel, Jakob
Totentanz. [Heidelberg: Heinrich Knobloch-
  tzer, um 1488/89]; 2° [Gw M4725510
  und M47257]: **80**
Totentanz → *Danse macabre*
Tratt, Hans von: *Ausschreiben über seinen
  Handel mit der Stadt Weissenburg.
  17.I.1497.* [Heidelberg: Heinrich
  Knoblochtzer, nach 17.I.1497].
  [Gw M47454 und M4745410]: **118**

Vergilius Maro, Publius: *Opera.* Heidelberg:
  Heinrich Knoblochtzer, 1495. 4°
  [Gw M4978110]: **63**
Versor, Johannes: *Super Donatum.* [Heidel-
  berg: Heinrich Knoblochtzer, nicht nach
  1491]. 4° [Gw M50208]: **37**
*Verteidigung der Rechte des Deutschen
  Ordens auf die Balleien Apulien und
  Sizilien.* [Heidelberg: Heinrich Knob-
  lochtzer, nicht vor August 1492];
  [Gw M50312]: **117**
Virdung, Johannes: *Almanach auf das Jahr
  1498,* deutsch. [Heidelberg: Heinrich

Knoblochtzer, um 1498]; [Gw M50711]:
  102
Virdung, Johannes: *Prognostikon auf das
  Jahr 1495,* deutsch. [Heidelberg:
  Heinrich Knoblochtzer, um 1495]; 4°
  [Gw M50739]: **104**
Virdung, Johannes: *Prognostikon auf das
  Jahr 1500,* deutsch. [Heidelberg:
  Heinrich Knoblochtzer(?), um
  1499/1500]; 4° [Gw M50749]: **106**
Vocabularius Curia palatium, lat.-deutsch.
  [Heidelberg: Heinrich Knoblochtzer]; 4°
  [Gw M51243]: **39**
Vocabularius de partibus indeclinabilibus.
  [Heidelberg: Drucker des Lindelbach
  (Heinrich Knoblochtzer)]; 4°
  [Gw M51289]: **35**
Vocabularius Ex quo. [Heidelberg: Heinrich
  Knoblochtzer, um 1485]; 4°
  [Gw M51056]: **24**

Walbrun, Hans und Philipp von: *Beschwerde
  über die Ermordung ihres Vaters Hans
  von Walbrun durch seinen Bruder.
  27.X.1498.* [Heidelberg: Heinrich
  Knoblochtzer, vor 13.I.1499];
  [Gw M51378]: **119**
Wann ein jeglicher Fisch am besten ist →
  Frankfurter, Philipp
Wie man Fische und Vögel fangen soll →
  *Büchlein, Wie man Fische und Vögel
  fangen soll*
*Wie man Höfe, Zehnte und Mühlen verleihen
  soll* → *Ordo iudiciarius*